Recasting America

Recasting America
Culture and Politics in the
Age of Cold War

Edited by Lary May

The University of Chicago Press   *Chicago and London*

Lary May, associate professor of American studies at the University of Minnesota, is the author of *Screening Out the Past: The Birth of Mass Culture and the Motion Picture Industry*.

The University of Chicago Press, Chicago 60637
The University of Chicago Press, Ltd., London

© 1989 by the University of Chicago
All rights reserved. Published 1989
Printed in the United States of America
98 97 96 95 94 93 92 91 90   5 4 3 2

A shorter version of chapter 7, "Movie Star Politics," by Lary May, appeared in *New Directions in California History: A Book of Readings*, edited by James J. Rawls (New York: McGraw-Hill, 1988), © 1988 by The University of Chicago. All rights reserved.

Library of Congress Cataloging-in-Publication Data

Recasting America : culture and politics in the age of cold war /
    edited by Lary May.
        p.   cm.
    Papers evolving from a national conference and speakers series,
    held 1987–1988 at the University of Minnesota.
    Includes index.
    ISBN 0-226-51175-8.   ISBN 0-226-51176-6 (pbk.)
    1. United States—Civilization—1945-   —Congresses. 2. United
States—Popular culture—History—20th century—Congresses.
3. United States—Politics and government—1945-   —Congresses.
4. Political culture—United States—History—20th century—
Congresses. I. May, Lary.
E169.12.R43   1989
973.92—dc19   88-21618
                                                                CIP

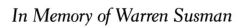

In Memory of Warren Susman

Contents

Part Four THE SEARCH FOR ALTERNATIVES: ART, MINORITIES,
AND POPULAR CULTURE

Acknowledgments

All those who embark upon the long process of creating a scholarly work realize that despite their individual efforts, and the sweaty palms and sleepless nights that seem theirs alone, they do get more than a little help from their friends. In a collection evolving from a national conference and speakers series, I have become especially conscious of the magnitude of individual and institutional support that brought this project to fruition.

A major grant from the College of Liberal Arts at the University of Minnesota provided the necessary funding to bring a diverse group of national scholars together in 1987–88. Professor Edward Griffin, Chairman of the American Studies Program at the University of Minnesota, encouraged the project and generously turned over the resources of the program to make that endeavor a success.

Among the scholars whom I wish especially to thank, David Noble is the first. He helped clarify my thinking about the shift in values after World War II, and spurred us to organize events that would explore the ways that transformation encouraged a series of cultural and political enterprises. Along the way, Lewis Erenberg was an endless source of stimulation and advice. Nor will I ever be able to forget the eager responses from the scholars I phoned around the country who enthusiastically agreed to come together to explore postwar America. No recollection of their names is required, since each is included as an author in the following pages.

At the point when I began to realize that with more research, expansion, and revision the papers would form the heart of an innovative collection, Douglas Mitchell of the University of Chicago Press jumped into the process with enthusiasm and energy. I also wish to thank the superb staff at the press, the anonymous reviewers whose astute criticisms helped bring the book to maturation, and Jennifer Delton for the superb index.

Throughout, my colleague and wife, Elaine Tyler May, brought to the task her constant encouragement, amid the excitements of teaching, deaning, writing her book, and helping raise our three children, Sarah, Daniel, and Michael. It literally could not have been done, nor been any fun, without her.

Above all, the keynote speaker at the conference deserves special mention: Warren Susman. Long before the gathering, Susman had been one of the most noted practitioners of American Studies and cultural history, widely known for his pioneering explorations of the interplay between intellectual and popular expression in the twentieth century. Embedded in my memory is the first contact with him by telephone in 1986. When told about our project, he exclaimed, "What a wonderful idea. I will come for nothing but expenses." In addition to such generosity, his opening address provided the focal point for the following discussions at that gathering, and his opening essay in this volume will no doubt continue to spark debates among its readers for many years to come. Unfortunately, before his untimely death he had only partially finished revising the essay for publication. But with the assistance of his wife, Beatrice Susman, and the sure editing of Edward Griffin, we have drawn on that transcript to complete his work. We offer this collection in memory of the dialog he sparked on at the Minnesota conference and fondly dedicate *Recasting America* to his memory.

Introduction

Lary May

The essays collected in *Recasting America* represent a new departure in our understanding of postwar culture in the United States. They emerged from a conference and a series of seminars sponsored by the American Studies Program at the University of Minnesota from 1985 to 1987. As the authors presented papers on art, politics, intellectual thought, and private life and as vigorous debates ensued, it gradually became clear that a significant shift in values occurred after World War II—one that begs for an explanation. Too often, scholars see the era simply as the end of the Depression and the coming of affluence, or as the backdrop to McCarthyism, Vietnam, and civil rights. Yet we still have little understanding of how the perceptions undergirding these events connect to the twentieth century as a whole or why Americans, in area after area, thought that the culture—the values and beliefs that gave form to their political and social actions—seemed so distinct from that of previous decades.

To gain perspective, let us listen to the voice of one who experienced that cultural transition from the inside. Writing his autobiography in the 1950s, the noted theater producer Harold Clurman, of the Group Theatre, found it puzzling that the world seemed so different from that of his youth. In the Great Depression, when hard times and bitter political conflicts predominated, he produced plays like *Waiting for Lefty* and *Awake and Sing* that portrayed the aspirations of ordinary people to change their world. The endeavors of the Group Theatre also merged with similar artistic and political movements to unify "the world's chaos, to live within the context of integrated thought and vision." Across various fields a unity of themes and symbols prevailed, as many "felt the need to believe . . . that they were working towards some valuable artistic, social and humanly significant goal." By the 1950s, his co-workers found even greater success on Broadway and in Hollywood, writing plays and training actors like James Dean and Marlon Brando in the new "method" style of acting. Yet, in a period of affluence and political harmony, Clurman lamented that his co-

1

workers felt anxious, living with a feeling that something had been lost along the way, a "sense of purpose, an ideal something to be achieved over and above a smash hit, a fat salary, rave notices."[1]

Why in the Depression did hardship and conflict yield expressions of unity and optimism, while, in the affluent and apparently tranquil fifties, success coexisted with fragmentation and anxiety? Undoubtedly, Clurman's disappointment emanated from the collapse of the Group Theatre and the fact that achievement often leaves one unsatisfied. Indeed, if the question had been asked in the fifties, when Clurman published his autobiography, most scholars would have observed that the producer's personal observations merely reflected his individual disappointment and contained no larger significance. For, in the fifties, when politics was characterized by consensus, the scholarly wisdom held that American history had always been dominated by class harmony centered on individual competition and a quest for success but underscored with anxieties about achievement and fragmentation. The well-informed scholar would thus have pointed out that the decade was not too different from earlier eras; it was just human nature that in hard times people band together and feel optimistic, but in the following good times prosperity arouses fear and anxiety.

Yet the research of the past twenty years suggests a much different view of human nature in America, one that gives plausibility to Clurman's observations. In fact, one reason why the postwar era seems so puzzling to the authors in this collection is that a new approach to American history has emerged since the fifties. Although these concepts have not been fully integrated into our view of the period after 1945, researchers using the tools of the new social history have shown how racial, ethnic, and class consciousness characterized earlier times. Rather than consensus, conflict and diversity informed the world of public and private life, as gender, populist protest, and minority tension repeatedly surfaced in social movements. In addition, historians have shown how these movements often validated an ideology of republican citizenship often in conflict with monopoly capital. In spite of economic ups and downs, that progressive ethos validated for over a century a Jeffersonian ideal of small producers and local control, qualities that presumably distinguished the nation from aristocratic Europe.[2]

Furthermore, the most recent scholarship on the Great Depression suggests that this progressive ethos continued into the thirties to provide the unity that Clurman saw animating his youth. Historians concentrating on ideology and social movements have found that a revival of traditional rhetoric inspired farmer, worker, and middle-class protest. Others have shown that the era's most noted novelists achieved popularity because their works emphasized a struggle against monopolistic interests, while regionalist painters turned to styles and subjects that validated the folk community, hostile to domestic and foreign tyrants. Likewise, that élan permeated popular culture, as the most noted filmmakers of the period, particularly John Ford and Frank Capra, attained success because their characters revived American ideals to overcome corruption and gain personal salvation—a promise typically dramatized in lesser productions like *All That Money Can Buy*. Based on Stephen Vincent Benet's short story, "The Devil and Daniel Webster," the film charts the story of a farmer who sells his soul to the devil but then finds redemption when the great senator tells a jury of traitors that "It was for freedom that we came to these shores in ships and boats. It was a long journey and a hard and bitter one. Yes, when the whips of the oppressors are broken and their names are forgotten, free men will be living under a free star. Yes, we have planted freedom on this earth. You Americans cannot be on the side of the oppressor. Gentlemen of the jury, do not let this country go to the Devil."[3]

Such a vision of the democracy as redeemed and different from Europe represents an updating of the American jeremiad so ably analyzed by Sacvan Bercovitch for earlier eras of our history—a traditional rhetoric that validated national exceptionalism from the Revolution to modern times. After the attack on Pearl Harbor, a similar progressive ethos continued to inspire a formerly isolationist country to carry its democratic élan into the battle against fascism and tyranny abroad. As evidenced in current investigations of the war, such as John Morton Blum's *V Was for Victory*, writers and artists portrayed the struggle against Japan and Germany as they had portrayed the domestic battle against monopoly and intolerance. Similarly, formerly marginal unions and ethnic groups appeared to be entering the mainstream, and, with the ensuing victory and prosperity, the postwar period offered the promise of renewed security and affluence.[4]

Yet, despite the appearance of continuity, a number of events suggest that after 1945 Americans entered a new phase in their history. One of the most thoroughly investigated by diplomatic scholars has been the coming of the cold war. A country which had traditionally developed economic relations with the rest of the world, but often defined its national identity as isolated from political and military alliances outside the continent, now moved into the international arena with treaties, foreign aid, and defense commitments around the globe. Scholars have debated who started the cold war and the nuclear-arms race, while an equally large number have concentrated on the rise of domestic anticommunism. Yet we still do not understand how these events might have altered American culture and political ideology as a whole. Red Scares, for example, had emerged periodically throughout the century, but the postwar crusade was different in its duration and unprecedented power to alter traditional policies, such as hostility to a permanent defense establishment and international involvements.[5]

Whether or not it was caused by the cold war and domestic anticommunism, a paradigm shift of major proportions also permeated intellectual life, with implications for how we conceive the American heritage. True, intellectuals frequently build on old foundations and reassess the ideas of their mentors. Yet the uniqueness of the postwar period was that writers who in earlier times had reached only a small readership with their critical ideas began to dominate intellectual life. After 1945, Lionel Trilling became among the most noted literary scholars with his assault on Vernon Parrington and the whole Progressive school of criticism; Perry Miller became the most esteemed interpreter of early America with his attacks on Vernon Parrington's and Frederick Jackson Turner's theory that the frontier bred a democratic culture. And the most influential historian of the generation, Richard Hofstadter, sought to demolish the similar arguments of Charles Beard that the people had been continually locked in a battle against the "interests" and monopoly capital.[6]

Essentially, each thinker rejected the older progressive conviction that the society had been dominated by a dualistic struggle between a democratic insurgency and un-American monopolists and advanced new ideas that captured a generation's faith. In a period when the atomic bomb had ended the war and nuclear power promised unlimited energy, scholars applauded Daniel Bell, who argued in *The End of Ideology* that social science yoked to modern technology would allow capitalism in the United States to realize a frontier of abundance, eliminating conflicts over limited resources. Soon historians of the rising "consensus" school went one step further and announced that, rather than a heritage of conflict, the nation's true legacy rested on pragmatism and economic growth. Across the country, a modern symbol of that ethos arose as architects constructed skyscrapers built in the "international style," which celebrated the power of technology. Faith in scientific wizardry permeated popular culture as well. At the end of the "Lone Ranger" radio show in 1947, for example, the hero looked at a shooting star, then remarked to his trusty Indian companion, Tonto, "We don't realize the forces that are in nature. The energy of the blasting powder is nothing compared to the forces of nature and lightning, the waves pounding the rocky beach and the power of the sun itself. If man can harness those forces and make them work for him, there is no limit to what might be accomplished."[7]

Translated into modern realms of power and economic life, that boundless faith also converged with the rise of a new style of nationalism. In the recent past, much of the middle class saw the nation as distinct from Europe because it was a republic where the producers opposed the nonproductive, aristocratic monopolists. Yet, in a period of international expansion and economic growth, public opinion polls no longer recorded strong antimonopoly sentiments. Instead, politicians and businessmen spoke with one voice in praise of the modern corporation and an affluent society where conflicts over scarce resources were a thing of the past. Striking evidence of that convergence occurred in 1959 when Vice President Richard Nixon visited the Soviet Union and engaged in the "kitchen debates" with Soviet Premier Nikita Khrushchev. At the American exhibition in Moscow, the vice president, surrounded by reporters from all over the world, pointed to a well-stocked ranch-style home, complete with kitchen appliances, as proof of capitalism's superiority to communism.[8]

In linking the home to a new "American Way," Nixon revealed in the famed kitchen debates another focal point of the time. Not only was the ideology of consensus grounded in the politics of the cold war, but it also interacted with major developments in family life. Although it had not been predicted by experts, Americans of all classes experienced an unprecedented domestic revival. Recently, sociologists, demographers, and historians have documented the change, but they still have not explained why millions of adults who had lived through the Depression and wartime disasters, now married earlier, slowed what had been an accelerating divorce rate, and generated a baby boom. And, in the expanding suburbs, these new families purchased homes designed in the ranch-house style that Nixon praised so lavishly. On the surface, that domestic ideal appeared a result of affluence—and undoubtedly that was part of it. Yet the vision of abundant home life also provided a focal point for an unprecedented quest for personal fulfillment and consumption that Nixon praised as the core of a new nationalism.[9]

Perhaps for this reason, the same modern homes were often photographed with artworks that displaced the older concerns with public symbols and representation. Grandma Moses's and Norman Rockwell's portrayals of small-town folk still retained great popularity, but official sponsors of international exhibits featured paintings that elevated the artist's personal expression as the essence of American freedom. In the process, Jackson Pollock was portrayed as the avant-garde hero who rebelled against the regionalism and folksy subject matter of his mentor, Thomas Hart Benton, to create a widely popular abstract expressionism. Recently, art historians have even linked that stylistic change directly to the ideology of the cold war, and still others have found its determinants in the formal developments initiated by a coterie of New York artists drawing on European developments in surrealism and cubism.[10]

Whichever interpretation gains precedence, it is important to realize that this modernist thrust was also part of a generational rebellion. By way of contrast, throughout the twenties and thirties, the trendsetters in literature and the arts arguing for the autonomy of each field remained a minority. But in the postwar period that minority became the majority. Now a full-blown modernism arose, with abstract expressionist and color-field canvases, free from referents outside itself; with an international school of architecture, stripped of historical imagery; with a literature focused on the inner life and stylistic innovation; with a New Criticism concerned with the nature of beauty and literary form divorced from social context.[11]

Ironically, the modernist thrust did generate one common theme across newly autonomous fields: a concern with anxiety. In some ways, of course, that concern was not new. Earlier American writers and painters, from Henry Adams, Herman Melville, and Mark Twain to Thomas Eakins, Winslow Homer, and Albert Ryder both dramatized pessimistic themes and created stylistic innovation. Yet their tragic visions did not penetrate very deeply into a culture grounded in Enlightenment ideals of historical progress. After 1945, however, the change could not have been more stark. In the performing arts, playwrights such as Tennessee Williams and Arthur Miller created dramas, particularly A Streetcar Named Desire and Death of a Salesman, which portrayed family disintegration and self-destruction. Best-selling novelists, led by Kurt Vonnegut, Jr., Norman Mailer, and Ralph Ellison, found large audiences by combining brilliant neomodernist experiments in narration with the portrayals of characters suffering despair and lost identity. Likewise, poets of the Beat Generation continued to admire earlier writers like Walt Whitman and Henry Thoreau but could realize their democratic ideals only by turning to separate bohemias and Eastern religions, far from the mainstream of modern life.[12]

The undercurrent of anxiety, moreover, that ran beneath the affluent consensus incorporated far more than alienated artists and youthful rebels.

Just as important were major thinkers who generated a series of remarkable innovations in the academic world. In the main current moved perhaps the most influential intellectual of the period, Reinhold Niebuhr, a theologian who shed his earlier commitment to progress and optimism and now portrayed mankind caught in sin and irony. Another tributary joined when the psychologist Erik Erikson perceived young people as undergoing identity crises and the sociologist David Riesman found in *The Lonely Crowd* a generation turning into "other-directed" Americans. Still another current merged when C. Wright Mills discovered a "new middle class" trapped in large organizations and the philosopher Herbert Marcuse critiqued the ensuing "one-dimensional" men. The river could even broaden to include future presidential advisers like the noted historian Arthur Schlesinger, Jr., who cautioned his contemporaries in 1949 that history was "not a redeemer, promising to solve all human problems in time; nor is man capable of transcending the limits of his being. Man is generally entangled in insoluble problems; history is a constant tragedy in which all are involved, whose keynote is anxiety and frustration, not progress and fulfillment."[13]

Skeptical observers, of course, have suggested that this unease characterized only a minority of elite intellectuals, far removed from the popular culture of the people. And it is true that the mass media were now characterized by a positive tone that reinforced the affluent consensus, as evidenced by the phenomenal success of Norman Vincent Peale, Bing Crosby, and family television shows. Yet what was also unprecedented was the rise of a large market for dark, pessimistic works whose cinematic forms manifested a stark beauty. Starting in the early forties, for example, a new type of gangster and detective film arose. The ensuing "film noir" genre portrayed the world in stark images, with antiheroes often psychically tormented. By the 1950s, science fiction, suspense, and juvenile delinquency films sparked artists such as Alfred Hitchcock to evoke the harmony of the affluent world, then slowly reveal the irrational terror beneath the placid surface.[14]

What is more, filmmakers often surrounded these dark images with musical innovations that shattered the older harmonies as well. In the Depression era, the most popular music was "swing," a unified sound which drew on American melodies and jazz. Yet, in the forties, innovators broke from that unity and created the more complex rhythms and dissonances of "bebop." Practiced by black musicians like Charles Parker and Dizzy Gillespie, bebop was both a break from sentimental melodies and an expression of black American existence outside the affluent consensus. But the polyrhythms and dissonance of bebop soon filled the soundtracks of numerous popular films and set the stage in the fifties for the phenomenal rise of "rock and roll." As the lyrics and rhythms of black artists, minorities, and working-class whites gained popularity, rock and roll became a well-publicized symbol of the era's most noticeable development—the rise of a rebellious youth culture.[15]

At this point, we have come full circle to where we began, making it possible to appreciate fully why Harold Clurman saw that from 1940 to 1960 his worldview had turned upside down. The American people had previously experienced economic downturns and wars, but never before had these social crises carried in their wake such a remarkable reorientation of national values and artistic forms. Although many of these alterations have been explored as innovations isolated to each field, a noted historian over twenty years ago pinpointed the larger issue that still awaits investigation. Upon reviewing Richard Hofstadter's *The Progressive Historians*, David Potter recognized that, while the author was a major contributor to the new consensus school of history arising after the war, his concentration on the internal evolution of the history profession had not clarified why the paradigms of the old Progressives—Turner, Beard, and Parrington—now seemed so dated. "Could Hofstadter have analyzed in a more direct way the specific changes in ideology," wrote Potter, "which made these writers, once so perfectly attuned to prevailing tendencies in social thought, so irrelevant," then our knowledge would be immeasurably richer.[16]

More than two decades have passed since that evaluation, and, if anything, the question looms larger than ever: Why in the Depression did hardship and conflict yield political optimism and artistic unity, but in the affluent fifties a widespread consensus was characterized by fragmentation and anxiety? Certainly one reason why this question remains unanswered is that the intellectual heritage created after the war still dominates the academic world. To explore a transformation in ideology—the values, beliefs, and worldview informing a people or group over time—would entail an investigation of the arts and political change in a process of interaction. However, the academic innovators after the war separated questions of value from historical contexts. Within the humanities, the New Critics and their theoretical descendants in literature and art were bent on analyzing texts and artifacts without reference to the wider historical context. At the same time, the innovators in the social sciences brought to full realization what had formerly been a powerful but still not dominant trend as they separated the observation of group behavior from the historical process that had traditionally been vested in their fields. As a consequence, humanists increasingly studied text without context, social scientists context without text, making it impossible to see the mutual interaction between art and society, history and ideology.[17]

Unfortunately, historians have not done much better. It is not just that those whose professional standing rests on the study of change over time have traditionally ignored the arts but that investigators of the postwar era have divided it into discrete themes or decades, making impossible a long-term view of ideological transformation. Discussions of cold war and domestic politics typically begin in 1945 and focus on who started the foreign conflict, or how the conservatives and liberals battled it out in the McCarthy period over the New Deal heritage, with little analysis of whether the values informing these events differed from those of earlier periods. More persuasive, but still not satisfying, are those scholars who focus on cultural themes or political concepts that distinguish the era, from the ideology of consensus and age of anxiety to the counterculture and civil rights rebellion of the "conservative" fifties. Yet, because these discussions avoid the paradigm shift that so absorbed contemporaries' attention, readers have no way of knowing how concepts like the consensus and "age of anxiety" came into being.[18]

The study of postwar America, in other words, is in need of a vigorous infusion of new ideas and approaches. Yet, by treating the period as a self-contained entity, historians have helped isolate their work from the innovations that might have furthered that reassessment. Starting in the sixties, those interested in the history of black Americans, followed by women, ethnics, and other groups, began to devise new methods, such as quantification, oral history, and demography to uncover experiences that had been ignored by practitioners of the consensus school. Similarly, pioneering humanists and cultural historians began to break down the divisions between the study of art, of politics, and of popular culture, with one result being that we now understand earlier social movements to be informed by a republican ideology at odds with monopoly capital. Yet, if it followed that our view of the American past was seriously revised and the uniqueness of the postwar consensus stood out in high relief, a difficult question remained for those who wanted to apply similar approaches to the postwar period: How was one to understand the transformation from the coherent cultures of the eighteenth and nineteenth centuries to an era characterized by art forms devoid of social referents, academic fragmentation, and ideological reorientation?[19]

Given that the authors in this collection sought to answer these questions, it is significant that they first gathered at a conference sponsored by the Program of American Studies at the University of Minnesota. American Studies provided an ideal meeting ground because it came into existence as an interdisciplinary field after World War II to resist the academic trend of separating art and values from their historical context. The founding generation also developed great skill in relating intellectual and popular thought to long-term social and cultural formations, be they worldviews, ethoses, or symbols. While the first generation was limited by their concentration on static, homogeneous, Anglo-Saxon myths of the nineteenth century, the past two decades have seen American Studies researchers also investigating issues of race, gender, and paradigm change. As articulated by scholars such as Thomas Kuhn, John Higham, Eric Foner, and Carlo Ginsberg, society no longer can be viewed as a static, harmonious system. Rather, culture is—in the words of the anthropologist Anthony Wallace— a "structure of conflict" in which separate parts are maintained, developed and changed by different groups and in many aspects experienced in slightly different ways by every individual.[20]

What distinguishes the contributors to *Recasting America*, then, is that, as they work within the context of these more dynamic approaches to cultural study, the result adds up to a new view of the United States from 1940 to 1960. In exploring key aspects of that change, this collection has brought together humanists, political theorists, and historians whose interdisciplinary explorations revolve around explaining a central process. Against the backdrop of the Great Depression, these authors examine high and popular culture by drawing on traditional techniques of American studies to treat these two spheres as moving simultaneously in a similar direction, and interacting with a common set of structural conflicts. Yet they also see that these common experiences are interpreted differently by each class and group. Particularly for alienated artists and subcultures, such as blacks, Chicanos, bop musicians, abstract expressionists, and participants in the new youth culture, the conflict stimulated utopian artistic forms and political possibilities.

Above all, as each author seeks to explain what *caused* that shift in culture, the aim is not to close off discussion but to spark debate and pose hypotheses for future research. Without distorting the nuances of each essay, we can divide that debate into three schools of thought. The first, represented by Warren Susman and Jackson Lears in the opening section, "Toward a Theory of Postwar America," demonstrates that a corporate order was fully legitimized after World War II. For Susman, that accomplishment fulfilled the earlier wishes of American thinkers and leaders fully to organize national life. But, with the work done, that accomplishment also released a sense of loss, a fact that explains the contradictory images of optimism and anxiety that characterized intellectual and popular culture. Lears, in turn, draws on the concepts of Antonio Gramsci to argue that a "new middle class" gained hegemony within the new corporate order, propagating monolithic values rooted in the promise of classless consumption. Yet beneath that consensus was the continuing reality of class, race, and psychological repression that sparked the undertone of discontent.

Another set of writers, however, offers a different causal explanation. As readers move to the next two sections, "The Intellectual Reorientation," and "The Making of Cold War Culture," they will participate in the second stage of the debate that followed Lears's and Susman's presentations. Although these authors acknowledge that something distinct occurred after 1945 and that a new corporate order came to power, the first set of writers argues that the unique qualities of the age were stimulated by the disintegration of an American identity that had informed national life for over a hundred years. In the thirties, that progressive ethos came to center on New Deal efforts to reform the corporations and remain isolated from international involvements. Yet, as best articulated by David Noble in his exploration of the historians Charles Beard and Richard Hofstadter, the coming of World War II saw that hostility to capitalism defeated by events. Some intellectuals responded with a pervasive sense of loss and despair. Others, as portrayed in Terence Ball's essay on social science and in Carl Schorske's personal memoir of a major cultural historian, launched intellectual innovations that reoriented academic thought.

Out of this larger crisis of the Progressive tradition, others explain why the consensus became so pervasive after 1945. Here, the critical factor was the cultural impact of anticommunism. As Norman Rosenberg argues in his study of legal thought, and I in my exploration of Hollywood politics, the postwar Red Scare was less an irrational crusade than a revolutionary ideology that legitimized the new corporate order and promised an escape from wars, depressions and hard times. Elaine Tyler May and Clifford Clark then demonstrate in their examinations of domestic ideology and suburban architecture that this political ideology deeply affected private values. In creating the ideology of abundance, experts now saw family life warding off communism and containing dangers associated with consumption and the moral revolution. The result served to focus wishes for freedom on the private home and helps explain the unprecedented family formation and baby boom that centered in the growing suburbs.

At the same time, the quest for cultural renewal that sparked the rising consensus moved others to question its deepest assumptions. In exploring how that led artists and alienated groups to reassess racial concepts and ways of life that had dominated American life for over two hundred years, the final section, "The Search for Alternatives: Art, Minorities, and Popular Culture," begins with Erika Doss's reinterpretation of the roots of abstract expressionism. Beginning with the thirties, she demonstrates that Thomas Hart Benton saw his art dramatizing New Deal reform and reorientation of Anglo-Saxon individualism. But when the larger Progressive culture turned into the entrapments and inertia of a consensus society, his student, Jackson Pollock, generated abstract expressionism to represent new forms of artistic and psychological exploration. A similar reorientation informs Lewis Erenberg's study of the path from swing music to bebop. In the wake of the war, he shows that boppers shed the sounds of swing and developed a postwar jazz scene to continue their search for a more vital, pluralistic community. Finally, John Wright's study of the major black novelist Ralph Ellison and George Lipsitz's discussion of Richie Valens and Chicano rock and roll take this analysis one step further. Each shows how these artists not only used their art to rework American racial concepts that formerly inhibited the rise of effective minority leaders but also forged a culture and politics attractive to their own people as well as rebellious white youth.

That contest, moreover, was not isolated to the United States. Indeed, as the economic and military power of the country spread around the globe, American images spread through a mass-media system that was now international in scope. To explore the consequences of that process, the collection ends with Reinhold Wagnleitner's discussion of how United States forces occupying Austria after the war tried to impose the newly made consensus on Europeans. Hoping to reverse the former relationship of a provincial American culture to the aristocratic civilization of Europe, policymakers exported books and plays to democratize people and win the cold war. Yet the Austrians rejected that "high" culture, which they still saw as inferior to their own, and turned instead to the popular art and ideas of America's formerly despised minorities. As rock and roll, bebop music, and movies spread through the free marketplace of mass communications, it excited European youth's admiration, and offered for many a means to contest the rigidities of the cold war consensus in the East and West.

Wagnleitner's essay also provides an ideal conclusion to the collection as a whole. For in focusing on the dualistic response to the unprecedented spread of American power and ideas into the intenational arena, his study brings into high relief the benefits and costs of the values that emerged in the age of cold war. Did the transformation of intellectual and popular thought, along with the full flowering of a consumption economy, generate passivity in the face of a highly organized social order, or did it release new forms of creativity and liberation? Some of our contributors argue that the reorientation of values in the cold war era severely constricted political and personal options. Others perceive that the crisis generated by the erosion of an older, Anglo-Saxon tradition allowed formerly repressed ideas and minorities to find expression and power. Whichever side of the debate appears more convincing, it is our hope that the readers of *Recasting America* will also be stimulated to rethink an era that, for better or worse, continues to influence the lives of people in the United States as well as foreign countries.

NOTES

1. Harold Clurman, *The Fervent Years: The Group Theatre and the 30's* (New York: Harcourt Brace Jovanovich, 1975), 281–313.

2. On consensus history, coupled with a critique, see John Higham, "Beyond Consensus: The Historian as Moral Critic," in *Writing American History: Essays on Modern Scholarship*, ed. John Higham (Bloomington: Indiana University Press, 1970), 139–56. A good overview of the new social history is Olivier Zunz, "The Synthesis of Social Change: Reflections on American Social History," in *Relieving the Past: The Worlds of Social History*, ed. Olivier Zunz (Chapel Hill: University of North Carolina Press, 1985). For an overview of the literature on the republican, producer ethic, see Gordon Wood, "Hellfire Politics," review of *The Lost Soul of American Politics*, by John Diggins, in *New York Review of Books* (February 28, 1985): 29–33.

3. On various aspects of politics and culture in the Great Depression, see Warren Susman, *Culture as History: The Transformation of American Culture in the 20th Century* (New York: Pantheon, 1985); Richard Pells, *Radical Visions and American Dreams: Culture and Social Thought in the Depression Years* (New York: Harper and Row, 1973); Alan Brinkley, *Voices of Protest: Huey Long, Father Coughlin and the Great Depression* (New York: Knopf, 1982); John Higham, "The Mobilization of Immigrants in Urban America, ed. Odd S. Lovel (Northfield, Minn.: Saint Olaf College Press, 1985), 1–29; Alfred Kazin, *On Native Grounds: An Interpretation of Modern American Prose Literature* (New York: Harcourt Brace Jovanovich, 1970); Gene Wise, *American Historical Explanations: A Strategy for Grounded Inquiry* (Minneapolis: University of Minnesota Press, 1980), 179–223; Marlene Park and Gerald E. Markowitz, *Democratic Vistas: Post Offices and Pub-*

lic Art in the New Deal (Philadelphia: Temple University Press, 1985); Robert Sklar, *Movie Made America: A Cultural History of American Movies* (New York: Vintage, 1975), 195–215; Roy Rosenzweig, "United Action Means Victory: Militant Americanism on Film," *Labor History* 24 (Spring 1983): 274–88; *The Devil and Daniel Webster* (RKO, 1941), also known as *All That Money Can Buy.*

4. Sacvan Bercovitch, *The American Jeremiad* (Madison: University of Wisconsin Press, 1978); John Morton Blum, *V Was for Victory: Politics and American Culture during World War II* (New York: Harcourt Brace Jovanovich, 1976).

5. A convenient summary of the scholarly debate on cold war diplomacy can be found in Thomas J. McCormick, "Drift or Mastery? A Corporatist Synthesis For American Diplomatic History," in *The Promise of American History: Progress and Prospects,* ed. Stanley I. Kutler and Stanley N. Katz (Baltimore: Johns Hopkins University Press, 1982), 318–30. A similar overview of domestic anticommunism can be found in Robert Griffith and Athan Theoharis, *The Specter: Original Essays in the Cold War and the Origins of McCarthyism* (New York: New Viewpoints, 1974).

6. Wise, *American Historical Explanations,* 179–359.

7. Daniel Bell, *The End of Ideology: On the Exhaustion of Political Ideas in the Fifties* (Glencoe, Ill.: Free Press, 1960). On the rise of the consensus in intellectual thought, see Robert Fowler, *Believing Skeptics* (Westport, Conn.: Greenwood, 1978), and Godfrey Hodgson, *America in Our Times: From World War II to Nixon* (New York: Doubleday, 1978), 67–98. William Jordy, *American Buildings and Their Architects: The Impact of European Modernism in the Mid-twentieth Century* (New York: Anchor, 1976). "Lone Ranger" radio show, "The Rays of the Sun," April 1947, in the J. Fred McDonald Personal Collection, Northeastern University, Chicago, Illinois.

8. The transformation in national identity as portrayed by historians from 1930 to 1960 is the main subject in David Noble, *The End of American History: Democracy, Capitalism, and the Metaphor of Two Worlds in Anglo-American Historical Writing, 1880–1980* (Minneapolis: University of Minnesota Press, 1985). On the change in polls, see Hodgson, *America in Our Time,* 67–98. For the Nixon "kitchen debate," see "The Two Worlds: A Day-long Debate," *New York Times* (July 25, 1959): 1, 3.

9. Andrew Cherlin, *Marriage, Divorce, Remarriage* (Cambridge: Harvard University Press, 1981).

10. On international exhibits and abstract expressionism, see Jane De Hart Matthews, "Art and Politics in Cold War America," *American Historical Review* 81 (October 1976): 762–87. For the two versions of the new style's origins, see Serge Guilbaut, *How New York Stole the Idea of Modern Art* (Chicago: University of Chicago Press, 1983); Irving Sandler, *The Triumph of American Painting: A History of Abstract Expressionism* (New York: Praeger, 1970); Meyer Schapiro, *Modern Art: 19th and 20th Centuries* (New York: Braziller, 1978), 179–232.

11. The roots of the new literary criticism in the thirties can be found in Kazin, *On Native Grounds,* 400–452. For the postwar era, see Grant Webster, *The Republic of Letters: A History of Post-War American Literary Opinion* (Baltimore: Johns Hopkins University Press, 1979). A good sampling of postwar modernism,

from both painters and critics, can be found in *Readings in American Art, 1900–1975*, ed. Barbara Rose (New York: Praeger, 1975), 103–46.

12. See, for example, Josephine Henden, *Vulnerable People: A View of American Fiction since 1945* (New York: Oxford University Press, 1978), and Howard M. Harper, Jr., *Desperate Faith* (Chapel Hill: University of North Carolina Press, 1967). And, for one among many contemporary statements, see Norman Mailer, "Hipsters," in *Advertisements for Myself* (New York: Putnam, 1959), pt. 4, and *The White Negro* (San Francisco: City Lights, 1957). *The Modern American Theatre*, ed. Alvan B. Kernan (Englewood Cliffs, N.J.: Prentice-Hall, 1967); Bruce Cook, *The Beat Generation* (New York: Scribners, 1971).

13. On Niebuhr, see Donald B. Meyer, *The Protestant Search for Political Realism, 1919–1941* (Berkeley: University of California Press, 1960); on the general trend of social criticism from the standpoint of personal alienation, see Peter Clecak, *Radical Paradoxes: Dilemmas of the American Left* (New York: Harper and Row, 1977); and Hodgson, *America in Our Time*, 67–99, 274–87; Fowler, *Believing Skeptics*. The Schlesinger quote is from his famous *Partisan Review* essay. See Arthur Schlesinger, Jr., "The Causes of the American Civil War: A Note on Historical Sentimentalism," in *The Causes of the American Civil War*, ed. E. C. Rozwenc (Boston: Heath, 1961).

14. Eric Goldman, in *The Crucial Decade—And After: America 1945–1960* (New York: Vintage, 1960), 305, observed that "the intellectuals satirized and gloomed and warned, and the general public did not listen." William O'Neill, in *Coming Apart: An Informal History of America in the 1960's* (Chicago: Quadrangle, 1971), 4, added that "Materialism and conformity prevailed everywhere, it was said, though few outside the intellectual community seemed to mind." A brilliant discussion of Peale and other optimistic postwar thinkers can be found in Donald Meyer, *The Positive Thinkers: Religion as Pop Psychology from Mary Baker Eddy to Oral Roberts* (New York: Pantheon, 1980). Barbara Deming, *Running Away from Myself: A Dream Portrait of America Drawn from the Films of the Forties* (New York: Grossman, 1969); John H. Lenihan, *Showdown: Confronting Modern America in the Western Film* (Urbana: University of Illinois Press, 1980).

15. For the best cultural account of the transition from swing to bop, see Imamu Amiri Baraka, *Blues People: The Negro Experience in White America and the Music That Developed from It* (New York: Morrow, 1963), 142–244.

16. David Potter, "Conflict, Consensus and Comity," review of *The Progressive Historians*, by Richard Hofstadter, in *History and American Society: Essays of David M. Potter*, ed. David E. Fehrenbacher (New York: Oxford University Press, 1973), 190.

17. I am using the term "ideology" in much the same way as that outlined in Eric Foner, *Free Soil, Free Labor, Free Men: The Ideology of the Republican Party before the Civil War* (New York: Oxford University Press, 1970), 4–5, and in Clifford Geertz, "Ideology as a Cultural System," in *The Interpretation of Cultures*, ed. Clifford Geertz, (New York: Basic, 1964), 193–233. For an account of the humanities, see Webster, *The Republic of Letters*, and for a contemporary criticism of the removal of the social science from historical and public issues, see C. Wright Mills, *The Sociological Imagination* (New York: Grove, 1961), 20–22,

42–43, 61–62, 143. For the roots of the process that came to completion after 1945, see Philip Abrams, "The Sense of the Past and the Origins of Sociology," *Past and Present* 55 (1972): 18–32, and Alvin Bauldner, *The Crisis of Western Sociology* (New York: Basic, 1970), 88–157.

18. The historical literature on the various parts of the postwar era is vast. The following, then is but a representative sample of the dominant trends. To grasp the foreign-policy debate, see McCormick, "Drift or Mastery?" For the self-contained, decade-by-decade approach to politics, see Eric Goldman's classic, *The Crucial Decade*. For the contrasting culture of each decade's analysis, stressing almost always the conservative 1950s with the rebellious 1960s, see Paul Carter, *Another Part of the Fifties* (New York: Columbia University Press, 1983); Benjamin DeMott, *Surviving the 70s* (New York: Dutton, 1977); Roland Stromberg, *After Everything: Western Intellectual History since 1945* (New York: St. Martin's, 1977). For those that stress the distinctive themes of the era, see William Leuchtenberg, *A Troubled Feast: American Society since 1945* (Boston: Little, Brown, 1973); Richard Polenberg, *One Nation Divisible: Race, Class and Ethnicity in the United States since 1938* (New York: Viking, 1980); Robert Wiebe, *The Segmented Society: An Introduction to the Meaning of America* (New York: Oxford University Press, 1975); Fowler, *Believing Skeptics*; Hodgson, *America in Our Time*; Clecak, *Radical Paradoxes*.

19. For a survey of the new social history, see Zunz, "The Synthesis of Social Change," and for criticism of its often apolitical, fragmented approach to the past, see Eric Foner, *Politics and Ideology in the Age of the Civil War* (New York: Oxford University Press, 1980), 3–15. For the new approaches to art history and political ideology, see the special issue "Art and Ideology," *Radical History Review* 38 (Spring, 1987): 3–154. On popular culture, theory, and history, see George Lipsitz, "'This Ain't No Side Show': Historians and Media Studies," *Critical Studies in Mass Communication* (June, 1988). For republicanism, see the overview by Wood, "Hellfire Politics."

20. The classic statement of American Studies' aims is Henry Nash Smith, "Can 'American Studies' Develop a Method?" in *The American Experience: Approaches to the Study of the United States*, ed., Hennig Cohen (Boston: Houghton Mifflin, 1968), 338–49. On the problem of conceptualizing cultural transitions, see John Higham, *Writing American History*, 40–102, and for the analysis of paradigm change, see Thomas Kuhn, *The Structure of Scientific Revolutions* (Chicago: University of Chicago Press, 1962); Eric Foner, *Politics and Ideology*, 1–53; Carlo Ginsberg, "Preface to the English Edition" in *The Cheese and the Worms*, trans. John and Anne Tedeschi (Baltimore: Johns Hopkins University Press, 1980), xi–xxvi; Anthony Wallace, *Rockdale: The Growth of an American Village in the Early Industrial Revolution* (New York: Knopf, 1978), xvi, 477–85.

PART ONE

Toward a Theory of
Postwar America

1   *Did Success Spoil the United States?*
Dual Representations in
Postwar America

Warren Susman
with the assistance of Edward Griffin

Naught's had, all's spent,
where our desire is got without content.
　　　　　　　　　—Macbeth

Can we define the America of the period following World War II as a distinct culture? I want to begin an answer with a partial assumption—one I think I can demonstrate. By the end of the war (certainly, let us say, by the period between the end of the war and 1955), America had succeeded, beyond anyone's expectations, in achieving many of its goals. Americans had produced on these shores the society and government which, since the late nineteenth century, many politicians and intellectuals had hoped for. Fulfilling those utopian dreams made the United States a success, not only in terms of winning the war, but also in terms of winning the battle to create the kind of world that in the previous century had been merely a wish.

Ironically, however, this moment of triumph was accompanied by something disturbing: a new self-consciousness of tragedy and sense of disappointment. The postwar success story was also the "age of anxiety."

I

In accounting for this irony, the matter of approach is, of course, crucial. I want to assert at the outset, therefore, that I am not interested in cultural history as a series of events. I do not argue that events are unimportant, or that events do not change things, or that events are insignificant. I do claim, however, that if one tries to develop a cultural analysis based on the assumption that particular events, such as wars or depressions, are causal, one will develop a traditional narrative demanding a traditional narrative logic. Yet that search will limit one's ability to see continuity and change outside those events. Hence, one will spend a good deal of time arguing about how the cold war did this or that and very little time wondering whether the cold war itself was not part of a larger cultural complex. From my perspective, however, the major problem of cultural history is to find that pattern which is not the logic of narrative but the logic of the way people operate within a culture. I wish to move beyond the notion of events as historically important in favor of other kinds of significant foci.

We take a useful step, therefore, in locating the patterns of postwar American life when we ask why so many social thinkers believed that after 1945 their earlier hopes had been realized. We can see, first, that a significant shift in government policy did take place at this time. Before 1945, reformers, from the Populists through the New Dealers, envisioned a democratic state which guarded the general welfare and managed the economy. Such a social order had begun emerging after the Civil War, but Harry Truman, between 1946 and 1948, did what no previous president had been able to do: he added the crucial final pieces.

One need cite only a few of those pieces to recognize the salient features. Probably the most significant was the Full Employment Act of 1946. Granted that social legislation was frequently watered down in practice and in subsequent legal amendments; nonetheless the Full Employment Act was very important as policy. It committed the government to responsibility for achieving total employment, and it affirmed the economic theories of John Maynard Keynes as the official economic doctrine of the United States. To assume such responsibility and to establish the Council of Economic Advisers was a new and significant step.[1]

This step was accompanied by another which established fresh relationships among the government, its agencies, and the major corporate powers of the nation. It was the passage of the Atomic Energy Act in 1946, a piece of legislation decidedly influential in bringing the new state into existence. It gave control of materials, facilities, products, research, and information to a special Atomic Energy Commission, and it signaled to Americans that, if modern industries and research brought risks, the government of the United States would bear them; if the new industries brought gains, private corporate power would make them.[2]

The modern state emerged on the foreign as well as the domestic scene. Government interest in foreign affairs had hitherto been largely defensive, but between 1946 and 1949 the United States launched a series of unprecedented international initiatives. In the name of "security," those initiatives engaged the government in arenas in which it had never before operated. The founding of the National Security Council and the Central Intelligence Agency, for example, along with the right to allocate whatever forces or resources might be needed in times of emergency, indicates the establishment of an elaborate system of protections. The system had domestic features as well. Internal investigations and loyalty legislation were joined with laws to extend security to families in the form of benefits to homeowners, children, and widows. A national housing act in 1954 (which was a most radical departure from past practice) further illustrates the fulfillment of the dreams of welfare-state advocates from the 1880s onward.[3]

Social commentators, therefore, saw emerging around them the outlines of an America which realized the visions of those who had wished to see the state assume responsibility for the economy and general welfare. They thought they saw what a modern capitalist society might become when it was liberated from the excesses of individual competition and cutthroat practice. They seemed to see it becoming a society of abundance and, as such, the fulfillment of yet another long-standing dream. It was a dream that Franklin Roosevelt had entertained; if one returns to his public papers of the Great Depression, one finds him saying that there *is* great abundance out there, but it is abundance we cannot appropriate because the mechanism has broken down. Once we repair the mechanism and get at all that wealth, Roosevelt promised, all our problems will essentially be solved.[4] And in the late 1940s and 1950s, precisely such a situation seemed to be developing. The long search for a comfortable life, a search unsatisfied throughout the history of the republic, appeared to have reached its end.

If we yearned for a consumer paradise, a world of abundance in which things would be easy to purchase, consume, and maintain, the unprecedented economic growth unfolding after World War II was making that wish come true for middle-class Americans. Perhaps, many thinkers speculated, the developing consumer marketplace could eliminate gross social inequalities and create conditions where we could all love automobiles, have refrigerators, and own ranch houses (which could be big or small but, above all, similar).

Symbolizing the world of new possibilities was the suburban ideal. Earlier in our history, the notion of suburban life, which began to unfold in the 1870s and 1880s, was a fantasy fulfilled only for the wealthy, and then only partially attained. It continued to be a dream, however, for less well-to-do Americans. Yet, in the postwar years, the new affluence allowed millions of ordinary Americans to acquire their suburban homes. With them, they hoped to attain the domestic perfection for which middle-class Americans had traditionally yearned, since there has been, throughout our history, an effort to connect our consciousness, civilization, and demography to the American home and the American Dream.[5]

Indeed, the literary, artistic, and photographic representations of the Depression and war foreshadow the concern for family that so characterizes the period after 1945: one can find it as far back as 1933, in Eugene O'Neill's *Ah, Wilderness,* with its sentimental yearnings about a little boy growing up in the bosom of a great family with a wonderful father—a prefiguration of the Andy Hardy vision of the American family that dominated the late thirties and early forties (and won, in 1942, a special Academy Award for Louis B. Mayer's use of the film to preserve the "American Way of Life"). One recalls Thornton Wilder's *The Skin of Our Teeth* (1942), with its primeval image: the primordial family, Adam and Eve and Cain and Abel, throughout wars and panics and disasters, survives. In the most dismal photographs of the Great Depression, in the home-front images of wartime, family unity is crucial and central.[6] One can typify that emphasis by remembering how Norman Rockwell turned the American "Four Freedoms" into family-centered events: "Freedom from Want" was the family at Thanksgiving gathered around the table; "Freedom from Fear" was the parents looking in on the sleeping child, a primal vision.

After the war, moreover, the government advanced support for dependent children, created housing acts, and instituted urban renewal, all in the name of the home. And by the fifties Father Patrick Peyton tried to get Americans to pray together, with his campaign motto "The family who prays together stays together," and popular magazines campaigned for marital "togetherness." Not to be outdone, the new medium of television found its function in domestic-centered television shows, from "I Love Lucy" to "I Remember Mama," all seen in the "family room." (Indeed, think of all the family words enveloping the new suburban life-style: family-size carton, family room, family car, family film, family restaurant, family vacation.) In essence, one can represent the new affluent society collectively in the image of the happy suburban home.[7]

II

At this point, however, we encounter a difficulty. In the very hour of achievement, of triumph over fascism and totalitarian government, doubts began to arise. An extraordinary heightening of consciousness occurred; its development is very important, for it signalled a startlingly new feature of our history. To highlight the unique quality of that phenomenon, let us linger over the serious point made in a marvelous spoof of the

Middle Ages, entitled *1066 and All That*. In it there is a wonderful passage purporting to state what the barons agreed to on that fateful day when the Magna Carta was finally signed. The last provision of that charter was "We pledge to keep up the Middle Ages." Now it is perfectly obvious that nobody in that period knew he was living in the Middle Ages. People were not conscious of themselves as living between epochs in this particular, dramatic way. The idea of the Middle Ages was something invented by historians in the eighteenth century to refer to an earlier period, for scholars frequently look back and discover all sorts of things that participants at the time did not know anything about.[8]

Yet, in contrast, people in the period from 1945 onward actually talked about living in an "age of anxiety." They saw themselves living in an age of crisis that they despised and during which they began to develop a vision of what life was like. What they discovered was not new, but their concern, particularly in its intensity, was new: it is rare for a people to be so self-aware, so self-conscious, so self-concerned. I can provide here only a brief introduction to this topic. Some of these observations will surprise you, some will not, but these discoveries were significant because they came in the wake of this optimistic dream of fulfillment and because they were originally defined in an entirely different sense.

One observes, first of all, that at the very point at which young America had achieved its fulfillment in the development of state influence and had produced one of the strongest governments the world had ever known, commentators began raising alarms about the dangers of such power. These alarms find expression in an enormous outpouring of literature about totalitarianism and the abuses of central governments. The sheer volume of writing on the topic is impressive, and an examination of these texts reveals a particularly telling fact: the new vision of totalitarianism reverses a series of formerly sacred principles.

One reversal focused on the ideal of mass participation in government. In the nineteenth century, of course, democratic dreamers had argued that the mass involvement of the citizenry realized the American dream. Now, questions arose about the possibility that such mass participation would encourage dogmatic ideology and lead to a totalitarian state. The irony is deep here because the older literature had celebrated the great vision of unity, coalescence, and agreement, the goal that the citizenry should assimilate those who were not American and create a system of shared, fundamental values. Trying to do so, leaders created an iconography of holidays, flags, and symbols.

Another principle undergoing rethinking was the power of government to interfere in the lives of the people. Obviously, the government was now active in places where it had not formerly intervened. The very functioning of the welfare state had moved in this direction. New writers, however, were sounding the alarm about the dangers. John Updike, as an example, came onto the scene as a new novelist during a time when planners had created the greatest welfare system they had ever dreamed about and in his first novel, *Poorhouse Fair*, told the story of people rebelling against the institution they live in—an institution sociologically run by the latest principles of welfarism.[9]

Everywhere we look, then, old ideals were now seen as new threats. Mass culture: fearful writers now produced a series of major tracts about it. Interestingly enough, if one had bothered to look, one would have discovered that many of the same critics who attacked mass culture in the 1940s and 1950s were, in the teens and twenties, its greatest proponents. Dwight Macdonald, for instance, had cheered on the rise of mass culture. Earlier in the century, he had written about and glorified the sudden rise of the popular arts and talked about the heroic status of Charles Chaplin, but he bemoaned in the 1950s what mass culture was doing and the kind of conformity that it had created.[10]

And in the 1950s Americans discovered violence. Of course, we have always been an aggressive people and have always talked about violence, but not until the 1950s did readers begin to see thousands of articles analyzing it as a fundamental character defect in American life. Social commentators began to see violence as a part of the process of historical development and as a characteristic American response which from the very beginning had depended upon those higher up for its solutions. I have often asked my classes this question: "When you see a Western in which the man in the black hat and the man in the white hat start down the street together, would you like to see one man reach for his revolver and then say, 'Hey, let's not fight it out, let's go to the saloon and reason together?'" Audiences would boo, hiss, and stamp their feet. They know there has to be a showdown at the OK Corral. Violence is built into the American mythology. Yet, in this period violence was suddenly defined as a major problem that society needed to solve.[11]

Connected with the growing apprehensions about violence was the shocking realization that in the supposedly wonderful world of suburbia juvenile crime—what came to be termed "juvenile delinquency"—was springing up. Juvenile delinquency, one might have assumed, had no place in the abundant environment of suburbia. It was supposed to be the consequence of slum living, of the sociological conditions of depressed people who do not have enough money. Yet, investigators discovered it in the affluent suburbs, where everybody had a car and access to all the goods and services that money could buy. Who, asked the social commentators, are those juvenile delinquents? The answer was chilling: they were "rebels without a cause," essentially psychopathic personalities.[12]

These discoveries—that things were not working out in practice precisely as theory had predicted—disturbed investigators, but even more frightening was the basic finding that America was in fact a hypocritical society, believing one thing and practicing another. Norman Mailer's first novel, his war novel, *The Naked and the Dead*, illustrates that point. The American army he describes, because of its fascist implications and its authoritarian general, is more of a threat than the violent enemy, although supposedly the enemy is fascism itself. Another illustration is Gunnar Myrdal's 1944 report on what he called "the American dilemma." The people believed in the democratic creed, but when it came to treating blacks equally, they did not really believe in the democratic creed. Or one might reflect on Estes Kefauver's televised senate investigations, which showed criminal activity by some of the country's most admired corporations. If one could find criminals in the high places of respected business authority, what else could one expect to find? Indeed, one of the most extraordinary revelations of the McCarthy investigations was the presence of presumably subversive communists in Hollywood, the churches, and the army of the United States.[13]

Even the new affluence came under attack. Numerous observers began to wonder what it meant to live in an abundant society. What could be done, for example, when the very world of leisure that people had so eagerly desired now engendered fear? The hero of the award-winning drama *Marty* stands on the street corner with his friends, unable to decide what to do with his time. James Dean and his friends in *Rebel without a Cause* wonder what they can do about the boring life which leisure represents; what they ultimately do, we know, leads to disaster.[14] So extraordinary was the pressure of leisure time that home owners in middle-class America busily began to fill in the spaces. They invented the do-it-yourself craze (everybody had to have a wood shop in the basement) because they could not waste all this leisure. They had to use it up somehow. Presumably, a person could do one thing today and another thing tomorrow: hunt in the morning, fish in the afternoon, breed cattle in the evening, and

criticize art after dinner without becoming a hunter, fisherman, herds-
man, or critic.

But that long-awaited ideal no longer satisfied, for people were conscious that something was going wrong. Surprisingly, the growing anxiety
also came to focus on the domestic ideal. By 1945, films like *The Best
Years of Our Lives* and *Since You Went Away* began to suggest that the war
may have destroyed the sanctity of domestic bliss. *Death of a Salesman* is
many things, but above all it is a play about the disintegration of the
American home. The theme pervades the writings of Tennessee Williams,
most dramatically of course in *Cat on a Hot Tin Roof* but even in *A Streetcar Named Desire* (1947), a play about a hideous rape taking place in the
bosom of the family. In 1957, with Eugene O'Neill's *A Long Day's Journey
into Night*, the home dissolves in full view of the audience, as theater provides an awesome portrait of the decline of the family as a possible agency
for the raising of children and the fulfillment of the American Dream. By
the end of the decade, with the plays of Edward Albee, the American
Dream turns into the decaying marriage, and the family is assaulted, as it
has never before been assaulted, as a total failure. With the failure of that
ideal imagery comes the collapse of everything sacred.[15]

III

I have argued so far that Americans in this age developed a dual
collective representation of themselves, nicely rendered by competing images of the family. Many ages, of course, develop collective representations, but few have done it so self-consciously as did this particular age.
Here, it is important to locate this development in terms of a larger thesis,
for this dualism reflects two fundamental visions of what constitutes the
United States and the Americans. Traditionally, the citizen has been an
optimistic, problem-solving, responsible participant in a culture, with a
sense of both social responsibility and individual self-reliance. The traditional collective ideal persisted, but with the discovery of the horrors and
hypocrisy of the modern world a new image, a new collective representation, was also called into existence: a new American discovered. To me,
the most fascinating aspect of this discovery is its source. It sprang from the
theologians and writers of comic books.

When the German theologian Reinhold Niebuhr, for example, gained
enormous influence with his understanding of man as essentially sinful,
anxious, unfulfilled, and pathetic, he assisted in the rise of a generally
tragic sense of life. Niebuhr insisted that humans, as inheritors of original

sin, cannot follow scientific rationalism to ultimate success, nor could the new promised vision of America solve people's problems. This growing consciousness, furthermore, had interesting consequences in worlds we might not have thought of.

In the late 1940s, for example, the American historian Arthur Schlesinger, Jr., in a famous and revealing essay, "The Causes of the American Civil War: A Note on Historical Sentimentalism," attacked the historians of the Civil War who wrote during the 1920s and 1930s. Why? Because that earlier generation considered the Civil War the consequence of blundering leadership. Living in the era of the New Deal, when Franklin Roosevelt seemed the world's great problem solver, these scholars thought that rational leaders could have avoided the Civil War. Not so, said Mr. Schlesinger. To think in this way is to indulge in historical sentimentalism. There come moments in the times of men when the moral logjam is so great that it can be destroyed only through violence. No amount of statesmanship can do anything about it. In a sinful world, men must kill other men because there is no other answer.[16]

Still, that was only part of the story. Remember the rebel without a cause? A psychologist named Robert Mitchell Lindner provided us with this term and with a key to an understanding of the 1950s. Three of his books were continuously in print into the 1970s. The most famous was *Rebel without a Cause*, but *The 50 Minute Hour* and *Must You Conform?* were also quite popular. Lindner began as a prison psychologist but moved from there to general psychology, concentrating on the young and the new nonconformists of the fifties. He called these people "rebels without a cause." There was no sociological explanation for their rebellion. They were essentially social psychopaths, and it was not necessarily bad that they were deranged. For they revolted against a society deserving revolt. Popular writers and professionals had thus arrived at the point where the disturbed personality should be regarded not as a villain but as a hero. Indeed, one of the extraordinary features of the period was the celebration of the psychopathic as heroic.[17]

One can pursue this phenomenon down to a very important level, one which historians often miss. In 1955, a University of California study discovered that during the late 1940s and up to 1953 one billion comic books were produced each year. The total cost to produce those comic books was $100 million dollars, four times the total book budgets of all the public libraries in the United States put together. And do not believe that comic books were read only by children. They were read by large numbers of people, in age groups that one might not expect. The comics themselves became a matter of major national concern, engendering a book by a noted psychologist, a congressional investigation, and a series of state laws. They gained attention because they were filled with sex, violence, and crimes against persons (especially against women).

Yet the comics dramatized the same kind of personality, the same kind of collective representation appearing in so many realms of postwar culture: the heroic figure who is a concerned, anxious sinner capable of the most dreadful acts and incapable of operating rationally in terms of a scientific society's norms. This psychopathic hero embodied what Schlesinger had realized—that sometimes you cannot solve a problem by statesmanship. He is a counterforce to the organization man that William Whyte talked about in 1957, and who was demanded by people who thought he would be able to master the problems of a complex world.[18]

The conflict between these collective representations is nicely put by Paul Goodman in his widely acclaimed book of 1960, *Growing Up Absurd*. Goodman describes the transition from the old clergyman society to the new managerial, organizational culture. In the following paragraph, his rhetoric illustrates my point:

> The pragmatism, instrumentalism, and technologism of James, Dewey, and Veblen were leveled against the abuses and ideals of the then dominant class: the Four Hundred and the Robber Barons—academic culture, caste morals, and formal religion, unsocial greed. The philosophers were concerned about abundant production, social harmony, practical virtues, and more honest perception and feeling, which would presumably pertain to the rising group of technicians, social-scientific administrators, and organized labor. . . . In that early turn of the century, these philosophers failed to predict that precisely with the success of the managers, technicians, and organized labor, the "achieved" values of efficient abundant production, social harmony, and one popular culture would produce even more devastatingly the things they did not want: an abstract and inhuman physical environment, a useless economy, a caste system, a dangerous conformity, a trivial and sensational leisure.[19]

I do not contend that what Goodman says is in fact the case. Rather, it is important that now people began to think that this was in fact the case;

Fig. 1.1. *Double Indemnity*, the classic film noir of 1944. A comfortable insurance salesman has just committed murder to attain another man's wife, and the good life. Such uncontrolled desires lead to horror and destruction. (Courtesy of the Museum of Modern Art/Film Stills Archive.)

they were aware of an optimistic world gone wrong. The most important contribution of a major subgenre of detective and gangster movies in the forties, film noir, similarly served to reduce the optimistic American vision to dust. In *Double Indemnity* (1944), for instance, the story begins in a beautiful suburban Los Angeles community, focusing on a very pretty little house on a very pretty little plot. The minute we get inside that house, however, it is dark, dismal, and gloomy, and we find a family so desperately monstrous that one can scarcely conjure up such relationships into any kind of reality. The woman in question is, of course, blonde, for, throughout American film history, blondes have traditionally represented the sweet and innocent. (One should fear the dark-haired beauty, not the blondes.) Yet Barbara Stanwyck is a blonde who, down to the bracelets on her ankles, represents everything monstrous and evil. One of the crucial

scenes takes place in a supermarket, a bright, shiny, glorified, wonderful
scene of commodity exchange—but what is desired is not the consumer
culture. In dark glasses, in a supermarket, the two main characters plot
murder (fig. 1.1).[20]

It is a wonderful set of images, and engrained in those images is a startling new reality. In Hollywood and in the America of the 1940s and early
1950s, the fulfillment of our sweetest desires leads inevitably to the brink of
danger and damnation. It is specifically the noir movie that shows the audience that its desires, which they can now fulfill in the modern world of
abundance, social welfare, and security, are fundamentally dangerous and
filled with evil possibilities. In this anxious world, people found ways of
alleviating anxiety. One answer was to pop pills. By 1956, tranquilizers—
anti-anxiety drugs—were the great solution. Drugs became common in
everyday life, not just among the junkies whom William Burroughs describes in his novels, like *Naked Lunch*, but among the personalities associated with the so-called Beat generation who glorified the psychotic
personality functioning in a world of immediate gratification.[21]

IV

At this juncture, it is also appropriate to suggest some hypotheses
about how this dual consciousness of an ideal, completed society and inner
rebellion developed. In any analysis of values and beliefs, one requires a
sense of what I call the "structure of desire" existing within any society. For
culture shapes desire, and desire helps shape the nature of the culture. In
this regard, both collective representations so pervasive in postwar America
become essential. One is not simply the criticism of the other. The vision
of man as alienated, anxious, psychopathic, and outside social bonds becomes part of the people's needs. Perhaps audiences did not fully comprehend the meaning of their desires, but that is why film noir and juvenile delinquency films and certain detective stories, particularly Mickey
Spillane's popular novels featuring the psychotic hero, Mike Hammer,
flourished. Watching these deranged heroes and heroines, audiences felt
genuinely sad that their illusions were hopeless. Yet they were also exhila-
rated by the living grace of the doomed heroes and heroines they saw on
the screen. In other words, when men or women saw themselves in the
mirror as alienated, weak, and anxious, they cherished that feeling every
bit as much as they did while characterizing themselves, in the other collective representation, as heroic and self-sacrificing.[22]

Why did this happen? Why did this alternation of images occur? My theory is that humans, by their very nature, repress certain things that must be denied if culture and civilization are to flourish. But the instinctual always seeks to return. In the postwar period, because of the new abundance, opportunities, freedom, possibilities, and new sense of liberation, the repressed came back. And on a deep psychological level, that return was welcomed. Those aspects of humanity that had been kept down were accepted and delighted in, for Americans actually desired the returning pleasure they had denied themselves and did not want to relinquish it. So, they simultaneously needed their image of a world in which things have been denied and some way to hold on to what had been repressed when, eventually, it returned. At the same time, the concept of man as sinful, anxious, and alien served specific fundamental cultural purposes.[23]

The tension between these conflicting, yet mutually reinforcing, desires energized what might be, from a cultural point of view, the most important achievement in the United States in the postwar period. In 1955, there opened on the outskirts of Los Angeles a fabulous amusement park. Built by Walt Disney, the world-famous cartoonist and creator of Mickey Mouse, it was an extraordinary effort to create a collective representation of a utopian and ideal American world, a very special kind of world. In contrast to other examinations, it is important to explore how Disneyland (and later Disney World) can be seen as an attempt to resolve the tensions within the structure of desire.[24]

Disneyland is a world of the self-contained. At its center, Main Street USA, is a community of consumption where you can buy everything you want. Yet it is also the ideal prototype, the expression of the ideal vision of America, with all the repressed instincts remaining repressed. Here, the instinctual has not returned, for the amusements and rides raise only those pleasures which can be satisfied within the limits of the Disneyland itself. They do not include hootchy-kootchy dancers or anybody else who might arouse desires which cannot be satisfied. As a matter of fact, the whole environment is ordered so that one can feel a sense of mastery as one participates in it. It makes one feel good about a society which is neatly balanced among the past (conveniently analyzed), the present, and the future. It is all contained; it tells the whole story; it provides the mythic essence of what life was supposed to be like in the 1940s and 1950s. As the patrons experience that whole story from beginning to end, the old society that they leave behind in favor of the new does not know what to do with its wealth, wastefully accumulates pirate treasures, and is not engaged in productive activity. It may be charming in an old-world sense, but this world is

Fig. 1.2. Disneyland, the postwar utopia. As the patrons move through the various lands, they progress through a historical world where all fears of uncontrolled desire are banished, a world that culminates in the modern home, Tomorrowland's "House of the Future," in the lower left-hand corner. (Courtesy of the Museum of Modern Art/Film Stills Archive.)

contained (and audiences know this) through the mechanical apparatus that creates it. On the other side, the patron sees what the American worlds of the present and future are like: essentially dominated by a benevolent technology and its fruits (fig. 1.2).

Disneyland thus projects a mythic history of the United States, a collective fantasy, an immense metaphor for the system of representations and values unique in postwar America. And, as the trip logically culminates in Tomorrowland, the visitor finds a special exhibit, appropriately called "American Journeys." Here, the visitor is no longer a participant but a spectator waiting to be told the final story. Immobilized and passive, having visited a world in which one can consume to the presumed satisfaction of all desires, one now sees pictures of nineteenth-century family life on the frontier, life in the early twentieth century, and life today—when families experience modern work, leisure, and fun—culminating in a Fourth of July celebration at the Statue of Liberty, complete with patriotic songs and fireworks.

Interestingly enough, we are back at the story I related about the centrality of the family in American life. Disney tells us that throughout human history the family remains the same in every single historical period. What changes for this abiding family is the number of appliances and the increased sophistication of the utensil-dominated human environment. Visitors see people progressively dominating this world of useful objects, and as they enjoy its pleasurable fruits, they accept the proposition that Marshall McLuhan made—the only civilization could invent: If people's needs are unfulfilled, those needs can be satisfied; people can create wtih technology more pleasure than they have.[25]

Yet Disneyland narrows the patrons' desires to what is contained within the park. It becomes utopian in that particular sense and for those particular purposes. Some might label the result a degenerate utopia. Disneyland, however, is not "degenerate" in the larger sense of hedonistic indulgence; on the contrary, it represents a structure of desire in which the repressed is held down, where nothing is dirty, where everything is manageable and life-size, where sex and social conflict are eliminated, where the family never changes except to receive more goods and services, where it seems possible for a world of modern culture to satisfy every conceivable want. Here the postwar American Dream and its collective representations are fulfilled on a new California frontier.

But it was not what America had become by 1955 or 1960. It was not, because the repressed had persisted in returning to haunt and delight. For the larger American Dream which is characterized most vividly by Disneyland is not all that the United States had become. That other collective representation, from the Beats through *Playboy*, from the comic book heroes through film noir, was a reality that audiences delighted in and refused to give up. They cultivated the return of the repressed and reveled in it. By the late fifties, the United States had become the self-conscious home of hypocrisy. The consequences, however, would be revealed in the 1960s when we were forced to deal with America as a degenerate utopia.

NOTES

1. On earlier quests for a unified state, see Robert H. Wiebe, *The Search for Order* (New York: Hill and Wang, 1967); Stephen Kemp Bailey, *Congress Makes a Law: The Story behind the Employment Act of 1946* (New York: Columbia

University Press, 1950); Edward Serrill Flash, *Economic Advice and Presidential Leadership: The Council of Economic Advisors* (New York: Columbia University Press, 1965).

2. See Paul S. Boyer, *By the Bomb's Early Light: American Thought and Culture at the Dawn of the Atomic Age* (New York: Pantheon, 1985); Lawrence S. Wittner, *Cold War America: From Hiroshima to Watergate* (New York: Praeger, 1974), 174–76.

3. On the new order, see Godfrey Hodgson, *America in Our Time* (New York: Random House, 1976), 3–134; Alonzo Hamby, *Beyond the New Deal* (New York: Columbia University Press, 1973), 13–85; Charles S. Maier, "The Politics of Productivity," *International Organization* 31, no. 4 (1977): 607–32; *The National Security: Its Theory and Practice, 1945–1960*, ed. Norman A. Graebner (New York: Oxford University Press, 1986).

4. Perhaps the best example is Franklin D. Roosevelt, "Commonwealth Club Address," in *The Public Papers and Addresses of Franklin D. Roosevelt* (New York: Random House, 1966), 1:742–56.

5. For the classic account of the new world of abundance, see John Kenneth Galbraith, *The Affluent Society* (Boston: Houghton Mifflin, 1958). On earlier suburbs, see Sam Bass Warner, *Streetcar Suburbs: The Process of Growth in Boston, 1870–1900* (Cambridge: Harvard University Press, 1962); the classic account of the postwar suburb is Herbert Gans, *The Levittowners: Ways of Life and Politics in a New Suburban Community* (New York: Pantheon, 1967); for an overview, see Kenneth Jackson, *Crabgrass Frontier: The Suburbanization of the United States* (New York: Oxford University Press, 1985). On consumerism, see Warren Susman, *Culture as History: The Transformation of American Society in the 20th Century* (New York: Pantheon, 1984); and *The Culture of Consumption*, ed. Richard Wightman Fox and T. J. Jackson Lears (New York: Pantheon, 1983).

6. The literature of the family and American ideology is vast, but, for examples that cover the time period, see Linda Kerber, *Women of the Republic: Intellect and Ideology in Revolutionary America* (Chapel Hill: University of North Carolina Press, 1980), and Ruth Milkman, "Women's Work and the Economic Crisis: Some Lessons from the Great Depression," *Review of Radical Economics* 8, no. 1 (September 1976): 73–97. On the relation of family ideology and nineteenth-century suburbs, see Gwendolyn Wright, *Moralism and the Model Home: Domestic Architecture and Cultural Conflict in Chicago* (Chicago: University of Chicago Press, 1980). For Depression photos, see especially James Agee and Walker Evans, *Let Us Now Praise Famous Men* (Boston: Houghton Mifflin, 1961). Eugene O'Neill, *Ah, Wilderness* (New York: Random House, 1933). On MGM, see *The 1943 Film Daily Yearbook*, ed. Jack Alicoate (New York: Wid's Film, 1943), 81, and Bosley Crowther, *The Lion's Share: The Story of an Entertainment Empire* (New York: Dutton, 1957), 257. Thornton Wilder, *The Skin of Our Teeth*, in *The Best Plays of 1942/43 and the Year Book of the Drama in America*, ed. Burns Mantle (New York: Dodd, Mead, 1943).

7. On Father Peyton, see "Rosary Rally: New York Joins Priest's Drive for Family Prayer," *Life* 27 (October 27, 1952). On the family, television, and consumerism, see George Lipsitz, "The Meaning of Memory: Family, Class and

Ethnicity in Early Network Television Programs," *Cultural Anthropology* 1, no. 4 (November 1986): 355–87.

8. Walter Carruthers Sellar and Robert Julian Yeatman, *1066 and All That* (London: Methuen, 1931).

9. The more important examples of the critique would include George Orwell, *1984: A Novel* (New York: New American Library, 1949); Friedrich August von Hayek, *The Road to Serfdom* (Chicago: University of Chicago Press, 1944); Carl J. Friedrich and Zbigniew K. Brzezinski, *Totalitarian Dictatorship and Autocracy* (Cambridge: Harvard University Press, 1956); Hannah Arrendt, *The Origins of Totalitarianism* (New York: Harcourt, Brace, 1951); Eric Hoffer, *The True Believer: Thoughts on the Nature of Mass Movements* (New York: Harper and Row, 1951); Daniel Bell, *Beyond Ideology: On the Exhaustion of Political Ideas in the Fifties* (New York: Free Press, 1962). On earlier attempts to Americanize the immigrants, see John Higham, *Send These to Me: Immigrants in Urban America* (Baltimore: Johns Hopkins University Press, 1984). On the Americanization drive of the thirties, see Susman, *Culture As History*, 15–211. John Updike, *The Poorhouse Fair* (New York: Knopf, 1959). Another novel with a similar point is, of course, Ken Kesey, *One Flew over the Cuckoo's Nest* (New York: New American Library, 1962). A contemporary scholarly criticism along the same lines is Christopher Lasch, *Haven in a Heartless World: The Family Beseiged* (New York: Basic, 1977).

10. See especially Dwight Macdonald, *Masscult and Midcult* (New York: Random House, 1961), as well as *Dwight Macdonald on Movies* (Englewood Cliffs, N.J.: Prentice-Hall, 1969).

11. For example, see Richard Hofstadter, *American Violence: A Documentary History* (New York: Knopf, 1970), and Hugh Davis Graham, *The History of Violence in America: Historical and Comparative Perspectives* (New York: Praeger, 1969).

12. See the recent study of postwar juvenile delinquency and its cultural impact, James Burkhart Gilbert, *A Cycle of Outrage: America's Reaction to the Juvenile Delinquent in the 1950's* (New York: Oxford University Press, 1986).

13. Norman Mailer, *The Naked and the Dead* (New York: Rinehart, 1948); Gunnar Myrdal, *An American Dilemma: The Negro Problem and Modern Democracy* (New York: Harper, 1944). On the Kefauver hearings, see Estes Kefauver, *Crime in America* (New York: Greenwood, 1968), and Estes Kefauver, with Irene Till, *In a Few Hands: Monopoly Power in America* (New York: Pantheon, 1965). On anticommunism, from a firsthand source, see Joseph McCarthy, *McCarthyism: The Fight for America* (New York: Devin-Adair, 1952). On the 1954 Army-McCarthy hearings, see the documentary film *Point of Order* (Sterling Movies, 1964), or read the transcript by Emile DeAntonio, *Point of Order! A Documentary of the Army-McCarthy Hearings* (New York: Norton, 1964).

14. See Galbraith, *The Affluent Society*, and for a current critique, Christopher Lasch, *The Culture of Narcissism: American Life in an Age of Diminishing Expectations* (New York: Norton, 1978). For *Marty*, see Paddy Chayefsky, *Television Plays* (New York: Simon and Schuster, 1954). *Rebel without a Cause* (Warner Brothers Pictures, 1955).

15. *The Best Years of Our Lives* (Metro-Goldwyn-Mayer, 1946). *Since You*

Went Away (United Artists, 1944). Arthur Miller, *Death of a Salesman* (New York: Viking, 1949); Tennessee Williams, *Cat on a Hot Tin Roof* (New York: New American Library, 1955) and *A Streetcar Named Desire* (New York: New Directions, 1947). Eugene O'Neill, *Long Day's Journey into Night* (New Haven: Yale University Press, 1955). For Edward Albee, see, for example, *The American Dream: A Comedy* (New York: Street and Smith, 1960).

16. On Niebuhr and his influence, see David W. Noble, *The End of American History: Democracy, Capitalism, and the Metaphor of Two Worlds in Anglo-American Historical Writing, 1880–1980* (Minneapolis: University of Minnesota Press, 1986), and Donald Meyer, *The Protestant Search for Political Realism, 1919–1941* (Berkeley: University of California Press, 1960). The Schlesinger essay was written in 1949; see Arthur Schlesinger, Jr., "The Causes of the American Civil War: A Note on Historical Sentimentalism," in *The Causes of the American Civil War*, ed. E. C. Rozwenc (Boston: Heath, 1961).

17. Robert Mitchell Lindner, *Rebel without a Cause: The Psychoanalysis of a Criminal Psychopath* (New York: Grune and Stratton, 1944), *The Fifty-Minute Hour: A Collection of True Psychoanalytic Tales* (New York: Rinehart, 1954), and *Must You Conform?* (New York: Rinehart, 1956).

18. The University of California study is in Edward L. Feder, *Comic Book Regulation* (Berkeley: Bureau of Public Administration, University of California, 1955); United States Congress, Senate Special Committee to Investigate Organized Crime in Interstate Commerce, *Juvenile Delinquency: A Compilation of Information and Suggestions Relative to the Incidence of Juvenile Delinquency in the United States and the Possible Influence Thereon of So-Called Crime Comic Books during the Period 1945 to 1950* (Washington, D.C.: Government Printing Office, 1950). William H. Whyte, *The Organization Man* (New York: Holt, Rinehart and Winston, 1955).

19. Paul Goodman, *Growing Up Absurd: Problems of Youth in the Organized System* (New York: Random House, 1960), 80.

20. *Double Indemnity* (Paramount, 1944). For the imagery and themes of this work and film noir generally, see *Film Noir*, ed. Alain Silver and Elizabeth Ward (Woodstock, N.Y.: Overlook, 1979), 1–6, 92–93.

21. William Burroughs, *Naked Lunch* (New York: Grove, 1959).

22. For a contemporary account of the juvenile delinquency films and their appeal, see Pauline Kael, "The Glamour of Delinquency," in *I Lost It at the Movies* (Boston: Little, Brown, 1965), 39–54. On Spillane and his popularity, see John G. Cawelti, *Adventure, Mystery, Romance: Formula Stories as Art and Popular Culture* (Chicago: University of Chicago Press, 1976).

23. For the theory that all cultures repress instincts, see the classic statement by Sigmund Freud, *Civilization and Its Discontents*, trans. James Strachey (New York: Norton, 1962). On the "return of the repressed," see Norman O. Brown, *Life against Death: The Psychoanalytical Meaning of History* (Middletown, Conn.: Wesleyan University Press, 1959). For the "structure of desire" theory and its relation to the modern economy, see Gilles Deleuze and Felix Guattari, *Anti-Oedipus: Capitalism and Schizophrenia* (New York: Viking, 1977), 1–50.

24. For other accounts, see Richard Schickel, *The Disney Version: The*

Life, Times, Art and Commerce of Walt Disney (New York: Simon and Schuster, 1968), and Christopher Finch, *The Art of Walt Disney: From Mickey Mouse to the Magic Kingdom* (New York: Abrams, 1973). Since the same analysis applies to Disney World and EPCOT in Florida, see Richard Beard, *Walt Disney's EPCOT Center: Creating a World of Tomorrow* (New York: Abrams, 1982); Peter Blake, "Walt Disney World," *Architectural Forum* 5 (January 1972): 24–41; Ionnis Pissimissis, "The Fragmentation of Space and Time and the Commodification of Leisure: The Case of Disney World and EPCOT in Florida," (Ph.D. diss., UCLA, 1983).

25. Marshall McLuhan, *Understanding Media: The Extensions of Man* (New York: McGraw-Hill, 1964), esp. 226–45.

2　A Matter of Taste:
Corporate Cultural Hegemony
in a Mass-Consumption Society

Jackson Lears

It is no secret that Anglo-American historiography has shown a persistent hostility to theory. At every turn, writers hear the constant refrain:
do not "impose your own framework" on the past, let the historical actors
speak for themselves, understand them through the categories and idioms
they created for themselves. This is a good idea, up to a point. Sympathetic
understanding—the elusive *verstehen*—is far more appealing than dissec-
tion or polemic.

But the distrust of theory can lead to problems. For example, investigators can be badly misled if they turn to the social thought of the 1940s
and 1950s—the thought generated by the historical actors themselves—as
a guide to understanding American culture and society in the postwar era.
By way of contrast, this essay proposes to get inside the social ideas of the
leading intellectuals during that era and to reconstruct a few of their major
preoccupations—especially the tendency to perceive mass consumption
and conformity as the defining characteristics of postwar American society.
Throughout, however, it will be imperative to suggest the incompleteness
of their perceptions, and to propose a way to supplement their understanding by assimilating some ideas of the Italian Marxist Antonio Gramsci to the
particular circumstance of the United States in the mid-twentieth century.

I

During the immediate postwar years, American intellectuals were
preoccupied with the possibility of returning economic depression. But by
the late forties, when the creation of the permanent war economy seemed
to be providing a floor for prosperity, they began to look about themselves.
And what they saw was good: a democratic polity of competing interest
groups, an extraordinarily fluid social structure, an emergent cultural consensus based on the spread of affluence and the promise of upward mobility.
Mary McCarthy articulated the nascent conventional wisdom when she
responded to Simone de Beauvoir's critique of American society in 1952:

> The society characterized by Mlle. de Beauvoir as "rigid,"
> "frozen," "closed" is in the process of great change. The
> mansions are torn down and the real estate "development"
> takes their place: serried rows of ranch type houses, painted
> in pastel colors, each with its own picture window and its
> garden, each equipped with deep freeze, oil-furnace, and
> automatic washer, spring up in the wilderness. Class bar-
> riers disappear or become porous; the factory worker is an
> economic aristocrat in comparison with the middle class
> clerk; even segregation is diminishing; consumption re-
> places acquisition as an incentive. The America invoked by
> Mlle. de Beauvoir as a country of vast inequalities and dra-
> matic contrasts is rapidly ceasing to exist.

McCarthy caught the emergent optimism that was affecting many of her contemporaries: the desire to dismiss intractable problems ("even segregation is diminishing") and accentuate hopeful signs. The problem was that it required some rhetorical sleight of hand: the distinction between consumption and acquisition, for example, was elusive; it suggested more about intellectuals' frame of mind than about the habits of the wider population. The intellectuals' focus of attention had shifted from Wall Street to Madison Avenue, from the financial power behind advanced capitalism to the cultural values associated with its products.[1]

The ostensible reason for that shift was not far to seek. Cultural commentators nearly all agreed that Americans were plucking the first fruits of a successful capitalist revolution. For the first time in American history, it was thought, the vast majority of the population had been economically enfranchised. The postwar bonanza of consumer goods held out the possibility of a classless society where factory workers ate porterhouse steaks and drove Buick Electras. To Philip Rieff, the old Marxist categories had only an ironic appropriateness to the new situation. "False consciousness is here to stay; it is the happy psychic condition of a mature and still dynamic industrial civilization that has worked back through a religion of transcendence to a religion of immanence based on a supra-primitive fetishism of infinitely variable commodities," he wrote in 1956. Werner Sombart's classic formulation appeared more apt than ever before: the dreams of socialist revolution had been wrecked on the shoals of roast beef and apple pie.[2]

And the economic transformation resonated in the realm of ideas. In 1952, the editors of *Partisan Review* introduced their symposium "Our Country and Our Culture" by announcing that, in just over a decade, "more and more writers have ceased to think of themselves as rebels and exiles. They now realize that their values, if they are to be realized at all, are to be realized in America and in relation to the actuality of American life." This new attitude is well known; so is the justification for it—the belief that the intelligentsia had awakened from the sentimental dreams of the thirties to "life's tragic complexities," that is, Soviet totalitarianism and the global responsibility to combat it. The new faith was sometimes expressed in the Freudian idiom of "maturity." As the literary critic Newton Arvin put it in his contribution to the symposium, "The negative relation to one's culture has great validity in certain periods; at others, it is simply sterile, even psychopathic, and ought to give way, as it has done here, in the last decade, to the positive relation. Anything else suggests too strongly the continuation into adult life of the negative Oedipal relations of adolescence—and in much of the alienation of the 20s and 30s there was just that quality of immaturity." Or the advocates of affirmation could adopt an overt cold war idiom, as Sidney Hook did. "I cannot understand," said Hook, "why American intellectuals are limited in their effective historical choice between endorsing a system of total terror and critically supporting our own imperfect democracy with all its promises and dangers." Hook's Manichaean vision of the world rendered the intellectual's "choice" absolute and made it difficult to imagine the precise nature of the criticism he expected to develop within "our own imperfect democracy." His language was symptomatic of the early fifties but also eerily anticipates our current cultural situation. To understand the quiescence of postwar intellectuals in terms of "the actors themselves," one need only turn to the current pages of *Partisan Review*, *New York Times Book Review*, or *Commentary*, and one will find the same fresh and challenging idioms—the attack on leftist intellectuals' alleged "failure of nerve" in confronting Soviet totalitarianism, for example—the same arguments, and often the same people making them.[3]

This dreary saga of accommodation among a self-constituted critical elite ought by now to be a familiar story; what is needed is a little more attention to the implicit frames of reference, the categories of understanding that were taken for granted by the intelligentsia when they attempted to focus their gaze on the America beyond the Hudson. They were, first of all, overwhelmingly struck by the homogeneity of American society and culture. This perception could be clothed in the jargon of functionalist sociology (Talcott Parsons's social system) or of culture and personality anthropology (David Riesman's lonely crowd). The serried ranks of identical houses spotted by Mary McCarthy (and a host of other travelers in suburbia) were the most visible material embodiments of a culture that was becoming everywhere the same. Or so it was thought.[4]

Whatever the idiom, the emphasis on homogeneity did not originate in the postwar period. It stemmed from tendencies that surfaced in the early twentieth century. Eugene Leach has perceptively shown how American social scientists detached crowd psychology from its moorings in European conservatism, replacing the "mob" with a "mass" that could be manipulated toward "progressive" ends by managerial elites. This benign vision of a homogenous population animated advertisers, public relations "experts," and other would-be social engineers between the wars. At the same time, as Warren Susman has observed, the worldwide cataclysms of the 1930s were promoting a sense of cultural homogeneity among middle-class Americans in general—the people who had something to lose. Amid the psychic ravages of the Great Depression, widespread longings for a secure sense of identity led to a quest for a sense of belonging in some comforting collective whole. It was no accident that the late thirties and forties saw the creation of some compelling myths of collectivity: a myth of an American past in which social conflict was concealed by a renewed stress on individual heroism, embodied in the resurgence of filiopietistic biography (Sandburg's Lincoln, Freeman's Lee) after decades of debunking; a myth of "the American people" as a classless, undifferentiated folk, enacted (for example) in John Ford's film bowdlerization of Steinbeck's *Grapes of Wrath*. These myths gradually converged in a larger one, a faith in what came to be called the American Way of Life. The convergence was reinforced by World War II, which was defined as a cultural war not only by policymakers but also by anthropologists such as Ruth Benedict and Margaret Mead.[5] The idea of a "peculiarly American" (and—despite rhetorical gestures toward pluralism—implicitly homogenous) national culture was carried aloft by waves of wartime nationalism and institutionalized after the war in dozens of American Studies programs, where students sought the philosophers' stone of "national character." The American Way of Life pervaded postwar thought from *Partisan Review* to the *Saturday Evening Post*.

There were many ironies involved in this surge of cultural nationalism. The idea of the virtuous American folk, a homegrown variant of the more sinister *Volkische* ideologies flourishing on the continent in these years, originated on the Left; it was encapsulated in Popular Front slogans and WPA murals. But it was picked up, popularized, and mass-marketed by corporate elites: media moguls, advertising executives, and finally business publicists eager to counterattack the New Deal by developing what William

Bird has called a "new vocabulary of business leadership." During the war, corporate-sponsored patriotism became increasingly pervasive. After the war, as foreign-policy elites orchestrated anticommunist fervor and corporations completed their appropriation of nationalistic imagery, the idiom of Americanism changed subtly but profoundly. To be sure, the Left did not give in without a struggle, as Lary May's carefully researched study of the Hollywood Screen Actors' Guild makes clear.[6] But by midcentury, the essence of the American Way of Life had shifted from a vague populism to an equally murky notion of free enterprise. What remained unchanged was the emphasis on national uniqueness and homogeneity. And that emphasis pervaded postwar social thought.

The tendency to see American culture as a monolithic and autonomous entity required a systematic inattention to power relations. The neglect of power could be justified in several ways. One was by reference to the stalemate among interest groups that had supposedly developed during the twenty years of New Deal/Fair Deal legislation. The mixed economy of welfare capitalism was characterized, according to John Kenneth Galbraith, by a system of "countervailing power." Other thinkers referred to the proliferation of interest groups rather than the stalemate of a few. As Daniel Bell wrote, "The growing complexity of society necessarily multiplies those interests, regional or functional, and in an open society the political arena . . . is a place where different interests fight it out for advantage. That is why, usually, the prism of 'class' is too crude to follow the swift play of diverse interest groups." Marxism was a convenient dead horse, always available for rhetorical flogging while the writer invoked the vision of American politics as a roistering egalitarian melee. For some social critics, the task of locating power in America was not merely difficult but impossible; they dismissed the human agents of power altogether. "Who *really* runs things?" David Riesman asked in 1950. "What people fail to see is that, while it may take leadership to start things running or to stop them, very little leadership is needed once things get underway. . . . The fact they do get done is no proof that there is someone in charge." In this case, what purported to be a tough-minded attempt to dissuade (unidentified) "people" from their naive conceptions of power turned out on closer inspection to be an astonishingly candid admission of befuddlement.[7]

The refusal to engage questions of power led to the reification of abstract concepts into things which acted autonomously on people. Parsons's "social system" was the most egregious example, though many others could be culled from the literature of "modernization" or from culture-

and-personality anthropology; the famous modal personality types in *The Lonely Crowd* (tradition-directed, inner-directed, other-directed) were formed, the authors assumed, "at the knee of society." The postwar quest for "national character" enticed historians to follow social scientists into the bogs of reification. David Potter's *People of Plenty* (1954), the national character study that was most widely respected among historians, was a straightforward exercise in behaviorist reification. In keeping with postwar preoccupations, Potter chose the abstraction "abundance" as the deus ex machina hovering over two centuries of American history. "As abundance raised the standard of living," Potter wrote, "*it* did far more than multiply the existing kinds of goods. *It* caused us to use new goods, new sources of energy, new services, and by doing so, *it* transformed our way of life more than once every generation." We were passive, abundance was active.[8]

The tendency to see abstractions (society, abundance, the economy, the organization) as omnipotent beings was reassuring but also disturbing. It signaled an implicit acceptance of bureaucratic systems, designed to promote productivity so efficiently that they seemed to run without need of human control. Yet there was a chill to that efficiency. Parsons and his students never felt it, but more thoughtful commentators did.

The achievement of affluence required the triumph of bureaucratic technique. And the triumph of technique seemed to mean a loss of purpose and value. This aimlessness was at the core of the emerging critique of "mass society." Some critics tried to revive older political frameworks of value: C. Wright Mills drew on Dewey and decentralist democratic tradition, Erich Fromm on the young Marx. Both espoused a democratic communitarianism; both were marginalized and misunderstood. Given the pervasive rejection of political protest as "sentimental" (in the cold war idiom) or "immature" (in the Freudian), and given the ambiguity of the malaise the intellectuals sought to combat, it should not be surprising that a religious idiom of protest enjoyed a brief revival. In *Protestant, Catholic, Jew* (1955), Will Herberg argued that the surrogate religion of the American Way of Life had supplanted the theological foundations of the Jewish and Christian traditions, and that only a (vaguely neo-orthodox) "biblical faith" could end the suffocating complacency of the suburban churches.[9] The fear of a kind of cultural asphyxiation was articulated more explicitly by Allen Tate in his Phi Beta Kappa address of 1953, "The Man of Letters in the Modern World." Americans' moral dilemmas, Tate argued, lay deeper than the pragmatic solution of balancing means and ends; for most Americans, Christian ends no longer existed. In Tate's view, we were choking on our own abundance, trapped by our own technological detritus. The disenchantment of the world meant the covering over of it by consumer goods.[10]

Tate's solution to the problem of "means without ends" was a return to traditional Christianity, but for more secular souls the dilemmas were more difficult. Riesman's anthology *Abundance for What?* perfectly captured the perplexity of intellectuals who believed that fundamental economic problems had been solved and that the old issues of power had become passé yet who still groped for a way to sustain their critical role. An absence of ultimate ends, of "national purpose" or personal purpose, seemed the besetting sin of their society. Yet they had no vocabulary to discuss ultimate ends. They had only a vague sense of disappointment. William H. Whyte, an editor at *Fortune*, expressed that feeling in his enormously influential *The Organization Man* (1956). "The fruits of social revolution are always more desirable in anticipation than fact, and the pink lamp shade in the picture window can be a sore disappointment to those who dreamed that the emancipation of the worker might take a more spiritual turn," he wrote. "It is a sight, however, that we can well endure."[11]

Whyte's "pink lamp shade in the picture window" was a significant choice of symbols. He implied that poor taste was a small price to pay for the economic "emancipation" of the majority of the population; criticism that focused on taste alone was, from this view, a dilettantish luxury. At the same time, though, Whyte—like many of those who were less able to endure the pink lamp shade in the picture window—tended to conflate aesthetics with more general "spiritual" issues. From his statement, one might infer that a more tasteful lamp shade would have indicated a more spiritual emancipation. If one assumed that Americans' common condition was a prosperous homogeneity, then the very sameness that signified the spread of economic security also revealed the rise of a new cultural presence, less palpable than poverty but not a whit less alarming: the specter of conformity.

Whyte's *Organization Man* was the locus classicus of the 1950s critique of conformity. In Whyte's view, the Protestant Ethic had been displaced by a Social Ethic. Its advocates defined the group rather than the individual as the source of creativity, asserted that "belongingness" was the ultimate need of the individual, and promoted behavioristic social engineering as a way to achieve the belongingness. These were the institutionalized consequences of the longings for collective identity located by Susman in the 1930s. The Social Ethic could be found in "progressive" public schools, where children were judged "uncooperative" if they wanted to be by themselves from time to time; in suburbs, where "inconspicuous consumption" prevailed and "the job is not to keep up with the Joneses . . . it's to keep *down* with them"; and above all in the modern corporation, where executives guided by personality testing rewarded the affable team player with economic security—which was all he really wanted in the first place.[12] Whyte's attack on corporate-induced conformity was pointed and well placed; the problem was that he presented few clear alternatives. Although he preferred cranky entrepreneurs to well-adjusted corporate executives, his ultimate ideal seemed to be a conception of individual autonomy that was as reified as the ideal of organization he aimed to resist. Here as elsewhere in postwar social thought, the lack of larger frameworks of meaning left the reader wondering, "Nonconformity for what?"

Perhaps the bleakest picture of the omnipotent organization encasing the fragile private self was provided by the sociologist Erving Goffman. In *Asylums* (1959), Goffman analyzed "total institutions"—prisons, mental hospitals, monasteries, ships at sea—places where behavior was monitored and controlled, and where the inmates developed theatrical role-playing strategies as a means of "adjustment" to the loss of autonomous selfhood. Throughout, there was the subtle suggestion that the modern corporation, with its demands for an endlessly manipulable (other-directed?) personality, was creating the same kind of fragmented personae that appeared in total institutions. The only solution that Goffman could imagine was an ironically detached acceptance of the fragmented role-playing self—the discontinuous identity promoted by the bureaucratic organization of experience. The self-conscious awareness that one was in fact engaging in a theatrical social performance constituted at best a Pyrrhic victory; the only triumph available was a psychological and aesthetic one—the role-player's realization that he was observing a flawless social performance: his own.[13]

Asylums was not as idiosyncratic as it might seem. The book contained many features that gradually came to typify postwar social thought: the sense of the irrelevance of politics; the feeling of entrapment in an all-encompassing system that fed the body but starved the soul; the tendency to cultivate a spectatorial, aesthetic outlook on the world. If economic problems were solved and questions of power were lost in the labyrinth of the bureaucratic system, the intellectual could still play a critical role: assaulting conformity, promoting more diverse and challenging standards of taste, serving as a kind of high-grade consumer adviser. If the American economy had reached W. W. Rostow's final stage of economic growth and public discourse had arrived at what Bell called the end of ideology, then for the intellectual consumption constituted the last frontier, the last opportunity to exercise some influence on society.[14] The aesthetic emphasis on consumption was not only politically safe, it was intellectually satisfying to men and women who had few frameworks of meaning left standing outside the temple of art.

In the mainstream discourse of the 1950s, even overtly political or religious protest tended to be redefined in aesthetic categories. Fromm became known for his assaults on "conformity"; Tate achieved his widest fame as a poet and New Critic. The dominance of New Criticism was itself evidence of the pervasive aestheticism of the 1950s—the tendency to make literature into a kind of surrogate religion, to elevate the text as a sacred gem above the vicissitudes of history or biography. And, among intellectuals, literary critics acquired a disproportionate influence. At a Museum of Modern Art panel, "The Role of the Intellectual in Modern Society," held in 1957, W. H. Auden looked about him and noticed that the panel members were all literary men. He took it as evidence of the zeitgeist. Had the panel been organized in the Middle Ages, Auden observed, the "panel members would have been mostly members of the clergy; in the sixteenth and seventeenth centuries . . . mostly natural scientists; in the twentieth century, we are mostly literary men." One need not accept Auden's oracular simplifications to acknowledge that during the 1950s, the touchstones of cultural criticism became questions of style and taste—questions, it was assumed, that literary intellectuals were well-equipped to answer. This was the period when Eisenhower's leadership was criticized as a case of "the bland leading the bland," and when the Dulles brothers' Latin American policy evoked no more contempt than the White House appearance of Fred Waring and the Pennsylvanians.[15] In such an atmosphere, aesthetic issues carried unprecedented weight.

Mass-culture criticism became especially portentous. To Lionel Trilling, for example, the novel's sickness unto death was symptomatic of broader cultural maladies. As he wrote in 1949, "If the novel is dead or dying, it is not alone in its mortality. The novel is a kind of summary and paradigm of our intellectual life, which is perhaps why we speak sooner of its death than of the death of any of our other forms of thought. It has been of all literary forms the most devoted to the celebration and investigation of the human will; and the will of our society is dying of its own excess. The religious will, the political will, the sexual will, the artistic will, each is dying of its own excess." It is not always easy to penetrate this sort of pronouncement, but Trilling seemed to be referring to the bureaucratization of bourgeois individualism in America, the tendency for spontaneous or even heroic individual exertions to become reduced to routine in a culture of mammoth organizations and mass-produced sensation. Dwight Macdonald struck similar notes of exhaustion, decay, and suffocation in 1953 when he warned that "there is slowly emerging a tepid, flaccid middlebrow culture that threatens to engulf everything in its spreading ooze." An apocalyptic idiom seems appropriate to the cold war era, except when one recalls that the apocalypse in question was not the threat of nuclear war but the triumph of middlebrow culture. The "spreading ooze" that was going to "engulf everything" was being promoted by the Book-of-the-Month Club. [16]

The same sense of a homogenized, asphyxiating dominant culture also affected those on the Left who were trying to preserve some sense of power relations. In *White Collar* (1951), C. Wright Mills prefigured Whyte and other critics of the organization. Mills presented "the white collar people . . . slipping quietly onto the stage of history" and soon becoming hopelessly entrapped in an "enormous file." In *The Power Elite* (1956), Mills elaborated this picture by presenting a complex account of the interlocking groups that formed the American power structure. By offering a forthright answer to the question that baffled functionalists—"Who really runs things?"—the book touched off the only interesting debate in mainstream sociology during the 1950s; nevertheless it tended to stay within the reigning paradigm in its assumption that the bulk of the American population constituted an inert, manipulable mass-consumption society. Those Frankfurt School theorists who had migrated to America also continued to use the idiom of masses. The best-known strand of their work culminated in Herbert Marcuse's *One-Dimensional Man* (1964), which made postwar America seem at a dead standstill, with all will to resistance sapped. Americans, from Marcuse's view, were passive consumers who defined themselves solely through their washing machines, cars, and trash compactors. What Marcuse called the process of "repressive desublimation" had drained whatever potential existed for a libidinous civilization into the tinsel tawdriness of Hollywood fan magazines and titillating advertisements. Id had become another item on the mass market. [17]

Across the political spectrum, celebrants and doubters alike accepted the same basic assumption that postwar America was a homogenous mass-consumption society. The very terms of the discussion promoted the primacy of consumption as a category of understanding: the endless chatter about conformity, the tendency to redefine questions of power as matters of taste. That redefinition could lead to handwringing, as it did for Mac-

donald, but it could also open the way for a more optimistic assessment of
American prospects even among the devotees of European high culture.
Lionel Trilling, decrying cultural death in some areas, found signs of new
life in others. Writing in 1950, Trilling applauded what he thought of as
new development in American civilization. "Wealth," he said, "now
shows a tendency to submit itself in some degree to the rule of mind and
imagination, to apologize for its existence by showing taste and sensitivity."
Middlebrow trends that might have driven Macdonald to despair—the rise
of Robert Hutchins's Fat Man's Class (a Great Books program for corporate
executives), the establishment in 1949 of the Aspen Institute—could also
be seen as a farewell to Babbittry. The modestly fixed as well as the rich
might be willing to submit to the direction of a cultural elite. Riesman, for
example, was encouraged in 1950 to see "the extremely rapid disavowal by
Detroit auto workers of overstuffed Grand Rapids furniture." He observed
hopefully that "many in the last several years have gone in for modern design." A preoccupation with taste spread across the political spectrum;
sometimes it seemed as if the chief issue dividing "Left" and "Right" was
whether all those concertgoers really liked Verdi or not—whether refined
aesthetic perceptions were trickling down among the mass of the population or whether the media's least-common-denominator approach was
mixing "the sacred and the profane, the genuine and the specious" into "a
single slushy compost." Even the sharpest critics seemed able to define dissent only in terms of taste. For Marcuse, by the 1960s, the sole escape from
"one-dimensional society" was *The Aesthetic Dimension*—the title of a
book he published in 1968.[18]

II

So, if we stick to the terms of the actors themselves, we are stuck
with a narrow, apolitical frame of reference as well as a monolithic conception of postwar consumer culture. And, if the past fifteen years of social
historiography have taught us anything, it is the segmented and discontinuous character of American life—the ways that social groups can carve
out separate enclaves of neighborhood or sisterhood or brotherhood, the
ways that mediating institutions of family, community, or faith can prevent
the individual's absorption by the all-encompassing system. And yet these
sorts of arguments have not been generally made with respect to postwar
America. As Leo Ribuffo has observed, the historians' rule seems to be that
American society has evolved from complexity to simplicity; the most obscure theological controversies are taken seriously when they occur in Pu-

ritan times, but rebellion in the 1960s is dismissed as "a kind of binge." As American society becomes more complex and diverse, historians' images of it become more standardized, more consensual.[19]

Why is this? The social theorists of the 1950s would have an answer: the standardizing influence of mass culture, mass media, mass marketing, and mass consumption. And there they would have a point—more of a point, really, than contemporary social historians might be willing to admit. As David Nye has shown in his wonderful book on photography at General Electric, historians have yet to grapple with the implications of corporate control over image production in the twentieth century.[20] Nevertheless, the argument for standardization flattens a great deal of social and cultural complexity by uncritically accepting the idiom of "the masses." I want to suggest a more flexible framework for understanding postwar American society and culture, one that transcends the idiom of "masses" (I hope) without ignoring power relations or corporate domination.

To begin, one must acknowledge the persistence of a certain degree of cultural pluralism even amid the postwar triumph of the American Way of Life. As early as the mid-1950s, defenders of mass culture were citing the importance of "the primary group" as an intervening influence between communications media and the individual citizen; "opinion leaders" in local communities were found to be at least as influential as the faceless hidden persuaders uncovered by Vance Packard. Tocqueville was ritually invoked in the 1950s, not only as the theorist of egalitarian conformity and anomic individualism but also as the discoverer of the "voluntary association"—the crucial mediating institution that (by decentralizing authority) would allegedly save Americans from the heartbreak of totalitarian democracy.[21]

The problem with the sociologists of the mediating institution in the 1950s and the social historians who followed their lead in the 1970s is that neither group paid much attention to the location of the primary group in the larger social structure or to the relationship between the culture of the group and the larger arenas of power, policy, and public discourse. It made no difference how eloquently convictions were expressed around kitchen tables or in church basements if those private points of view were never admitted into the charmed circle of "responsible opinion." Some groups had more power than others, including the power to set the boundaries of permissible debate, to legitimate some ideas and values while declaring others "tasteless" or "irresponsible." Deliberately or unconsciously, dominant social groups could use gender, race, ethnicity, and other barriers to screen out entire subcultures by dismissing or ignoring them. That does not mean those subcultures ceased to exist—on the contrary, they may have flourished as never before—but they were rendered marginal or even invisible to the wider public culture.

This process is nicely captured by Gramsci's concept of cultural hegemony. The essence of hegemony is not manipulation but legitimation. It does not require a vision of a scheming elite and a passive populace. Rather, cultural hegemony is exercised by what Gramsci called a "historical bloc"—a loose coalition of groups cemented by cultural as well as economic bonds. In pluralistic, parliamentary states especially, the ruling coalition is likely to be fluid rather than rigid: constantly changing shape as some groups peel away and others adhere but maintaining cultural as well as political dominance until successfully challenged by another set of groups that have formed a counterhegemonic historical bloc. A hegemonic historical bloc identifies its own problems and interests with those of society and indeed humanity at large. Other groups' problems and interests are systematically marginalized and diminished—"the Negro Problem," "the unemployment problem," "the paranoid style of American isolationism," "the Jesse Jackson phenomenon." "Reality" is what coincides with the ruling groups' worldview. [22]

It is possible to argue that in postwar America a hegemonic historical bloc was formed by the groups often characterized as a "new class" of salaried managers, administrators, academics, technicians, and journalists—people who manipulated symbols rather than made things, whose stock in trade consisted of their organizational, technical, conceptual, or verbal skills. [23] This historical bloc had been in the process of formation since the early twentieth century; James Burnham had made it the subject of popular controversy with *The Managerial Revolution* (1941). But by the postwar period it was apparent that the "new class" had come into its own. There were more opportunities for institutionalized employment of intellectual expertise than ever before: in the rapidly expanding universities; in advertising, publishing, and the mass media; in foundations; and in the emerging military-industrial complex. By 1950, Lionel Trilling was able to observe that "intellect has associated itself with power, perhaps as never before in history, and is now conceded to be itself a kind of power." Irving Howe was not sure about the capacity of intellect to exercise autonomous power, though he agreed in 1953 that "established power and the dominant intellectual tendencies have come together in a harmony such as this country has not seen since the Gilded Age; and this, of course, makes the temptations of conformism all the more acute. The carrots, for once, are real." Howe, an editor at *Time* before he struck out on his own to found *Dissent* magazine, knew whereof he spoke.[24]

The "new class" may not have constituted a class in any coherent or unified sense. But it did constitute a historical bloc—a coalition of groups which differed in many ways but which were bound together (up to a point) by common interests, common experiences, and a common worldview. The members of those groups tended to be rootless urbanites or suburbanites; they worked for big organizations that prized instrumentalist values; they sent their children to progressive schools and worried about sexual satisfaction in marriage; they were affluent enough to be at the cutting edge of mass consumption. They believed there was such a thing as an American Way of Life—fundamentally benign though sometimes suffocatingly vulgar; they believed their own interests and those of the nation were best served by pragmatic interest-group politics and an expanded "mixed economy" undergirded by business-government cooperation. They feared "extremist" crusades at home and an implacable Soviet threat abroad. On the basis of these experiences and values, the professional/managerial groups were able to form cross-class alliances and constitute—for a time—a hegemonic historical bloc.

But where does the working-class majority fit into the picture? What was the relationship between subordinate cultures and the dominant culture created by professional and managerial elites? Those questions are difficult to answer on the basis of standard sources. The promoters of the dominant worldview in the postwar period conflated their own experiences and attitudes with American culture as a whole. The lists of "American" traits compiled by seekers of national character bore a suspicious resemblance to the values enshrined by the corporate sponsors of the American Way of Life. "The American" was devoted to practical labor but fond of material comfort, jealous of his private independence but eager for the public approval of others; above all he (always "he") was pragmatic and optimistic, not given to unproductive speculation or brooding.[25] For many analysts, pragmatic optimism explained our economic success as well as our cultural failures. It promoted a can-do attitude but also a bland indifference to the darker dimensions of life. That upbeat banality was what so annoyed critics like Riesman, but the only examples of it he could adduce were fiction and advice literature produced by and for the enlightened upper-middle classes.[26] Nearly all the traits that were alleged to characterize American culture as a whole were projections of hegemonic values onto a wider population that did not necessarily share them.

Available evidence suggests that during the postwar period, working-

class participation in a national consensus remained limited and ambiguous. As the sociologist Michael Mann wrote, summarizing survey data in
1970, "It is not value-consensus which keeps the working class compliant,
but rather a *lack* of consensus in the crucial area where concrete experiences and vague populism might be translated into radical politics." Schools
and mass media, in the postwar era as before in our history, presented a
picture of competitive strivers within a benevolent nation state. Rather
than engaging in indoctrination, "the liberal democratic state" has perpetuated "values that do not aid the working class to interpret the reality it
actually experiences." In other words, working-class people could not see
themselves in the picture of "America" presented by the dominant culture.
As a result they felt an inescapable sense of inner conflict, as Richard Sennett and Jonathan Cobb have thoughtfully demonstrated. Although working-class people had their own resources for dignity and solidarity, they
could not escape the effect of dominant values: they deemed their class
inferiority a sign of personal failure, even as many realized they had
been constrained by class origins they could not control. And contrary to
Marcuse, who claimed that workers shared the taste for commodities promoted by the dominant culture, Sennett and Cobb insisted that mass-
consumption patterns were not simple expressions of a drive for pleasure
through material gratification. Instead, they wrote, "material things are
aids to creating an inner self which is complex, variegated, not easily fath-
omed by others, because only with such psychological armor can a person
hope to establish some freedom in the terms of class society." Whatever
one thinks of this interpretation, it is intriguing to ponder the complexity of
the personal conflicts that must have existed inside all those allegedly identical houses in suburbia.[27]

The assumption that the United States was covered by a seamless web of
consumer culture not only denied psychological complexity, it obscured
the vitality and variety of subordinate cultures flourishing outside the
mainstream. Kent Blaser and George Lipsitz (among others) have begun to
remind us of that diversity, but what is amazing is how long the conventional picture of postwar homogeneity has remained embedded in textbooks and monographs.[28] The evangelical ethos that sustained the black
civil rights movement offers the most dramatic piece of counterevidence,
but consider another of many possible examples: the realm of popular music. During the late forties and fifties, black blues and white "hillbilly music" provided a powerful alternative to the saccharine formulas of Tin Pan
Alley; Billie Holiday and Hank Williams sang to huge audiences that were

anything but blandly optimistic; indeed, judging by those singers' lyrics, they were popular precisely because they were given to unproductive brooding on the intractable sadness of life. Black and white working-class music converged in early rock 'n' roll and was imported to the suburbs, where it posed a direct but ambiguous challenge to the hegemonic culture.

When the hegemonic culture began to fray at the seams, though, it was not as a result of rock 'n' roll–induced hysteria from below. Within the ruling historical bloc, many alliances were tenuous at best. There were important differences among various groups in temperament, outlook, and interest. The key fissure was between technicians and literati. The first group favored the language of expertise and power, the second the language of taste and style. There was a world of difference, after all, between the Rand Corporation and the New Criticism. The attempt to yoke together the cultural contradictions of capitalism began to break down during the 1960s.[29] Humanists had never been comfortable with the instrumentalist orientation of many technicians and social scientists; Tate and Whyte and others had articulated this discomfort when they had complained about the divorce of technique from content and means from ends. But the issue had remained philosophical and moral during the 1950s; the Vietnam War politicized it. The war revealed the myriad ways that the denatured language of expertise could sanitize a sordid rearguard defense of imperial prerogatives. It provoked an unprecedented rejection of technical prowess in the service of illegitimate power. In the name of humane values, many intellectuals and academics split off from the dominant direction of the "new class" to join with students in forming a counterhegemonic culture. Neoconservative snipings at a privileged "new class" do get at a fundamental social fact, though in a distorted and incomplete way: the counterculture *was* bred in the precincts of the "new class"—but only in some of its precincts, and in direct opposition to the instrumentalist orientation of its most powerful sectors.

The drive toward counterhegemony was only fitfully successful. The key to the diffusion of protest lay in language as well as power—as Gramsci, an accomplished linguistic theorist, would have well understood.[30] The problem was the prevalence of a dominant idiom that stressed the centrality of consumption, that fixated on matters of taste. Constrained by this inheritance from the 1950s, the rebellion of the 1960s lost its grasp of power relations and degenerated into a search for "alternative life-styles."

By now, this is a familiar indictment of the counterculture; it should not be construed to mean that the assault on technocratic thinking and suburban blandness was mistaken, only that the critique was incomplete. The rebels of the 1960s quite properly recognized that there was no neat fit between the needs of the individual and the requirements of the "social system" reified by Parsons and his followers; they articulated longings for personal autonomy that had often remained inchoate in the writings of social critics in the 1950s; they embraced rock 'n' roll—that amalgam of underground musical traditions from the white and black working class—as a means of dramatizing their desire for release from the stifling normality of an overorganized society.

The rise of rock 'n' roll provides some evidence for the argument that consumers need not be mere passive receptors of hegemonic cultural artifacts. They can locate other cultural artifacts outside the dominant culture and use them as a focus for resistance. Or they can take products that are squarely in the corporate mainstream and reinterpret them according to their own needs and interests: the Teddy Boy in the Edwardian suit, the working-class kid with the customized Oldsmobile. A few intellectuals, notably David Riesman, recognized this in the 1950s; a few others in the 1980s are beginning to resurrect those arguments under the imprimatur of Mikhail Bakhtin or Stuart Hall. A matter of taste, from this view, is not always a trivial matter.[31]

Yet troubling questions remain. How significant is the consumer's struggle to appropriate meaning? How successfully is it translated into discourse in the public arena? How likely that it could challenge existing inequalities? My own answers would not be reassuring. In postwar America, the tendency for protest to become a matter of taste has meant the devaluation of public discourse, the reduction of politics to questions of personality and style. These maladies affect "responsible" journalists, writers for *People* magazine, and those ordinary voters who disagreed with many of Ronald Reagan's policies but planned to vote for him because of his alleged "personal gallantry." Until the maladies run their course, the heirs apparent of the "new class" will continue to risk the fate of their forebears in the 1950s—men and women who were haunted by a fear of cultural asphyxiation, restless for stylistic novelty, and unaware that the task of resuscitation involved more than a breath of fresh air from Camelot.

NOTES

1. Mary McCarthy, "Mlle. Gulliver en Amérique," *Reporter* 6, no. 2 (January 22, 1952): 36.

2. Philip Rieff, "Socialism and Sociology," review of C. Wright Mills, *The*

Power Elite, Partisan Review 23, no. 3 (Summer 1956): 369; Werner Sombart, *Why Is There No Socialism in the United States?*, trans. Patricia M. Hocking and C. T. Husbands (1906; reprint, London: Macmillan, 1976). Sombart's words are translated as "All Socialist utopias come to nothing on roast beef and apple pie" on p. 106 of this edition.

    3. "Editorial Statement," *Partisan Review* 19, no. 3 (May –June 1952): 284; Newton Arvin, in ibid., 287; Sidney Hook, in ibid., no. 5 (September–October 1952): 569.

    4. Talcott Parsons, *The Social System* (Glencoe, Ill.: Free Press, 1951); David Riesman, with Nathan Glazer and Reuel Denney, *The Lonely Crowd: A Study in the Changing American Character* (1950; reprint, New Haven: Yale University Press, 1969).

    5. Eugene E. Leach, "Mastering the Crowd: Collective Behavior and Mass Society in American Social Thought, 1917–1939," *American Studies* 27 (Spring 1986): 99–114; Warren Susman, *Culture as History: The Transformation of American Society in the Twentieth Century* (New York: Pantheon, 1984), 150–210.

    6. William L. Bird, Jr. "Order, Efficiency, and Control: The Evolution of the Political Spot Advertisement, 1936–1956," (Ph.D. diss., Georgetown University, 1985), 62–77; Lary May, "Movie Star Politics: The Screen Actors' Guild, Cultural Conversion, and the Hollywood Red Scare," chap. 7 in this volume. For other accounts of the corporate appropriation of the American Way, see Robert Griffith, "The Selling of America: The Advertising Council and American Politics, 1942–1960," *Business History Review* 57, no. 3 (Autumn 1983): 388–412; John Morton Blum, *V Was for Victory: Politics and Culture during the Second World War* (New York: Knopf, 1979); and Charles F. McGovern, "Selling the American Way: Democracy, Advertisers, and Consumers in World War II," paper presented at National Museum of American History, Smithsonian Institution, Washington, D.C., June 23, 1987. For an account of one historian's effort to preserve an independent Left perspective amid the celebration of the American Way of Life, see Christopher Lasch, "On Richard Hofstadter," *New York Review of Books* (March 8, 1973): 7–13.

    7. John Kenneth Galbraith, *American Capitalism: The Concept of Countervailing Power* (Boston: Houghton Mifflin, 1952); Daniel Bell, "The *Power Elite* Reconsidered" (1958), in *C. Wright Mills and the Power Elite*, comp. G. William Domhoff and Hoyt B. Ballard (Boston: Beacon, 1968), 198–216; Riesman, *Lonely Crowd*, 220.

    8. Riesman, *Lonely Crowd*, 3; David Potter, *People of Plenty: Economic Abundance and the American Character* (Chicago: University of Chicago Press, 1954), 68; emphasis mine.

    9. Will Herberg, *Protestant, Catholic, Jew: An Essay in American Religious Sociology* (Garden City, N.Y.: Doubleday, 1955). For the influence of Dewey on Mills, see Irving Louis Horowitz, *C. Wright Mills: An American Utopian* (New York: Oxford University Press, 1983). For Fromm's use of Marx, see John Schaar, *Escape from Authority: The Perspectives of Erich Fromm* (New York: Harper and Row, 1964), esp. 183–92.

10. Allen Tate, "The Man of Letters in the Modern World," Phi Beta Kappa Address, University of Minnesota, May 1, 1952, reprinted in his *The Forlorn Demon* (Chicago: Regnery, 1953), 10. For other critiques of the elevation of technique over content, see Erich Fromm, *The Sane Society* (New York: Rinehart, 1955), esp. 110–20, and F. H. Heinemann, *Existentialism and the Modern Predicament* (New York: Harper, 1958).

11. *Abundance for What?* ed. David Riesman (Glencoe, Ill.: Free Press, 1964); William H. Whyte, *The Organization Man* (New York: Simon and Schuster, 1956), 310. See also John W. Jeffries, "The 'Quest for National Purpose' of 1960," *American Quarterly* 30, no. 4 (Fall 1978): 451–70.

12. Whyte, *Organization Man*, esp. 7, 17–18, 312ff., 384.

13. Erving Goffman, *Asylums* (Garden City, N.Y.: Doubleday, 1959).

14. W. W. Rostow, *The Stages of Economic Growth* (New York: Cambridge University Press, 1960); Daniel Bell, *The End of Ideology* (Glencoe, Ill.: Free Press, 1960). On the predominance of this "end-of-the-line" argument, see Winston White, *Beyond Conformity* (Glencoe, Ill.: Free Press, 1961), 160–61.

15. Auden, quoted in Bennet M. Berger, "Sociology and the Intellectuals," *Antioch Review* 27, no. 3 (Fall 1957): 281–82. "The bland leading the bland" is from Eric Goldman, *The Crucial Decade—And After: America 1945–1960* (New York: Knopf, 1973), 344. The reference to Fred Waring is in Paul Goodman, *Growing Up Absurd* (New York: Random House, 1960), 109.

16. Lionel Trilling, *The Liberal Imagination* (New York: Viking, 1950), 266; Dwight MacDonald, "A Theory of Mass Culture," in *Mass Culture: The Popular Arts in America*, ed. Bernard Rosenberg and David Manning White (Glencoe, Ill.: Free Press, 1957), 59–73.

17. C. Wright Mills, *White Collar: The American Middle Classes* (New York: Oxford University Press, 1951), ix, 189–214, and *The Power Elite* (New York: Oxford University Press, 1956); Herbert Marcuse, *One-Dimensional Man: Studies in the Sociology of Advanced Industrial Society* (Boston: Beacon, 1964).

18. Trilling, in "Our Country and Culture," *Partisan Review* 19, no. 3 (May–June 1952): 319; James Sloan Allen, *The Romance of Commerce and Culture* (Chicago: University of Chicago Press, 1983); Riesman, *Lonely Crowd*, 298n.; Bernard Rosenberg, "Mass Culture in America," in Rosenberg and White, *Mass Culture*, 5; Herbert Marcuse, *The Aesthetic Dimension* (Boston: Beacon, 1968).

19. Leo Ribuffo, "Introduction: The Burdens of Recent History," *American Quarterly* 35, nos. 1–2 (Spring/Summer 1983): 3.

20. David Nye, *Image Worlds: Photography at General Electric, 1890–1930* (Cambridge: MIT Press, 1984). Mills also raised a central issue overlooked by social historians in chap. 13 of *The Power Elite*, where he discussed the transformation of the nineteenth-century "public" into a modern mass "audience."

21. Daniel Bell, "The Theory of Mass Society: A Critique," *Commentary* 22 (July 1956): 75–83; White, *Beyond Conformity*, 142–43. For Tocqueville as prophet of conformity, see Whyte, *Organizational Man*, 395, and Louis Hartz, *The Liberal Tradition in America* (New York: Harcourt, Brace, 1955), 11, 56–57. On voluntary associations, see, for example, Henry Steele Commager, *The American Mind* (New Haven: Yale University Press, 1950), 22–23. Vance Packard's *The*

Hidden Persuaders (New York: McKay, 1957) popularized the notion of a mass of consumers manipulated by corporate elites.

22. I have explored Gramsci's ideas at greater length in "The Concept of Cultural Hegemony: Problems and Possibilities," *American Historical Review* 90 (June 1985): 567–93.

23. Jean-Christophe Agnew ably summarizes the literature on the professional/managerial class in "A Touch of Class," *democracy* 3 (Spring 1983). See also *Between Labor and Capital,* ed. Barbara and John Ehrenreich (Boston: South End, 1980).

24. Trilling, "Our Country and Our Culture," 320; Irving Howe, "This Age of Conformity," *Partisan Review* 21, no. 1 (January–February 1954): 20, reprinted in his *A World More Attractive* (New York: Horizon, 1963).

25. For representative examples, see Commager, *American Mind,* 5–6, 409–10; Hartz, *Liberal Tradition,* 6–7.

26. Riesman, *Lonely Crowd,* esp. chap. 7.

27. Michael Mann, "The Social Cohesion of Liberal Democracy," *American Sociological Review* 35 (1970): 423–39, emphasis in original; Richard Sennett and Jonathan Cobb, *The Hidden Injuries of Class* (New York: Vintage, 1972), 159ff., 168–69, 218ff.

28. See Kent Blaser, "'Pictures from Life's Other Side': Hank Williams, Country Music, and Popular Culture in America," *South Atlantic Quarterly* 84, no. 1 (Winter 1985): 12–26; George Lipsitz, *Class and Culture in Cold War America: A Rainbow at Midnight* (South Hadley, Mass.: Bergin and Garvey, 1981).

29. Daniel Bell, *The Cultural Contradictions of Capitalism* (New York: Basic, 1978), discusses the conflict between a commitment to efficient productivity in the economic realm and a desire for personal fulfillment in the cultural realm.

30. On the importance of language in maintaining hegemony, see "The Concept of Cultural Hegemony," 591–93.

31. See Mikhail Bakhtin, *The Dialogical Imagination,* trans. Michael Holquist and Caryl Emerson (Austin: University of Texas Press, 1981); *Culture, Media, Language,* ed. Stuart Hall et al. (Atlantic Highlands, N.J.: Humanities, 1981); *Resistance through Rituals,* ed. Stuart Hall and Tony Jefferson (Wolfeboro, N.H.: Longwood, 1984); Dick Hebdige, *Subculture: The Meaning of Style* (London: Methuen, 1979). Riesman's comments on the liberating possibilities of "consumership" are in *Lonely Crowd,* chap. 15.

PART TWO

The Intellectual Reorientation

3   The Reconstruction of Progress: Charles Beard, Richard Hofstadter, and Postwar Historical Thought

David W. Noble

At the end of World War II, a new way of comprehending the American past swept over the history profession. In the academic world, scholars who had once admired Charles Beard as the leading intellectual of the Progressive school now turned to ideas propounded by the most famous advocate of the new understanding, Richard Hofstadter. Looking back in 1968 on the distinctive qualities of that alteration, Hofstadter wrote a memorable work comparing his vision with that of the previous generation. The result was *The Progressive Historians* (1968), an analysis of Vernon L. Parrington, Frederick Jackson Turner, and Charles A. Beard, who, in the author's judgment, "gave us the pivotal ideals of the first half of the twentieth century." Not only had their histories provided American liberals with a national identity, but he had chosen to become a historian "under the inspiration that came from reading Charles and Mary Beard's *The Rise of American Civilization*."[1]

Yet, far from Hofstadter's intellectual departure generating a sense of optimism, something resembling a troubled youth informs this recollection. As he looked back on that lost world of Progressive ideas and beliefs, Hofstadter acknowledged that "I started this book out of a personal engagement with the subject, out of some sense of incompleteness of my reckoning with my intellectual forebears." It was also more than just a reckoning. Rather, he recognized that his writings represented that "perennial battle we wage with our intellectual fathers," and that his major accomplishments were in many ways "my own parricidal forays."[2]

Obviously, words like these suggest a restructuring of selfhood as well as of the conceptual themes guiding the writing of history. What, then, was this older historical tradition and why should the rise of newer concepts be linked to ideas of oedipal revolt? As outlined by Gene Wise in his major study, *American Historical Explanations*, the fundamental paradigms by which scholars had organized their narratives underwent a dramatic shift from a Progressive to a consensus vision during the 1940s. An earlier generation of writers followed the ideas of Charles Beard and saw the patterns of American development as simple, straightforward, and predictable. There was for them a conflict between the people and the "interests." Behind the people stood virtue, democracy, and an ideal republic, while behind the interests stood alien monopolists associated with the evils of Europe, aristocracy, and capitalism. Inexorably, progress was pushed forward by the battle between good and evil unfolding in America. Then, led by the dazzling writer Richard Hofstadter, a new generation saw that time was not a simple evolution of democracy's triumph over false power. Nor could progress be defined as the inevitable victory of good over evil. Rather, American history found its character in progress guided by experts, coupled to ambiguity, irony, unpredictability, and even personal tragedy.[3]

Over the past decade, the meaning behind that change, moreover, has increasingly become a focal point of intense scholarly debate. Despite Wise's invaluable work, we still do not know what forced younger historians suddenly to abandon a mode of analysis that seemed convincing for much of the century. Some, like John Diggins, have sought to deny that a generational shift ever occurred, arguing that Progressive, republican ideas never took root in the United States and that the dominant thought of the twentieth century was defined by interest-group liberalism, not very different from consensus history itself. But this view cannot explain why Hofstadter should admit his own debt to the Progressives and affirm that he had to liberate himself from the power of the parental generation with "parricidal forays." In dealing with that intellectual reconstruction, this essay will show how the earth-shaking impact of World War II fundamentally altered the conditions necessary to sustain the belief in an ideal republic, giving rise to a generation seeking to alter not just historical paradigms but their own sense of progress and national identity.[4]

In order to understand that restructuring, let us look at the origins of the Progressive tradition that dominated the historical profession until 1945. As first formalized by Frederick Jackson Turner, the historian to whom all Progressive scholars traced their roots, the nation had reached a crisis in 1890. On the one hand, he announced at the Chicago World's Fair in 1893 that the very core of America's distinctness from Europe lay in the frontier and democracy. In contrast to Europe, where the structure of power was overwhelmingly weighted to favor the capitalists and aristocrats, the New World offered a potential escape from greed and oppression. Instead of a concentration of property, the opportunity to acquire free land provided the people with the resources to create a democratic culture guided by reason.

Around that struggle between democracy and oppression, Turner wove his narratives. To Turner, the American Revolution provided the democratic republicans with the opportunity to purge the New World of capitalists dominated by aristocratic, European ideas. Next, the Jeffersonians had to contest Alexander Hamilton and his desire to make monopoly and European ideas predominate. Yet, when it appeared that capital might conquer, it became the manifest destiny of the new republic to push westward across the vast continent and bring free land to the people. As conceived by participants in the republican tradition, such spatial expansion infinitely multiplied the area of productive property owned by virtuous farmers and small businessmen, providing a rational state of nature to counterbalance the dynamism of capitalism and the corrupting power of eastern monopolists. It followed that the democratic heroes were the presidents who released the energies of the people, battled the interests, and expanded the frontier. Indeed, the Progressives deified Jefferson, Jackson, and Abraham Lincoln, for in the name of the people they overcame the bankers and speculators.[5]

What is now clear, moreover, is that these ideas also represented a long tradition in Western thought. Although Turner was certain that American democracy did not owe its origins to European ideas, recent scholarship suggests that his key concepts merely transplanted the ideology of English republicanism to national soil. Turner identified the farmers with virtue and independence, but in so doing he rearticulated the Atlantic republican tradition so ably described by J. G. A. Pocock in *The Machiavellian Moment*. Originating in Renaissance Italy, and informing political thought in seventeenth- and eighteenth-century England and the North American colonies, republicanism presented a pre-Marxist critique of capitalism by making an absolute distinction between productive private property and parasitical capitalism. Capitalism embodied the tyranny, accidents, and irrationality of history, while a polity grounded in freehold property conformed to reason and universal law. Inasmuch as the citizenry needed to be independent and productive to preserve justice and the larger public good, Pocock saw the free land of the United States offering the full flowering of the republican ideal in the nineteenth century. The New World thus provided the place where the people could avoid the tragedies of Old World history and create a new Eden, in touch with divine progress.[6]

Just as Turner's frontier thesis reworked traditional republican ideals for nineteenth-century America, so the end of the frontier aroused fears that America's unique identity would be lost. Indeed, that omnipresent fear was at the heart of Turner's germinal paper read amid the splendor of the 1893

Chicago World's Fair, sponsored by the great capitalists who were building the new corporate order. As Turner saw the future, the danger was not that men would be without property or that upward mobility would be blocked. Rather, citizens accustomed to managing their own civic and economic fates would find their destinies determined by more powerful men. The clear implication was that the United States would no longer have a republic different from aristocratic Europe. "The transformations through which the United States is passing in our day are so profound, so far-reaching," he wrote, "that we are witnessing the birth of a new nation." Yet Turner lamented these events and asked, "Under the forms of American democracy, is there in reality evolving such a concentration of economic and social power in the hands of a comparatively few men as to make political democracy an appearance rather than a reality?" The tragic answer was yes, because "the free lands are gone. The material forces that gave vitality to Western democracy are passing away."[7]

On that somber note, Turner defined the key dilemma for future historians. And, exactly at this intellectual crossroads, Charles Beard began his career. Yet, instead of despairing, he soon would become the most influential historian of the early twentieth century because he provided a convincing intellectual framework for regenerating a progressive American identity. Rather than seeing the end of the frontier as a tragedy, he thought republican virtue could be reborn when the people learned how modern society worked and used participatory democracy to master industry. In so doing, Beard believed that the new means of control would come as the people gained access to the fundamental laws of science and technology—laws that he saw as universal and working for the good of all humanity. Then, through a political uprising dedicated to reform, they would be able to apply these principles against the irrational forces embodied in monopoly capital.

So between 1900 and 1919, the most noted historian of the day was deeply engaged in public issues and civic life, celebrating the liberating power of social science, a theme which informed his first major work, *The Industrial Revolution* (1901). The overall pattern of history as evolutionary progress was rational and universal, he argued, and through the power of reason, all nations could transcend an outmoded culture. The end of the frontier was thus not the destruction of a virtuous American democracy, as Turner feared. With the aid of public-spirited social scientists, the enlightened citizenry could discern history's laws and construct new institutions to control that reality. In this framework, he agreed with the tradition of republican virtue that capitalism was irrational, antidemocratic, and corrupting. But capitalism did not pose a threat, because it represented a chaotic stage of evolution between a reactionary medieval aristocracy and a progressive democracy. Harnessed to social science, the Progressive movement would triumph everywhere in the world because it expressed the universal laws of reason.[8]

In many ways, this interpretation of history paralleled the capitalist critique of Karl Marx. Yet, unlike the Marxists, Beard and his academic contemporaries in the Progressive movement saw no need for violent revolution to overthrow capitalism. Experiencing new democratic initiatives all across the land, and seeing their wishes embodied in the successful reform efforts of Presidents Theodore Roosevelt and Woodrow Wilson, these Progressive intellectuals believed that most of the American middle class participated in the virtue and rationality of production. For Beard, therefore, this middle class was against monopolists who exploited a dependent work force in the name of irrational greed and profit. And he could look with admiration on Progressive laws—based on social science investigations and recommendations—to control the corporations. Further, he could make a tremendous commitment to World War I, with its promise of "making the world safe for democracy," as a threshold experience when all humanity would pass over from the Egyptian bondage of capitalism to the promised land of industrial democracy. He predicted that "the years, 1917–1918, as surely as the age of the American and French Revolutions, will mark the opening of a new epoch in the rise of government by the people and in the growth of a concert among the nations."[9]

Like many other Americans after World War I, however, Beard was thrown into intellectual despair by the failure of this prophecy of a new international system after the war. As Progressivism collapsed and the Treaty of Versailles seemed to restore the old order in Europe and America, he responded by angrily rejecting his previous view that history expressed universal laws. Yet, instead of participating in the experience of the "lost generation" that informed literary intellectuals, Beard began to reassess his view of progress. In a dramatic reversal of his old faith, he now argued that the natural human experience was to be a participant in a national tradition. The unnatural or abnormal, he declared, was represented by such universalist philosophies as capitalism, Marxism, and Roman Catholicism. In contrast, the uniqueness of America was that it had created a democratic culture that had to be protected from the corrupting self-interest of these international philosophies. Indeed, for the rest of his life, he would insist that reform rested on the truth that the United States was an exceptional egalitarian culture isolated from a world where aristocracy and capitalism had great power.

Above all, isolationism provided the strength for the true American tradition and the knowledge generated by social science would help master the corporations in the United States. Articulating the outlines of that view, Charles and his wife, Mary, wrote the most influential work of history between the wars, *The Rise of American Civilization* (1927). Together, they developed a philosophy which brought them closer to Turner's view of a unique American culture, but which still tried to avoid Turner's tragic impasses. Like the great exponent of the frontier, they argued that when the United States began in 1789, its cultural foundation did not rest on an undemocratic heritage, as was the case with all other nations. Radiating optimism in describing a people rooted in the frontier experience, Beard celebrated America in a poetic prose of loving respect. "In this immense domain sprang up a social order without marked class or caste, a society of people substantially equal in worldly goods," he declared, and "in its folkways there was a rugged freedom—the freedom of hardy men and women, taut of muscle and bronzed by sun and rain and wind, working with their hands in abundant materials." [10]

The vision of an isolated, organic nationalism unique in world history also allowed Beard to explain the defeat of the reform movement, something he had not been able to do in 1920. Progressive democracy, he explained, had begun in the 1890s to defeat the capitalists, who after the Civil War had established a beachhead in the Northeast. But when the United States entered World War I, the nation had been caught up in internationalism, the environment in which rootless capitalism flourished. The result by the 1920s was the momentary victory of the monopolists. Nonetheless, inspired by the vision of a unique people armed with democratic culture and a patriotic social science, Beard was certain that reform would once again reassert itself.

In contrast to his earlier writings, moreover, this evocation of an American identity unique in world history made an enormous impression on the general reading public and the history profession. Against the backdrop of a failed crusade to make the world safe for democracy and the disillusion of the twenties, the *Rise* immediately sold more than one hundred thousand copies and was distributed by the Book-of-the-Month Club. Professionally, Beard was elected president of the American Historical Association, and, when coupled with the writings of Turner, his Progressive view of American uniqueness began to influence the writing of a generation of scholars. Older men trained their students to organize their materials around the new conceptual framework, and Beard set an example of the publicly engaged intellectual.[11]

Nowhere was that influence more evident than on the young man who was to dominate the profession after World War II, Richard Hofstadter. Starting his graduate career in the thirties, Hofstadter, in his first book, *Social Darwinism in American Thought* (1944), provided an extended footnote to the Beards' thesis about the dangers of monopoly power and internationalism. Focusing his attention on social scientific thought at the turn of the century, Hofstadter argued that Social Darwinism gained power after the Civil War as the philosophic sanction for laissez-faire capitalism and derived its central ideas from Europe. Yet this period of alien influence was soon challenged by popular uprisings of the people, armed with the ideas of social scientists like Lester Frank Ward. Soon the people applied that social science in a democratic uprising, purging the country of unrestrained monopolistic greed. As he wrote, "American social thought had been optimistic, confident of the special destiny of the country, humanitarian, democratic." And Ward's ability to formulate an alternative to rampant individualism, Hofstadter concluded, "stemmed from his democratic faith."[12]

In accord with Charles Beard's assertion of an isolated American tradition, Hofstadter also saw that uprising interacting with a non-Marxist opposition to capitalism. "The change in the political outlook of the common man," Hofstadter declared, "was responsible for a change in the fundamental mechanisms of thought among workers in the social sciences." Also giving scholarly form to that democratic élan were the theories of Progressive intellectuals who followed Ward, especially John Dewey and, by implication, Charles Beard. Hofstadter, moreover, followed the Progressive theme by ending his book with the frustration of the people's faith in World War I, when "the reformers of the era were destined to tragic failure." For capitalism was "being made to fit the mold of international conflict just when its inapplicability to domestic economics was becoming apparent." Yet, despite the declension, Hofstadter also faced the new gilded age with hope because, as he wrote, despite "the interruption of the 'twenties,' the trend toward social cohesion kept growing."[13]

The coming of the Great Depression, moreover, seemed to validate the accuracy of that prophecy. Early in the economic downturn, neither Beard nor his followers despaired. Rather, they were enormously optimistic. The capitalists had fallen with the stock-market crash, and, after 1932, the people once again had a great tribune and democratic hero, President Franklin Roosevelt. Repeatedly, Beard praised Roosevelt's efforts to isolate the country's unique heritage from an undemocratic world, mobilizing the people to conquer the "European" monopoly tradition at home. As the new president initiated the New Deal and used social science to understand the crisis and its solution, Beard wrote of Roosevelt as one in a long line of democratic heroes, the equal of Jackson and Lincoln.

Yet events of the late thirties caused a severe strain in that Progressive faith. The crisis came from the second great issue of the day: how to interpret the meaning of World War II and the president's response. Far from being a salvation figure of the democratic national identity, Roosevelt was now portrayed by Beard as a schemer plotting to take the United States into the war which was breaking out in Europe, an international initiative that once again would subvert the reform effort and bring monopoly to power. With that prospect, Beard by 1941 had reached a position comparable to Turner's in 1893. Once more capitalism was about to defeat democracy and the unique democratic heritage of a frontier nation. Once more, Europe was about to destroy American virtue. And, like Turner fifty years earlier, he could no longer write a narrative which separated virtuous America from corrupt Europe.[14]

Given that historical expectations were being defeated by the war, the critical question now became, How would Beard's followers deal with the failure of the Progressive tradition to explain history and create a non-capitalist nation? Would they discard or reconstruct the Progressive tradition? From the standpoint of Richard Hofstadter, it was clear that similar questions were very much on his mind. Self-confident and optimistic in 1940, when he followed the Beardian thesis and started to write *Social Darwinism*, he now described his views in dramatically different terms. Writing to a friend, he confessed that "I am by temperament a conservative and timid and acquiescent." It is due, he concluded, "among other things to a pervasive inner despair."[15] His next book, *The American Political Tradition* (1948), not only expressed his attempt to transform this despair into anger, but also became in the immediate postwar era the most influential work among a younger scholarly generation as well as the general reading public.

It was not hard to see why. If in 1945 Beard's Progressivism failed to explain why capitalism had not been defeated by democracy and why the country was no longer isolationist, Hofstadter sought to find an alternative means of understanding the course of history. The answer was first found by shedding the Progressive paradigm he unfolded in *Social Darwinism* and turning to the international, Marxist analysis he had held as an undergraduate. No longer did he see in the American tradition of reform a conflict between productive, democratic property and parasitical, capitalist property. There was no conflict between the "interests" and the people, for a commitment to private property and to capitalism had always, as in Europe, been the dominant tradition in the United States. A belief in a unique national tradition that could master international capitalism was thus an illusion that inhibited understanding. In effect, Hofstadter was replacing the conflict theory of American history with a new consensus approach. As he recalled, "My own assertion of consensus history in 1948 had its sources in the Marxism of the 1930s." [16]

That assertion brought with it an angry assault on the Progressive tradition with which he had formerly structured his narratives. In seeking to destroy the false consciousness perpetuated by his intellectual mentors, not the least of whom was his own doctoral adviser and follower of Beard, Merle Curti, Hofstadter made the opening pages of *The American Political Tradition* drip with irony. The "quest for the American past," he declared, was "carried on in a spirit of sentimental appreciation rather than critical analysis." But "the following studies in the ideology of American statesmanship," he continued, "have convinced me of the need for a reinterpretation of our political traditions which emphasized the common climate of American opinion. The existence of such a climate of opinion has been much obscured by the tendency to place political conflict in the foreground of history." Using a Marxist perspective, Hofstadter argued that, "even when some property right had been challenged—as it was by followers of Jefferson and Jackson, the challenge . . . when translated into practical policy, has actually been urged on behalf of some other kind of property." And the depth of his disillusionment became apparent when he complained that ours had been a "democracy of cupidity rather than a democracy of fraternity." [17]

Disappointed with the democratic heritage that he had inherited, Hofstadter saw his teachers' value judgments as essentially unrealistic. He pointed out that all the heroic American presidents whom Beard and other Progressives had identified as spokesmen for American democracy were covert capitalists. In chapter after chapter, he brought home this message. "Thomas Jefferson: The Aristocrat as Democrat" led into "Andrew Jackson and the Rise of Liberal Capitalism," followed by "Abraham Lincoln and the Self-made Myth," about a man whose ambition and democratic spirit led to the presidency but who was accompanied by deep personal anxiety and tragedy. Hofstadter's satire reached its peak as he described the presidents whom his mentors had followed in their own lives, especially "Theodore Roosevelt: The Conservative as Progressive." The author depicted "TR" as a warlike spokesman for the Social Darwinism that had dominated foreign policy before World War I and led to world chaos. Roosevelt, he wrote, was a masterful demagogue who had an "uncanny instinct for unpalpable falsehoods" and whose speeches contained "a string of plausible superficialities."[18]

Finally, he concluded that the democratic tradition reached a dead end when the economy crashed in 1929, leaving President Hoover a tragic figure whose imaginative world reflected the realities of the nineteenth century, realities that no longer provided an adequate guide to modern economic organization. With regret, he used the next president who had to deal with the Depression, Franklin Roosevelt, as emblematic of his generation's inheritance. The president was "neither systematic nor consistent, and he provided no clearly articulated break with the inherited faith." Roosevelt thus engaged in "month-to-month improvisation, without trying to achieve a more inclusive and systematic conception of what is happening in the world." Yet the Roosevelt presented by Hofstadter differed from that of Beard in being a pragmatic realist who recognized American's international responsibility to resist Nazi Germany.[19]

At the same time, the completion of the *The American Political Tradition* left the author with a quandary: What would replace the older culture and politics? Who and what social force might master a dangerous world order as well as the omnipresent instability of capitalism and the international arena? At first, the answer was by no means clear. By 1948, he explicitly rejected the Progressive historical understanding which he saw had "been intensely nationalistic and for the most part isolationist" and called for a new pluralism, "corporate and consolidated, demanding international responsibility." Yet, despite his use of a Marxist analysis, he could not take the next step and envision a socialist producer democracy's coming to the United States. In response, Hofstadter slowly began to create a new vision of progress for managing a chaotic world and rampant industrialism: a pluralistic society defined by capitalism, guided by experts armed with social science, removed from the "people" and a democratic tradition rooted in false consciousness.[20]

The full implications of that restructuring emerged full blown in

Hofstadter's next book, *The Age of Reform* (1955), a study of the Progressive tradition from the late nineteenth century to World War II. Borrowing terminology from Henry Nash Smith's *The Virgin Land: The American West as Symbol and Myth* (1950), he described the Populist uprising of the 1890s, which earlier historians had seen as the roots of modern reform, as an expression of irrational myth. Populists believed that farmers lived in harmony with the timelessness of nature, and they feared that capitalist dynamism would drag them away from an Edenic state, undermining their virtuous republic. Hofstadter criticized the farmers for believing that capitalism was a conspiracy and for their subsequent "paranoid" politics.[21]

Hofstadter similarly portrayed the next generation of reformers as reactionaries unable to adjust to the large-scale structures of the twentieth century and the realities of internationalism.[22] In so doing, he reversed the older themes of good and evil and stood the symbols of traditional reform on their heads. Earlier, in *Social Darwinism in American Thought*, Hofstadter followed Beard in presenting the capitalists as hopelessly nostalgic for nineteenth-century individualism and the chief cause of the failures of reform at home and abroad. Good thus resided in the people and their leaders, who were the practical visionaries seeking world peace and popular control. Yet by 1955 evil resided less in the corporate leaders than in the tribunes of the people, the Populist and Progressive leaders who "had not been brought up to think of the well-being of society merely in structural terms, as something resting upon the sum of technique and efficiency, but in moral terms, as a reward for the sum total of individual qualities and personal merits." Domestically, this destructive tradition led to irrational crusades against capitalist organizations, while, internationally, the reform impulse failed to bring peace. When President Wilson linked World War I "as intimately as possible to the Progressive values and Progressive language he was unintentionally insuring that the reaction against Progressivism and moral idealism would be as intense as it could be."[23]

In sharp contrast, Hofstadter now found an alternative to the Progressive faith in the pragmatic, nonideological policies of Franklin Roosevelt. Without fanfare, he reported a momentous change in American history. "Viewing the history of the New Deal as a whole," he wrote, "what seems outstanding about it is the drastic new departure that it marks in the history of American reformism." Contrasting Franklin D. Roosevelt with the great Progressive presidents, Theodore Roosevelt and Woodrow Wilson, Hofstadter pointed out that these earlier leaders had led crusades against special interest groups, particularly immigrant machines. But he praised the New

Deal leader for stepping outside the Yankee-Protestant tradition of moral absolutes, since FDR "was thoroughly at home in the realities of machine techniques of accommodation" and made "no effort to put an end to bossism and corruption, but simply ignored the entire problem." And, as "for the restoration of democracy," Hofstadter concluded, "he seemed well satisfied with his feeling that the broadest public needs were at least being served by the state and that there was an excellent rapport between the people and their executive leadership."[24]

Finally, he pointed to the books written in the 1930s by Roosevelt's attorney general, Thurman Arnold—*The Symbols of Government* and *The Folklore of Capitalism*—as exemplars of a more pragmatic way of mastering the economy. In Hofstadter's analysis, these tracts were part of a "sharp and sustained attack upon ideologies, rational principles, and moralism in politics." He commended FDR and thinkers like Arnold for their recognition of tolerance and pluralism, for managing "an economy in such a way as to restore prosperity," for discarding moral absolutes and questions of democratic control.[25] As these new managers laid the foundation for guiding capitalism through its periodic cycles, they avoided the disruption that resided in the emotional appeal of democratic politics. Indeed, he suggested that there were dangerous parallels between the totalitarian regimes of Europe and the folk democracy that Populists and Progressives admired. Fortunately, he argued, these reactionary residues were being inexorably eroded by the evolution of large-scale enterprise, and, with the entry of the United States into the international arena, Americans were "thrust into a situation in which their domestic life is largely determined by the demands of foreign policy and national defense. With this change came the final involvement of the nation in all the realities it had sought to avoid, for now it was not only mechanized and urbanized, but internationalized as well."[26]

In their ability to master this problem in a presumably disinterested way, Hofstadter saw the experts as the new heroes of progress. Yet, at the same time, there also flowed from this reformulation a different American identity than that which he had advocated when he had adhered to the Progressive tradition. Frederick Jackson Turner set the terms of the debate when he despaired in 1893 that the development of corporations and cities had undermined the pattern of freehold property which was the economic basis for a frontier democracy. Charles Beard, however, regenerated the national mission when he told historians that Turner's prophecy was wrong because the ideal of republican virtue could be revived through social science yoked to participatory democracy. For the great historian of the twenties and thirties, only an isolated, democratic America could overcome a foreign capitalism and realize the wonders of industry and technology. But, with the coming of World War II, Hofstadter lost faith in the power of Beard's ideas to predict events. Now, he came to agree with Turner that a twentieth-century America, dominated by cities, corporations, labor unions, and government bureaucracies would be more like Europe than the rural, decentralized United States of 1890. Seeking to restructure a vision of progress, however, Hofstadter argued that Americans had to shed their democratic culture and widespread citizen participation and let experts armed with a pure social science deal with the dangers of industry and world power.

As Hofstadter's writings gained enormous popularity with the educated public and professional historians in postwar America, his emphasis on a flawed democratic culture reaching back to the early nineteenth century helped obscure the dramatic transformation of national identity that had occurred in the author's own lifetime. Yet the tone of his books between 1944 and 1955 also suggests that the conversion wrought by the dilemmas of World War II had not been fully overcome. In *Social Darwinism in American Thought*, he followed Beard in praising the optimistic, participatory spirit of a people not only committed to democracy but also segregated from international capitalism and Marxism. The struggle against the fascists abroad, however, shattered that understanding, and the tone of Hofstadter's *The American Political Tradition* and *The Age of Reform* was by turns restrained, disappointed, and angry. Teaching Americans to accept capitalism and their international role, not as a declension from the virtuous past, but as the best that could be expected was not an experience that could evoke the kind of ecstatic prose Beard had used in *The Rise of America Civilization* to describe the succession of presidents who pioneered a unique democratic nation, isolated from a flawed world. At best, Hofstadter painted the earlier chief executives as self-interested and deluded, and Franklin Roosevelt was an ironic Moses figure who disabused his people of their illusions that they were a chosen people in a democratic promised land. Freed of their former faith, the people were now expected to accept as the true American reality all that many reformers had formerly seen as anathema: a capitalistic marketplace gaining strength from its expansion into the world arena.

At this point, we have come full circle back to the question with which we began and can discern why, when Hofstadter wrote his last great work, *The Progressive Historians*, he saw himself completing an act of parricide against his intellectual fathers. In the two major books written after 1945, *The American Political Tradition* and *The Age of Reform*, he faced the crisis within the Progressive tradition and concluded that capitalism was the organic experience of the American people, while populist democracy was their false consciousness. The clear implication followed that, for progress and order to be restored, the majority should shed their older emotional commitment to widespread participatory democracy and turn civic and economic power over to experts better qualified to direct the nation through dangerous waters. The result was that the most influential historian of his generation served as midwife to the two reigning ideas in postwar academic thought: a national identity rooted in consensus and a polity best served by social scientists removed from an irrational democratic tradition.

NOTES

1. Richard Hofstadter, *The Progressive Historians* (New York: Knopf, 1968), xiv.

2. Ibid.

3. Gene Wise, *American Historical Explanations* (Minneapolis: University of Minnesota Press, 1980), 82–112, 179–222.

4. Ibid., 223–350. Bernard Sternsher, *Consensus, Conflict, and American Historians* (Bloomington: Indiana University Press, 1975). John Diggins, *The Lost Soul of American Politics* (New York: Basic, 1984), and "Republicanism and Progressivism," *American Quarterly* 37 (Fall 1985): 572–98.

5. See the discussions of Turner in Henry Nash Smith, *The Virgin Land: The American West as Symbol and Myth* (Cambridge: Harvard University Press, 1950); Gene Wise, *Explanations*; and David W. Noble, *The End of American History: Democracy, Capitalism and the Metaphor of Two Worlds in Anglo-American Historical Writing* (Minneapolis: University of Minnesota Press, 1985).

6. J. G. A. Pocock, *The Machiavellian Moment* (Princeton, Princeton University Press, 1975). Dorothy Ross discusses the influence of republicanism in "The Liberal Tradition Revisited and the Republican Tradition Addressed," in *New Directions in American Intellectual History*, ed. John Higham and Paul Conkin, (Baltimore: Johns Hopkins University Press, 1979), 116–31.

7. Frederick Jackson Turner, *The Frontier in American History* (New York: Holt, 1921), 261.

8. Charles Beard, *The Industrial Revolution* (London: Allen and Unwin, 1901). Ellen Nore, *Charles A. Beard: An Intellectual Biography* (Carbondale: Southern Illinois University Press, 1983), provides the fullest overview of Beard's writings. See the discussion of Beard's vision of the industrial revolution in Noble, *The End of American History*, and David W. Noble and Michael Fores, "The Metaphor of Two Worlds: The American West, Industrial Revolution in England and Modernization Theory," *Soundings* 67 (Summer 1985): 139–59.

9. Frederic A. Ogg and Charles Beard, *National Government and the World War* (New York: Macmillan, 1919), 2.

10. See the discussion in Noble, *The End of American History,* 41–46; Charles and Mary Beard, *The Rise of American Civilization* (New York: Macmillan, 1927), 514, 516–17.

11. See the discussion in Gene Wise, *Explanations,* vii–viii, 123–34, 179–215, for the persuasiveness of the Progressive paradigm; Thomas Bender, "The New History—Then and Now," *Reviews in American History* 12 (December 1984): 613–22.

12. Richard Hofstadter, *Social Darwinism in American Thought* (Philadelphia: University of Pennsylvania Press, 1944), 50–51, 65. Hofstadter is discussed in Marian J. Morton, *The Terrors of Ideological Politics: Liberal Historians in a Conservative Mood* (Cleveland: Case Western Reserve University Press, 1972); Daniel Joseph Singal, "Beyond Consensus: Richard Hofstadter and American Historiography," *American Historical Review* 89 (October 1984): 976–1004; and Susan Stout Baker, *Radical Beginnings: Richard Hofstadter and the 1930s* (Westport, Conn.: Greenwood, 1985). Baker points out that Hofstadter explicitly designed his undergraduate thesis and his master's thesis to expand on points made by the Beards. She also describes Hofstadter's rejection of his youthful Marxism as he began his dissertation, which also depended on the Beards' Progressive paradigm.

13. Hofstadter, *Social Darwinism,* 101, 144, 145, 175.

14. See the discussion in Noble, *The End of American History,* 55–59.

15. Quoted in Baker, *Radical Beginnings,* 180–81.

16. Richard Hofstadter, *The American Political Tradition and the Men Who Made It* (New York: Knopf, 1948), and *The Progressive Historians,* 452, n. 9.

17. Hofstadter, *The American Political Tradition,* v, vii, viii.

18. Ibid., 227, 294–95.

19. Ibid., viii.

20. Ibid., x.

21. Richard Hofstadter, *The Age of Reform* (New York: Knopf, 1955), 38, 39, 46, 49–130.

22. Ibid., 202, 217.

23. Ibid., 223, 278.

24. Ibid., 203, 306, 307.

25. Ibid.

26. Ibid., 326. For a different interpretation of Thurman Arnold's writings during the thirties, see Norman Rosenberg's essay in this collection. For a discussion of Hofstadter's participation in the new theories of democratic elitism that informed a younger generation of political scientists and social scientists after the war, see Noble, *The End of American History,* 90–114. Also see David Danbom, *The World of Hope: Progressives and the Struggle for an Ethical Public Life* (Philadelphia: Temple University Press, 1987). Since Banbom emphasizes that the reformers were fighting against the concept of interest-group politics, his book thus helps to clarify the distinctiveness of Hofstadter's rejection of Progressivism in *The Age of Reform* and his new celebration of interest-group politics.

4 *The Politics of Social Science in Postwar America*

Terence Ball

The idea that there exists a connection between politics and social science in postwar America might seem a curious one. After all, science and politics, like oil and water, are not supposed to mix. Politics is the interest-laden quest for power, and science is the disinterested search for knowledge. Therefore, the social sciences, qua science, cannot be said to be political, nor to have a politics. Like much that passes for conventional wisdom, however, this claim cannot withstand close critical scrutiny. The welfare-warfare state that emerged in the Depression and cold war eras created the conditions which the various social sciences—economics, psychology, sociology, anthropology, and political science—became valuable, if not indispensable, adjuncts of corporate and state power.

The result of that process is now a commonplace of contemporary academic life, namely that the social sciences depend to a very great degree upon government grants and others monies. Indeed, it is almost impossible to imagine them flourishing as they have since World War II without a high level of largess from foundations and other funding sources. As one observer joked, anthropologists who study South Pacific cargo cults have come to expect and receive research grants as much as Melanesians expect to receive cargo.[1] Much the same can be said of other researchers in the social sciences, almost all of whom are, to one degree or another, dependent on government grants, foundation funding, corporate support, or some combination of the three. So commonplace is this situation that it is easy to forget how recent this development is and to overlook the causes and consequences of that intimate interchange between science and the pursuit of political power.

None of these developments occurred in isolation. On the contrary, the social sciences generally, and the so-called policy sciences in particular,

For criticizing an earlier version of this paper, I am grateful to Carl Schorske, Donald Meyer, Jackson Lears, Barbara Laslett, and Lary May, none of whom should be held responsible for what I have done (or failed to do) with their criticisms and suggestions.

came to enjoy prominence as a result of three major events that confronted Americans from 1930 to 1950. The creation of the welfare state, the coming of World War II, and the politics of the cold war created the climate in which the claims of these disciplines acquired a powerful appeal. After the war, there emerged for the first time a vast institutional infrastructure— government granting agencies, private foundations, and the modern multiversity, in which the increasing professionalization of the social sciences proceeded apace—for supporting research and training. Through this combination of circumstances, the disciplines of the social sciences that had been evolving since the 1890s came into their own, overcoming popular resistance and attaining a degree of legitimacy that they had not previously known.

I

Yet little of that rise to prominence makes sense unless we explore why it was that first in the 1930s the people and their leaders increasingly turned to the appeal of the social sciences. As a watershed in the nation's history, the Great Depression sparked the coming of the New Deal and the birth of the American welfare state. And along with these developments came a whole host of changed attitudes about the proper relation between citizens and their government. These include changing beliefs about government's responsibility for alleviating social ills, for engaging in limited economic planning (by, among other things, controlling the money supply, bolstering the banking system by regulating banking practices, insuring individual deposits, and the like), for mediating between the interests of capital and labor, and generally checking the worst social and economic excesses of an otherwise untrammeled laissez-faire market economy.

Even as America experimented with the New Deal, Nazis came to power in Germany, and fascists extended their hold over Italy and Spain. Social and economic ills were explained by these regimes as the results of the machinations of Jews, communists, and other unpopular minorities whose members were already being marked for mass extermination. Labor unions and working-class political parties were outlawed, their members silenced, and their leaders imprisoned or killed. And in the erstwhile workers' paradise to the east, Stalin in a series of purges succeeded in consolidating his power over the party that had seized state power in the name of the proletariat. Repression was rife, and all across Europe the threat of another world war was palpable.

These developments did not go unnoticed or unfelt in the United States, which had its share of native crackpots, political schemers, sophisticated ideologues, and stem-winding orators. The simple solutions promised by partisans of almost every political and ideological stripe—from Father Coughlin and Huey Long on the populist Right to communists like Earl Browder and home-spun democratic socialists like Norman Thomas on the Left—appealed to an ever-larger audience of the dispossessed and the downtrodden. The New Deal was in no small part an attempt by Progressives to undercut the appeals of radicals of the Right and the Left by offering a more moderate, and arguably more democratic, alternative. All these developments are familiar enough. Less familiar, perhaps, is the revolution wrought in, and by, the social sciences during the prewar period.

The reasons for the social sciences' rise to prominence during this period are, broadly, of two kinds. The first—about which I shall have more to say later—has to do with the particular political, social, and economic conditions of the time. The second set of reasons has to do with the logical and epistemological features characteristic of a particular understanding of the social sciences themselves.

According to nineteenth-century positivists and their twentieth-century successors, the logical positivists (or logical empiricists), all the "positive" sciences—natural and social—are alike not in their subject matters but in their method. The scientific method of controlled inquiry and observation enables them to provide not merely information but knowledge of a particular kind. Nomological knowledge—that is, scientific knowledge of the universal laws or principles operative in nature and in human society— could prove particularly useful not only in explaining natural and social phenomena but also in predicting and controlling them. If we know that X causes Y—if, that is, there is some universal law according to which the occurrence of X is a necessary if not sufficient condition for the occurrence of Y—then we can, in principle, bring about Y by bringing about X. Conversely, if Y is deemed undesirable, we can preclude its occurrence by preventing X. Once armed with such nomological knowledge, moreover, we are in a position to predict particular classes of outcomes.[2] If X is observed to occur, we can predict that Y will follow; if X fails to occur, Y will not happen. Hence, to be able to control antecedent conditions is to have the power to produce outcomes deemed desirable and to prevent those thought to be undesirable. Nomological knowledge is therefore the epistemic prerequisite for social engineering. As Auguste Comte put it, "*Savoir pour prevoir, prevoir pour pouvoir*"—to know in order to predict, to predict in order to control. The possession of such nomological knowledge enables social sciences to be, in Comte's phrase, a "science of order."[3]

II

In a period of dislocation and disorder which was at the same time an age of astounding scientific and technological progress, the hope of reconstructing society along more surely scientific lines was bound to have a certain appeal, at least in some quarters. This was perhaps especially true of those order-minded Progressives who saw America faced with the choice between anarchy and planning. As early as 1914, Walter Lippmann contrasted the "drift" of the older order to the "mastery" promised by the more rational system of economic planning and social control.[4] In a variety of ways, the theme was reiterated by John Dewey, Charles A. Beard, Herbert Croly (whose debt to Comte he happily acknowledged), and the *New Republic* and other organs of Progressive opinion. But calling for reform was one thing; planning and carrying it out in detail was something else again. It was just here that the social sciences seemed to offer a measure of hope. Their business was to identify and describe social problems, discover their causes, trace their consequences, and analyze the effectiveness of alternative proposals and policies. Above all, the social sciences were to be objective, detached, and disinterested. As a source of normatively neutral and instrumentally rational knowledge, the social sciences seemed ideally suited to serve the ostensibly nonpartisan aims of the Progressives. Disgusted with the petty partisan wrangling that characterized traditional politics, the Progressives favored a nontraditional politics of nonpartisanship and professional expertise enlisted in the service of some higher public good. Hence, it became necessary, as Barry Karl has observed, to begin to develop "the methods and instruments in the social sciences that would make progressivism work and would, indeed, be one of its chief legacies."[5]

These themes appear in Robert Lynd's *Knowledge for What?* published in 1939. The distinguished sociologist and coauthor of the *Middletown* series suggested that society had become so complex and its problems so intractable as to defy solution by traditional nonscientific means. The wiles and intuitions of the neighborhood politician, and for that matter his national counterpart, were too narrowly partisan, too parochial—and above all, too uninformed—to be rationally relied upon in governing a society as large and as complex as America had become. True to the tenets of his Progressive faith, Lynd opined that politics should become less an avocation for amateurs than a vocation open to expert professionals and planners more devoted to the public good than to narrowly partisan interests. Henceforth, politicians were to be replaced by professionals, and mayors by managers. And both were to be advised, if not replaced, by social scientists, the disinterested savants of a new and more rational social order.[6]

Although advanced as "outrageous hypotheses," Lynd's suggestions were not entirely novel. For, from the 1930s on, social scientists from a variety of disciplines had become increasingly active and visible servants in both the private and the public sectors. In the former, for example, psychologists and other social scientists carried out research on the morale and productivity of workers in various industries; devised time-and-motion studies to assess workers' efficiency; designed and administered tests to determine which prospective employees would be misfits and malcontents and which could be counted on to be compliant; proposed strategies for increasing the efficiency, productivity, and profitability of large firms; and so on. Elton Mayo and the "human relations" school of industrial psychology stressed the importance of inexpensive nonmaterial incentives in increasing worker morale and productivity, and hence the profitability of the firms for which they worked.[7] The findings of the social sciences—and the discipline of industrial psychology in particular—were in the 1920s and 1930s applied by management in hopes of exercising more subtle forms of control over workers who might otherwise be attracted to trade unionism or, worse still, to socialism.[8] The pages of *Business Week* and the *Harvard Business Review* regularly reported the latest research findings of social scientists studying worker morale, consumer motivation, and the like. As a prominent psychologist was later to remind readers of the *Harvard Business Review*, "The social sciences are an especially pertinent subject for businessmen to consider, for they deal . . . with the organization of people and the control of behavior."[9]

The presence of social scientists in the public sector was, if anything, even more pronounced. As Bernard Barber notes, "The use of social scientists by the Government . . . passed a major turning point during the Depression of the 1930's. With the generally increased scope of Government activities which began in that period, a great many social scientists from the fields of economics, political science, and sociology entered the permanent [or part-time] employ of the Government."[10] The "alphabet agencies" of the New Deal—the FHA, NRA, RFC, WPA, SEC, and others—were staffed largely by social scientists. Daniel Lerner does not exaggerate when he observes that "The New Deal . . . appeared to be a government of social scientists in its early years. . . . The New Deal codified a relationship between social research and social policy. . . . Social research has [since] become an indispensable instrument of public policy, regardless of party, in the complex urban industrial society of modern America."[11] Yet, important as it was in institutionalizing and legitimizing the social sciences, the Depression pales in comparison with World War II.

III

In some respects, the war was a godsend for the social sciences. It increased, in ways that the Depression never had, opportunities for research and disciplinary advancement. Before 1940, most social science research was funded from private sources. Even during the Depression, government monies allocated for social science research were spent mainly on gathering and publishing statistical information.[12] The war changed all that. "World War II," writes Harry Alpert of the National Science Foundation, "was undoubtedly the major catalytic event leading to the expansion of the federal government's programs in [the social science] field." Indeed, he adds, the present-day prominence of the social sciences in America

> is a product of World War II and of the postwar era and represents novel developments both with respect to the magnitude of the funds involved and the types of problems and disciplines supported. The events of the war on both the military and civil fronts, and the problems of postwar readjustment . . . , provided the social sciences with dramatic opportunities to demonstrate their practical value and essential role in modern society. As a result, social science research firmly established its legitimacy as a fundamental contributor to our national life.[13]

A report released by the Russell Sage Foundation in 1950 noted that in "the prosecution of World War II . . . social scientists were converted into social practitioners. Their services were comparable to the function of engineers and other specialized technologists in applying knowledge of the physical scientists [sic]."[14] Physicists might say how atoms behaved and engineers how weapons worked, but social scientists could explain, predict—and possibly alter—the behavior of those who pulled the triggers.

Not surprisingly, then, a good deal of effort was devoted to studying the attitudes and behavior of wartime GIs. One of the classic studies—The American Soldier, by social psychologist Samuel Stouffer and his associates—was originally undertaken for the very practical purpose of improving the selection, training, and performance of military personnel.[15] Yet this massive research project represented only one small part of a larger development in which social scientists were to an ever-greater extent becoming social engineers in the employ of the state.[16] Economists, for example, took advantage of a wartime milieu even more congenial to economic research and planning than that of the Depression. They drew up plans for rationing consumer goods, allocating war materiel, and overseeing the de facto nationalizing of some sectors of production and distri-

bution (steel, shipping, rubber, textiles, coal and oil, even agriculture). As
John Kenneth Galbraith—then a young agricultural economist working
for the Office of Price Administration—was later to observe, economists in
wartime Washington had their differences, but what none of them disagreed about was that they belonged in the corridors of power.[17]

Nor were the psychologists and economists alone in getting a piece of
the wartime action. The "policy sciences"—political science, public administration, and allied disciplines—got a leg up by analyzing the effects
and assessing the effectiveness of various wartime policies.[18] These social
scientists studied farm subsidy programs, recycling schemes, ad campaigns
for war bonds, the draft-registration system, the beliefs and behavior of the
American soldier, the determinants of military morale, race relations in
the military, the social effects of the bombing and shelling of civilians, the
effectiveness of different kinds of propaganda, the social causes of the
spread of venereal disease, and dozens of other war-related phenomena.[19]
So much in demand were social scientists that training, finding, and recruiting them became a considerable problem in its own right.[20] At war's
end, most social scientists returned to the academy whence they had come.

IV

One war was over, but another had begun. While World War II
had been a war of weapons—preeminently and ultimately of the most fear-
some weapon of all—the cold war was above all a war of ideas and ideologies, of psychology and propaganda. It was, in a phrase not yet coined, a
struggle for the hearts and minds of men. In this long twilight struggle, the
social scientist had, or purported to have, something special to contribute.
In the in-house literature and public pronouncements of the postwar period, social scientists are likened repeatedly to technicians, to engineers,
even to physicians concerned with the "health" of American society. In
1947 the SSRC's Pendleton Herring put it this way:

> One of the greatest needs in the social sciences is for the
> development of skilled practitioners who can use social data
> for the cure of social ills. . . . The term *social science tech-*
> *nician* [refers to] an individual who has been professionally
> trained to apply to practical situations the facts, generaliza-
> tions, principles, rules, laws, or formulae uncovered by
> social science research. . . . Social engineering [is] the ap-
> plication of knowledge of social phenomena to specific
> problems.

"Social engineering," he concluded, "is a meaningful conception, worthy of considerable expansion."[21]

And expand it did. Measured in almost any terms—monies allocated, scope and size of foundation funding, professorships endowed and filled, fellowships awarded, surveys conducted, number of books and articles published, dissertations written, degrees granted, and so on—the postwar period proved a bountiful one for the social sciences. These developments were scarcely accidental ones having merely to do with the changing tastes, whims, and vicissitudes of the American academy. Quite the contrary. The remarkable growth of the social sciences in postwar America was intimately tied to the growth of American power abroad and of the central government at home. It is no less closely tied to the connection between the American university—or multiversity, as Clark Kerr was later to call it[22]—whose professionalized faculty is increasingly dependent for funding and academic advancement and prestige upon the large foundations, public and private, and upon government grants and contracts related to national defense, military and civilian intelligence, internal security, and the operation of the welfare state. These developments have, moreover, created a new, but by now thoroughly familiar, figure in the American academy and in departments of social science in particular: the academic entrepreneur or grantsman skilled in the art of securing government and foundation funding. Little wonder, then, that this new figure on the academic scene was soon to be singled out for special censure by C. Wright Mills and, later, by spokesmen for the New Left.[23]

It is tempting and altogether too easy to follow in the footsteps of C. Wright Mills and the New Left, detecting in these developments a massive conspiracy to co-opt and corrupt American academicians. That there was, and is, some measure of co-optation and corruption would be difficult to deny. But these developments doubtless had more to do with functional imperatives than with the conscious conspiratorial designs of a power elite. It is worth considering, in conclusion, one of these imperatives and its implications.

V

Consider again the question of cost. Modern social science research has proved to be enormously expensive. The funding for such research has come, more often than not, from either federal agencies or private or public foundations. One might suppose that here, as elsewhere, the old adage applies: He who pays the piper calls the tune. If so, it is not called consciously and directly but unconsciously and indirectly. That is, these agencies and foundations by no means predetermine the specific outcomes or findings of social science research. They do, however, determine the sorts of questions that researchers ask and answer and the sorts of inquiries and investigations deemed worthy of support and, thereby, less directly, of reporting in conferences, symposia, publications, and even, eventually, pedagogy.

By way of illustration, consider my own field of political science. In the 1950s, say Somit and Tannenhaus,

> An unprecedented flow of foundation funds helped further ease the rigors of scholarly life. Whereas a $10,000 grant was a major event in the 1930's or even 1940's, so modest an amount barely occasioned mention by the late 1950's. Carnegie and Rockefeller multiplied manyfold their support of political science. Of even greater moment was the appearance of a new giant—the Ford Foundation. The lavish beneficence of this leviathan late-comer dwarfed the combined giving of the older agencies. Taking the twenty years as a whole, it would be conservative to say that the Ford complex provided 90 per cent of the money channeled to political science by American philanthropic institutions.

"Under these circumstances," they continue, "political scientists would have been less than human were they not tempted to manifest a deep interest in the kinds of research known to be favored by Ford Foundation staff and advisers." And, although they add that "this is a point to which we will later return," they never mention the matter again.[24] In a wide-ranging retrospective published in 1961, Robert Dahl acknowledges

> the influence of those uniquely American institutions, the great philanthropic foundations—especially Carnegie, Rockefeller and . . . Ford—which because of their enormous financial contributions to scholarly research, and the inevitable selection among competing proposals that these entail, exert a considerable effect upon the scholarly community. . . . [B]ecause even foundation resources are scarce, the[ir] policies . . . must inevitably encourage or facilitate some lines of research more than others. If the foundations had been hostile to the behavioral approach, . . . it would have had very rough sledding indeed. For characteristically, behavioral research costs a good deal more than is

needed by the single scholar in the library—and sometimes . . . behavioral research is enormously expensive. [25]

Other costs—less tangible but no less real—are also incurred by social
scientists doing research of this kind. We might even couch this in terms
of a lawlike generalization to the effect that the more expensive her re-
searches, the less independent the researcher. As Marian Irish remarks,
rather matter-of-factly, "There is an understandable tendency in university
circles to direct one's research where the money is available rather than
into independent research. Even the most scientific research—for example, basic research in comparative politics, cross-national studies, the
politics of violence, or the politics of race relations—may be mission-
supporting." [26] Translated into plain English, "mission-supporting" means
that such knowledge may be useful in one group's efforts to control, coerce,
repress, suppress, or subvert another. [27]

There is yet another sense in which scholarly integrity and independence may be compromised. To the extent that social scientists are dependent upon governmental or foundation funding, they are less likely to ask
certain kinds of questions. And foremost among these are questions about
the locus, distribution, and uses of power. As David Easton observed
in 1953,

> Entrenched power groups in society, those who have a firm
> hold on a particular pattern of distribution of social goods,
> material or spiritual, have a special reason to look askance at
> this probing into the nature and source of their social posi-
> tions and activities. They are prone to stimulate research of
> a kind that does not inquire into the fundamentals of the
> existing arrangement of things. . . . History has yet to show
> us empowered groups who welcomed investigation into the
> roots and distribution of their strength. [28]

These postwar warnings echo a fear voiced earlier by the Progressive historian Charles A. Beard. Beard, who had the double distinction of being
president of the American Historical Association and the American Political Science Association, warned of the corrupting effects of corporate and
government philanthropy on critical and original thinking. [29] His postwar
successors seemed to be less troubled by the specter of scholarly compromise or corruption.

One can of course compile a long list of social scientific books and
articles published during the postwar period, almost all of which were

funded by corporate or government agencies and few of which show any
overt ideological or political bias in their conclusions. If there are biases,
they are of a more subtle sort, having more to do with the kinds of issues
addressed, the unarticulated premises from which they begin, and the
questions that remain unasked. This can be seen even in the most distinguished work. Consider, for example, the seminal studies of prejudice, tolerance, and intolerance conducted during the postwar period. Two of the
most important and influential of these—Adorno, Frenkl-Brunswick, and
Levinson's *The Authoritarian Personality* (1949) and Samuel Stouffer's
Communism, Conformity, and Civil Liberties (1955)—share as their fundamental guiding assumption the belief that tolerance is the preeminent
political virtue. That tolerance may indeed be a virtue in a diverse and
pluralistic society like ours I do not deny. But two points are worth noting.
The first is that the issue is never framed in the "normative" language of
civic virtue. And the second is that (the virtue of) tolerance is predicated
on a particular political theory—interest-group liberalism—whose practices (and prejudices) these studies of (in)tolerance then serve to legitimize
if not insulate from criticism.[30]

The postwar period also saw the publication of numerous studies of the
theory, practice, and psychological appeals of communism. One of the most
important of these—Gabriel Almond's *The Appeals of Communism*, sponsored by the Carnegie Corporation—attempted to discover the sources of
communism's appeal in hopes that effective psychological and propagan-
distic means might be found to counter it.[31] In this and in many other
ways, the social sciences became valuable additions to America's cold war
arsenal.

It is surely ironic that, during the postwar period, the old staple of political description and analysis—"the state"—virtually disappeared from the
social scientists' vocabulary, even as the American state was becoming
more powerful than ever. Structuralists, functionalists, and structural-
functional "systems" theorists like Talcott Parsons and David Easton preferred to speak instead of "the political system" as a "subsystem" of a larger
and more benign entity, "the social system." Characterized by widespread
normative consensus and the virtual absence of protracted conflict (especially class conflict), the social system looked a lot like an abstract version
of the America being portrayed by the consensus historians and by the social scientists who in the late 1950s announced "the end of ideology."[32]

Despite such notable exceptions as David Riesman's *The Lonely Crowd*
(1955), C. Wright Mills's *White Collar* (1958), and J. K. Galbraith's *The*

Affluent Society (1958), much of "mainstream" social science in the post-war period tended to be more celebratory than critical. No need to search for the good society, said one distinguished sociologist, since it is already here. American-style democracy, wrote Seymour Martin Lipset, is "the good society itself in operation."[33] Even our defects turned out, upon closer examination, to be virtues. For example, survey researchers discovered that most Americans are politically ill informed, inactive, and apathetic. By "traditional" democratic lights, this was cause for considerable alarm. Yet, according to the newly emergent "elite theory" of democracy, it is widespread political participation that poses the greatest danger to democracy. Fortunately, an antidote is readily available. That antidote is apathy. Widespread apathy allows well-educated and affluent "democratic elites" to have a disproportionate say in the shaping of political possibilities.[34]

In these and many other ways the groundwork was being laid for a post-Progressive vision of a "consultative commonwealth," a "knowledge society" guided by the "epistemocratic authority" of experts.[35]

VI

Although most of the social scientists educated in the postwar years stayed in the academy, some went to work for government agencies and corporations. Sometimes, though, it was difficult to tell the difference between them. For even those remaining within the professional departments in the multiversity often worked under contract on "mission-supporting" projects. Called "the new Mandarins" by their critics and "the defense intellectuals" or "policy scientists" by their defenders, they attempted to contract a marriage between knowledge and power. From that marriage came numerous offspring, some benign and some not. Project Camelot and the Vietnam war were arguably among the most notorious and visible of these progeny.[36] Under the guise of objectivity and value freedom, some social scientists sold their skills and services without asking any hard moral questions, either of themselves or of their sponsors. As Stuart Hampshire has noted,

> An illusory image of rationality distorted the moral judgment of the American policy-makers. They thought that their [critics] were sentimental and guided only by their unreflective emotions, while they, the policy-makers, were computing consequences with precision and objectivity, using quasi-quantitative methods. . . . Under the influence

> of bad social science, and the bad moral philosophy that
> usually goes with it, they over-simplified the moral issues
> and provided an example of false rationality.[37]

Much of the groundwork for such social science was laid in the postwar era. The cold war, threats of communist expansion, America's new pre-eminence as a world power, the coming of the welfare-warfare state, the rise of the multiversity, and the largess of the large philanthropic founda-tions were among the conditions that created the climate in which a positivistic vision of an instrumentally useful and normative neutral social science could take root and flourish.

By the late 1960s, however, this vision began to come under consider-able strain. Not only was the luster of the social sciences tarnished by the Vietnam War and earlier "counterinsurgency" research programs like Project Camelot, but their demonstrable lack of explanatory and predictive power was becoming increasingly obvious. Thus, for example, ideology, far from ending, as predicted in the late fifties, enjoyed a resurgence in the sixties and afterward; economic forecasts have proved particularly un-reliable; all the theories of revolution have come a cropper; theories of modernization and secularization have proved singularly unsuccessful in explaining or predicting developments in the Middle East and elsewhere; and so on. Even the discipline of economics—sometimes called the queen of the social sciences (usually by economists)—has come in for consider-able criticism, much of it from economists themselves.[38] Successes there have doubtless been, though they seem in retrospect to be few and far between.[39]

Ironically, the present predicament of the social sciences may well have been brought about less by the failures of their theories and explanations than by their unparalleled political success in securing support from foun-dations and government. And, as we have seen, this support stemmed in no small part from the enormously successful self-promotion of the social sciences during the postwar period. Promises were made, or at least im-plied, and credit was extended. From the relative penury of the late forties and early fifties, the social sciences came to enjoy unprecedented pros-perity in the sixties. If federal and foundation funding is any index of sup-port, the social sciences were well supported during the 1960s.[40] A war abroad and the Great Society at home proved to be a profitable combina-tion of circumstances.

The boom did not, and perhaps could not, last. To recount the reasons for this change of fortune must, however, remain another story for another time.

NOTES

1. Alasdair MacIntyre, "Ideology, Social Science, and Revolution," *Comparative Politics* 5 (April 1973), 312–42.

2. This "deductive-nomological" or "covering-law" view of explanation has a venerable ancestry, going back to the scientific revolution of the seventeenth century. Its boldest and clearest statements are to be found in the writings of nineteenth-century positivists like Auguste Comte and J. S. Mill and their twentieth-century descendants, the logical positivists. For the latter see, among others, Carl G. Hempel, "The Function of General Laws in History," *Journal of Philosophy* 39 (1942): 35–48.

3. Auguste Comte, in *Auguste Comte and Positivism*, ed. Gertrud Lenzer (New York: Harper, 1975), esp. 56–59, 88–90.

4. Walter Lippmann, *Drift and Mastery* (New York: Kennerly, 1914).

5. Barry D. Karl, *The Uneasy State: The United States from 1915 to 1945* (Chicago: University of Chicago Press, 1983), 31. Karl's is one of the few general histories of the period to take note of the social sciences' intimate connection with Progressivism. For a more specialized study of a single social science discipline, see Raymond Seidelman and Edward J. Harpham, *Disenchanted Realists: Political Science and the American Crisis, 1884–1984* (Albany: State University of New York Press, 1985), esp. chaps. 3, 4. The eclipse of the Progressive spirit in the various social sciences may be partly explained by the increasing influence of distinguished European social scientists who emigrated to the United States in the 1930s and early 1940s, bringing with them quite different political orientations and traditions. The history of that episode has yet to be written, although H. Stuart Hughes's *The Sea Change: The Migration of Social Thought, 1930–1965* (New York: Harper and Row, 1975), marks a good start.

6. Robert S. Lynd, *Knowledge for What? The Place of Social Science in American Culture* (Princeton: Princeton University Press, 1939), esp. chap. 6.

7. Elton Mayo, *Human Problems of an Industrial Civilization* (New York: Macmillan, 1933); Thomas North Whitehead, *The Industrial Worker* (New York: Oxford University Press, 1938). For overviews and criticisms, see Harold L. Sheppard, "The Social and Historical Philosophy of Elton Mayo," and Louis Schneider, "An Industrial Sociology—For What Ends?" both in *Antioch Review* 10 (1950): 396–417; Sheldon S. Wolin, *Politics and Vision* (Boston: Little, Brown, 1960), chap. 10. On other specific episodes in the history of American social science, see Thomas L. Haskell, *The Emergence of Professional Social Science: The American Social Science Association and the Nineteenth-Century Crisis of Authority* (Urbana: University of Illinois Press, 1977); Edward T. Silva and Sheila A. Slaughter, *Serving Power: The Making of the Academic Social Science Expert* (Westport, Conn.: Greenwood, 1984); Donald T. Critchlow, *The Brookings Institution, 1916–1952: Expertise and the Public Interest in a Democratic Society* (Carbondale: Northern Illinois University Press, 1986).

8. See Loren Baritz's seminal study, *The Servants of Power: A History of the Uses of Social Science in American Industry* (Middletown, Conn.: Wesleyan University Press, 1960).

9. Raymond A. Bauer, "Our Big Advantage: The Social Sciences," *Harvard Business Review* 36 (May–June 1958): 125–36, at 125.

10. Bernard Barber, *Science and the Social Order* (Glencoe, Ill.: Free Press, 1952), 252.

11. Daniel Lerner, "Social Sciences: Whence and Whither?" in *The Human Meaning of the Social Sciences*, ed. Daniel Lerner (Cleveland: World, 1959), 22.

12. A. H. Dupree, *Science in the Federal Government* (Cambridge: Harvard University Press, 1957), 335.

13. Harry Alpert, "The Growth of Social Research in the United States," in Lerner, *Human Meaning*, 79.

14. Russell Sage Foundation, *Effective Use of Social Science Research in the Federal Services* (New York: Russell Sage, 1950), 42.

15. Samuel Stouffer et al., *The American Soldier*, 2 vols. (Princeton: Princeton University Press, 1949).

16. See Paul F. Lazarsfeld, *"The American Soldier*—An Expository Review," *Public Opinion Quarterly* 13 (1949): 377–404.

17. John Kenneth Galbraith, *A Life in Our Times* (Boston: Houghton Mifflin, 1981), chaps. 9–11.

18. Harold D. Lasswell, "The Policy Orientation," in *The Policy Sciences*, ed. Daniel Lerner and Harold D. Lasswell (Stanford: Stanford University Press, 1951), 3–15.

19. Russell Sage Foundation, *Effective Use*, 14–20.

20. John McDiarmid, "The Mobilization of Social Scientists," in *Civil Service in Wartime*, ed. Leonard D. White, (Chicago: University of Chicago Press, 1945), 73–96.

21. Pendleton Herring, "The Social Sciences in Modern Society," Social Science Research Council *Items* (March 1947): 5–6.

22. Clark Kerr, *The Uses of the University* (Cambridge: Harvard University Press, 1964), chap. 1.

23. See C. Wright Mills, *The Sociological Imagination* (New York: Grove, 1959), chaps. 4, 5.

24. Albert Somit and Joseph Tannenhaus, *The Development of American Political Science* (Boston: Allyn and Bacon, 1967), 167.

25. Robert A. Dahl, "The Behavioral Approach in Political Science: Epitaph for a Monument to a Successful Protest," *American Political Science Review* 60 (December 1961): 763–72, at 765.

26. Marian D. Irish, "Advance of the Discipline?" in *Political Science: Advance of the Discipline*, ed. Marian D. Irish (Englewood Cliffs, N.J.: Prentice-Hall, 1968), 19.

27. On the social sciences' repeated attempts to "sanitize" the language of political description, see my "In the Shadow of Babel: The 'Scientific' Reconstruc-

tion of Political Discourse," in *Political Discourse*, ed. Bhiku Parekh and Thomas Pantham (Beverly Hills: Sage, 1987), 23–46.

28. David Easton, *The Political System* (New York: Knopf, 1953), 50–51.

29. See Charles A. Beard, "Time, Technology, and the Creative Spirit in Political Science," *American Political Science Review* 21 (February 1927): 1–11.

30. See Robert Paul Wolff, "Beyond Tolerance," in Wolff, Barrington Moore, Jr., and Herbert Marcuse, *A Critique of Pure Tolerance* (Boston: Beacon, 1965), 3–52.

31. Gabriel A. Almond, *The Appeals of Communism* (Princeton: Princeton University Press, 1954).

32. On the "systems" approach to political and social analysis, see Easton, *Political System*, and Talcott Parsons, *The Social System* (Glencoe, Ill: Free Press, 1951). For one version of consensus history, see Louis Hartz, *The Liberal Tradition in America* (New York: Harcourt, Brace, 1955). On the end-of-ideology thesis, see Edward Shils, "The End of Ideology?" *Encounter* 5 (November 1955): 52–58, and Daniel Bell, *The End of Ideology* (New York: Free Press, 1960). Note the shift from Shils's interrogative to Bell's declarative.

33. Seymour Martin Lipset, *Political Man* (Garden City, N.Y.: Doubleday, 1959), 439.

34. See Bernard Berelson's concluding chapter, "Democratic Practice and Democratic Theory," in Berelson et al., *Voting* (Chicago: University of Chicago Press, 1954); and the incisive critiques by Graeme Duncan and Steven Lukes, "The New Democracy," *Political Studies* 11 (1963): 156–77, and Lane Davis, "The Cost of Realism: Contemporary Restatements of Democracy," *Western Political Quarterly* 17 (1964): 37–46.

35. See, respectively, Heinz Eulau, "Skill Revolution and Consultative Commonwealth," 1972 APSA presidential address, in *American Political Science Review* 67 (March 1973): 169–91, and Daniel Bell, *The Coming of Post-Industrial Society* (New York: Basic, 1973), esp. chap. 6. For a critique of these and other visions of "epistemocratic authority," see my "Authority and Conceptual Change," in *NOMOS XXIX: Authority Revisited*, ed. J. Roland Pennock and John Chapman (New York: New York University Press, 1987), 39–58.

36. See Noam Chomsky, *American Power and the New Mandarins* (New York: Pantheon, 1967), and the essays in *The Rise and Fall of Project Camelot*, ed. Irving Louis Horowitz (Cambridge: MIT Press, 1967).

37. Stuart Hampshire, *Public and Private Morality* (Cambridge: Cambridge University Press, 1978), 51.

38. For critiques of these failures see, e.g., Alasdair MacIntyre, "The End of Ideology and the End of the End of Ideology," in his *Against the Self-Images of the Age* (Notre Dame: University of Notre Dame Press, 1978), chap. 1, and his *After Virtue* (Notre Dame: University of Notre Dame Press, 1981), chaps. 7, 8; Walter Laqueur, "A Reflection on Violence," *Encounter* 38 (April 1972): 3–10. The explanatory and predictive pretentions of economics—arguably the most influential of the policy sciences—have come under withering scrutiny by a number of critically minded economists. See, e.g., the essays on "The Crisis of Economic

Theory" in the 1890 special issue of *Public Interest*; Amartya K. Sen, "Rational Fools: A Critique of the Behavioral Foundations of Economic Theory," *Philosophy and Public Affairs* 6 (1977): 317–44; Steven Kelman, *What Price Incentives? Economists and the Environment* (Boston: Auburn House, 1981); Robert Kuttner, "The Poverty of Economics," *Atlantic Monthly* (February 1985): 74–84; and Donald N. McClosky, *The Rhetoric of Economics* (Madison: University of Wisconsin Press, 1986).

39. See the claims of social-scientific success by Karl Deutsch, John Platt, and Dieter Senghors in *Science* (March 1971), and MacIntyre's critique in *After Virtue*, chap. 8.

40. Between 1960 and 1967, federal funding for social science research increased fivefold, from less than $73 million to more than $380 million. This figure covers only federal expenditures for domestic programs. See *The Use of Social Research in Federal Domestic Programs*, a staff study for the Research and Technical Programs Subcommittee of the Committee on Government Operations, U.S. House of Representatives (Washington, D.C.: Government Printing Office, 1967), pt. 1.

5 A Life of Learning

Carl E. Schorske

My first encounter with the world of learning took place, if family account is to be believed, when I entered kindergarten in Scarsdale, New York. To break the ice among the little strangers, my teacher, Miss Howl, asked her pupils to volunteer a song. I gladly offered a German one, called "Morgenrot." It was a rather gloomy number that I had learned at home, about a soldier fatalistically contemplating his death in battle at dawn. The year was 1919, and America's hatred of the Hun still ran strong. Miss Howl was outraged at my performance. She took what she called her "little enemy" by the hand and marched him off to the principal's office. That wise administrator resolved in my interest the problem of politics and the academy. She promoted me at once to the first grade under Mrs. Beyer, a fine teacher, who expected me to work but not to sing.

Was this episode a portent of my life in the halls of learning? Hardly. But it was my unwitting introduction to the interaction of culture and politics, my later field of scholarly interest. . . .

As far as I know, my parents had no deliberate idea of pushing me toward an academic career. Autodidacts both, they respected learning, but what they cultivated was not scholarship but a kind of natural intellectuality. The concerts, theaters, and museums that were their recreation became the children's education. They fostered our musical interests not just with private lessons but by taking us with them into their choral societies. On my father's two-week vacations we went by rail and ship on intensive sight-seeing trips: to New England's historic sites such as Concord or the old ports of Maine; Civil War battlefields where my grandfather had fought in a New York German regiment; the great cities of the East and the Midwest from Philadelphia to St. Paul.

This essay was written in a longer version as the Charles Homer Haskins Lecture of the American Council of Learned Societies, published as ACLS Occasional Paper, no. 1, April 23, 1987. I wish to thank the ACLS for allowing me to reproduce those portions of it conveying the transformation of academic culture addressed by Professor Schorske at the Minnesota Conference. —Ed.

Along with all the elite cultural equipment, my parents introduced us children, through their lives as well as by precept, to the realm of politics. My father, son of a German-born cigar maker, inherited the radical propensities that went with that socially ambiguous trade. As a young New Yorker, father had campaigned for Henry George and Seth Low in their mayoral races, and followed the radical free-thinker Robert Ingersoll. World War I made father, despite his profession as banker, a life-long socialist. His deep-seated hostility to America's entry into the war—both as an anti-imperialist and an ethnic German—gave his political orientation, though still progressive in substance, a bitter, alienated quality by the time I came along in his forty-fifth year. I inherited a marginal's sensibility from him as a German. When my mother, who, unlike my father, was Jewish, encountered unpleasant social prejudice during my high-school years, I acquired a second marginal identity. Perhaps this sense of marginality enhanced history's fascination for me and shaped my attitude toward it, at once wary and engaged. For me, as for my parents, politics acquired particular importance, both as a major determining force in life and as an ethical responsibility.

In 1932 I entered Columbia College. From Seth Low Library the statue of Alma Mater looked upon a space that contained the principal tensions of the university's life: In the foreground was 116th Street, New York City's bisecting presence at the center of the campus. On the south side of the street stood the Sun Dial, a great sphere of granite, Columbia's Hyde Park Corner. Here were held the rallies for Norman Thomas, who swept the student presidential poll in 1932. Here too I took the Oxford Oath, pledging never to support my government in any war it might undertake. Here too I watched in ambivalent confusion as antiwar sentiment slowly turned into its own opposite, militant antifascism, after Hitler occupied the Rhineland and Mussolini invaded Ethiopia. Political radicalism then bore no relation to university rebellion; it only invigorated the university's intellectual life.

In Columbia's strongly defined academic culture, Clio still presided over much of the curriculum. It is hard for us to remember in our day of disciplinary differentiation and autonomy how much all subjects were then permeated with a historical perspective. Having deposed philosophy and become queen of the world of learning in the 19th Century, Clio, though not as glamorous as she had been still enjoyed pervasive influence. She dominated the only compulsory course for undergraduates, a two-year introduction, Contemporary Civilization in the West. It was designed in the spirit of the New History of the early twentieth century, that amalgam of pragmatism, democracy and social radicalism that James Harvey Robinson, Charles Beard and John Dewey had injected into Columbia's university culture. The course presented us in the first year with three textbooks in modern European history—one economic, one social and political and one intellectual. Our task was to generate out of these materials a synoptic vision of the European past, leading, in the sophomore year, to analysis of the American present.

The structure of undergraduate major programs also reflected the primacy of history as a mode of understanding in contrast to the intradisciplinary analytic and theoretical concerns that tend to govern the program in most fields of the human sciences today. The programs in literature, philosophy, even economics, were saturated with the historical perspective on human affairs.

I avoided a history major, which I felt would tie me down. Instead I enrolled in Columbia's two-year humanities Colloquium, which allowed one to construct one's own program. Colloquium was centered in great books seminars conceived in a more classical spirit than usual in the university's prevailing pragmatist culture. The seminars were team-taught by truly outstanding young faculty members, such as Moses Hadas and Theodoric Westbrook, Lionel Trilling and Jacques Barzun. Watching their play of minds on the texts awoke in me for the first time a sense of the sheer intellectual delight of ideas.

The thought of an academic vocation, however, was slow in coming. Actually, I aspired to a career in singing, which I had studied since high school days. By my junior year, the sad truth grew upon me that my voice simply had not the quality to support a career in *Lieder* and the kind of Mozart roles I dreamt of. In the same year, I enrolled in young Jacques Barzun's course in nineteenth-century intellectual history. Barzun simply overwhelmed his few students with the range of the subject and the brilliance of his exploration of it. At work on his biography of Hector Berlioz, Barzun injected much musical material into his course. While I shared with my classmates the exciting experience that this course turned out to be, I drew one rather personal conclusion from it: intellectual history was a field in which two principal extra-academic interests—music and politics—could be studied not in their usual isolations, but in their relationship under the ordinance of time. I was ready to pursue it.

Yet something held me back. I felt myself to be an intellectual, interested in ideas; but could I be a scholar? Oddly enough, my Columbia experience offered no basis for an answer. As an undergraduate, I had only once been asked to prepare a research paper. Written exercises took the form of essays, oriented toward appreciation and interpretation of an issue or a text, with no particular attention to the state of scholarship or to the marshalling of empirical material to sustain a point of view. I found scholarly works often uninteresting; and when they truly impressed or captivated me, I found them daunting, far beyond my power to emulate.

The hue of resolution thus sicklied o'er by the pale cast of doubt, I sought advice. It was arranged for me to see Charles Beard, who was attending the American Historical Association's 1935 convention in New York. Perched on the bed in his overheated room in the Hotel Pennsylvania, Beard poured forth his scorn for the pusillanimity and triviality of a historical scholarship that had lost all sense of its critical function in the civic realm. He gave me a formula for a fine scholarly career: "Choose a commodity, like tin, in some African colony. Write your first seminar paper on it. Write your thesis on it. Broaden it to another country or two and write a book on it. As you sink your mental life into it, your livelihood and an esteemed place in the halls of learning will be assured."

The second counselor to whom I turned, Lionel Trilling, then in the fourth of his six years as an instructor in a still basically anti-semitic Columbia University, almost exploded at me. What folly to embark, as a half-Jew, upon an academic career in the midst of depression! Thus both of my gloomy advisors spoke out of personal experiences that confirmed the gap between the high calling of learning and some seamier realities of the academy. Neither, however, could touch my central doubt, which was about my own fitness for scholarly research. There seemed no solution to that but to put it to the test. When I entered Harvard Graduate School in the fall of 1936, it was in a receptive spirit, but hardly with a strong vocation.

To pass from Columbia to Harvard was to enter another world—socially, politically and intellectually. My undergraduate stereotypes of the two institutions doubtless led me to exaggerate their differences. But stereotypes can have roots in realities. The very physical structure of Harvard seemed to express a conception of the relation between university and society different from that of Columbia.

Harvard was in the city but not of it. Where Seth Low Library looked upon the city street, Widener Library faced the Yard, a greenspace walled off from the surrounding town. The Harvard houses, with their luxurious suites, dining halls with maidservants, separate libraries and resident tutors, expressed a unity of wealth and learning in which each lent luster to the other. Whatever its social elitism, Harvard was, as Columbia was not, a citadel of learning seemingly impervious to political tensions. Harvard had no Sun Dial, no central space for student rallies. The students must have felt no need for one. If politics had a presence here, it did not meet the newcomer's eye. I was glad, given my self-doubts about a scholarly career, to take advantage of the opportunity that the University's calm environment offered for submersion in the work of learning.

The form of instruction at Harvard differed even more strikingly from Columbia's than its architectural form. At Columbia, we thought of our instructors as teachers, guides in the exploration of texts to make us generate intellectual responses. At Harvard, the instructors were more like professors, learned authorities dispensing their organized knowledge in lectures. The prevailing nineteenth-century idea of history, with its strong architecture of development and narrative structure, reinforced the authoritative lecture mode. . . .

The comparative quiet of Harvard's political scene that I found on my arrival in 1936 soon changed. After 1938, when America began to face the menacing international situation in earnest, political concern became more general and intense within the university—and in me. Divisions on the issue of intervention ran deep, and many of us, young and old, felt impelled to debate it publicly. When political passions run strong, the relation between one's obligations to the republic of letters and to the civic republic can become dangerously conflated. Two personal experiences at Harvard brought this problem home to me.

The first occurred in 1940 in History I, the freshman course in which I served as a graduate teaching assistant. Its professor, Roger B. Merriman, a colorful, salty personality of the old school, passionately devoted to aristocratic Britain, believed, along with a few other staff members, that instructors had a public responsibility to get in there and tell the little gentlemen what the war was all about, to make them realize the importance of America's intervention. A few of us, across the often bitter barriers of political division, joined hands to resist the use of the classroom as an instrument of political indoctrination. My two partners in this effort were Barnaby C. Keeney, later the first director of the National Endowment for the Humanities, and Robert Lee Wolff, who became professor of Byzantine history at Harvard. Quite aside from the principle involved, the experience of History I taught me how shared academic values could sustain friendships that political differences might destroy.

The second experience, of an intellectual nature, left a permanent mark on my consciousness as a historian. The graduate history club had organized a series of what were called in jocular tribute to Communist terminology of the day, "cells," in which the student members prepared papers on problems that were not being dealt with in regular seminars. My cell took up the problem of contemporary historiography. We inquired into historical work in different countries as it evolved under the Weimar Republic and the Third Reich, not merely in terms of the political pressures upon them, but also in terms of the way in which specific cultural traditions in historiography, in confrontation with a new present, led to new visions of the past. I was astounded to discover that some of the most nationalist historians justified their doctrinaire nationalism by an explicit philosophic relativism. The value of this exercise in the sociology of knowledge was not only in understanding the work of historians of other nations. It also sensitized me and my fellow-apprentices in history to the fact that we too live in the stream of history, a condition that can both enhance and impede the understanding of the past. Above all, it made us aware as our elders, in their positivistic faith in objectivity, were not, of distortions that can result from our positions in society.

The Research and Analysis Branch of the Office of Strategic Services, which I joined a few months before Pearl Harbor, has been rightly known as a second graduate school. My own intellectual debt to my colleagues there—especially to the German emigres and to a stellar group of economists, some Keynesian, some Marxist—is not easy to calculate. The whole experience, however, taught me that, much as I enjoyed contemporary political research, I was not by temperament a policy-oriented scholar.

When I was released from service in 1946—over thirty, the father of two children, without a Ph.D.—I found what proved to be an ideal teaching post at Wesleyan University. I was to stay for fourteen years. Of all my mature educational experiences, that of Wesleyan probably had the strongest impact on the substance of my intellectual life and my self-definition as a historian. Basic to both were the larger shift in America's politics and academic culture in the late forties and fifties. I would have encountered them in any university. But only a small college could have provided the openness of discourse that made it possible to confront the cultural transformation across the borders of increasingly autonomous disciplines. At Wesleyan in particular, thanks to President Victor Butterfield's selection of imaginative faculty members at the war's end, an atmosphere of vital critical exploration prevailed. From my colleagues, I received the multidisciplinary education for the kind of cultural history I soon felt drawn to pursue.

In the first two years at Wesleyan, I had no sense of either the intellectual dilemmas about to appear or the new horizons that opened with them. Like most returning veterans, whether students or professors, I felt only a joyful sense of resuming academic life where I had left it five years before. The freshman Western Civilization course that I was asked to teach had just been introduced by assistant professors fresh from Columbia. For me it was a throwback to my freshman year fourteen years earlier. Teaching four sections, I had more than enough opportunity to explore the riches of the course. Once again I encountered there, in all its optimistic fullness, the premise that the progress of mind and the progress of state and society go hand in hand, however painful the tensions and interactions may sometimes be.

In framing an advanced course in European 19th-century history, I also returned to a prewar pattern to explore the relationship between domestic national histories and international development. Even my European intellectual history course, though fairly original in its comparative national approach to the history of ideas, bore the stamp of the American neo-Enlightenment in which I had been formed at home and at Columbia. Its central theme was the history of rationalism and its relation to political and social change. Viable enough for constructing an architecture of intellectual development before the mid-19th century, the theme proved less and less useful as the 20th century approached, when both rationalism and the historicist vision allied with it lost their binding power on the European cultural imagination.

In the face of the fragmentation of modern thought and art, I fastened on Nietzsche as the principal intellectual herald of the modern condition. He stood at the threshold between the cultural cosmos in which I was reared and a post-Enlightenment mental world just then emergent in America—a world at once bewildering, almost threatening, in its conceptual multiplicity, yet enticing in its openness. After Nietzsche, whirl was king, and I felt rudderless. The conceptual crisis in my course set the broad question for my later research: the emergence of cultural modernism and its break from historical consciousness.

While in my teaching I tested the dark waters of modern culture, my research was still cast in terms set by my political experience and values from the years of the New Deal and the War. I could not bear, after five years of engagement with National Socialism in the OSS, to resume my dissertation on its intellectual origins, despite a substantial prewar investment in the subject. Instead I turned to German Social Democracy as a thesis topic, and concurrently, to a more general study of the problem of

modern Germany. Behind both lay a pressing concern with the direction
of world politics. The two superpowers were in the process of creating
through their occupation policies two Germanies in their own images: one
socialist and antidemocratic, the other democratic and antisocialist. Accordingly, the saw-toothed course of the divide between East and West in
German politics ran between the two working-class parties, Communist
and Social Democratic. Before World War I, these two groupings had been
part of a single party committed to both socialism and democracy. Why
had that unity failed to hold together? What was the historical dynamic
that made democracy and socialism incompatible in Germany? Contemporary questions surely stimulated my historical research, though they did
not, I hope, determine its results. I realize now that I was writing not only
analytic history, but a kind of elegy for a once creative movement that history had destroyed.

Parallel to the historical work on German Social Democracy, I explored
directly the contemporary problem of Germany and American policy toward it for the Council on Foreign Relations. There I had an experience of
the life of learning quite different from that of either government or aca-
demia. The members of the Council's German Study Group, headed by
Allan Dulles, were intelligent, influential members of America's business
and political elite. Most of them viewed German policy not as an area in
which, as in Austria or Finland, some kind of accommodation was to be
sought with the Soviet Union, but as a counter in the fundamental conflict
between the two powers. I continued to believe in the goal of a unified but
permanently neutralized Germany. That policy, which had been espoused
by the OSS group with which I had worked, still seemed to me the only
way of redeeming in some measure the damage of the Yalta accord and of
preventing the permanent division of Europe. Although the Council generously published my analysis of the German problem, it rejected my policy recommendations. It was my last fling at influencing U.S. policy from
within the establishment.

The swift transformation of the East-West wartime alliance into the
systemically structured antagonism of the Cold War had profound consequences for American culture, not the least for academic culture. It
was not simply that the universities became a prey to outer forces that saw
them as centers of Communist subversion. The break-up of the broad,
rather fluid liberal-radical continuum of the New Deal into hostile camps
of center and left deeply affected the whole intellectual community. The
political climax of that division was Henry Wallace's presidential campaign

in 1948, in which I myself was active. The bitter feelings left in its wake only served to conceal a more general change in climate by which most intellectuals were affected, namely the revolution of falling expectations in the decade after 1947. The coming of the Cold War—and with it, McCarthyism—forced a shift in the optimistic social and philosophic outlook in which liberal and radical political positions alike had been embedded.

Wesleyan was a wonderful prism through which these changes were refracted. Several liberal activists of the social science faculty, including nonreligious ones, turned to the new Orthodox Protestantism of Reinhold Niebuhr to refound their politics in a tragic vision. Young scholars in American studies transferred their allegiance from Parrington and his democratic culture of the open frontier to the tough moral realism of Perry Miller's Puritans. For undergraduates, a new set of cultural authorities arose. Jacob Burckhardt, with his resigned patrician wisdom in approaching problems of power, and the paradoxical pessimism of Kierkegaard elicited more interest than John Stuart Mill's ethical rationalism or Marx's agonistic vision. Existentialism, a stoical form of liberalism came into its own, with Camus attracting some, Sartre others, according to their political persuasion.

Nothing made a greater impression on me in the midst of this transvaluation of cultural values than the sudden blaze of interest in Sigmund Freud. Scholars of the most diverse persuasions to whom my own ties were close brought the tendency home. Two of my teachers turned to Freud: the conservative William Langer used him to deepen his politics of interest; while the liberal Lionel Trilling, now battling the Marxists, espoused Freud to temper his humanistic rationalism with the acknowledgment of the power of instinct. Nor can I forget the day in 1952 when two of my radical friends, the Wesleyan classicist Norman O. Brown and the philosopher Herbert Marcuse, suddenly encountered each other on the road from Marx to Freud, from political to cultural radicalism. Truly the premises for understanding man and society seemed to be shifting from the social-historical to the psychological scene.

All these tendencies pointed American intellectuals in a direction that Europeans, with the exception of the Marxists, had gone half a century before: a loss of faith in history as progress. At a less creedal level, but one actually more important for the world of learning, history lost its attractiveness as a source of meaning. Formalism and abstraction, refined internal analysis, and a new primacy of the theoretical spread rapidly from one discipline to another as all turned away from the historical mode of understanding of their subjects. For intellectual history, this tendency had two consequences, one relating to its educational function, the other to its scholarly method.

Students now came to intellectual history expecting consideration of thinkers no longer studied in the disciplines to which they belonged. Thus in philosophy, the rising Anglo-American analytic school defined questions in such a way that many previously significant philosophers lost their relevance and stature. The historian became a residuary legatee at the deathbed of the history of philosophy, inheriting responsibility for preserving the thought of such figures as Schopenhauer or Fichte from oblivion. In economic thought, a similar function passed to intellectual history as the economists abandoned their historical heritage of general social theory and even questions of social policy to pursue an exciting new affair with mathematics.

An opportunity for intellectual historians, you say? Yes and no. We were simply not equipped to assume such responsibilities. At best we had paid little attention to the internal structure of the thought with which we dealt. We had a way of skimming the ideological cream off the intellectual milk, reducing complex works of art and intellect to mere illustrations of historical tendencies or movements. The new ways of analyzing cultural products developed by the several disciplines revealed such impressionistic procedures as woefully inadequate. The historian thus faced two challenges at once: to show the continued importance of history for understanding the branches of culture whose scholars were rejecting it; and to do this at a moment when the historian's own methods of analysis were being revealed as obsolete and shallow by the very ahistorial analytic methods against which he wished to defend his vision.

For me, the issue first came to focus in dealing with literature. When I charged my Wesleyan friends in the New Criticism with depriving literary works of the historical context that conditioned their very existence, they accused me of destroying the nature of the text by my excess of relativization. One irritated colleague hurled at me the injunction of e.e. cummings: "let the poem be." But he taught me how to read literature anew, how the analysis of form could reveal meanings to the historian inaccessible if he stayed only on the level of ideas, of discursive content. Other colleagues in architecture, painting, theology, etc., similarly taught me the rudiments of formal analysis so that I could utilize their specialized techniques to pursue historical analysis with greater conceptual rigor.

By the fifties, the problems I have thus far described—the changes in politics with the external and internal Cold War, the dehistorization of academic culture, and the need for higher precision in intellectual history—all converged to define my scholarly agenda. I resolved to explore the historical genesis of the modern cultural consciousness, with its deliberate rejection of history. Only in a circumscribed historical context, so it seemed to me, could a common social experience be assessed for its impact on cultural creativity. Hence, a city seemed the most promising unit of study. Like Goldilocks in the house of the three bears, I tried out several—Paris, Berlin, London, Vienna—in seminars with Wesleyan students. I chose Vienna as the one that was "just right." It was indisputably a generative center in many important branches of twentieth-century culture, with a close and well-defined intellectual elite that was yet open to the larger currents of European thought. Thanks to my Wesleyan colleagues, I had acquired enough intellectual foundation to embark upon a multidisciplinary study, in which the new analytical methods of the humanities could be harnessed to a social conception of cultural change. . . .

During much of my scholarly life, I worked to bring the arts into history as essential constituents of its processes. In the last years, I have partly reversed the effort, trying to project historical understandings into the world of the arts, through work with museums, architecture schools and critical writing for the larger public. The venue may change, the forms of one's engagement alter as one grows older and the world changes. Preparing this account, however, has made me realize all too clearly that I have not moved very far from the issues that arose in my formative years, when the value claims of intellectual culture and the structure of social power first appeared in a complex interaction that has never ceased to engage me.

PART THREE

The Making of Cold War Culture

6   Gideon's Trumpet: Sounding the Retreat From Legal Realism

Norman L. Rosenberg

Legal writing, a well-known practitioner of the craft once claimed, must aim at very diverse audiences. At the highest level, according to Karl Llewellyn, are works "for the hundred," for specialists who can fathom the difference between complex legal doctrines such as libel per se and libel per quod. Then, there is "jurisprudence for the hundred thousand," for members of the bar and nonlawyers interested in general, and perhaps even somewhat technical, legal matters. Finally, there is popular "juris-prudence for the hundred million." [1]

Anthony Lewis's *Gideon's Trumpet* defies such pigeonholing. First pub-lished in book form in 1964, *Gideon's Trumpet* has likely reached "the hundred million," especially after the book inspired both a prime-time television documentary and a subsequent "docudrama" starring Henry Fonda which celebrated the resilience and pluck of ordinary people. At the same time, however, Lewis's journalistic study charmed the legal elite, as well as the "hundred thousand" in between. Reviewing the book in 1964, law professor Charles Alan Wright concluded that the "principal reaction a lawyer will have on reading Mr. Lewis' book is pride, pride in being a member of a profession with such an honorable tradition of helping the helpless. . . ." More than twenty years later, editors of the *Michigan Law Review* still recommended *Gideon* to prospective law students and praised its explication of the judicial process. [2]

Gideon's Trumpet did offer more than drama; it also celebrated a legal-constitutional system that expressed ideals considered necessary to winning the cold war and fine-tuning the New Deal–Fair Deal–welfare state. Re-peatedly, Lewis praised the Warren Court for exemplifying both the "judi-cial process" and "reasoned elaboration" at their very best. And he finds the justices shouldering weighty political burdens as well. In an era of international tensions, when the United States had become "a nation with world responsibility," the Court needed to speak to the rest of the globe as "a national voice . . . on questions such as those posed by the Gideon

case." The justices became national schoolmasters, instructing the less enlightened about liberal progress. In "its steady march toward higher standards" in constitutional law, the Court "was not reflecting popular ideas"
but actually instructing the citizenry.[3]

Anthony Lewis, the prominent liberal journalist who served in the early
1960s as Supreme Court correspondent for the *New York Times*, related
these legal ideals to an uplifting story. Clarence Earl Gideon, a "fifty-one-
year-old white man who had been in and out of prisons much of his life,"
initiates his own appeal. Imprisoned for breaking into a Florida pool hall,
Gideon files a pencil-written petition, asking the United States Supreme
Court to release him because the trial judge, following the High Court's
own precedent in *Betts v. Brady* (1942), had refused a request for state-paid
legal assistance. Only one appeal in piles of similar petitions, Gideon's case
is selected for the Supreme Court's docket.[4]

This "real-life" drama apparently ended happily. The Supreme Court
accepts Gideon's claim that Florida had unconstitutionally denied him
professional counsel, overturns the *Betts* rule (which had forced states to
provide attorneys only in "special" circumstances), and requires all states
to furnish lawyers for felony defendants too poor to employ their own legal
counsel. After the justices order Gideon retried, his attorney uncovers new
evidence and gains his client's acquittal.

Lewis skillfully integrated this human-interest tale with a disarmingly
simple account of how the legal-constitutional system "really" worked. He
offers the story of the "right to counsel" guarantee, from the cases of the
"Scottsboro boys" in the 1930s to *Gideon* in the 1960s, as a "fascinating
example of how constitutional doctrine develops . . . slowly, deliberately,
case by case." Invoking an evolutionary paradigm, Lewis sees legal change
emerging from an elaborate process of legal reasoning, and he views the
creation of legal rules as a coherent and essentially nonpolitical enterprise.
The legal world, in other words, called for specially trained talents, and it
required a fundamentally different, and more elevated, kind of discourse
than that used in ordinary political discussions. The "search for principle"
constituted "the essence of the judicial process." "It can never be enough"
for courts to make decisions purely on the basis of vote tallies or political
calculations; especially in the Supreme Court, "every decision should be
supported by reasons that appeal to the intellectual and ethical sense of
Americans."[5]

But, still wanting to link this process, at least for some purposes, to politics, Lewis also argued that Gideon, the "poorest and least powerful of

men—a convict with not even a friend to visit him in prison," was "not really alone."⁶ If the "judicial process" serves as one heroic force in *Gideon's Trumpet,* a set of real-life heroes, members of the postwar legal elite who aided Gideon's cause, also become central players in this legal drama. Indeed, Gideon's lawyers for the Supreme Court appeal came from the Washington office of Arnold, Fortas, and Porter. Byron ("Abe") Fortas, confidant of Lyndon Johnson and friend of the Supreme Court's liberal activists, managed Gideon's appeal and argued his cause before the High Court. Thurman Arnold, the firm's senior partner, had taught at Yale Law School in the 1930s and later served in the New Deal administration as Franklin Roosevelt's attorney general. Both lawyers had been associated with pre–World War II "legal realism" at Yale, and Lewis's book credits them with helping to bring this approach to law out of the academy and into Washington's power centers.

The combination of lessons in current politics, constitutional history, judicial processes, and Washington's legal life bolstered the appeal of Lewis's book. Still widely admired, *Gideon's Trumpet* must also be seen as a primary source for the study of cold war culture. The book not only celebrated the postwar legal system but also heralded the "retreat" of critical realism, a controversial style that had dominated "law talk" during the interwar period. Because of the prominence Lewis assigns to Fortas and Arnold, closely associated with Yale in the 1930s, the book provides a convenient focus for examining legal realism and some of the ways in which legal discourse changed between the Depression and cold war eras. It further suggests why the legal system, as portrayed by writers such as Lewis, became a key element in the political culture unfolding after World War II. Finally, a critical reading of *Gideon's Trumpet* can underscore the need to consider how major shifts in cultural values and political consciousness helped to redefine not only law but also other aspects of post-World War II life.

I

What was the "realistic" style of law that Lewis saw inspiring the Fortas-Arnold law firm? The question defies easy answers. A corpus of legal writing, which later came to be called "legal realism," first emerged at prestigious law schools during the 1920s; the so-called realists eventually came to dominate law-school debates of the early 1930s. By mid-decade, they became firmly identified with Yale Law School, and many later staffed the federal bureaucracies established during the New Deal.

Although Lewis notes that realists had once been controversial figures, his emphasis on positive, consensual strains in legal-constitutional history leads him to view realism as just another stage in the progressive evolution of the legal process in the United States: "The realists emphasized what judges did, as opposed to what they said, and recognized that law was not logic alone. . . ." By reducing 1930s-style realism to a commonsense concern for looking at what law "really did," Lewis ignores the more troubling insights of realists, including those of Thurman Arnold himself.[7]

In truth, the heyday of legal realism remains a complex, often maligned era in American legal culture. Historians have credited, or blamed, legal realists for introducing empirical research into legal studies, offering new philosophical approaches to law, and stimulating practical changes in legal procedure. Yet the rise of the realists owed a great deal to the general intellectual ferment in both the scientific and social communities of the early twentieth century. The philosopher-historian Morton White links legal realism to the broader "revolt against formalism," while Edward Purcell relates it to the emergence of "scientific naturalism," a movement in the social sciences that rejected the search for a priori universal "truths" in favor of empirical investigations into the ways in which social phenomena, including legal ones, "really operated."[8]

Most generalizations about a "movement" called "legal realism" tend to break down when the writings and politics of individual "realists" are scrutinized, but common themes do appear. Most strikingly, realists rebelled against assumptions that legal elites—especially judges—could accurately describe social life through scientific, transcendent, objective, neutral juridical principles and "distinctly legal" categories. Realists split over exactly how to approach legal materials but generally agreed that words and phrases long used by lawyers, treatise writers, and judges could not be accepted at face value as the bases for accurate, neutral, or even rational accounts of complex social relationships. Appealing to nonlegal disciplines, especially functionalist social science and psychology, they argued that legal language must be taken apart—"deconstructed," to use a term from current literary criticism—in order to unmask the deeper realities concealed by the abstract, unreal quality of traditional legal words and categories. Even Llewellyn, one of the most cautious realists, wanted legal writers to reject the usual approaches: "See it fresh, see it clean," he urged.[9]

More iconoclastic realists went further. Advocating the need for significant social change, they charged that the supposedly rational, neutral language of the "classical legal style" served to steer legal discussions away from issues of poverty, inequality, and injustice—social problems that demanded immediate attention. The mission of realists, they insisted, was to

open up legal language; to reveal the purely rhetorical and apologetic nature of legal doctrines; and, they hoped, to point the way toward more
fruitful ways of confronting pressing socioeconomic questions. [10]

Although generally liberal reformers rather than political radicals, the
most critical of the realists rebelled against their profession's traditional reverence for legal argumentation and language. During the 1930s, Thurman
Arnold, for example, did more than seek "to puncture the myths about
judges" and to focus upon what judges did, in addition to what they said.
He and other realists tried to strip away law's self-congratulatory mystique,
especially the idea that lawyers could talk meaningfully about fundamental, suprahistorical or evolutionary principles in the language of the law. In
The Symbols of Government (1935), Arnold ridiculed those jurists who,
despite "all the irrefutable logic of the realists," persisted in "believing that
there are fundamental principles of law which exist apart from any particular case, or any particular human activity." Continuing, Arnold also dismissed the view that "these principles must be sought with a reverential
attitude; that they are being improved constantly; and that our sacrifices of
efficiency and humanitarianism are leading us to a better government."
The role of law had not been so much "to guide society" in progressive
directions "as to comfort it." Incantation of familiar legal slogans filled psychic needs, helping to satisfy "a deep-seated popular demand that governmental institutions symbolize a beautiful dream within the confines of
which principles operate, independently of individuals." [11]

Another noted realist, Felix Cohen, extended the critique of legal language. In a now-classic 1935 law-review article, he characterized legal debate as "a special branch of the science of transcendental nonsense." In
"every field of law," the realist could find "the same habit of ignoring practical questions" in favor of elaborating legal doctrines that added "precisely
as much to our knowledge as Moliere's physician's discovery that opium
puts men to sleep because it contains a dormative principle." Legal language displayed the same circularity: it revolved around terms that were
"necessarily circular, since those terms are themselves creations of law." To
privilege the words and phrases of the law, "the protective camouflage
of transcendental nonsense," was wrongly to view legal decisions as the
"products of logical parthenogenesis born of pre-existing legal principles"
rather than to examine them for what they "really" were: "social events
with social causes and consequences." [12]

The politics of the 1930s led some realists to expand their critique to
constitutional law and the Supreme Court. Robert Lee Hale, Columbia
Law School's most iconoclastic realist, for example, wove various strands of

critical realism into a blanket indictment of the nation's highest tribunal. Hale, along with other realists, had focused in the 1920s on "private" law areas, especially contract and property doctrines. Highlighting what he saw as the clearly "public" implications of traditional law and viewing classical legal doctrines against the backdrop of inequalities in distributions of economic wealth *and* access to state power, Hale slashed through phrases such as "freedom of contract" and "private" property rights. During the 1930s, Hale extended Cohen's attack on legal language and categories, turning it against the rhetoric of Supreme Court opinions. Constitutional guarantees and legal rights, no matter how sublimely elaborated, could never be viewed apart from the social-economic realities of liberal capitalism, Hale insisted.

In "Equivocal Constitutional Guarantees" (1939), published after FDR had reformed the Supreme Court, Hale issued a stern jeremiad: formalistic liberties supposedly guaranteed by Supreme Court decisions could be "manipulated out of existence," not simply by government officials but also, in the "real" world, by private individuals and groups that possessed greater knowledge and power than others. Indeed, legal doctrines that justified the "private" property rights of some stood, in reality, as barriers against the nonproperty rights of others. For instance, by enforcing, under the rubric of freedom of contract, "private agreements" that really expressed the superior bargaining power of one part against the other, the language of the law conveniently ignored the realities of power and knowledge. Law could never treat people equally or guarantee them equal rights "as long as we have inequality in private property," Hale concluded. "This fact is obscured and often denied." [13]

Hale's work epitomized critical realism. Beginning with the problem of language—and thus questions about how lawyers and judges can "really" know about the social relationships they purport to describe accurately and then to adjudicate neutrally—Hale proceeded to address fundamental questions of power. [14] He probed the formalistic slogan of "equality before the law," a phrase that rang especially hollow in the critical areas of property and contract law. In a 1927 essay, Hale dismissed the idea that all people had "the same legal rights and duties" as "clearly untrue in anything but name." To Hale, judicial claims about equality before the law were simply inconsistent with reality: the vast inequality in property. "Is the right of property of some unemployed tramp equal to the right of property of the owner of the La Salle Hotel? If all have equal property rights, why are the courts so occupied with disputes over the title to property?" [15]

Such language and ideas ultimately reached a wide audience. To be sure, realism began as "insider talk," as phrases such as Cohen's "logical parthenogenesis" might suggest, for the law-school elite, but some realists also found a market for their ideas. In addition to *Symbols*, Thurman Arnold wrote *The Folklore of Capitalism* (1937); Jerome Frank, another prominent realist who joined FDR's New Deal, published a series of popularly oriented works, beginning with *Law and the Modern Mind* (1930); and Yale's Fred Rodell wrote almost entirely for nonacademic audiences. Never a person who could equivocate, Rodell made his critique of traditional legal styles succinct: "There are two things wrong with almost all legal writing. One is its style. The other is its content. That, I think, about covers the ground." Rodell did not limit himself to condemnation. He offered a seminar for law students who wanted to write for the general public, and he wrote numerous popular articles and two book-length studies during the 1930s.[16]

In *Fifty-Five Men* (1936), Rodell linked issues of language, knowledge, and power—questions at the heart of critical realism—to the literature produced by Progressive historians and economists. Drawing upon Charles Beard's economic interpretation of the Constitution, Rodell argued that the political insiders who had drafted the document of 1787 knew that "it would not be the words they put on paper that counted, when it came down to the actual checking of laws." The meaning of constitutional guarantees would inevitably remain both uncertain and ever-changing, and the founders realized it "would be the men who used those words, and the way they used them" that would determine the content and shape of American constitutional law.[17]

This historical analysis helped to ground Rodell's infamous *Woe unto You, Lawyers!* a popular exposé of law and politics first published in 1939. Although lawyers actually dealt with "the stuff of living," with real people ensnared in concrete problems, they used an artificial language that evaded the essence of life. Manipulation of legal language, by people with insiders' knowledge and a disproportionate share of power, could best be compared with "learning to work cryptograms or playing bridge." But lawyers, unlike cryptographers and bridge players, were taken in by the mystique of their "high-class racket" and could never admit "that their mental efforts, however difficult and involved," had no real "significance beyond the game they are playing." "Like the medicine men of tribal times and the priests of the Middle Ages," lawyers "actually believe their own nonsense."

Tribal nonsense reigned supreme, Rodell argued, in the ritualistic celebration of the Constitution, which attained its sesquicentennial in 1937. Rodell gave the document little deference: it was "made up of abstract principles which mean nothing until brought down to earth by lawyers." But anyone who then viewed their earthly prose in terms of some heavenly logic, principles, and orderly development was badly mistaken. As "a matter of fact," legal-constitutional language could be "all things to all lawyers simply because the principles on which it is built are so vague and abstract and irrelevant that it is possible to find in those principles both a justification and a prohibition of every human action or activity under the sun." Following Felix Cohen, Rodell insisted that what judges claimed to be their reasons for a certain decision were nothing more than a restatement, in different words, of their result. More refined legal reasoning, or what Anthony Lewis would later call the "maturing of collective thought," offered no remedy. Given underlying inequalities in the distribution of power and knowledge, "the chief function which legal language performs is not to convey ideas clearly but rather to . . . conceal the confusion and vagueness and emptiness of legal thinking" itself.[18]

II

As the soothing tones of *Gideon's Trumpet* suggest, Rodell's hard-boiled legal style fell out of fashion during the postwar era. By 1962, for example, Rodell's Yale colleague Alexander Bickel indicted the aging realists as "nihilists," amoral skeptics who could not understand the underlying "morality" of the legal process. Bickel's *The Least Dangerous Branch*, a leading postwar legal text, dismissed the older realism as "arrested realism or surrealism" and charged its proponents with embracing "cynicism pure and simple." And, here, as in other realms, Bickel concluded, "cynicism is . . . 'the only deadly sin.'"[19]

Although most scholars, following the lead of writers such as Bickel, correctly see the significance of the break between pre- and postwar legal culture, there is much less clarity in tracing the precise ways in which the critical realists were deflected. How could writers so deftly veer away from the realism of the 1930s and discard its critical insights? Much more research needs to be done, but I want briefly to suggest some of the stratagems, skillfully popularized in *Gideon's Trumpet*, by which leading legal writers tried to defuse and discard that older legal discourse.

An appropriate place to begin is with one of the heroes of *Gideon's Trumpet*, Thurman Arnold. At first glance, Arnold seems an unlikely symbol for the retreat from realism. During the 1930s, for example, he had never adopted one of the traits—uncritical reverence for social-science methodology—that some historians have cited for realism's failure.[20] And though staunchly anticommunist, Arnold risked the accusation hurled at so many older realists—sympathy for "totalitarian" approaches to law by defending the alleged agents of "Soviet totalitarianism," including the historians William A. Williams and Owen Lattimore, from the postwar Red Scare.[21] Finally, Arnold remained identified, in various intramural legal battles, with the old realist cause. He simultaneously infuriated the dons at Harvard Law School, by accusing them of subtly preaching the old nineteenth-century legal "theology," and earned Alexander Bickel's wrath for allegedly corrupting Yale Law School with "nihilism" and "surrealism."[22]

On further reflection, though, Anthony Lewis is perfectly correct in finding few differences, on fundamental questions, between Arnold and "mainstream" legalists such as Bickel. Indeed, a review of Rodell's *Woe unto You Lawyers*, published in the *Progressive* in 1957, revealed the ways in which Arnold had "retreated" from the critical realism of the 1930s. In agreeing to write the review, Arnold confessed that he genuinely liked his old Yale colleague, and the prospect of publicly attacking Rodell's book troubled him. (Besides, he confided, Rodell's unrelenting scorn for the Harvard-oriented Justice Felix Frankfurter merited the highest praise.) But Arnold also thought that Rodell's work, and the strand of realism it exemplified, failed to address the "real" issues of the era. Following a more general trend in postwar legal writing, Arnold put critical realist writings into an evolutionary, functionalist narrative of constitutional-political history. He accordingly viewed realist critics of the twenties and thirties as vital to the discrediting of nineteenth-century ideas about law and limited government, and he praised them for helping to "prepare the way for the tremendous adjustments of our basic ideals of law to our revolutionized industrial structure." As a "serious" work about legal thought, though, Rodell's book was tainted by a fatal, sophomoric strain and outflanked by the progressive march of history.[23]

In a more enlightened postwar era, Arnold insisted, realist critiques had little to offer. At home, the New Deal mixed economy had replaced an outdated, unjust, and inefficient political economy. And the rise of the Soviet Union overseas underscored the naive facets of critical realism. Unfurling the banner of "maturity," Arnold represented Rodell's criticism of traditional legal classicism as "well intentioned" but flawed musings that failed to recognize the value of the ideal of the "rule of law" in a more dangerous world. "Remember that in its inception Communism was a humanitarian movement," Arnold warned. Appealing to higher law ideas he himself had once ridiculed, Arnold now claimed that the "Law with a capital L is the only way of thinking about a free society."

By the late 1950s, then, Thurman Arnold was backing away from the agenda of prewar realists, especially efforts to critique "Law with a capital L" and to relate specific legal doctrines to issues of knowledge and power. Instead, Arnold now accepted the legitimating role of legal-constitutionalism and warned of the corrosive effect of critical realism if it were revived and redirected against the New Deal and the work of the post-1937 "liberal" Supreme Court. Undiluted realism, he confessed, was not "effective in giving our judicial institutions the public respect required to symbolize the great ideal of the law above men." Political necessities of the cold war era required belief rather than skepticism: "The faith that dignifies the Supreme Court is the belief that through logic and reason it may discover the impartial principles of law that are independent of the whims, prejudices, or the economic philosophy of the justices."[24] Having once decried legal "myths" for stalling political change, Arnold now applauded similar ideas when they helped to justify decisions by the Supreme Court that served, in retrospect, to complete the translation of the New Deal-Fair Deal political agenda into legal-constitutional writ.[25]

As Arnold's review suggests, the apparent completion of the New Deal helped to cripple critical realism. At one level, of course, the New Deal state provided law-school realists with career opportunities in Washington; Roosevelt's domestic programs, which Jerold Auerbach has called the "Lawyer's Deal," brought onetime inconoclasts into the federal bureaucracy. Presumably, the result was that, when people such as Arnold, Fortas, and Frank became "insiders," they "accepted the institutional restraints and abided by professional expectations." As a judge, Frank reproduced the kind of "transcendental nonsense" he had once detested.[26] And, as time went on, academic legal scholars increasingly shaped research projects away from critical analyses about "law" and society toward "policy"-oriented studies acceptable to powerful lawmaking interests.[27]

The relationship between postwar liberalism and legal culture, however, extended far beyond simple careerism. First, as recent scholarship on capitalist-state relations in the twentieth century has argued, the welfare state produced new roles for both lawyers and the "law." The political reformation of the 1930s, for example, placed a new emphasis upon "rights," for the "welfare state utilized law as well as money in the attempt to compensate all citizens for disadvantaged interests." Cases such as *Gideon*, viewed from this perspective, encapsulate the core of welfare liberalism: a benevolent government, staffed by liberal administrators and assisted by public spirited professionals, will guarantee delivery of various services, including legal ones, to their "clients." [28]

Second, the wartime battle against fascism and the postwar crusade against communism helped to shift the emphasis away from criticism toward what Eugene Rostow, who left Yale Law School to join the Kennedy administration, called "positive" and "affirmative" constitutionalism. The legal ideals lauded by Anthony Lewis became part of cold war liberals' "fighting faith." And here again many of the older realists, such as Thurman Arnold, did not dissent. Even if the rule of law were a symbol, Arnold wrote, the "cost" of the clinging to the "old symbols . . . must be paid because without them, as we can see in the case of Russia and Germany, men may lose themselves in the greatest illusion of all, the illusion that absolute power may be benevolently exercised." [29]

Neoconstitutionalism thus became one of the cold war liberals' favorite antidotes against "totalitarianism" overseas and injustice at home. But the new constitutionalists, such as Bickel, went beyond the nineteenth-century legal classicists and claimed at least part of the old realist legacy. Considering themselves the true heirs of "realism"—one of the keywords of cold war liberals—writers such as Bickel embraced what might be called the "constructive" or "instrumental" side of prewar legal-realist writings. Since any tough-minded postwar "realist" began by assuming the legitimacy of liberal capitalism and rejecting "utopias," legal discussions could focus on how to conceptualize, and then use properly, the unique tools of law in social life. And, rather than trying to understand legal phenomena against the backdrop of a search for a more egalitarian democracy, most postwar legal writers tried, along with their brethren in political science, to reconceptualize democratic theory in ways that justified existing institutions. [30]

III

In the broadest sense, then, older styles of critical realism ran afoul of the "believing skepticism" of cold war thinkers. But did the complementary retreat from critical realism and the rise of a new faith in legal-constitutionalism truly contribute to a progressive postwar society in the United States? Ironically, as current scholars probe the nature of cold war legal culture, they confront a reality that recalls realist warnings about how legal guarantees can be manipulated out of existence. In the postwar era, the courts did erect an elaborate set of legal safeguards, and there was, in Milton Konvitz's phrase, a conceptual body of "expanding liberties." Yet, at the same time, the growing national security bureaucracy and private security institutions also emerged to challenge the practical values of the new legal rights. As a result, legal scholars have to face a basic question: What is the value of a formal constitutional guarantee in an age of surveillance?[31]

In response, one might posit a complicated tale of postwar writers and progressive lawyers having to retreat from critical realism not simply as a response to the New Deal state, or the rise of foreign totalitarianism, but as a way of protecting themselves and clients from domestic anticommunist repression. A case study for testing that hypothesis might be the history of the National Lawyers Guild after 1945. Attracting radical and progressive attorneys drawn to the realist critique, the organization formed in the thirties as an alternative to the American Bar Association. But, during the late forties, left-leaning lawyers confronted charges of belonging to a subversive, procommunist group. Despite the accusers' failure to document this charge, members of the Lawyers Guild faced a steady attack from J. Edgar Hoover's Federal Bureau of Investigation (FBI), from Truman's Justice Department, and from powerful private groups, including the media.[32]

The postwar career of the guild and one of its officers, Thomas Emerson of Yale Law School, showed the difficulty of maintaining a critical, realist-oriented approach to questions raised by the national security state. Initially, Emerson and others tried to link issues about the legality of recent "national security" measures to broader questions of power in foreign affairs and domestic surveillance. In 1948, for example, Emerson and David Helfeld wrote an essay attacking Truman's "loyalty program." Though not openly critical of classical legal arguments about rights, the article rested on a basic realist message: all the legal procedures offered by the administration's liberal lawyers and all the most streamlined procedural safeguards might not prevent Hoover's FBI from becoming the real power behind the program. A really effective program, they pointed out, would require an "initial screening and continuous surveillance of all applicants for [governmental service] and employees." It would entail the "maintenance of a large investigative force which can obtain information from all possible sources about the daily life and daily thoughts of numerous individuals who depart in some way from the established norm." Emerson and his Yale colleague further speculated that the FBI was already engaged in illegal surveillance. Prophetically, they concluded that a "secret police established to investigate the 'loyalty' of American citizens can develop into a grave and ruthless menace to democratic processes. There are signs the FBI is moving dangerously in this direction."[33]

Hoover's response was swift. Secret informants had already reported on the article's preparation, and the FBI apparently pilfered a draft copy for Hoover's use in drafting a speedy, anticommunist reply, one that appeared in a subsequent issue of the *Yale Law Journal*. Next, the FBI chief made Emerson—known at Yale as "Tommy the Commie"—and the guild targets of a harassment campaign. At the same time, the guild's efforts to expose the reality of the loyalty program ran into dangerous dead ends. Realistically, guild lawyers could not expect to acquire information from the bureau's files and document their claims of FBI dirty tricks. Likewise, Hoover's critics lacked both his immense political power and the bureau's positive image, one nurtured in the popular media. And, as the guild's campaign to obtain a high-level investigation of the FBI stalled, the bureau counterattacked with a carefully orchestrated media assault on the guild and surveillance of its leaders.[34]

Under siege, the guild found protection in reorienting its approach to legal-political issues. As late as 1951, for example, the guild's leaders tried to frame First Amendment concerns in political and economic terms. At its annual convention, a symposium entitled "Underlying Causes of the Crisis in Civil Liberties" included several sessions: one about the "influence of economic factors" and the "need for solution of basic economic problems" and another on the relation between United States foreign policy and domestic civil liberties. Yet, by the late fifties, after lengthy court battles to stay off the attorney general's list of "subversive" organizations, the guild subtly narrowed its focus on free-speech issues to a more legalistic approach, one that de-emphasized the broader call for social justice and a new foreign policy and elevated legal-constitutionalism.

Paradoxically, then, under the pressure of domestic anticommunism, even the most committed legal realists might find themselves drawn to the appeal of legal principles presumably divorced from issues of power and knowledge. When cold war liberals such as Thurman Arnold defended targets of "McCarthyism," they also helped to legitimate claims that surveillance institutions could operate within the boundaries established by the "rule of law," and to fit these bureaucracies into the framework of the postwar legal-constitutional order. At the same time, the accused, like those in the Lawyer's Guild, found themselves forced to temper critiques honed in the 1930s and to embrace "transcendental" discourses, especially ones that celebrated rather than debunked the value of legal rights. Needing to protect themselves from the power of the surveillance state, they hoped that emphasis on "rights" and "rule of law" would shield dissident groups and lawyers who defended unpopular political causes.[35]

In a very profound way, then, the postwar retreat from realism and the rise of constitutionalism pitted tactical legal issues against moral and political ones, the kinds of fundamental dilemmas that Victor Navasky detailed in his study of "blacklisting" and informing in Hollywood. In one sense, the retreat might be reviled as a failure of nerve or the result of intellectual blindness. But, given the shrinking options available to progressives and the reorientation of legal culture (with its implicit support of a liberal consensus), the reliance upon traditional forms of legal discourse (with the emphasis upon judicially enforced rights) promised one of the safest defensive strategies against state surveillance and domestic anticommunist attacks.[36]

IV

At this point, we can appreciate more fully the reasons why Gideon's Trumpet was hailed by both the wider public and the legal profession. In Anthony Lewis's story, legal decisions such as Gideon represented constructive, instrumental means for dealing with issues involved in the "powerful currents of history." The book accordingly embraced postwar legal orthodoxy by elevating constitutional discussions to a privileged position above ordinary political considerations for transforming power. In so doing, legal writers like Lewis ignored the major insights of the critical realists of the 1930s, who viewed "law" and "society" as inseparable spheres. As the contemporary critical legal theorist Gerald Frug suggests, law and society are "inextricably interlinked. . . . Society is constituted in part by law, and law is constituted, in part, by society."[37]

Yet Gideon's Trumpet, as did most other examples of postwar legal writing, repressed many troubling questions about the relationship between "law" and "society." In contrast to the critical realists, who emphasized the complicity of legal rules and leaders in pervasive patterns of socioeconomic injustice, Lewis treated judicial decision making as effectively insulated from political results and nonlegal origins. Though Clarence Earl Gideon's desperate life on the margins of postwar society said a good deal about the continuing existence of poverty and the powerlessness of the poor, Lewis ultimately narrowed Gideon's story to the frame offered by the Supreme Court: Gideon's case "represented a progressive step in the evolution of the 'right to counsel.'" Though accurate at one level, such a judgment retreated from the critical legal style of the twenties and thirties and utterly failed to probe the role of law and rights in the age of the postwar welfare and national security state.

The retreat from realism, therefore, raises broader questions about post-war America. Despite their limitations, the critical realists of the thirties did begin to develop fundamental analyses of the links between "private" law and "public relationships."[38] In considering why their legacy was not transmitted to the next generation, students must rethink the place of law in the wider culture and also confront the major shifts in power that accompanied the New Deal and the cold war at home and abroad. Is it just accidental that the penchant of postwar legalists, for example, to narrow their focus to the precise meanings of legal texts and to de-emphasize questions of economic power and social context echoed the techniques coming into favor with the "new critics" in art and literature or with many of the practitioners of the new consensus history and behavioral sciences? Similarly, was it accidental that, when cold war politics unraveled in the sixties and seventies, a new generation of legal analysts revived in more modified and sophisticated forms the agenda of the critical realists?[39]

Perhaps the law professor Sanford Levinson has offered the most appropriate reason for trying to understand the demise of legal realism in the years after 1945. Any satisfactory view of legal culture must, he points out, "come to terms with the various realist critiques . . . that can no longer be repressed, except (as Freud taught) at the price of creating yet more severe neurosis."[40]

NOTES

1. Quoted in William Twining, *Karl Llewellyn and the Realist Movement* (Norman: University of Oklahoma Press, 1985), 173.

2. Anthony Lewis, *Gideon's Trumpet* (New York: Random House, 1964); Charles Alan Wright, "Review," *Texas Law Review* 42 (1964): 939; "A New List of Recommended Reading for Prospective Law Students," *Michigan Law Review* 83 (1985): 664.

3. Lewis, *Gideon's Trumpet*, 218. On "reasoned elaboration" and "process jurisprudence," see G. Edward White, "The Evolution of Reasoned Elaboration: Jurisprudential Criticism and Social Change," in his *Patterns of American Legal Thought* (Indianapolis: Bobbs-Merrill, 1978), 136–63.

4. Lewis, *Gideon's Trumpet*, 5. *Betts v. Brady*, 316 U.S. 455 (1942). For a very different, far less dramatic, account of how Gideon's case arrived at the Supreme Court, see Bernard Schwartz, *Super Chief: Earl Warren and His Supreme Court: A Judicial Biography* (New York: New York University Press, 1983), 457–63.

5. Lewis, *Gideon's Trumpet*, 105, 214. On the Scottsboro cases, see Dan T. Carter, *Scottsboro: A Tragedy of the American South* (New York: Oxford University Press, 1969).

6. Lewis, *Gideon's Trumpet*, 208.

7. Ibid., 49. There is a sizeable, oftentimes contradictory literature on legal realism. For this study, I have relied upon the following: Edward Purcell, *The*

Crisis of Democratic Theory: Scientific Naturalism and the Problem of Value (Lexington: University of Kentucky Press, 1973), 74–94, 159–78; G. Edward White, *Tort Law in America: An Intellectual History* (New York: Oxford University Press, 1980), 63–113; Laura Kalman, *Legal Realism at Yale, 1927–1960* (Chapel Hill: University of North Carolina Press, 1986); Twining, *Karl Llewellyn and the Realist Movement*; Twining, "Talk about Realism," *New York University Law Review* 60 (1985): 329–84, esp. 339–40 n. 24, 343–47; John Henry Schlegal, "American Legal Realism and Empirical Social Science: From the Yale Experience," *Buffalo Law Review* 28 (1979): 459–586; and "American Legal Realism and Empirical Social Science: The Singular Case of Underhill Moore," *Buffalo Law Review* 29 (1980): 195–323; James Boyle, "The Politics of Reason: Critical Legal Theory and Local Social Thought," *University of Pennsylvania Law Review* 133 (1985): 685–780, esp. 708–20; Gary Peller, "The Metaphysics of American Law," *California Law Review* 74 (1985): 1152–1290.

8. Morton White, *Social Thought in America: The Revolt against Formalism* (Boston: Beacon, 1957), 3, 8, 61–75; Purcell, *The Crisis of Democratic Theory*, 74–94, 159–78.

9. Quoted in Twining, "Talk about Realism," 376.

10. For a concise and penetrating analysis of the "classical" legal style, see Thomas C. Grey, "Langdell's Orthodoxy," *University of Pittsburgh Law Review* 45 (1983): 1–53.

11. Lewis, *Gideon's Trumpet*, 49; Thurman W. Arnold, *The Symbols of Government* (New Haven: Yale University Press, 1935), 32–33, 34–35.

12. Felix Cohen, "Transcendental Nonsense and the Functional Approach," in *The Legal Conscience: Selected Papers of Felix S. Cohen*, ed. Lucy Kramer Cohen (New Haven: Yale University Press, 1960), 33–76, at 45, 46, 75.

13. Robert Hale, "Our Equivocal Constitutional Guarantees," *Columbia Law Review* 39 (1939): 563–94, at 587.

14. On the relationship between legal discourse and questions of knowledge and power, see Clare Dalton, "Deconstructing Contract Doctrine," *Yale Law Journal* 94 (1985): 997–1114.

15. Robert Hale, "Economics and Law," in *The Social Sciences and Their Interrelation*, ed. William F. Ogburn and Alexander Goldenweiser (Boston: Houghton Mifflin, 1927), 135–36, and "Rate Making and the Revision of the Property Concept," *Columbia Law Review* 22 (1922): 212. See also Warren J. Samuels, "The Economy as a System of Power and Its Legal Bases: The Legal Economics of Robert Lee Hale," *University of Miami Law Review* 27 (1973): 261–371.

16. In addition to Arnold's already-cited *Symbols of Government*, see his *Folklore of Capitalism* (New Haven: Yale University Press, [1937] 1962), and Frank's *Law and the Modern Mind* (Garden City, N.Y.: Anchor, [1930] 1963). Fred Rodell, "Goodbye to Law Reviews," *Virginia Law Review* 23 (1936): 38.

17. Fred Rodell, *Fifty-Five Men* (New York: Harrisburg Telegraph, 1936), 221.

18. Fred Rodell, *Woe unto You, Lawyers!* (New York: Reynal and Hitchcock, 1939), 10, 15, 17, 32, 35, 189.

19. Alexander J. Bickel, *The Least Dangerous Branch: The Supreme Court at the Bar of Politics* (Indianapolis: Bobbs-Merrill, 1962), 83–84.

20. Grant Gilmore, *The Ages of American Law* (New Haven: Yale University Press, 1977), 87.

21. Purcell, *Crisis of Democratic Theory*, 159–78, and White, *Evolution of Reasoned Elaboration*, 140–42; both emphasize the effect of "totalitarian" charges on realist writers.

22. Thurman Arnold, "Professor [Henry] Hart's Theology," *Harvard Law Review* 73 (1960): 1298–1317; Bickel, *Least Dangerous Branch*, 82–83.

23. *Voltaire and the Cowboy: The Letters of Thurman Arnold*, ed. Eugene Gressley (Boulder: Colorado Associated University Press, 1977), 423; Thurman Arnold, "Liberating Force," *Progressive* (October 1957): 35–36.

24. Thurman Arnold, *Fair Fights Foul: A Dissenting Lawyer's Life* (New York: Harcourt Brace, 1965), 69, 71. On the importance of the word "maturity" in different contexts of cold war culture, see Barbara Ehrenreich, *The Hearts of Men* (New York: Anchor, 1983), 14–28, and William Graebner, "Coming of Age in Buffalo: The Ideology of Maturity in Postwar America," *Radical History Review* 34 (1986): 53–74.

25. On the general relation between the Warren Court's jurisprudence and New Deal political culture, see Martin Shapiro, "Fathers and Sons: The Court, the Commentators, and the Search for Values," in *The Burger Court: The Counter-Revolution That Wasn't*, ed. Vincent Blasi (New Haven: Yale University Press, 1983), 226, and Mark Tushnet, "The Optimist's Tale," *University of Pennsylvania Law Review* 132 (1984): 1660–62, 1670–73.

26. Jerold Auerbach, *Unequal Justice: Lawyers and Social Change in Modern America* (New York: Oxford University Press, 1976), 191–230; Glennon, *Iconoclast as Reformer*, 138; Schlegal, "American Legal Realism and the Yale Experience," 585. Also compare Bruce Ackerman, *Reconstructing American Law* (Cambridge: Harvard University Press, 1984), with the critique of Alan David Freeman and John Henry Schlegal, "Sex, Power and Silliness: An Essay on Ackerman's Reconstructing American Law," *Cardozo Law Review* 6 (1985): 851.

27. See, for example, G. Edward White, "From Realism to Critical Legal Studies: A Truncated Intellectual History," *Southwestern Law Journal* 40 (1986): 825–27.

28. David Kettler, "Legal Reconstitution of the Welfare State: A Latent Social Democratic Legacy," *Law and Society Review* 21 (1987): 10.

29. For Rostow, see "Reviews," *Yale Law Journal* 56 (1947): 1472, 1473; quoted in Simon Verdun-Jones, "Jurisprudence Washed with Cynical Acid: Thurman Arnold and the Psychological Bases of Scientific Jurisprudence," *Dalhousie Law Journal* 3 (1976): 581.

30. My emphasis follows Peller, "Metaphysics of American Law," 1288–89; on the general trend toward redefining democratic theory, see Raymond Seidelman and Edward J. Harpham, *Disenchanted Realists: Political Science and the American Crisis, 1884–1984* (Albany: State University of New York Press, 1984), 151, 157–59, 185–86; and on the realist label, see Robert Fowler, *Believing Skeptics: American Political Intellectuals, 1945–1964* (Westport, Conn.: Greenwood, 1978), 135–44, 230–31, 239.

31. Compare, for example, the positions of Frank J. Donner, *The Age of Surveillance* (New York: Random House, 1980), xix, 7–9, and Stanley I. Kutler,

The American Inquisition: Justice and Injustice in the Cold War (New York: Hill and Wang, 1982), 243–46.

32. On the composition, aims, and problems of the National Lawyers Guild, see Percival R. Bailey, "The Case of the National Lawyers Guild, 1939–1958," in *Beyond the Hiss Case: The FBI, Congress, and the Cold War*, ed. Athan G. Theoharis (Philadelphia: Temple University Press, 1982), 129–75, and Auerbach, *Unequal Justice*, 198–200, 234–36.

33. Thomas I. Emerson and David M. Helfeld, "Loyalty among Government Employees," *Yale Law Journal* 58 (1948–49): 67, 141.

34. *Yale Law Journal* 58 (1948–49): 401–425, contained a reply by Hoover, a response by Emerson and Helfeld, and a rejoinder by Hoover. On FBI activities at Yale, see Bailey, "Case of the Lawyers Guild," 135, and Sigmund Diamond, "Surveillance in the Academy: Harry B. Fisher and Yale University, 1927–1952," *American Quarterly* 36 (1984): 7–43. On FBI attacks on the guild, see Bailey, "Case of the Lawyer's Guild," 135–63; for the surveillance of Emerson, see Donner, *Age of Surveillance*, 149–50.

35. Compare the changing emphasis, for example, in *New York Guild Lawyer* 9 (September 1951): 1; Ibid. (October 1951): 7; Ibid. 13 (September 1955): 4–5; Ibid. 15 (November 1957), 1, 3–9. And for Emerson's explicit rejection of realist analysis in First Amendment thought, see Thomas I. Emerson, *Toward a General Theory of the First Amendment* (New York: Random House, 1963), 29–30 n. 3.

36. Victor S. Navasky, *Naming Names* (New York: Viking, 1980). For a defense of traditionalist legal arguments by a participant in the cold war legal battles, see Ed Sparer, "Fundamental Human Rights, Legal Entitlements, and the Social Struggle: A Friendly Critique of the Critical Legal Studies Movement," *Stanford Law Review* 36 (1984): 539–47. For a thoughtful, historical analysis of the promise and peril of rights talk, see Hendrik Hartog, "The Constitution of Aspiration and 'The Rights That Belong to Us All,'" *Journal of American History* 74 (1987): 1013–34.

37. Gerald Frug, "The Ideology of Bureaucracy in American Law," *Harvard Law Review* 97 (1984): 1288–89.

38. For a critique of Rodell's "law as mere babble" approach, see Joan Williams, "Review—The Development of the Public/Private Distinction in American Law," *Texas Law Review* 64 (1985): 243; and for realists' vulnerability to traditional critiques, see Robert Gordon, "J. Willard Hurst and the Common Law Tradition in American Legal History," *Law and Society Review* 10 (1975): 39.

39. See, for example, Mark Kelman *A Guide to Critical Legal Studies* (Cambridge: Harvard University Press, 1987), and Susan S. Silbey and Austin Sarat, "Critical Traditions in Law and Society Research," *Law and Society Review* 21 (1987): 165–74.

40. Sanford Levinson, "Law," *American Quarterly* 35 (1983): 204.

7 Movie Star Politics: The Screen Actors' Guild, Cultural Conversion, and the Hollywood Red Scare

Lary May

> Coming out of the cage of the Army . . . a series of hard nosed
> happenings began to change my whole view of American
> dangers. Most of them tied in directly with my own bailiwick of
> acting. . . . From being an active (though unconscious) partisan
> in what now and then turned out to be communist causes, I little
> by little became disillusioned or perhaps, in my case, I should
> say reawakened.
>
> *Ronald Reagan, former president*
> *of the Screen Actors' Guild, 1960*

> Really and truly, the triumph of McCarthyism was, in effect, the
> cutting off of a generalized social movement that began before
> the war. . . . The picking on the Hollywood people . . . received
> a lot of attention because everybody knew who the stars were.
> What I'm trying to say is that you're not dealing with an isolated
> event, but the focus of such a national event as it happened in
> Hollywood.[1]
>
> *Abraham Polansky,*
> *blacklisted film director, 1970*

The year in which Ronald Reagan recalled being reawakened, and
Abraham Polansky saw anticommunism sweeping through Hollywood,
there appeared on the front page of the Screen Actors' Guild (SAG) magazine an article entitled "Utopia is Production." Written by Eric Johnston,
the new head of the Motion Picture Producers' Association, the author
tried to convince Hollywood leaders in the spring of 1946 that they epitomized a new era in American history. Like a Puritan minister, Johnston
saw that the citizenry in earlier times had created an exceptional nation

I wish to thank Kim Felner and Mark Locher of the Screen Actors' Guild for their assistance
with the archival research, as well as my colleagues David Noble, George Lipsitz, Lewis
Erenberg, Carl Schorske, James Rawls, Elaine Tyler May, Barbara and Stephen Lassonde,
the graduate students in American Studies 8259 at the University of Minnesota in 1988 and
the fellows of the Wesleyan University Humanities Center in 1987 for making this a better
essay than it would have been without their probing questions and help.

free of European exploitation and conflicts. The rise of big business at the
end of the nineteenth century, however, aroused fears that the frontier was
gone. Later, the Great Depression had given rise to New Deal politicians
who generated a "nightmare" of "class rhetoric." Yet Johnston saw that the
continuation of the wartime cooperation between labor and capital would
convert the people back to the true national identity of "democratic capitalism." In order to thwart communist threats to that dream at home and
abroad, Johnston saw that Hollywood had a great role to play: "It is no exaggeration to say that the modern motion picture industry sets the styles for
half the world. There is not one of us who isn't aware that the motion picture industry is the most powerful medium for the influencing of people
that man has ever built. . . . We can set new styles of living and the doctrine of production must be made completely popular."[2]

Johnston's words were not mere platitudes. His views reflected those of
corporate leaders who backed the publisher of *Time* and *Life*, Henry Luce,
in the vision of a new "American Century." Coming to head the industry's
major trade association from his tenure as president of the United States
Chamber of Commerce, Johnston had argued in his book, *America Unlimited* (1944), that to create full production and abundance, the people
needed to put aside "foreign" ideas of class conflict and build an international order rooted in anticommunism and defense against the Soviet
Union. The eruption after the war of the greatest strike wave in the country's history, however, showed Johnston's domestic dream was far from
being realized. Particularly in the film capital, the militant Conference of
Studio Unions (CSU) endorsed the "Century of the Common Man" propounded by Franklin Roosevelt's former vice president, Henry Wallace. As
CSU members left their jobs in 1946 and were joined by stars like John
Garfield and Charles Chaplin on the picket lines, the strikers also validated
the promise of abundance and peace. But they saw it realized through
democratic hostility to monopoly capital and the continuation of the wartime cooperation with the Soviet Union.[3]

Given Johnston's business interests, it was not surprising that he would
try to convince the Screen Actors' Guild to side with the producers against
their traditional allies in the CSU. Yet it is surprising that Johnston saw the
outcome of that contest as critical to creating a new political and cultural
order for the nation. Certainly one reason why current scholars might have
difficulty in comprehending this ideological conflict lies not only in how
we have been taught to understand the film industry and its relation to
modern society, but in how we have been taught to comprehend the ori-

gins of postwar anticommunism. Whether the story was told by Marxists, liberals, or conservatives, Hollywood presumably created entertainment that took filmmakers and their audiences' imaginations away from the nature of work and class relations. Following that logic, those who analyze the Red Scare in the motion-picture industry argue that the coming of the House Un-American Activities Committee to Hollywood in 1947 was part of an irrational crusade led by provincial conservatives that destroyed careers and undercut the left-wing activities of exceptional writers and artists. But the result had little bearing on issues of national politics or popular culture.[4]

Johnston's article, however, offers a twofold corrective to these views. First, it suggests that the Hollywood Red Scare was not an isolated episode but had deep affinities with political transformations occurring across the country. Second, it highlights that far from anticommunism in 1947 being dominated by reactionary, small-town conservatives, it was more a revolutionary effort sparked by corporate leaders who hoped to convert national values and popular imagery away from doctrines hostile to modern capitalism. Taking Johnston's efforts as the entry point, this essay will focus on the object of his appeal in 1946, the Screen Actors' Guild, an organization in which popular culture and politics were intimately intertwined from 1932 to 1950. In so doing, it will be possible to reassess the larger meaning of the Hollywood Red Scare and gain a fresh understanding of the industry's place in creating after 1947 the new "American" ideology of corporate consensus, class harmony, and abundance.

To begin this examination, it is important to understand why Eric Johnston saw that the film industry was so critical for reformulating the coordinates of modern national culture and politics. Generally, we tend to reject such a linkage because we have been taught that the revolution in manners and morals that came to center on the "movies" occurred separately from the vast economic and political changes that altered the face of modern society. Yet for the filmmakers and audience created after 1914, these two developments were intimately intertwined. Clues to that symbiosis can be seen in studies that chart the rise of the new corporate order and a modern "middle class." Like the workers of immigrant stock pouring into the cities, the salaried employees that came to dominate the twentieth-century American bourgeoisie were also losing control over private property and becoming subject to the authority of large firms. And as the corporate order became the predominant form of business organization, the workers as well as the middle classes used their higher wages to pioneer a leisure realm that became the centerpiece for a widely recognized revolution in manners and morals identified with a rising consumer culture.[5]

The visual imagery of that new morality, moreover, was spread to millions by the new motion-picture industry centered in Hollywood. Yet the coming of the Great Depression saw the new corporate order and the promise of abundance come crashing down. In response, employees in Hollywood did what workers in other industries were doing: they helped launch the major mass movement of the day, labor organizing. And there were good reasons. Like much of their audience, the Hollywood players were part of a new middle and working class employed by large corporations. But with the stock-market crash, big business and the studio system collapsed, producers cut salaries, and unemployment spread. Searching for alternatives, industry employees voted by 1936 more than six to one for the reform administration of President Franklin Roosevelt, and a complex business that was virtually unorganized in 1929 became by 1945 one hundred percent unionized, a percentage far ahead of national trends.

At the forefront of that development, moreover, were the most famous actors and actresses of the day. Mobilized in the Screen Actors' Guild, their presidents, activist board of directors, and prominent members included major box-office attractions such as Eddie Cantor, Charles Chaplin, Joan Crawford, John Garfield, Jane Wyman, James Cagney, Robert Montgomery, and Edward Arnold. After the performers received a contract from the studios in 1937, guaranteeing minimum wages and better working conditions, SAG's power grew, so that by 1940 it contained nearly fifty percent of all the artists, and twenty-five percent of all the workers in a labor force that ranged from 26,000 to 34,000 employees. With this power to control the ingredients without which no film could be made—the stars and performers—SAG became the single most powerful union in the industry and also became, unlike the other, newly created writers' and directors' guilds, a powerful local branch of the American Federation of Labor (AFL).[6]

What captured so much attention was that this development also represented a remarkable shift in middle-class politics. Seven years after the players organized, for example, a study funded by the Carnegie Foundation examined all guild members and found that, excluding the unskilled extras (who had no speaking lines in films), more than fifty-four individuals made over $100,000 a year, higher than any other trade in the film capital. When the family backgrounds of the membership were tabulated, researchers found that fewer than ten percent came from worker or farmer backgrounds. But over eighty percent came from families with professional or proprietary skills, small merchants and tradespeople. Over sixty percent entered the industry in the thirties, and almost fifty percent were under the age of thirty-five. The overwhelming majority had finished high school, and nearly half the membership had gone to universities. As one writer observed, these young people had created "something new in America, a pioneer organization of professional people. Its birth and steady growth make one of the most significant labor developments of the last ten years."[7]

That significant development was not accomplished simply to advance the interests of the successful. On the contrary, the guild helped forge an unprecedented cross-class alliance. In many ways, this was a necessity of life. For ever since the early thirties, the International Association of Studio and Stage Employees (IA) dominated labor relations in the film capital. The IA emerged within the AFL, where it had been policy for over fifty years to mobilize elite craftsmen in bureaucratic organizations far removed from the unskilled and white-collar employees. The Hollywood branch accentuated that policy because it was dominated by gangsters who received payoffs from producers to keep wages low and the main work force immobilized. Guild leaders responded by supporting the efforts of an ex-boxer and set painter, Herbert Sorrell, to organize unskilled, technical, and white-collar workers into an alternative union, the Conference of Studio Unions (CSU), and by successfully working to put the gangsters and their producer allies in jail.[8]

In creating this cross-class alliance, the actors' activities were not isolated to Hollywood. Rather, they soon became involved with radical groups seeking to transform the larger national labor movement. No doubt the most important were the Congress of Industrial Organizations (CIO), which broke from the AFL in order to unionize mass-production workers on an industrywide basis, and the American Communist Party. Despite the fact that the Hollywood insurgents remained within the AFL and found that a host of issues divided them from party members in their organizations (ranging from a disdain for secrecy, to different strike tactics, to a belief in proper democratic procedures and respect for religion), the guild welcomed these militant groups in their common struggle against monopoly capital. Along these lines, SAG and its allies repeatedly condemned the producers' and the IA's "red baiting," arguing it was "un-American" and "fascist." And when their enemies attacked Harry Bridges and the Longshoremen's Union in 1936, SAG's board of directors praised this CIO and communist-influenced union, commending its aid in keeping strike-breakers off studio sets and its belief in

> solidarity . . . regardless of apparent immediate advantages. In the long run the slogan "one for all, all for one" is the proper guide for union action. Following this line of action they have built one of the strongest labor organizations in America. They have eradicated gangster control, raised wages, shortened hours and elevated the spirit of their men not only by educating them into the important role they are playing in their locality but making them conscious of their duty to aid American labor in its progressive march.[9]

Yet in spite of the charges of conservatives shocked by this militancy, it was not communist ideology or Marxism that inspired such radicalism. Indeed, long before the party formed its popular front with democratic groups and parties in 1935, the performers and the CSU mobilized behind an American, republican tradition that had sustained hostility to monopoly capital for over a century. In identifying their movement with the progress of the nation as a whole, the guild leaders spoke of themselves as the true producers of wealth who were exploited by the speculators and capitalists—un-American enemies identified with aristocratic Europe. Seeing their movement reviving that national identity, guild leaders attacked "economic royalists" and "oppressive corporate practices" whose activities demanded a new "Declaration of Independence" to free the modern "slave class." The guild leader, Eddie Cantor, thus told President Franklin Roosevelt in 1932 that the actors were "patriotic Americans," aligned against "monopolistic tyrants" and "financial pirates" who took "oppressive measures in their race for power." To recover their American "birthright," the performers had to reject delusions about class collaboration. "When the millennium comes," wrote Cantor, "the lion may lie down with the lamb, but in the present the Guild thinks it indiscreet of the lamb to lie down with the lion."[10]

Furthermore, the guild served to modernize that republican vision of progress to include formerly ostracized groups. After all, one reason why unionization in the United States was the least developed in the Western world was that a largely Anglo-Saxon bourgeoisie remained separated from a racially and ethnically divided working class. However, amid the crisis of the dominant culture that occurred with the Depression, the guild represented a shattering of that social division. In an industry composed of many groups from outside the mainstream, one-quarter of the guild membership was foreign born, and at least that many were the sons and daughters of immigrants. Repeatedly, their press condemned the Anglo-Saxon America of the Ku Klux Klan and racial exclusionism, equating it with European fascism. "Scratch an anti-Semite, anti-Catholic or anti-Negro," commented one cartoon, "and you will find an enemy of labor." Similarly, women (such as board member Gale Sondergaard), who composed almost fifty percent of the membership, saw their participation as a means to break from older gender categories. Members of racial or ethnic backgrounds, such as Lena Horne, Eddie Cantor, George Murphy, Ronald Reagan, and James Cagney, also saw their union serving to legitimize the new peoples and actors as responsible citizens. Exemplifying that process, a skeptical producer signed a guild contract after being assured that the Rich Brothers, a comedy team noted for its zaniness and tardiness, would be required to "show up on time." [11]

Naturally, observers accustomed to associating Hollywood with escapism and the high life often asked how and why the stars should become models of a highly visible shift in middle-class political culture. One answer was that the wealthy stars only joined the union movement to protect their salaries from wage cuts. Another answer was that their efforts were inspired by communist organizers. Neither assumption, however, can explain why the guild organized before the Communist Party came to Hollywood, or why, long after salaries rose, the same performers continued militantly to support the cause of labor. No, something more was going on, and that something more was constantly commented on in the guild press. A typical writer framed the issue by asking a fictitious actor, "Are We Laborers?" If the answer was no, then the respondent did not understand modern realities. In the nineteenth century, individuals could escape from European tyranny and monopoly power by moving into an open frontier of small property. But that democratic "safety valve" was no longer available. Corporate leaders like the Hollywood producers, "corresponding in a sense to the hereditary feudal lords, grew steadily in number and more concentrated." One might find, during the twenties, success in large organizations and freedom on the new frontier of leisure. But when the crash came, monopolists fired actors and subjected the rest to the "tyranny" of foremen who worked them long hours for lowered wages. [12]

Yet in seeking a cultural ideal to unite the middle with the working classes, the guild drew on the innovations unfolding in mass culture as a valuable resource. Before the rise of twentieth-century mass culture,

Americans were divided not only at work but also in leisure. Especially in the world of entertainments, distinctions of class, sex, and ethnicity predominated. Yet in the years after 1900 this Victorian demarcation broke down as young people mingled in amusements formerly associated with immigrant vice and began to borrow music, dances, and dress styles from blacks, Mediterranean Catholics, and other outsiders. Periodic censorship crusades by Anglo-Saxon moralists tried to contain this mass culture, but they proved largely ineffective.

By the 1920s, a movie industry dominated by producers of immigrant background began to dramatize the imagery of that moral experimentation. Expressing the rise of values at odds with conventional institutions, the film stars played characters restless in the old culture as well as under the constraints of a corporate workplace. But in the twenties, they showed how to rebel against and resolve that tension in private ways. The idea was not to resist the hierarchical economy or public life dominated by Anglo-Saxon mores. Rather, men worked to have the money for freedom in leisure, and young women validated the emancipated home. In order to provide exemplars of the new style, and keep it separate from civic values, stars like Douglas Fairbanks and Mary Pickford had to "stay in character on and off the screen" and live the happy ending on that new frontier of Hollywood.

With the collapse of the corporate order in the Great Depression, however, the private, "foreign" styles spread by Hollywood in the twenties began to alter. As critics in the guild press explained it, filmmakers in the early thirties found that fans patronized tragic films that showed men and women destroyed by a corrupt society. Yet after a period of trial and error, producers found that new stars like James Cagney, Eddie Cantor, Bette Davis, and Joan Crawford displayed through language and toughness the strength to overcome crippling injuries and hard times. To dramatize formulas more engaged with public life, directors showed characters who underwent a conversion experience to arouse the little people to overcome established politicians and immoral businessmen. Such a renewal, best dramatized in the enormously popular films of Charles Chaplin, Frank Capra, and even Busby Berkeley musicals, drew on the experimentation of popular culture to include the outsiders and ethnic Americans in the promise of abundance.[13]

Most strikingly, as spread by the guild, that promise did not remain isolated to the screen. In an industry where the star was expected to live his film image on and off the screen, the guild identified the star's persona with spreading the dreams of modern consumption far beyond the realms of the rich. That merger of art and politics surfaced when the stars preached hostility to monopoly and to injustice on their weekly radio shows sponsored by labor and the guild, appeared at labor exhibits in world's fairs, and entertained at White House birthday parties for President Roosevelt. It happened when they mobilized members at widely publicized rodeos, picnics, and "Films Stars Frolics" (fig. 7.1) and auctioned off President Roosevelt's hat to support Hollywood retirement homes. It accelerated when the celebrities advocated union boycotts, backed farm workers' organizing efforts, and presented humorous calls to spread the word of organized labor. A prime example was the appeal made by Robert Montgomery upon the birth of his son. Under the infant's byline, the president of SAG wrote to the members that, "since my advent into this world at the Cedars of Lebanon Hospital, I have in my small way done a certain amount of work which may be of interest to you. I have organized the children in the nursery into the Junior Guild and we have now pickets outside the door bearing placards 'Cedars of Lebanon nurses are unfair to union babies.' You may be interested to learn that we discovered a child who claimed to be related to a producer in the motion picture business. We took care of him!" [14]

Behind these playful, but serious, expressions lay a major reformulation of political ideology. Far from undercutting resistance to capitalism, the fusion of popular culture with the republican, antimonopoly tradition generated a renewed militancy. To realize the dream of abundance in real life, guild leaders and their allies argued that union demands for high wages would increase purchasing power and generate a return to full production. When the call for a rising standard of living merged with popular attacks on the intransigence of monopoly capital, that cultural symbiosis generated unity between the guild members and their working-class allies. Throughout the late thirties and the war, the CSU press, for example, combined labor militancy with beauty contests to choose the "Queen of the Picket Line," with waiters' inside accounts of what screen personalities like Orson Welles ate, with publicized benefits where stars performed to elevate union morale and then joined the workers on the pickets outside studio gates. Drawing on that élan, Herb Sorrell justified the CSU's successful strike against Disney Studios so that his "happy bunch of kids" could "dress like the stars." [15]

On the eve of World War II, therefore, the innovations associated with Hollywood—the mobilization of the studio employees into a mass labor

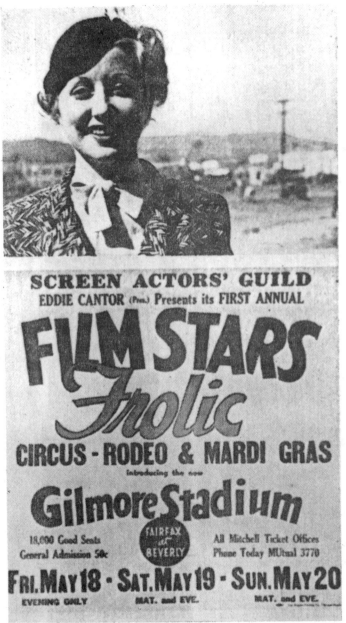

Fig. 7.1. The Film Stars Frolic, 1933. An advertisement in the SA exemplifies the public activities that mixed the stars' appeal, popular culture, and the serious business of mobilizing support for unionization. (Courtesy of the Screen Actors' Guild.)

Fig. 7.2. The Labor Day parade of 1937, Los Angeles. Preceded by a car containing Screen Actors' Guild leaders Boris Karloff and Robert Montgomery and floats carrying diverse racial and national groups, this group of guild veterans linked the modern culture and politics dramatized in the parade with traditional values of patriotism. (Courtesy of the Screen Actors' Guild.)

movement, the modernization of antimonopoly traditions, the validation of racial pluralism and abundance—all converged on a widely publicized joining of screen ideals to life. Nowhere was that convergence better dramatized than in the Los Angeles Labor Day Parade of 1937 (figs. 7.2–7.4). After a moribund period, New Dealers revived the event, and the union press ran photos of Franklin Roosevelt with captions explaining that the president was "loved by labor for the enemies he has made." Next came a cartoon proclaiming that high wages provided the purchasing power to restore full production, and a reporter observed that in preparation for the parade SAG was "going the limit to contribute all the fanfare of show business at its command." On the big day, the labor press reported that SAG "stole the show," with cars carrying Robert Montgomery, Edward Arnold, and "Brother" Eddie Cantor; with floats displaying "bathing beauties" serenaded by a swing band; with "cowboy and Indian" rider groups;

Fig. 7.3. The Actors' Guild leaders in the 1937 Labor Day parade, Los Angeles. From left to right, Chester Morris, Bob Montgomery, Lucile Gleason, Boris Karloff, and Claude King. (Courtesy of the Screen Actors' Guild.)

with marchers dressed in their native garbs from Eastern Europe, the South Seas, Africa, the East Indies, and China. Along the way, an actor dressed as Abraham Lincoln proclaimed all racial groups deserved the fruits of their labor, and Popeye and the Keystone Cops chased away "scabs." At the end of the march, the Los Angeles mayor led a crowd estimated to be "300,000 strong" in singing the Star Spangled Banner, and newspaper reporters observed that the marchers were "irresistibly headed for victory over the forces that have so long blocked the way." [16]

In retrospect, it is not surprising that the new culture unfolding in Hollywood captured widespread attention during the Great Depression, for in the best-publicized industry in the country, the stars offered the vision of a new America founded on a more abundant life and pluralism. Yet it would be a serious error to think that this reorientation of national values was just compensation for or escapism from hard times. In fact, the advent of the war and widespread prosperity represented less a discarding of the culture pioneered in the thirties than its diffusion to an even wider audience around the world. As the government mobilized Hollywood for the war effort, the most popular film of the war, *This Is the Army,* featuring a current and a future president of SAG, George Murphy and Ronald Reagan, celebrated a new America revitalized by consumerism, urban culture, and the new peoples of the city (fig. 7.5). In keeping with the merging of the stars' screen image with real life, guild members enlisted in the armed ser-

Fig. 7.4. "Its the Keystone to Recovery," an editorial cartoon in the local labor press that described the guild's participation in the Labor Day parade of 1937. It symbolically equates unions' demands for higher wages with stimulating the demand that will make the wheels of industry turn. (Courtesy, Hollywood Strike File, Special Collections, UCLA.)

Fig. 7.5. The climactic scene in *This Is the Army* (1943) features a theater production performed before a Washington, D.C., audience, including President Franklin Roosevelt and his family. This Irving Berlin musical was the most popular film
of the war, starred two presidents of SAG, Ronald Reagan and George Murphy,
and celebrated the new culture of consumerism and ethnic diversity as a force re-
newing American nationalism and state power. (Courtesy of the Museum of Modern Art/Film Stills Archive.)

vices, held premieres that boosted war morale, toured on bond drives, and
entertained the troops around the globe. Their magazine, in turn, promoted the new patriotism in splashy nightclub revues, and cartoons
displayed the world's seven continents, with captions exclaiming that a
"public once limited to the physical capacity of a single theatre has expanded through film and radio to global proportions."[17]

Yet while the war spread the culture identified with Hollywood to an
international audience, the highly organized war effort also transformed
the guild's political relation to the larger political order and the American
economy. In a defense effort characterized by total mobilization and rigid
authority, the government brought labor and business into state-run war

industry boards. However, as their leaders began to cooperate with corporate leaders in the enforcement of price guidelines and no-strike clauses, rank-and-file members soon demanded higher wages to keep up with inflation. But when their demands were refused, they launched a series of wildcat strikes. That national conflict assumed epic proportions in Hollywood as the extras—the unskilled of the actor's profession—asked that, because vast profits now came to producers and because the stars could receive waivers for their high salaries, they too be allowed to renegotiate their contracts. The board of directors' refusal sparked the dissidents to align with none other than the guild's old ally, Herb Sorrell, who expanded the membership of the CSU in the war and repeatedly took his members out on wildcat strikes. In response to these wartime strikes, the guild dismissed hundreds of "incorrigibles" and formed their own "patriotic" extras group. This generated a series of jurisdictional disputes between the CSU and SAG, and the guild's chief counsel, Kenneth Thomson, almost got into a fistfight with the insurgent's leaders in court and wrote the board a long report claiming that the insurgent "extras" were a "Frankenstein monster" which could "destroy us." [18]

The monster, of course, did not destroy SAG. But the series of conflicts within the union movement encouraged labor leaders to be much more cooperative with management. In Hollywood, that transformation was symbolized when the SAG leadership attained in 1945 a charter for their own loyal extras group from their older adversary, the IA, now presumably reformed and cleansed of its gangster leadership. Shortly thereafter, a delegation composed of the producers and IA leaders asked the board to support a lockout of the CSU. The minutes of that secret meeting show that despite the unwillingness of a vocal minority, the leadership found that it would be "hard to refuse" in light of their former enemies' "unsolicited support in the extras dispute." The result was that the actors proclaimed their neutrality and attempted to arbitrate the ensuing "jurisdictional" strike. But in reality they cooperated with the producers and crossed the picket lines to join the IA in maintaining full production. Over the next year, Sorrell's members responded with a national boycott of the stars' films, symbolizing the unravelling of an alliance that had lasted for over a decade (fig. 7.6A and B). [19]

At this point, it is also possible to see why guild leaders might be more than willing to listen to the call for political transformation advocated by Eric Johnston, the new head of the producers association. Speaking for corporate leaders who wished to overcome the attacks on monopoly capital

that plagued twentieth-century politics, and to create a new order against
the resistance of New Deal militants, Johnston argued that the ideological
basis for that transformation had been created in the wartime cooperation
with business and labor. To carry that same spirit into the postwar years, he
saw that the mass-communications industry centered in Hollywood had to
become a model of consensus. He accordingly asked the guild leaders, the
heroes and heroines of the screen, whom he saw as the most widely emulated figures in the world, to put aside their former New Deal "class rhetoric" and join with him in a struggle against the dangers of "communism" at
home and abroad.

Most guild leaders, of course, had grown accustomed to labeling such
anticommunist rhetoric as a negative doctrine that carried a deep hostility
to unions and the new culture of the city. Yet at a time when the war effort
had yielded conflicts not so much with monopoly capital as with rank-and-
file union members themselves, many guild leaders began to see Johnston's
call as a continuation of their own positive reform efforts. For one thing,
unlike the small businessmen and politicians who inspired Red Scares after

Fig. 7.6 (A and B). The Conference of Studio Unions press stereotypes Ronald Reagan during the 1946 strike as a dummy manipulated by a fat capitalist, and another cartoon dramatizes the impact of the national boycott of actors on the studios. (Courtesy, Hollywood Strike File, Special Collections, UCLA.)

World War I and later, Johnston spoke for modern corporate leaders who sought to sanction ethnic pluralism, the welfare state, "mature unions," and the promise of consumerism. Yet, more important, this modern form of anticommunism was seen as a positive doctrine that promised to generate national security as well as a rebirth of American power and prosperity.[20]

Nowhere was the success of Johnston's call more evident than in the rise of Ronald Reagan to undisputed power within the guild from 1947 to 1952. Similar to most of the membership making the transition from the thirties to the war years, Reagan had been a Roosevelt supporter, a loyalty he inherited from his father, a midwestern Irish-Catholic who was financially ruined by the Depression and often drowned his troubles in alcohol. Driven to escape a deeply insecure past, Ronald came to Hollywood, where he performed as a salaried player for the most pro-Roosevelt of all the studios, Warner Brothers. On the screen, he portrayed heroes triumphing over corrupt businessmen and foreign enemies. Off the screen, he worked to advance the new democratic politics and middle-class culture advanced by the guild. And as late as 1945, he belonged to Hollywood organizations that condemned "red baiting" and supported antimonopoly politics, militant labor, and the CSU.

The youthful Ronald Reagan, however, was also quite different from the earlier generation of guild leadership. His arrival in Hollywood in 1937 meant that he had missed the great unionizing drives of the thirties; indeed, he joined only after the guild's closed-shop agreements made it virtually mandatory. Nor did he rise to leadership by mobilizing the mass support of the members. Rather, in the highly organized guild of the war years, Reagan was appointed to the board and later the presidency, where he ran unopposed through the early fifties. Deeply committed to security and high-level consumption—he had eight insurance policies, two homes, a horse stable, and two Cadillacs when his wife divorced him in the late forties—he found his aspirations realized less in the union struggles of the thirties than in the patriotic expansion spurred by the defense effort. Small wonder that as the extras and CSU conflict erupted, as Eric Johnston identified anticommunism with realizing a "utopia of production," Reagan became an undercover agent for the Federal Bureau of Investigation and dropped his involvement in progressive groups or "communist fronts," seeing them as tools of the enemy. "I learned my lesson, the bulk of communist work is done by people who are sucked into carrying out red policy without knowing what they are doing."[21]

As Reagan shed his former loyalties, he also sought to "bring about the regeneration of the world I believed should have automatically appeared following the war." Believing with Johnston that Hollywood should become a model of "democratic capitalism," he first served as an arbiter of the jurisdictional strikes. But he ended up giving a major speech—against the vocal opposition of Katherine Hepburn, Edward G. Robinson, and others—persuading the members to back the IA and cross the CSU picket lines. Shortly thereafter, the extras legitimately complained that the board was made up of actors who had become producers; the leadership resigned, and Reagan became SAG's president. Jack Dales, the executive secretary of the organization, recalled that Reagan not only "disliked the extras tremendously," but also became convinced he was fighting "his own people, the pro-Russian Americans." Within months, the Reagan-led board condemned their own CSU supporters as "foreign dictators" who would "enslave people." To stop the "Reds" from taking over the industry, the leadership altered the SAG constitution to make petitions and popular initiative from the membership virtually impossible, with the result that the organization became much more bureaucratic and centralized.[22]

More important still, the utopian aspirations undergirding these battles were soon projected on a national screen as the House Committee on Un-American Activities (HUAC) came to Hollywood in 1947. Exactly what internal motivations spurred the committee to launch the most celebrated investigation of the postwar era will perhaps never be known. Yet it is possible to gauge its enormous impact on the industry by putting the process in historical perspective. HUAC represented an older anticommunist tradition that had generated Red Scares after World War I and was centered mainly in small-property, Anglo-Saxon Americans hostile to unions and the new culture of the cities. Seeing embodied in the industry all that was wrong with twentieth-century life—moral experimentation, cultural mixing, a militant labor movement and middle-class activism—HUAC found it natural to label Hollywood a hotbed of un-Americanism. With these ideas, the committee came in the late thirties to investigate the writers and performers, but with New Deal insurgency dominating the industry, the newly formed guilds and unions resisted the moral and political implications of their efforts, making HUAC ineffective.

By 1946, however, the situation had considerably altered. It was not just that the cold war had started with the Soviet Union and the Truman administration resisted the postwar strikes, but anticommunist rhetoric was now the common currency of Hollywood politics. Looking to make the industry a model of the new political and cultural order, Eric Johnston, the producers, and the new guild leaders now cooperated with the committee to discover and jail party members, who became known as the "Hollywood Ten." At the same time, they associated the traditional antimonopoly politics of the CSU with subversion, for with the Soviet Union hostile to both the United States and capitalism, opposition to big business was now equated with unpatriotic beliefs. As Eric Johnston pointed out, ideas of class conflict were foreign to "American Civilization," and its adherents were, at best, potential traitors, and at worst, irrational "crackpots" under the influence of a "delusion." [23]

Above all, the hearings now provided a national stage for curing Hollywood radicals, and by implication the mass audience, of a republican ideology that had been hostile to monopoly capital for over a century. The first act began when HUAC and industry leaders demanded of artists who wished to work again that they "name names" of their former communist associates. The second act saw the accused shed a middle-class ideology that had served to support so many political innovations in the film industry of the thirties. The finale occurred when the sinners confessed in widely publicized testimonials to their rebirth. A real-life dramatization of the entire process unfolded when the noted director Edward Dmytryck confessed in 1951 to the *Saturday Evening Post*. On the first page was a photo of Dmytryck holding a newspaper with the headline, "Trial Board Convicts Sorrell." After visually linking his own fall to the CSU's, he explained that his former belief that democracy was opposed to the corporate order led him to support Progressive causes and then join communist organizations. But the advent of the cold war, and his jailing as a member of the Hollywood Ten, brought the realization that abundance and racial tolerance could be attained only through the true American tradition of class unity.

Once this conversion process began, there could be no end to it. After all, the president of SAG and many on the board of directors had once been aligned with the CSU and proudly proclaimed a democratic ideology hostile to capitalism. To prove themselves willing converts to the new consensus, the Hollywood leaders now created industry-wide clearing boards to ward off false accusations. Yet in spite of their best efforts, the newly formed Motion Picture Industry Council (MPIC) found that mistakes invariably occurred. A prime example surfaced when SAG received in 1953 a letter from an executive at Columbia Pictures apologizing to the new Mrs. Ronald Reagan. Presumably, Nancy Davis had been denied work because she had the same maiden name as a woman who had signed a petition supporting free speech for the Hollywood Ten. As the executive explained, "You are aware we make a check on all actors, writers, directors being considered for employment. This is a regular routine. This investigation is made by a reputable organization in New York City." Despite the fact that a mistake had occurred, "I question whether your criticism of the organization that checks for us is justified. Of course we could have taken it for granted that the wife of Ronald Reagan could not be of questionable loyalty, and we could have disregarded the report." Although Nancy Reagan could prove her innocence, others were not so lucky. As Jack Dales, the executive secretary of the guild, recalled years later,

> What I have debated about since is that so many people were tarred by that brush who I don't think should have been now. . . . Even at the time, I'm saying my doubts came to the fore. I was not Ronnie Reagan or Roy Brewer. . . . I would argue about how far we were going, particularly when it got to be this clearing depot, you know, for work. I think of people who were terribly, unfairly treated like Larry Parks, Marsha Hunt, who had viewpoints that were different from the majority of the Board members, but they were far from communist agents. . . . They were just strong liberal people who took their lumps. . . . The producers carried it to ridiculous extremes and we did not stand up fairly to call a fair line. A line should have been called. . . .[24]

Such a line was so difficult to draw, however, because the reformers were also trying to transform the biggest prize of all—a popular culture that so many stars had identified with their personas on and off the screen. Looking to the screen as a major vehicle for spreading a new American Way to the world, Eric Johnston minced no words in explaining, "We'll have no more *Grapes of Wrath*, we'll have no more *Tobacco Roads*. We'll have no more films that show the seamy side of American life. We'll have no pictures that deal with labor strikes. We'll have no pictures that deal with the banker as villain." To ensure that result, Johnston, Brewer, and Reagan helped distribute a new film code written by the novelist and militant anticommunist, Ayn Rand—A *Screen Guide for Americans*. Under broad headlines, it preached "Don't Smear the Free Enterprise System," "Don't Deify the Common Man," "Don't Show That Poverty Is a Virtue . . . and Failure Is Noble." The "nobility" of the "little people" was now labeled the "drooling of weaklings." In this atmosphere, dramatists of the commoners' former hostility to monopoly, even the militantly anticommunist director

Frank Capra, found their security clearances taken away, and writers whose work for years had featured American heroes whose "fortune and happiness were threatened by a banker holding a mortgage over their heads," suddenly found these themes unmarketable.[25]

It followed that similar pressures affected the stars' public lives as well. In the wake of HUAC, for example, a reporter found that many performers "are afraid that the public might have received a very wrong impression about them, because of having seen them portray, say, a legendary hero who stole from the rich to give to the poor, or an honest, crusading district attorney, or a lonely, poetic, antisocial gangster." In response, the guild no longer held vast parades supporting militant labor unions, published ads calling for boycotts, mobilized their members in vast meetings with antimonopoly rhetoric, or condemned anticommunist attacks. Rather, the leaders funded industry organizations to dramatize the collaboration between labor and capital, expelled the CSU from Hollywood, and gave highly visible loyalty oaths in support of the cold war. As one actor remarked in 1948, "We've got to resolve any conflicts between what we are and what the public has been led to believe we are. We can't afford to have people think we're a band of strongmen or crusaders."

The guild, in turn, sought to resolve that conflict by turning the stars' imagery from public to private life. A striking example was a series of unprecedented speeches produced by the guild after 1947. Each standardized "talk" was to be given to civic groups around the country, emphasizing that the stars now embodied the rejuvenated family life unfolding in the suburbs. As such, the stars' glamour and consumer élan still represented a break from the stuffy styles of Victorianism. But their vernacular, or common, touch was no longer an ideal with which to question established institutions or power. Rather, the stars' marriages were presumably more stable than the rest of the country's, and the postwar consumer culture provided the foundation for happy marriages and healthy children, free of irrational ideas and conflicts. Listening to Ronald Reagan present that ideal to an audience in his boyhood home of Dixon, Illinois, a reporter recorded that "Dutch gave a stirring defense of his new home town, Hollywood. . . . He explained that it was only a few years ago that some churches wouldn't even bury an actor. That attitude, he explained, has changed today, because the film actors, unlike the thespians of old, now settle in one place, build homes, raise their children, attend school and churches and become part of the community. 'You certainly couldn't expect an actor to live out of a trunk to do that.'"[26]

Ironically, the drive to make the communications capital a model of the status quo might well have killed the goose that laid the golden egg. In the aftermath of the first HUAC investigations in 1948, producers and union leaders made a startling discovery: box office receipts that had risen for over a decade and half fell dramatically. As a consequence, SAG's membership dropped from 7,898 in 1946 to 6,533 in 1949. Much of the audience decline, of course, has been attributed to the baby boom that began in the postwar era and the rise of television. But it is well to remember that the baby boom started as early as 1941, and it was not until 1950 that even ten percent of American families had televisions. A more plausible explanation is that the Hollywood crusaders destroyed the appeal of modern popular culture, with its linkage to free social space outside power and authority. Indeed, the crusaders blacklisted their most popular writers and performers, pressured filmmakers to alter film plots, and prevented the distribution of "undesirable" works, such as *Salt of the Earth*. [27]

Even more damaging, the crusaders destroyed the careers of major stars like Charles Chaplin and John Garfield. Each attracted the ire of Hollywood's anticommunists for continuing to make socially critical films, for refusing to cross picket lines, and for supporting the Progressive campaign of Henry Wallace calling for a continuation of domestic radicalism and cooperation with the Soviet Union. In response Brewer, Reagan, and Johnston, mobilized in groups like the Americans for Democratic Action and MPIC, labeled these efforts close to treason. Then, when the Federal Bureau of Investigation launched an inquiry into Chaplin's activities, and when the Hollywood unions and the American Legion generated a national boycott of his films, Roy Brewer of the IA justified the star's departure from the country because "Chaplin has shown nothing but contempt for America and her institutions. His most recent statements that Hollywood has succumbed to thought control so far as I am concerned confirms the fact that his thinking is still in the communist orbit of influence. This is strictly Party line. . . . Nothing he has said or done would justify our assuming that he is on our side in this fight. Until we get such assurances, we are justified in resisting any further efforts to add to his fortune or influence." [28]

Years later, the screen's lovable American tramp lay buried in Europe, and the anticommunist guild leader rose to become president of the United States, appointing the IA leader Roy Brewer to a high post in the Labor Department. Hollywood gave Reagan and Brewer their political baptisms, but what conclusions can we draw from these events? By now it should be clear that the Hollywood Red Scare served as more than a reactionary or irrational crusade sparked by conservatives hostile to modern life. Rather, the industry attracted the attention of corporate leaders because the stars were living examples of a popular culture rooted in affluence and city life. When that consumer promise had collapsed in the Depression, the most noted personalities of the day aligned with workers in a radical labor movement dedicated to redistributing wealth and power. Drawing on the experimentation unfolding in mass culture and reconstructing an older democratic tradition hostile to capitalism, SAG advanced a New Deal politics intent on realizing a new nationalism rooted in the welfare state, ethnicity, and consumption. The apolitical process of defense mobilization in World War II brought the cultural side of that promise to fruition, while mass strikes within the guild and the country brought the leadership into a close relationship with big business.

Given these altered conditions, corporate leaders like Eric Johnston sought to make Hollywood a model of an unprecedented American identity rooted in consensus and consumption. To accomplish that ideological conversion, Johnston and his allies drew on a new form of anticommunism to discredit opposition to monopoly capital and generate support for building a new world order. Indeed, as the cold war began in 1947, and as the HUAC hearings discredited militant labor unions, the stars came to personify a corporate consensus in which labor unions as well as ethnic and racial minorities were presumably legitimized. Equality, however, was found less in the workplace than in a consumer-oriented home, centered in the affluent worker and new middle-class suburbs. Small wonder that when the politics and culture of the cold war faltered in the late sixties and seventies, Ronald Reagan would leave the film capital to revive the "democratic capitalism" he had helped to create. Nor was it incidental that a reporter interviewing him during his successful run for the presidency in 1980 found that these earlier events were still very much on his mind:

> Reagan, with no prompting from me, in what seems in fact to be a compulsive non sequitur, had resurrected events that took place some thirty years earlier, his wounds still raw and his hatred of the enemy unyielding. Most curious of all is that his view of the Soviet menace today is so deeply colored by events that took place in Hollywood more than a generation ago, as if today's Soviet government were simply the Hollywood communists projected on a larger screen.[29]

Strong testimony, indeed, to the way the events unfolding in postwar Hollywood helped to create the culture of the cold war.

NOTES

1. Ronald Reagan and Richard C. Hubler, *Where's the Rest of Me?* (New York: Dell, 1981), 162–64, 189. Abraham Polansky, "How the Blacklist Worked in Hollywood," *Film Culture* 50–51 (Fall 1970): 44.

2. Eric Johnston, "Utopia Is Production," *Screen Actor* 14 (April 1946): 7 (hereafter cited as *SA*).

3. For a full exposition of the "New Century" context, see Eric Johnston, *America Unlimited* (Garden City, N.J.: Doubleday, 1944), and Karl Schriftgiesser, *Business Comes of Age: The Story of the Committee for Economic Development and Its Impact upon the Economic Policies of the United States, 1942–1960* (New York: Harper, 1960), 13, 23, 73–75. On postwar strikes, see George Lipsitz, *Class and Culture in Cold War America: A Rainbow at Midnight* (New York: Praeger, 1983); Anthony Dawson, "Hollywood's Labor Troubles," *Industrial Labor Relations Review* 1 (July 1948): 638–47; *Life* (October 14, 1946): 29–33.

4. The literature dedicated to the escapist and Marxist view of popular culture is vast. A good introduction to the whole can be found in Patrick Brantlinger, *Bread and Circuses: Theories of Mass Culture as Social Decay* (Ithaca, N.Y.: Cornell University Press, 1984). For a typical example of anticommunism in the postwar period as another example of provincial nationalism, see Jane De Hart Matthews, "Art and Politics in Cold War America," *American Historical Review* 81 (October 1976): 762–87. This view is not wrong, but it needs to be complemented by what I see as a far more important development: the rise of a far more effective anticommunism spread by corporate leaders. For a survey of the prolific writings and scholarship on the Hollywood Red Scare, and a welcome corrective to the position that these events had no effect on the movies or politics, see Thom Andersen, "Red Hollywood," in *Literature and the Visual Arts in Contemporary Society*, ed. Suzanne Ferguson and Barbara Groseclose (Columbus: Ohio State University Press, 1986), 141–96.

5. See Lary May, *Screening Out the Past: The Birth of Mass Culture and the Motion Picture Industry* (Chicago: University of Chicago Press, 1983), chaps. 1–6.

6. For New Deal voting, see the poll in *Hollywood Reporter* October 8, 1936. On the industry work force, see Leo C. Rosten, *Hollywood: The Movie Colony, The Movie Makers* (New York: Harcourt and Brace, 1941), 373, 381–94. "The Guild and the Labor Movement," *SA* (July 1936): 4–5.

7. Rosten, *Hollywood*, 301–94; Editorial, "The Guild and the Labor Movement," *SA* (July 1936): 4–5.

8. Murray Ross, *Stars and Strikes: The Unionization of Hollywood* (New York: Columbia University Press, 1941), and Louis B. Perry and Richard S. Perry, *A History of the Los Angeles Labor Movement, 1911–1941* (Berkeley: University of California Press, 1963). Herbert Sorrell, "You Don't Choose Your Friends: The

Memoirs of Herbert Knott Sorrell," UCLA Oral History Project 1963, Special Collections, UCLA, 20–50, and Robert Montgomery, SAG Oral History Project, Screen Actors' Guild Files, Los Angeles, California (hereinafter known as SAG Files and UCLA Oral History Project, respectively).

9. For the CIO, see David Brody, *Workers in Industrial America* (New York: Oxford University Press, 1980), 82–173. On the CSU, SAG, and their common anticommunism, see Sorrell, "Memoir," 50–51, 86–87, 77–78, 134, 143–50, and Testimony of Herbert Sorrell, Hearings before a Special Committee on Education and Labor, House of Representatives, *Jurisdictional Disputes in the Motion Picture Industry*, 80th Cong., 1st sess., 1948, 784–805, 1860–1903 (hereafter known as *Jurisdictional Disputes*). Testimony of Father George Dunne, *Jurisdictional Disputes*, 403–33, 443–56, and "Christian Advocacy and Labor Strife in Hollywood," UCLA Oral History Project, 1981, 52. For SAG, see Montgomery, SAG Oral History Project. For common guild and Hollywood insurgent alliances, see Minutes, April 15, 1937; February 21, 1938, 683, 714; June 13, 1938, 802; October 1938. For the Longshoreman quote, see Minutes, March 1, 1937, 483.

10. Unsigned, "I Am an Individual," SA (January 1936): 5. Eddie Cantor, "What the Guild Stands for . . ." SA (March 1934): 2. "The Wire to President Roosevelt and the Executive Order," SA (May 15, 1933): 4, 16; "Text of Eddie Cantor's Speech at Annual Meeting," SA (May 15, 1934): 1, 12; Editors, "The Menace of the Academy," SA (April 15, 1934). For a summary of the scholarly literature on republicanism, see Sara M. Evans and Harry C. Boyte, *Free Spaces: The Sources of Democratic Change in America* (New York: Harper and Row, 1986), 1–25.

11. Rosten, *Hollywood*, 335. For guild leaders' recollection of their break with the old middle-class cultural inheritance, see Jack Dales, Gale Sondergaard, Robert Montgomery, Leon Ames, SAG Oral History Interviews, 1979, SAG Files. On racial tolerance, see "Guild Combats Danger of Minority Baiting," SA (April 1946): 7, 8, and Board of Directors' Minutes, November 9, 1939, 1307, SAG Files (hereafter known as Minutes).

12. For a recent account that incorrectly portrays a conservative guild in the thirties, see Garry Wills, *Reagan's America: Innocents at Home* (Garden City, N.Y.: Doubleday, 1987), 215–23. Roy Brewer, president of the IA, told the author in an interview that the Hollywood guilds were a communist idea in the thirties. Frank Scully, "Is the Middle Class in the Middle?" SA (December 1936): 8–9. Nunnally Johnson, "American Epic," SA (August 1934): 4; Fred Keating, "Are We Laborers? Under Conditions of Modern Economic Society Motion Picture Actors Are Laborers Whether They Admit It or Not," SA (August 1934): 4, 18–21.

13. May, *Screening Out the Past*, chaps. 1–6; Lary May, with the assistance of Stephen Lassonde, "Making the American Way: Modern Theatres, Audiences and the Film Industry, 1929–1945," *Prospects* (May 1987): 89–130. For film styles with protest themes, see Lawrence Levine, "Hollywood's Washington: Film Images of National Politics during the Great Depression," *Prospects* 10 (1985): 169–95, and Andrew Bergman, *We're in the Money* (New York: New York University Press, 1971).

14. See almost any issue of SA from 1935 to 1945 for the merging of labor

news and consumption. For boycotts, fairs, balls, and radio shows, respectively, see Minutes, February 21, 1938, 714; August 23, 1937; February 19, 1940, 1454; January 3, 1938, 657; and May 15, 1939, 1162; and "Screen Guild Theatre over CBS," SA (April 1941): 6. On FDR's hat, see SA (April 1941): 6. For the Montgomery letter, see Minutes, March 2, 1936.

15. On consumerism, mass production, and higher wages, see Los Angeles Citizen 3 and 10 (1936); 3 and 11 (1937). On CSU, see "Cafe Man Lifts Light on Hollywood Night Life," Hollywood Sun July 25, 1945. For Sorrell, see "Memoir," 77.

16. "Labor Day Parade," Los Angeles Citizen 3 and 10 (September 1936); 3 and 11 (September 1937). "Brother Eddie Cantor," Los Angeles Citizen 10 (September 1936). "Guild Joins in Labor Day Parade," SA (August 1936): 3.

17. On wartime nationalism and consumption, see John Morton Blum, V Was for Victory: Politics and Culture during World War II (New York: Harcourt Brace Jovanovich, 1979), 31–54, 90–117; and, for Hollywood and the guild's role, see This Is the Army File, Museum of Modern Art Film Library, New York City, New York; "Radio," SA (July 1942): 4; "Mobilization," SA (June 1943): 4; "Marching Men," SA (June 1942): 13; "SAG Cited by Army and Navy," SA (April 1946): 4; and James Cagney, "Spirit of '42," SA (June 1942): 9.

18. On wartime and postwar national strikes, see Lipsitz, Class and Culture; for Sorrell's participation in these events at the local level, see Jurisdictional Disputes, 1233. For the extras controversy, see Minutes, December 30, 1943; January 5, 1943; February 21, 1943; March 1, 1943; April 12, 1943; May 24, 1943, 2353; and December 18, 1944, 2704; October 17, 1945. The guild executive secretary explained in reference to the extras during the war that "there was a quite understandable feeling that we had our heads in the sand, that we really did not understand their problems . . . and we viewed them as a bunch of malcontents who really didn't have a stake in the business." See Dales, SAG Interview. Sorrell, "Memoir," 70–77. Kenneth Thomson, "Report on Extras," Minutes, March 14, 1943, SAG Files.

19. As late as 1945, the guild supported Sorrell's strikes. See Minutes, October 16, 1945, 2884–92, 2915. But then the Minutes of February 18, 1946, state that the IA will give replacements for striking CSU members, but not unless the IA has "the support of the Guild." The Minutes of August 20, 1945, 2853–54 added that SAG gave that support because the board "found itself in a position of being unable to refuse . . . because of the unsolicited, militant support which the IA has given" to SAG's extras' union. In the wake of that secret bargain, the new guild president, Ronald Reagan, later told congressional investigators that the "charge of conspiracy and collusion between the producers and the IA" and SAG was "groundless" and "ridiculous." See Ronald Reagan to Honorable Ralph W. Gwinn, March 2, 1948, SAG Files. CSU News June–August 1946; Hollywood Strike, folder 226, University of California at Los Angeles Special Collections (hereafter known as Strike Folder), also documents that for the pickets, the "actors seem to be a special object of their wrath."

20. See Eric Johnston, American Unlimited, 34–60; We're All in It (New York: Dutton, 1948), 1–60, as well as Eric Johnston, Testimony, House Commit-

tee on Un-American Activities, *Hearings Regarding the Communist Infiltration of the Motion Picture Industry*, 80th Cong., 1st sess., 1947, 305–10 (hereafter known as HUAC 1947). For the larger context of the new ideology, see Charles Maier, "The Politics of Productivity," *International Organization* 31, no. 4 (1977): 607–32. In order to compare Johnston's ideology with earlier anticommunism after World War I, see John Higham, *Strangers in the Land: Patterns of American Nativism, 1860–1925* (New York: Atheneum, 1971), 194–234.

21. For the recognition of Reagan as the most important anticommunist in the Hollywood unions, see the president of the IA's comments, Testimony of Roy Brewer, Committee on Un-American Activities, House of Representatives, 82d Cong., 1st sess., 1951, 517 (hereafter known as HUAC 1951). Reagan and Hubler, *Where's the Rest of Me?* 1–65, 147–230; Wills, *Reagan's America*, 247–50. For his films and political views, see Stephen Vaughn, "The Secret Service Films of Ronald Reagan," *American Quarterly* (Fall 1987): 355–81. On Reagan's divorce, see *Reagan v. Reagan*, Superior Court of the State of California, June 12, 1948, in Los Angeles County Archives, Los Angeles, California, no. D360058. The quote is from "Ronald Reagan Testifies He Didn't Know Jeffers," *Los Angeles Times*, unpaginated, undated clipping (probably January 1951), in Ronald Reagan File, *Los Angeles Times* library, Los Angeles, California.

22. Reagan and Hubler, *Where's the Rest of Me?* 160–61. Dales, SAG Oral History Project, 38; Dales, UCLA Oral History, 34, 51. Minutes, Annual Meeting, October 2, 1946, 3092; "Special Membership Meeting," *SA* (January 1947): 4–12. *Screen Actors' Guild Intelligence Report* (May 15 and June 16, 1947). The result was that petitions no longer could come from the floor at annual meetings; more class "A" members had to sign petitions to call a special meeting (a proposal that effectively silenced those without speaking parts in films, especially the extras; no alternative recommendations to the boards were allowed on the ballots; and secret ballots, rather than public debate, determined decisions. Further, the board eliminated the efforts of civil rights groups to pressure the producers to alter the "Sambo" type roles given to Negro actors. See Minutes, May 24, 1943, and October 20, 1947.

23. See Andersen, "Red Hollywood," for a survey of the literature on the Hollywood HUAC hearings. The tragedy, of course, was that in their dedication to a republican, antimonopoly tradition, the CSU and Sorrell tolerated party members but were militantly anticommunist. The CSU not only went out on strike against party policy in the war but also did not allow party members to hold offices in the union. For the best discussion of how they were falsely accused of being communist agents, see Wills, *Reagan's America*, 231–61. For Sorrell's progressive ideology, see Testimony of Hebert Sorrell, *Jurisdictional Disputes*, 186–200, 1930; and Sorrell, "Oral History," 50–51, 86–87, 134, 169–70, 208. Testimony of Father Dunne, *Jurisdictional Disputes*, 403–33, 443–56. Johnston, *America Unlimited*, 152–60.

24. For the Dmytryck interview, see Richard English, "What Makes a Hollywood Communist?" *Saturday Evening Post* (May 19, 1951): 30–31, 147–48. Wills, *Reagan's America*, 251–61. B. B. Kahane to Mrs. Ronald Reagan, January 7, 1953, SAG Files; Jack Dales, SAG Oral History, 1979, 12–13, SAG Files. For

an insightful view of the larger political implications of HUAC in Hollywood, see Abraham Polansky, "How the Blacklist Worked in Hollywood," *Film Culture* 50–51 (Fall 1970): 44.

25. For films and foreign-policy imagery, see Testimony of Eric Johnston, HUAC 1947, 305–10. Eric Johnston, *The Hollywood Hearings* (Washington, D.C.: Motion Picture Producers' Association, 1948), 1–10. For the Johnston quote, see Murray Schumach, *The Face on the Cutting Room Floor: The Story of Movie and Television Censorship* (New York: Harper and Row, 1964), 129. *Screen Guide for Americans* (Beverly Hills: Motion Picture Alliance for the Preservation of American Ideals, 1948), 1–12. Lillian Ross, "Onward and Upward with the Arts," *New Yorker* (February 21, 1948), 32–48. Frank Capra, *The Name above the Title: An Autobiography* (New York: Random House, 1971), 425–30.

26. The elimination of public activities is based on a survey of the *Intelligence Report*, the journal which replaced *Screen Actor* after 1946. Eric Johnston, "Motion Picture Industry Council," *New York Daily News*, unpaginated, undated article, 1948, in MPIC File, Academy of Motion Picture Arts and Sciences Library, Los Angeles, California (hereafter known as MPIC). For loyalty oaths, see SAG Press Release, April 10, 1951; Board of Directors to Miss Gale Sondergaard, March 20, 1951; "Speakers Kit," probably designed in 1948; Ronald Reagan, "Special Editorial to the *Hartford Times*," October 8, 1951—all the above in SAG Files. The quote is from *Dixon Evening Telegraph*, August 22, 1950, cited in Wills, *Reagan's America*, 144.

27. For evidence documenting the audience decline and rise of television, see Michael Conant, *Anti-Trust in the Motion Picture Industry* (Berkeley: University of California Press, 1960), tables 1, 4, 6; *Historical Statistics of the United States*, pt. 2, 796. For a similar account, but different conclusion, see Douglas Gomery, "The Coming of Television and the 'Lost' Motion Picture Audience," *Journal of Film and Video*, 37, no. 3 (1985): 5–12. On guild membership see, *Intelligence Report* (July 22, 1949), SAG Files. Herbert Biberman, *Salt of the Earth* (Boston: Beacon, 1965), and *Salt of the Earth* File, SAG Files. For boycotts, see "Film Council Asks Ban on Import of Red Movies," *Los Angeles Times* August 26, 1952.

28. For Garfield, see Andersen, "Red Hollywood," 177–91. For stories and pictures of Chaplin supporting the CSU, see *CSU News* May 24, 1947. Eric Johnston, "Mr. Wallace Proposes Appeasement" (unpaginated clipping, MPIC), and *Los Angeles Times* January 16, 1948. *Los Angeles Times* October 5, 1948, reported Ronald Reagan as chairman of AFL Film Council; its first statement was to "denounce Wallace." On the CSU and Wallace campaign, see *CSU News* May 24, 1947, and *Hollywood Citizen* January 1948; *California Progressive* June–January 1948, in Hollywood Strike Folder, 226. On Chaplin and the FBI, see Timothy J. Lyons, "The United States v. Charlie Chaplin," *American Film* 10 (September 1984): 29–34. "Roy Brewer Blasts Lessing for Branding IA 'Selfish,' Takes New Jab at Chaplin," *Variety* 1952, unpaginated, undated clipping, MPIC.

29. Robert Scheer, *With Enough Shovels: Reagan, Bush and Nuclear War* (New York: Random House, 1982), 42–43.

8 Explosive Issues: Sex, Women, and the Bomb

Elaine Tyler May

In 1951, Charles Walter Clarke, a Harvard physician and executive director of the American Social Hygiene Association, published a major article in the *Journal of Social Hygiene* on the dangers of atomic attack. "Following an atom bomb explosion," he wrote, "families would become separated and lost from each other in confusion. Supports of normal family and community life would be broken down . . . there would develop among many people, especially youths . . . the reckless psychological state often seen following great disasters." The preparedness plan that Clarke devised to cope with this possibility centered not on death and destruction or psychological damage but on the potential for sexual chaos. "Under such conditions," he continued, "moral standards would relax and promiscuity would increase." Clarke predicted that such postbomb sexual promiscuity would lead to a "1,000 percent increase" in venereal disease unless "drastic preventive measures" were taken. He then called upon public health professionals to help ensure that in the event of an atomic attack there would be adequate supplies of penicillin on hand in potential target areas, and "strict policing . . . vigorous repression of prostitution, and measures to discourage promiscuity, drunkenness, and disorder."[1]

Clarke's preoccupation with sexual chaos may seem rather absurd in the face of the incomprehensible horror of nuclear holocaust. Clearly, he did not represent mainstream medical opinion, since his organization had been preoccupied with venereal disease for decades. Nevertheless, his ideas struck a responsive chord among many fellow professionals who shared his concern with sexual order in the atomic age. When he sent a draft of the article to over seventy experts in medicine and public health around the country, most responded that they shared his concerns and endorsed his preparedness plan.[2] By linking fears of sexuality out of control with the insecurities of the cold war era, Clark articulated a symbolic connection that found widespread expression during these years, from professional writings to the popular culture. Indeed, he was one of many postwar experts who prescribed family stability as an antidote to these related dangers.

Historians should not be surprised to find fears over sexuality surfacing with the birth of the atomic age, for concern over the impending doom of the family has accompanied many crises in American history. Most scholars of the Progressive era, for example, have recognized that the combined forces of immigration, urbanization, and changing roles for women unleashed anxieties over sex and family life that motivated a great deal of reform activity. Progressivism lasted from 1900 to World War I and culminated in a number of measures intended to control these dangers, such as Prohibition, immigration restriction, women's suffrage, and the licensing and censoring of urban amusements. Presumably, by the 1920s the moral revolution had been institutionalized. Yet Clarke's article suggests that similar fears, coupled to the call for a renewed dedication to family life, had not died. Rather, the unresolved anxiety concerning modern sexuality and female roles continued into the postwar era as well.

Nor was Clarke's call for a revitalization of domesticity mere rhetoric, for it was accompanied by an astounding rush into family life. Indeed, scholars have long noted the unprecedented rise in the marriage rate and the dramatic decline in the marriage age that occurred after World War II. At the same time, the birthrate climbed to a twentieth-century high, yielding an equally well-noted baby boom. In searching for an explanation for that change, scholars have usually argued that in the wake of a major depression and world war, Americans turned avidly to a newly affluent and secure home life. Yet this demographic explosion went far beyond what might be expected from a return to peace and prosperity. The trends appear especially perplexing when we consider the experiences of American women at the time. The female labor force expanded in the postwar years, providing a potential alternative to early marriage and child rearing. In addition, more women as well as men entered institutions of higher education. These opportunities, combined with the increasing availability of contraception, might have encouraged women—as they did in the sixties and seventies—to postpone marriage and motherhood in order to pursue educational or occupational goals. Why, then, after World War II did they rush into marriage and childbearing instead?[3] This study seeks to answer that question by exploring a previously unrecognized facet of the postwar era: that profound connections existed among anxieties over sexual roles, the cold war, and a burgeoning family ideology.

In exploring that connection between private and public life, the writings of professionals offer a useful starting point. Whether or not all Americans read or believed the professionals, there can be little doubt that postwar America was the era of the expert. By articulating cultural norms, they expressed as well as helped to shape American values. Of course, Americans had valued expertise for many decades, but the postwar years marked a heightening of the status of the professional. Armed with scientific techniques and presumably inhabiting a world above popular passions, the experts had brought us into the atomic age. Physicists developed the bomb, strategists created the cold war, and scientific managers built the military-industrial complex. Science and technology seemed to have invaded virtually every aspect of life, from the most public to the most private. Whether in medicine, child rearing, or even the intimate areas of sex and marriage, expertise gained legitimacy as familiar, "old-fashioned" ways were called into question. As the readers of *Look* magazine were assured, there was no reason to worry about radioactivity, for if ever the time arrived when you would need to understand its dangers, "the experts will be ready to tell you."[4]

Americans consulted experts not only in print but also in person. One recent study by a team of sociologists examined the attitudes and habits of over 4,000 Americans in 1957 and found that reliance on expertise was one of the most striking developments of the postwar years. Long-term individual therapy also reached its peak of popularity in the mid-1950s; fourteen percent of the population said they had sought the help of professionals—lawyers, clergy, social workers, psychiatrists, and the like—at some point in their lives. The authors concluded, "Experts took over the role of psychic healer, but they also assumed a much broader and more important role in directing the behavior, goals, and ideals of normal people. They became the teachers and norm setters who would tell people how to approach and live life. . . . They would provide advice and counsel about raising and responding to children, how to behave in marriage, and what to see in that relationship. . . . Science moved in because people needed and wanted guidance." As other studies confirmed these findings, it seemed evident that people were quick to seek professional help for their personal problems. Clearly, when the experts spoke, postwar Americans listened.[5]

Yet in spite of public perceptions of aloofness and objectivity, professionals themselves were not far removed from the uncertainties of the day. Rather, they groped for appropriate ways to conceptualize and resolve them. Frequently, they framed public problems in terms of the family. For these experts, public problems thus merged with private ones, and the family appeared besieged as never before. The Massachusetts Society for Social Health, for example, focused its 1951 meeting on defense. It featured a panel discussion, "Social Hygiene in Total Mobilization." Bringing together physicians, clergy, social workers, military officers, and civil defense administrators, the Advisory Committee on Defense Activities outlined several areas for discussion, including "promiscuity and prostitution." The society saw that the increasing expression of female sexuality and women's entering the paid labor force were two sides of the same dangerous coin. The implicit criticism of both women's sexuality and employment was aimed at married as well as single women mingling in the world of men. Inside and outside the home, women who challenged traditional roles and restraints placed the security of the nation at risk. The experts warned that young women were drawn to public amusement areas, which would lead them to sexual promiscuity, while the employment of married women led to "unsupervised homes where both parents are working." The society cited both trends as major causes for the decline of sexual morality among youth and a weakening of the nation's moral fiber at a time when the country had to be strong.[6]

Despite warnings such as these, women remained in the paid labor force after the war, most notably vast numbers of married women who had joined the ranks of the employed for the first time. Yet anxiety continued to surround working women, especially since an essential ingredient in winning the cold war was presumably the rearing of strong and able offspring. Indeed, among many experts, the influx of women into jobs revived an older eugenic cry of "race suicide," a concern expressed by numerous observers who failed to notice that the baby boom was well under way. One scholar at Stanford University reported that the "talented" Americans were reproducing at a very low rate. Presumably, there would be a critical shortage of "talented" scientists and experts to sustain American technical superiority and world leadership. In response, a writer in the *Ladies Home Journal* complained that the perceived failure of the educated to reproduce adequately

> undoubtedly has to do with the so-called "emancipation" of women. Every field is open to women today, and every year thousands of women leave our colleges and universities determined to make careers for themselves. They often marry, but find reasons to postpone having children. Often Nature, as well as birth control measures, assist them in this. Women who lead very active lives, under conditions of nervous stress and strain, often do not conceive, and when they do, they miscarry. These women are violating their own biological natures; and for this they pay a heavy price. . . . The

feminist movement was an attempt to break from into a
"man's world"—and in the process, through envy, accepted
to an alarming extent the values of men.[7]

At the same time, many experts saw that the combined dangers of race
suicide, sexual promiscuity, and careerism might be avoided by adhering
to traditional family values. Above all, the containment of premarital sex
was central to this effort. Although the idea of chastity certainly was not
new in these years, the behavior advocated for achieving it was. Unlike the
authors of the prescriptive literature of the past who called for the repression of sexual desires, the postwar experts recognized that premarital sexual
experimentation was taking place to such an extent that calls for abstinence
would be futile. The goal now was to teach young people already indulging
in "petting" how to achieve restraint and keep sex under control. Even the
most outspoken advocates of healthy sexual expression, such as the noted
physician Mary Calderone, advised young people to save intercourse for
marriage. It is also worth noting that, for her advocacy of sex education,
Calderone was labeled a "communist." One method of containing sex was
through elaborate courtship etiquette. Dating became a ritual in itself. Until the mid-1950s, the term did not even appear in the guide to periodic
literature, and only a few articles were listed under the heading "courtship." After that time, however, it became a major category, with a proliferation of articles telling the do's and dont's of dating. Experts repeatedly
explained that it was up to young women to "draw the line" and exercise
sexual restraint, thereby safeguarding the stability of their future families.

Nevertheless, public health professionals, clergy, social workers, and
popular writers realized that appeals to moral rectitude and patriotism were
not likely to eradicate sexuality among young people. The best way to contain sex was through early marriage. Sex among young people would not
be dangerous if the young people were married. Hence, for the first time in
the postwar years, writers of prescriptive literature began to advocate early
marriage as the prerequisite for a healthy family and sexual life. As one
professional explained, "Psychologists observe increasing difficulties of sexual abstinence for those who have not trained themselves in self-control
and filled their lives with absorbing purposes and activities to the exclusion
of sexual experience. . . . Marriage is better late than never. But early
marriage gives more opportunity for happy comradeship, mutual development and physical adjustment, for having and training children, building a
home, promoting family life as a community asset, and observing one's
grandchildren start their careers."[8]

Most guidelines gave twenty-one as a healthy age for marriage, and pub-lic opinion polls indicated that most Americans agreed. Moreover, it was the woman's responsibility to achieve it. One typical guidebook, entitled *Win Your Man and Keep Him*, stressed the need for young women to culti-vate good looks, personality, and cheerful subservience. The authors ad-vised, "If you are more than 23 years old . . . perhaps you have begun to wonder whether Mr. Right would ever come along for you. Your chances are still good; you can increase them appreciably by taking actions which this book advocates." Another text offered a similar rational, scientific for-mula: "A girl who reaches the middle twenties without a proposal ought to consider carefully whether she really wishes to remain single. If she does not, she should try to discover why marriage hasn't come her way, and per-haps take steps to make herself more interesting and attractive."[9]

In order to provide this domestic quest with a sense of urgency, women's domestic roles needed to be infused with national purpose. It was not the first time that motherhood provided the female version of civic virtue. In-deed, as Linda Kerber has shown, ever since the era of the American Revo-lution, the nation's political ideology has held a special place for women as the nurturers and educators of future citizens. This idea of republican motherhood held unique power in the nineteenth century, when women were not allowed to vote but were encouraged to exercise their civic re-sponsibility through enlightened motherhood. In the post–World War II years, this dimension of female domesticity took a new form to fit the cold war. One way to add new purpose to women's domestic role was to provide the family with special functions to deal with the possibility of nuclear war. Domestic responsibilities based on expertise might also serve to give women in the home an elevated role at one with national purpose, much as their work in defense industries during the war had served a patriotic cause. Ex-perts called upon women to embrace domesticity in service to the nation in the same spirit that they had come to the country's aid by taking wartime jobs. To meet the challenge of the postwar era, women were to marshal their energies into a "New Family Type for the Space Age."[10]

A central institution involved in developing the concept of profession-alized homemaking for the atomic age was the Federal Civil Defense Ad-ministration (FCDA). Several women held key positions in this agency. Their task was to help formulate the role for American women in the area of civil defense. One central figure in this effort was Jean Wood Fuller, director of women's activities in the FCDA. Her role had an immediate public impact because, rather than simply formulating proposals to en-act in the event of an atomic attack, she was responsible for educational programs to be implemented in localities across the country. Born in Los Angeles, Fuller had been in the retail trade in Beverly Hills before World War II. During the war, she served in the Red Cross and the Home Services Corps, and from 1950 to 1954 she was president of the California Federation of Republican Women. Fuller actively promoted the various ways in which women could take leading roles in civil defense. In her work for the FCDA, she claimed that women could cope with atomic war. During the atomic test of 1955 in the Nevada desert, Fuller served, as she put it, as a "female guinea pig" in a trench 3,500 yards from ground zero. After the blast, the *Los Angeles Times* quoted her as saying it was "terrific, interesting and exciting. . . . My experience this morning shows conclusively that women can stand the shock and strain of an atomic explosion just as well as men. . . . It also proved that with the proper precautions, entire communities can survive an atomic bombing." Glowing from the experience, she spoke of "the beauty of [the mushroom cloud] . . . the colors and just before dawn you could get a sort of lovely background." [11]

Fuller's experience watching the blast led her to develop a program of "Home Protection and Safety." With chilling cheerfulness, she called for "positive action instead of negative" to overcome anxiety about the new age: "I always like to do something on a positive basis and this new threat of the H-bomb certainly gives us an opportunity." She was critical of women's groups that opposed the tests, such as the American Association of University Women, and urged them instead to contribute to preparedness. Women should draw on their unique domestic expertise to find new roles suited to the cold war. Home nursing was one important area. Mothers could learn first aid in order to enhance and professionalize their nurturing role. In the event of a nuclear attack, they would then, presumably, be equipped to tend to injured family members. Another skill to cultivate was the power of persuasion. They should convince public officials to become interested in civil defense by approaching them "in your own feminine way—but never be belligerent, please." Fuller appealed to rural as well as urban housewives, and particularly to church women: "It's second nature for them to put on large dinners. Aren't they just perfect naturals for our mass feeding groups?" Along with learning how to feed the survivors of a nuclear attack, women had to teach the children, too: "Civil defense training is almost akin to religious training. . . . We must teach our children protection. . . . A mother must calm the fears of her child. Make a game out of it: Playing Civil Defense." [12]

One of Fuller's most ardent campaigns was for women to prepare their homes for a nuclear attack. Radiation, she claimed, was not so dangerous as it used to be: "Our chances of living through the worst that the enemy can do are greater than his. . . . We must have a strong civil defense program . . . to help us get up off the floor after a surprise attack, and fight back and win." In an effort to recruit the nation's women to their role in this effort, Fuller along with other civil defense experts devised several campaigns which drew upon women's traditional domestic functions to equip them for a nuclear emergency. One of the most extensively publicized was "Grandma's Pantry," the home bomb shelter. With the help of the National Grocers' Association, several pharmaceutical houses, and the American National Dietetic Association, Fuller drew up guidelines for withstanding a nuclear holocaust.

The campaign appealed to time-honored values and rested on conservatism and nostalgia. Evoking memories of a simpler past, the slogan read, "Grandma's pantry was always ready. She was ready when the preacher came on Sunday or she was ready when the relatives arrived from Nebraska. Grandma's Pantry was ready—Is Your Pantry Ready in Event of Emergency?" Drawing on traditional virtues to face the unthinkable, the brochure featured a picture of an old-fashioned and well-supplied kitchen and included a long list of foods, canned goods, medical supplies, and other helpful items such as first-aid kits, soap, candles, buckets, and pet foods. Instructions taught women to rotate canned goods regularly, change bottled water every three months, and wrap glass items for protection: "With a well-stocked pantry you can be just as self-sufficient as Grandma was. Add a first aid kit, flashlight, and a portable radio to this supply, and you will have taken the first important step in family preparedness." [13]

Grandma's Pantry was only one way women could draw on their traditional skills to protect their families in the face of an atomic blast. There were also a number of widely publicized disaster feeding drills that took place around the country. Women were instructed in the art of cooking with makeshift utensils, "how to use this and that to make do with bricks and rubble and grates that you might find so that you could cook." Women were assured that, if they learned first aid, home nursing, fire fighting, and how to supply a bomb shelter, they could face the danger of an atomic attack without fear. Fuller taught women how to construct simple shelters in their basements from a large board leaning against a wall. To underscore the importance of this project, she showed detailed photographs taken at the Nevada test site which depicted child-sized mannequins under shelters still standing after the blast, while those outside the lean-tos were maimed. [14]

Nowhere is the image of the home as bulwark against the dangers of the atomic age more vivid than in the bomb-shelter boom of the postwar years. Jean Fuller and the civil defense establishment were not the only ones pre-occupied with family bomb shelters. Contractors commercialized the idea by creating a variety of styles and sizes to fit consumer tastes, from a "$13.50 foxhole shelter" to a "$5,000 deluxe 'suite' with telephone, escape hatches, bunks, toilets, and geiger counter." These private shelters symbol-ized family security and togetherness in the face of a frightening world. The popular press poured out numerous articles on the uses of home bomb shelters during peace as well as war, which centered on women's home-making tasks. As one woman wrote of her new shelter, "It will make a won-derful place for the kids to play in. And it will be a good storehouse, too. I do a lot of canning and bottling, you know."[15] Similarly, the *New York Times* reported that a boom in rural real estate was occurring because the countryside offered the appeal of escape from nuclear attack and a retreat into a vision of old-fashioned family life—much like Grandma's Pantry.[16]

In these ways, civil defense merged with widespread popular wishes for family security. Frequently, creators of popular culture portrayed marriage itself as a refuge against danger. In one of the most explicit symbolic repre-sentations of this fusion, *Life* magazine featured a newlywed couple about to descend into their own new bomb shelter just after their wedding. Under the boldface headline that proclaimed "Their Sheltered Honeymoon," a large photograph depicted the smiling young couple seated in front of their shelter, where they spent the next two weeks. Even their honeymoon was purposeful, setting the tone for what promised to be a life of usefulness. For, even in their newlywed bliss, they were advancing the cause of science and civil defense. As *Life* noted, "Mr. and Mrs. Melvin Minonson this month subjected their budding marriage to the strain of 14 days (the cru-cial period of fallout danger) of unbroken togetherness in a 22-ton, steel and concrete 8 × 11–foot shelter twelve feet underground. When they emerged last week the Minonsons were in fine spirits and the stunt had produced some useful evidence on underground survival."[17]

By coping with the threat of nuclear war through familiar and tangible realities such as Grandma's Pantry, a retreat to rural life, or home shelters, civil defense strategies served to tame fears of the atomic age by linking survival and security to traditional family values. In keeping with these val-ues, much of the postwar social science literature connected the functions of the family directly to the cold war. In one study funded by the Ford Foundation, two Harvard sociologists examined 60,000 "successful Ameri-can families" to determine what made them successful. Family success was defined in the study as the ability to keep children in school through high school. The reason for this concern was articulated by the authors:

> Early in January, 1957, Russia exploded an atomic bomb, and American scientists monitored its fallout of fission products. Non-stop simulated bomber flights in the upper atmosphere were now reported by the U.S. as traveling around the world in about forty-five hours. Trouble arose in the Middle East. Hungary broke into revolution. Then came Sputnik, space vehicles, ICBM's and crash programs for training more scientists. The world is like a volcano that breaks out repeatedly. . . . The world approaches this critical period with a grave disruption of the family system. . . . The new age demands a stronger, more resolute and better equipped individual. . . . To produce such persons will demand a reorganization of the present family system and the building of one that is stronger emotionally and morally.[18]

Here, we come to the heart of the concern, for it was not just the cold war that worried these professionals, but the "grave disruption of the family system." The key to successful families, the authors concluded, was moral homes in which men and women adhered to traditional gender roles. Even civil defense strategies infused the traditional role of women in the home with new meaning and importance, which would in turn help to fortify the homes as a place of security amid the cold war. In the ultimate chaos of an atomic attack, appropriate gender roles would presumably prevail. A 1950 civil defense plan put men in charge of such duties as fire fighting, rescue work, street clearing, and rebuilding, while women were to attend to child care, hospital work, social work, and emergency feeding. Above all, women, as professionalized homemakers, would fortify the home as a place of safety. In addition, parents should set good examples for their children, stay together and not divorce, and associate with like-minded families who shared common values and moral principles. Stable families conforming to respectable behavior held the key to the future. In keeping with the American tradition of republican motherhood, it was up to women to achieve successful families: if they fulfilled their domestic roles as adapted to the atomic age, they would be able to rear children who would avoid juvenile delinquency, stay in school, and become future scientists and experts to defeat the Russians in the cold war.[19]

So pervasive and lasting was the connection between fears of the atomic age and worries about disruptive sexuality that as late as 1972 a civil de-

Fig. 8.1. This illustration from a government civil defense pamphlet personifies dangerous radioactive rays as sexually flirtatious women. The pamphlet explained that "like energy from the sun, these rays are potentially both harmful and helpful." (Source: *Your Chance to Live*, Government Civil Defense Pamphlet, Defense Preparedness Agency, 1972, 79.)

fense pamphlet published by the government actually personified dangerous radioactive rays as sexy female "bombshells." The pamphlet made explicit the message that sexually liberated women were potentially destructive creatures who might, like atomic energy, be tamed and domesticated for social benefit. To illustrate the dangers of fallout, the authors wrote, "Radioactivity is also energy—but this time the rays come invisibly; alpha, beta, and gamma rays cause varying degrees of silent damage. Alpha's cannot penetrate, but can irritate the skin; betas cause body burns; and gammas can go right through you—and thus damage cells, which can make you ill, or kill you. Like energy from the sun, these rays are potentially both harmful and helpful" (fig. 8.1).

Beside this explanation was a drawing of the three "harmful and helpful" rays, personified as sexy and flirtatious women in seductive poses. The large-breasted bathing beauties wore ribbons across their torsos as if they were beauty queens, with the names "Alpha," "Beta," and "Gamma" emblazoned across each figure's chest. On the following pages of the pamphlet, other drawings indicated how to find safety by avoiding or containing these dangers: mom, dad, and baby huddled together in a home bomb shelter as chaos reigns above, and a detailed drawing of a well-equipped basement bomb shelter with "Home Sweet Home" tacked on the wall. Even though the fervor of the cold war had waned considerably by 1972, the images used as illustrations in this government pamphlet are powerful testimony to the symbolic connections among the fears of atomic power, sex, and women out of control.[20] In this vision of the atomic age family, women were the focus of concern: recognize their increasing sexual and economic emancipation but focus those energies within the family. Outside the home, they would yield a dangerous, destructive force. This subtle message was not so subtly expressed in the literature surrounding the cold war, civil defense, and the family.

These images were not confined to the civil defense literature but surfaced throughout the wider culture. Appropriately, during these years, a slang term for a sexy woman was a "bombshell." Although the term had been in use since the 1930s, female sexuality as a dangerous force found additional symbolic representation in World War II, when pilots named their bombers after their sweethearts and decorated their planes with erotic portraits. The wartime emergency called for fashion adaptations that would conserve fabric, giving rise to the two-piece bathing suit, which also appeared dangerous. The *Wall Street Journal* noted ominously that "the saving has been effected in the region of the midriff. . . . The difficulties and dangers of the situation are obvious." A photograph of Hollywood sex symbol Rita Hayworth was actually attached to the bomb dropped on the Bikini Islands. The island itself provided the name for the abbreviated swimsuit the female "bombshells" would wear. The designer of the revealing suit chose the name "bikini" to suggest the swimwear's explosive potential.[21] Similar images infused popular culture. Movies in the film noir genre portrayed more ominous visions of the destructive power of female sexuality. But this power was not so dangerous if it was contained and domesticated.[22]

In response, symbols of sexual containment proliferated in other areas as well. Even the female fashions of the fifties reflected that change. Gone was the look of boyish freedom that characterized the flapper of the twenties, along with the shoulder-padded strength that appeared in fashions of the thirties and early forties. Now quasi-Victorian crinolines and frills were back, along with exaggerated bust lines and curves which provided an aura of untouchable eroticism. Female sexuality was once again pushed into stays, girdles, and padded bras which pinched waists and elevated breasts. But the body itself was protected in a fortress of undergarments, warding off sexual contact but promising erotic excitement in the marital bed.[23]

In marriage, however, female sexuality could be safely unleashed, where it would provide a positive force to enhance family life. Domesticity would not only protect the public world from chaos; it would infuse the private world with excitement. It is no wonder, then, that professionals attempted to promote a vision of the family that would harness the social, sexual, and political dangers of the day.[24] At the same time, it appears that Americans at the time were not unresponsive to this prescriptive advise. One study of 300 postwar couples suggests that both sexes turned toward marriage as their own personal form of containment and that efforts to restrict sex to marriage may well have contributed to the drop in the marriage age during these years. Typical was the comment of one respondent who wrote, "The fact that we had been intimate, I am certain, made my mind set for marriage to him . . . made me feel I must marry this boy with whom I had been intimate." Another concurred: "Probably because I became sexually dependent on my wife before marriage was one of the reasons I married her, and also my guilty feelings toward a terminated pregnancy was another reason for marrying. However, neither of these two reasons were good ones for getting married."

Yet a study of over four thousand adults in the period found that the majority believed that people who did not marry were sick, immoral, selfish, or neurotic. Women in particular frequently viewed homemaking as a career, much as the experts advocated. Many saw their domestic role as having significance beyond the walls of their individual homes. As one woman in a postwar survey wrote of her decision to give up an outside career, "I think I have probably contributed more to the world in the life I have lived." Another former career woman wrote of her new position as wife and mother: "The new career is equally as good or better than the old." Many men in the same survey claimed that their families gave them a sense of purpose in their lives; some said it inspired them to hold religious and patriotic values. One respondent actually described his family in quasi–cold war terms: it provided "a sense of responsibility, a feeling of being a member of a group that in spite of many disagreements internally always will face its external enemies together."[25]

As the poll and survey data indicate, many undoubtedly believed in the formulas for successful family life expounded by experts. And no doubt

because of the Depression and war, many focused their wishes for affluence and security on the home. Yet, equally important, the continuing
anxiety surrounding women's changing sexual and economic roles helps
explain the unprecedented rush into family life and the baby boom of the
postwar era. Such concerns were reinforced by the rise of a domestic cold
war ideology and by the culture surrounding it as well. Stable family life
not only seemed necessary to national security, civil defense, and the
struggle for supremacy over the Soviet Union; it also promised to connect
the traditions of the past with the uncertainties of the present and the
future.

The postwar experts articulated these connections in concrete and symbolic terms. They expressed sentiments that were widely shared throughout
the population as a whole and gave substantial clues to what drove Americans into young marriage and pronatalism. Although further research is
necessary before we will fully understand the origins and implications of
this connection, it is clear that the ramifications are still with us today. For,
as the twentieth-century moral revolution revived in the sixties, traditional
gender roles and sexual mores once more came under attack. Reversing
the immediate postwar trends, the marriage age began to climb, the birthrate dropped, and premarital sex increased among youth. In addition, the
long-dormant feminist movement emerged as a powerful force, assaulting
the domestic ideology that had been prevalent since 1945. Nor did critics
of the postwar status quo fail to see the connection between this moral experimentation and its implicit questioning of cold war assumptions. To cite
one famous example, Stanley Kubrick, in his very successful film, *Dr.
Strangelove; or, How I Learned to Stop Worrying and Love the Bomb*,
equated the madness of the cold war with Americans' unresolved sexual
neuroses.[26]

It is also no accident that amid this attack on traditional sexual roles and
militant anticommunism, the Moral Majority emerged in the 1980s as a
powerful political force with the dual aim of reviving the cold war and re-
asserting the ideology of domesticity. The most vigorous opponent of the
Equal Rights Amendment, for example, was Phyllis Schlafly. Sounding
remarkably similar to Jean Fuller in the 1950s, Schlafly began her career as
an avid cold warrior and stated in 1983 that "the purpose of nuclear weapons is to protect lives." Her concerns move easily from attacking Henry
Kissinger for being too soft on communism, to opposing the ERA for its
alleged threat to the family, to pointing to herpes and AIDS as the most
recent form of punishment for sexual promiscuity. In essence, as the cold

war reaches new heights of reckless rhetoric in the 1980s, the incomprehensible is again reduced to the tangible. We have come full circle from Grandma's Pantry to four feet of backyard dirt as protection against a nuclear attack; from fire-fighting training for housewives to new civil defense home first-aid manuals, and from the call for penicillin in target areas to a new condemnation of female sexuality as leading to epidemic venereal disease. Although historians are still far from comprehending these complexities, it is clear that sex, women, and the bomb are still explosive issues.[27]

NOTES

1. Charles Walter Clarke, "Social Hygiene and Civil Defense," *Journal of Social Hygiene* 37, no. 1 (January 1951): 3–7.

2. The draft of Clark's article, along with Clarke's cover letter requesting comments, and the responses of those he surveyed, are contained in the file, "Walter Clarke, V.D. in Atom Bombed Areas, 1950," Papers of the American Social Hygiene Association, Social Welfare History Archives, University of Minnesota (hereafter cited as ASHA).

3. The literature on sexual concerns in the Progressive era is vast. Much of the material is summarized in Elaine Tyler May, *Great Expectations: Marriage and Divorce in Post-Victorian America* (Chicago: University of Chicago Press, 1980), chaps. 1–3. For the demographic trends of family life, see U.S. Department of Commerce, Bureau of the Census, *Historical Statistics of the United States, Colonial Times to 1970* (Washington, D.C.: Government Printing Office, 1975), pt. 1, 49, 54, 55, 64. For the historical implications of these trends, see Andrew Cherlin, *Marriage, Divorce, Remarriage* (Cambridge: Harvard University Press, 1981).

4. On the experts, see Joseph Veroff, Richard A. Kulka, and Elizabeth Douvan, *The Inner American: A Self-Portrait from 1957 to 1976* (New York: Basic, 1981), 194. The quote is from an unpaginated and undated clipping from *Look* magazine in the early fifties, in ASHA, box 94.

5. Joseph Veroff, Richard A. Kulka, and Elizabeth Douvan, *Mental Health in America: Patterns of Help-Seeking from 1957 to 1976* (New York: Basic, 1981), 8, 10, 226. Data on the frequency of consultation with professionals are from a survey done by E. Lowell Kelly, Kelly Longitudinal Study, Henry Murray Research Center, Radcliffe College, Cambridge, Mass.

6. Massachusetts Society for Social Health, Executive Committee Meeting Minutes, December 11, 1950; Minutes of Advisory Committee on Defense, January 19, 1951; List of Members of Executive Committee Advisory Committee on Defense Activities 1951–52; Memo to Committee members from Nicholas J. Fiumara, M.D., chair and director to MSSH, April 6, 1951—all in Massachusetts Society for Social Health Papers, MC 203, boxes 1 and 2, Schlesinger Library, Radcliffe College, Cambridge, Massachusetts (hereafter cited as Schlesinger).

7. Dorothy Thompson, "Race Suicide of the Intelligent," *Ladies Home Journal* 66, no. 5 (May 1949): 11. The article is in response to the address given by

Dr. Lewis M. Terman, a Stanford psychologist, to the International Council for Exceptional Children.

8. These prescriptions are in pamphlets and articles contained in ASHA, boxes 93, 94, 95. Mary Steichen Calderone Papers, box 1, file 1, Schlesinger. One poll taken by the *Ladies Home Journal* asked teenage boys about dating and sex. Most boys polled said they expected girls to set the limits. See "Sex Freedom and Morals in the United States," *Ladies Home Journal* (June 1949): 48, 89. See also Esther Emerson Sweeney, "Dates and Dating" (1958) ASHA, and "Behavior in Courtship," undated, unpaginated clipping from *Look* magazine—both in ASHA box 94. William F. Snow, "Marriage and Parenthood" (1949) pamphlet A542, 6, ASHA.

9. Jean and Eugene Benge, *Win Your Man and Keep Him* (Chicago: Windsor, 1948), 24; "Health for Girls" (1952) pamphlet A604, ASHA.

10. See Linda K. Kerber, *Women of the Republic: Intellect and Ideology in Revolutionary America* (Chapel Hill: University of North Carolina Press, 1980); Carl C. Zimmerman and Lucius F. Cervantes, *Successful American Families* (New York: Pageant, 1960), 12.

11. Jean Wood Fuller and Katherine Graham Howard, for example, worked extensively with other women in the Office of Defense Mobilization during the 1950s. See Howard Papers, A-64, and Fuller Papers, F-96, Schlesinger; Jean Wood Fuller, "Los Angeles Woman in Trench at A-Blast," *Los Angeles Times* (May 6, 1955): pt. 1, 2, in Fuller Papers, F-96, Schlesinger.

12. Fuller, "Wisdom is Defense," address before state meeting of Women in Civil Defense, Richmond Hotel, Augusta, Georgia, November 10, 1954, 2, 4, 6–8, Fuller Papers, F-96, Schlesinger. Criticism of the American Association of University Women is in the Fuller interview, Women in Politics Oral History Project, Berkeley, California: *Organizing Women: Careers in Volunteer Projects and Government Administration*, 218, Schlesinger.

13. Quote is from address to Dade Civil Defense Council, Miami, November 15, 1954, 2, 7, Fuller Papers, F-96; "By, For and About Women in Civil Defense: Grandma's Pantry Belongs in Your Kitchen" (Washington, D.C.: Government Printing Office, 1958).

14. Grandma's Pantry and the other civil defense crusades for women are discussed in the Fuller interview, Women in Politics Oral History Project, 189–91, 203–4B. Of course, many women and women's groups were for peace and advocated disarmament rather than civil defense. They, too, appealed to women's domesticity. See, for example, Dorothy Thompson, "We Live in the Atomic Age," *Ladies Home Journal* 63 (February 1946): 24–25; and Bruce Gould, "Last Trump," *Ladies Home Journal* 63 (January 1946): 6, which claims that women can save the world by love.

15. "Wonderful to Play In," *Time* February 5, 1951, National Affairs Section. See also "What Kind of Shelters?" *Architectural Record* January 1951; "Atomic Cave" *Time* September 11, 1950.

16. "Rural Areas Offer Escape from Nuclear Targets," *New York Times* April 21, 1950.

17. "Their Sheltered Honeymoon," *Life* (August 10, 1959): 51–52.

18. Quoted in Zimmerman and Cervantes, *Successful American Families*, 13.

19. Paul Boyer, *By the Bomb's Early Light* (New York: Pantheon, 1985), 311.

20. Defense Civil Preparedness Agency, *Your Chance to Live* (San Francisco: Far West Laboratory for Educational Research and Development, 1972).

21. Quote is from John Morton Blum, *V Was for Victory: Politics and American Culture during World War II* (New York: Harcourt Brace Jovanovich, 1976), 95; on the bikini, see Véronique Mistial, "Le Bikini a 40 ans," *Journal Français d'Amérique* 8, nos. 14–15 (July 4–31, 1986). The designer named the daring swimsuit four days after the Bikini test.

22. See, for example, Molly Haskell, *From Reverence to Rape: The Treatment of Women in the Movies* (New York: Holt, Rinehart and Winston, 1974), 189–211.

23. Susan M. Hartmann, *The Home Front and Beyond: American Women in the 1940s* (Boston: Twayne, 1982), 203–4. See also Lois Banner, *American Beauty* (New York: Knopf, 1983), chap. 13.

24. On atomic energy, see Boyer, *By the Bomb's Early Light*, chaps. 25, 26.

25. Quotes are from Kelly Longitudinal Study; Veroff, Douvan, and Kulka, *The Inner American*, 147.

26. The film created a storm of controversy, yet it broke records at the box office. See *Dr. Strangelove* file, New York Public Library Theater Arts Collection, Lincoln Center, New York. Demographic trends are documented in *Historical Statistics*, 49, 52, 54, 55, 64. On the rise of feminism, see Sara Evans, *Personal Politics: The Roots of Women's Liberation in the Civil Rights Movement and the New Left* (New York: Knopf, 1979).

27. See Carol Felsenthal, *The Sweetheart of the Silent Majority: The Biography of Phyllis Schlafly* (New York: Doubleday, 1981). See also Eileen Shanahan, "Antifeminist Says U.S. Helps Equal Rights Group," *New York Times* June 5, 1975, unpaginated clipping, Schlafly Biography File, Schlesinger. For the new civil defense propaganda, see Robert Scheer, *With Enough Shovels: Reagan, Bush, and Nuclear War* (New York: Random House, 1982). On herpes and the threat of promiscuity, see the cover story of *Time* magazine, August 2, 1982, which refers to herpes as "today's Scarlet Letter" and blames the epidemic on the Vietnam war, the sixties, and the "pill." The article contains subtle messages against the feminist movement and endorses motherhood while condemning "promiscuity." For an insightful analysis of the *Time* article, see Amy Wilents, "As *Time* Gloats By: Fanning the Herpes Scare," *Nation* 235, no. 10 (October 2, 1982): 298–300. A fuller exploration of the themes contained in this essay can be found in Elaine Tyler May, *Homeward Bound: American Families in the Cold War Era* (New York: Basic, 1988).

9 Ranch-House Suburbia: Ideals and Realities

Clifford E. Clark, Jr.

One of the most remarkable features of post–World War II America was the rise of an unprecedented consensus which saw affluence as the core of a new order. Politicians celebrated the new abundance, and, while intellectuals have often feared its conformist aspects, we have rarely looked at the cultural style surrounding the domestic revival and baby boom, the private aspirations that began to unfold in the new suburbias that sprang up all over the nation, filled with modern "ranch-style" houses. To many Americans, this remarkable house boom appeared at the time to be a reaffirmation of the American Dream of prosperity and security. In contrast to those who had defended bungalow houses during the 1920s and 1930s, which were pictured as a healthy, efficient, and simple antidote to the potential evils of a consumer society, the sponsors of the new housing boom argued that the ranch house represented the ultimate in "livability," "comfort," and "convenience." In house magazines and advice manuals in the 1950s, they asserted that it was now possible for middle-class Americans to fulfill their fondest hopes for a happy and secure family life. The 1950s housing crusade was thus a central part of a larger perfectionist impulse that swept through postwar American society. Like the crusade to halt the spread of communism and the belief that antibiotics would eliminate germs forever, the justification for the postwar housing boom was part of a one-dimensional frame of mind that stressed the possibility of creating the perfect society.[1]

For millions of middle-class Americans, this perfectionist vision of the family and home possessed immense power. Despite the cries of critics who saw the movement to the suburbs as evidence of a frightening rise in conformity, middle-class Americans took advantage of their new opportunities for home ownership to fulfill many of their long-sought-after desires. In the decade of the 1950s, before anxieties about affluence settled on them, middle-class Americans built upon these hopes to create a remarkably stable family structure. Yet, almost by definition, the perfectionist vision raised expectations too high, and by the end of the decade these same expectations had begun to erode the dream itself.

It is not surprising that the middle-class dream of establishing the ideal American family exerted such a powerful influence over the public consciousness in the 1950s. During the lean Depression years, when housing starts fell by over ninety percent, middle-class Americans had yearned for better homes and a more stable family life. The war years, with their drain on manpower, money, and resources, exacerbated middle-class frustrations. Two generations of Americans had scrimped and saved, postponing their hopes until the day when they could have better housing and a more relaxed and positive home life. Building-materials companies during the war, such as the Andersen Corporation, which produced windows, had fueled these hopes by selling scrapbooks for collecting ideas for future "dream houses." When the war ended in 1945 and more than 13 million servicemen and servicewomen returned home, therefore, it was not surprising to find an explosion of effort on the part of businessmen attempting to define a new American Dream of the perfect house and family.

This ideal vision of the house and family was first sketched in the advertisements of appliance makers and building-materials manufacturers in popular magazines such as *Life* and *Better Homes and Gardens* in the late 1940s and early 1950s. As part of their massive public campaign to sell products for the family and the home, they presented a new model of middle-class family life. At the center of this model was the image of the family as the focus of fun and recreation. Happiness came from raising happy, independent kids, decorating the home to one's own tastes, and sitting back in the evening with other family members and relaxing in front of the new TV set. Television, together with the ever-present radio, brought entertainment directly to the home and thereby reduced the necessity for getting out of the house often. Happiness came also from working together to improve the home, taking family vacations together, and enjoying the outdoor "patio" and backyard barbeque. Even the child-rearing advice columns in the magazines were designed to make marriages happier by reducing the anxiety involved in care of children.[2]

The second basic premise underlying the 1950s model of the ideal American family was the belief that family life was not static. Instead of the nineteenth-century view of the family, with its acceptance of large numbers of children and a relatively short life expectancy, social commentators and magazine advertisers pictured a conjugal unit that went through several stages. *Life* magazine explained to its readers that, during the average forty-year marriage, the family would first expand and then contract. The first two or three years would be childless and would be spent in a small apartment. Then would come the "crowded" phase, when the family bought a house and the average 2.17 children were born. During the "peak" years, defined as the period when the youngest child reached the age of seven, heavy demands would be placed on the parents and on their living quarters. But the last fifteen years of marriage would be spent together in a childless household. Even the classic sociological textbook on the family during this period—Clifford Kirkpatrick's *The Family as Process and Institution*—recognized the stages of family life in its title.[3]

The emphasis on happiness and the stage theory of family life put contradictory pressures on women in the 1950s that were reflected most clearly in the way women were depicted in magazine advertisements and on television. Single women were usually presented in beverage and cigarette advertisements as attractive, independent, and carefree—what Marshall McLuhan called the "frisky Coke-ad girl." Married women in the housemagazine advertisements, similarly, were often depicted as being creative and having fun. In contrast, married women in television family serials such as "I Love Lucy," "Ozzie and Harriet," and "The Honeymooners," often faced difficult and trying problems. Situation comedies made fun of the inept father whose harebrained ideas would have wrecked the family were it not for the common sense and hard work of the wife. Keeping the family together was a constant struggle.[4]

The common ideal that was supported by both television series and house magazines was the image of the efficient, hard-working wife who, whether she held a job outside the house or stayed at home, stabilized family life. But even this ideal was never consistently supported. Magazine advertisements, in particular, also occasionally depicted her, in the words of the National Advertising Review Board, as "stupid—too dumb to cope with familiar everyday chores, unless instructed by children, or by a man, or assisted by a man, or assisted by a supernatural male symbol," as with the advertisement for "Mr. Clean."[5]

This tension between self-sufficiency and ineptitude, which was expressed in Dr. Spock's contradictory emphasis on both personal self-reliance and professional expertise, placed women in an ambivalent position. As the decade of the 1950s wore on, the contradictory advertising images, together with the increasing number of women who were working outside the home, began to erode the image of the contented housewife. The contrast could be seen in *Life* magazine. When *Life* ran a special issue in

1956, entitled "The American Woman," Catherine Marshall insisted that her great achievements were not her job but her first date, her marriage, and her children. In "Love and Marriage," the editors insisted that the old-fashioned wife and mother, who was totally dedicated to her home and husband, and the "companion type" of wife being glorified in the movies and TV serials was being replaced by the new "career" woman, who would now be a full partner in marriage because her earnings would ensure "full and equal treatment."[6]

This shifting image of the ideal woman and the family in the 1950s was bound to influence the conception of the ideal home environment projected in the popular press. The household magazines not only suggested that with the right lawn tools and the latest cooking ranges the husband and wife could do a more professional job—special lawn mowers and never-fail cake mixes would take all chance of failure out of lawn work and baking—but they also insisted that a properly designed modern ranch house would solve the family's needs for work and recreation. Such specially designed homes could match the fun-loving companionate family's needs for a home environment that would be useful, convenient, and enjoyable.

From their beginnings in the 1930s to their enthusiastic promotion by home magazines in the 1940s and 1950s, ranch houses were identified with the new ideal of the family. The basic features of the ranch house—its simple, informal, one-story structure, its low-pitched eaves, its large expanse of glass, which included "picture" windows or "window walls"—were fused in the public mind with the easygoing lifestyle that was identified with the Southwest and the West Coast. When *Sunset* magazine reviewed a history of architect Cliff May's western ranch houses, it went out of its way to praise May's approach. "What made Cliff May exciting to anyone interested in those early days," wrote the editors, "was this drive to perpetuate ideas in livability rather than form and facade. His passion was not so much architecture as the way people wanted to live." May's houses were described as relaxed, comfortable, and casual. They were designed around a generous, open patio—the perfect complement to the informal family that loved the out-of-doors.[7]

Sunset magazine went even further and suggested that the ranch house was not so much a style as an "approach to living." One major feature of the ranch house was its low silhouette. The editors of *House and Garden* praised the low profile of one Oregon ranch house for the way in which it blended into the natural landscape. The house was both very "personal

Fig. 9.1. This ranch house, built in Bennington, Vermont, in 1956, was copied from plans in *Good Housekeeping*. (Photograph by Clifford E. Clark, Jr.)

and yet a thoroughly adaptable background for good living." Another magazine explained that the universal appeal of the ranch house was its simple, efficient look—"a long, low silhouette with a gentle sloping and overhanging roof sheltering the house against sun and rain." These popular house magazines invariably pictured the ranch house in a country landscape, overlooking a valley or nestled under the brow of a hill. (figs. 9.1, 9.2).[8]

A few designers saw the new ranch house as a healthy rebellion against the older compressed, boxlike bungalow house that had dominated house construction from the turn of the century until the 1930s. Although the

Fig. 9.2. This 1944 advertisement stressed the use of large picture windows to allow nature to be incorporated directly into the house. (Photograph courtesy of the Andersen Corp.)

Fig. 9.3. A semibungalow in the Tudor style, built in Milwaukee, Wisconsin, about 1910. (Photograph by Clifford E. Clark, Jr.)

bungalow was also essentially a one-floor design, it had been praised by architects and family reformers during its heyday as simple, efficient, and informal—a healthy antidote to its stuffy, cluttered Victorian predecessors. The bungalow, with its popular association with simple mountain cabins and summer homes, had been associated in the popular imagination with the healthy simplicity and self-control seen as necessary to withstand the allure of an overly commercialized society. The same values helped the bungalow remain popular during the Depression of the 1930s, when an ethic of scarcity and restraint seemed appropriate (fig. 9.3).

Where the shift from the Victorian house to the bungalow had been based on a wholesale rejection of previous popular designs, most advocates of the ranch house were less concerned about style and more interested in the function and convenience of the interior plan. As long as the house was handsome and had relatively little decorative detail, a variety of external styles was acceptable. As the authors of *Tomorrow's House* admitted in 1946, "even a poor architect has a hard time making a spreading, one-story house unattractive."[9]

In addition to having a low silhouette and rambling plan that made it fit well with the western landscape, the ranch house was also designed to allow Americans to recreate the California way of life elsewhere. Given the fascination with the West Coast and Southwest, which was reflected in the startling increase in the population of the Pacific states between 1940 and 1960, it was not surprising that Americans tried to duplicate the West Coast way of life in other parts of the country. By 1963, California had replaced New York as the number-one state in population. Many magazines not only praised the sunny openness of the California ranch house, with its inviting picture windows and large areas of glass, but they also explained how the new heating and cooling technologies would allow California ranch houses to be built anywhere in the country. Radiant heat with zone controls, porches with jalousie-type windows, and home air-conditioning systems would allow any American to enjoy a mild, temperate climate equivalent to that of the West Coast. Excessive heat and freezing cold could quickly be transformed by modern technology into a uniform zone of comfort. As the editors of *American Home* explained about a Detroit ranch house, "Mr. Rush said Mrs. Rush was the inspiration behind the interior planning—she, being a California gal whose dreams of a truly western ranch house with lots of refreshing color, was not deterred by the Michigan traditions of a somber house." Given the existence of cheap en-

ergy and the potential of the new technology, the ranch house could recreate a California environment anywhere.[10]

As a part of the attempt to sell the ranch house as a perfect place for
duplicating the California way of life, magazine designers and interior
decorators insisted that the ranch house established a new relationship between the house and nature. Reflecting on the changes that had taken
place in domestic architecture in the past thirty years, William Scheick, in
Parents' Magazine, suggested that the ranch house created an indoor-
outdoor unity that reflected the modern style of living. Large, insulated
plate-glass windows and the new "sliding glass walls" (called, by the 1960s,
sliding glass doors) made the seasons into an ever-changing wall decoration—a design feature that architect Philip Johnson extended to its logical
conclusion when he built his all-glass-walled house in New Caanan, Con-
necticut, in 1949. The interior walls of the house literally changed color
with the seasons and made nature a direct part of the home decor. Not
satisfied with the shifting scenery of the picture window, some interior
decorators designed photomural wallpapers that re-created the Rockies or a
seashore scene across an entire wall. These photomurals were often used in
doctors' offices that lacked windows.[11]

Given the high cost of house construction and the related reduction of
interior space, architects and magazine designers used patios, breezeways,
and, in the expensive houses, interior atriums to enhance the feeling
of ranch-house spaciousness. By building both house and patio on the
ground level, so that family members could come and go without stepping
up or down, the ranch-house designer helped create a sense of continuity
between the indoors and the outside. By removing the customary thresh-
olds and moldings that had traditionally marked the boundaries of rooms,
designers made patios appear to be outdoor extensions of indoor living
space. Where glass was the main component of the wall, ceiling beams or
walls were continued out into the yard to extend the interior and destroy
the feeling of barriers in the home. As one designer put it, such devices
make "the structure fraternize with nature" and create a sense of interior
and exterior unity.[12]

In the more expensive "Hallmark houses" in *House and Garden* and in
the Better Homes for All America series in *Better Homes and Gardens*,
various devices were used to mediate between the house and nature. In
addition to the ever-present patio, these magazines used pierced roof
beams over a recessed door to create a garden area at the house entrance
and a glass-walled interior atrium to bring a sense of nature inside the

house. Most often what resulted was a highly stylized version of nature. As one magazine put it, the entrance-area paintings were "simple, smart, just right for the setting." Since the typical ranch houses had low profiles, architects and decorators scaled down the natural world to fit them by using clumps of miniature birch trees, Russian olive bushes, and low-spreading yews. The ranch house was thus seen as creating a unity with nature, but it was a unity that pictured nature as a tamed and open environment. Like the technological re-creation of the temperate California climate, the 1950s designs conceived of the natural world in a simplified and controlled way that eliminated anything that was wild or irregular. Photographs of the suburban ranch house invariably showed a broad expanse of perfect lawn without weeds or dandelions.[13]

This fascination with nature, with its vision of the home nestled in a "natural setting," rested on the restorative vision of the natural world that had been inherited from the Progressive period with its preoccupation with national parks, boy scout and girl scout experiences, and healthy outdoor exercise. It also drew from the continuing traditional desire to avoid the grinding noise, dirt, and impersonality associated with cities. By living in a protected suburban environment, not only middle-class Americans but also, increasingly, upwardly mobile skilled workers hoped to restore a sense of peace and tranquillity to family life.

In addition to the access to nature and the long, rambling plan, another feature common to most ranch-house designs was separation of the interior into three different "zones": the housework center, the area of living activities, and the private area. Most architects urged builders of ranch houses to create a "utility core" of kitchen, bathrooms, and laundry at the center of the house for reasons of efficiency and convenience. The typical ranch house changed the kitchen from its earlier idea as hygienic service area into an attractive living space for the whole family. Kitchens were no longer relegated to the back of the house but were now placed to the front, often at the end of the house, where they could be entered directly from the garage. Kitchens were built in a U-shape, separated from other rooms only by a low counter. Because they were now open to the view of guests as well as of family members, kitchens also became the focus of decorators' attention. New tile and linoleum designs, pastel colors for stoves and refrigerators, and the use of brick walls and natural wood cabinets all helped to soften the austere lines inherited from the turn-of-the-century room. As the editors of *House and Garden* suggested, "instead of looking like a clinic, the kitchen is now a friendly, congenial common room."[14]

Convenience, efficiency, flexibility, and excellence were the terms most often applied to kitchen designs by magazine writers. The latest in cooking, refrigeration, and washing technologies were all used as sales pitches that would allow women to become better mothers. Not only could a woman now cook the perfect meal and wash the whitest clothes, but she could also get her housework done more quickly than her own mother had been able to do, thus allowing her to spend more time with the children. In extolling the benefit of the newly designed kitchen, some magazine writers, using terminology developed during the debate over the cold war, likened it to a military command post. By opening up the kitchen directly to the living room, designers allowed a woman to run the house without ever leaving the kitchen. She could cook a gourmet meal for guests and still talk with them as she prepared the food. Or she could do the laundry and still keep an eye on the children.

This new idea of the multipurpose kitchen was in keeping with the popular image of the multiple roles that needed to be played by women. Mothers, in the advice-book literature, were supposed to be jacks-of-all-trades: child psychologist, homemaker, cook, cleaner, and consultant on consumer products. For the increasing number of women who had outside jobs as well, the ranch-house kitchen, full of electric appliances, was absolutely necessary for accomplishing the many tasks that were expected of her.

The kitchen usually opened out into the second major "zone" of the house—the living and family room spaces. *Parents' Magazine* defended the need for "family" or "play" rooms as "don't-say-no" places for children and teenagers. Given the more permissive attitude toward child rearing encouraged by Dr. Spock and others, families felt that they needed a room where the children could play without disturbing the adults or threatening the furniture. In *House and Garden's* "House of Ideas," a model home built outside New York City in 1951 to exhibit the very latest in comfort, children were given a large space, divided by a partition, to play with their trains and Hopalong Cassidy cowboy clothes. Other designers insisted that the playroom be made of durable materials so that free play without rules would not be inhibited.[15]

Another reason for having a family or playroom in addition to the living room was to separate the world of the television from that of the adults, who might want to read or have some peace and quiet to themselves. The 1950s improvement in television and record-playing technologies—together with the surge in rock 'n' roll music and the emergence of a distinctive teenage culture—created a desire among parents to differentiate household functions. A separate family or playroom allowed the children to play their music or to engage in more active games with their friends without disturbing the other members of the house.

The remaining zone of the house consisted of the bedrooms and baths. As the home-building magazines made abundantly clear, the "private" areas of the house were to be just that—private. One mechanism for increasing the privacy of the suburban ranch house was to add more bathrooms. Even economy homes usually boasted of a second lavatory or half-bathroom for guests. Whereas the bungalow predecessors in the Midwest had placed a toilet in the basement for delivery men to use, the new ranch houses put a half-bath on the first floor and added a sink. In so doing, ranch houses made it easier to keep nonfamily members away from the occupants' own bathrooms and bedrooms. More expensive homes went one step further, adding a separate bathroom directly to the master bedroom. "Parents and children can have as much privacy as they like to concentrate on their separate interests," wrote one designer for *House and Garden*, implying that for all the rhetoric about families being together, there was also need to be alone.

Another magazine designer was even more candid about the need for private bedroom spaces. "Much as you may enjoy the friendliness of a house with a minimum of walls and a maximum of glass," he suggested, "there comes a time when everyone longs for privacy." The very openness of the ranch-house plan, with its emphasis on increasing the sense of spaciousness, meant that privacy was more difficult to find. Additional bathrooms and master-bedroom suites helped redress the balance between public and private.[16]

The other feature of the private area of the house—the bath and bedrooms—that was stressed in the magazine designs for ranch houses was the added amount of closet space. The increasing number of consumer goods, which ranged from board games such as Monopoly to clothes, created storage problems for many families in the 1950s. This problem was alleviated by using storage areas in the cellar or in the two-car garage that was connected directly to the house. But most homeowners demanded more built-ins, including wardrobes with sliding doors for business clothes and leisure wear.

What is clear from the flood of magazines promoting the suburban ranch house in the 1950s, with their endless pictures of built-in closets and "exciting" kitchens, was that the plans pictured did not aim simply to satisfy minimal housing needs. The plans were designed, as their predecessors had been, to create a new image of family life. In place of the more austere and antiseptic vision of the Progressive period, the ranch house was designed to facilitate a more comfortable existence. For the generations who had grown up with the ever-present legacy of Depression frugality, the new home stressed the pleasures of consumption—the emphasis on relaxation, children, and enjoyment. As television commercials suggested, now the family could have fun together, cooking hamburgers on its barbecue and playing catch in the backyard.

The constant emphasis on family rooms and master-bedroom suites in the magazine literature also implied the decreasing force of the older ideals of separate male and female spheres. In place of the nineteenth-century view of specialized spaces for each member of the family, a new vision of a more companionate marriage and a more interactive family had emerged. While the ideal was not fully realized and the father sometimes still had his workbench in the basement and occasionally a den, the nineteenth-century ideal of distinct male and female areas of the house had been significantly eroded. The space restraints of the ranch house together with the emphasis on family interaction created a positive vision of harmonious family life.

What was new about the image of the ranch house as the focus for family fun and relaxation was not that the ideal home would be a retreat from the hardships of the working world, which had been the view of the mid-nineteenth century. What was new was the glorification of self-indulgence. Convenience rather than style, comfort rather than some formal idea of beauty, became the hallmarks of the new designs. In 1956, one commentator on the changes in housing put it this way: "To the Average Family—that indescribable but extraordinarily powerful influence—the changes in housing over the last three decades would add up to something like this: thirty years ago they somehow had to fit themselves into the house, now the house is planned to fit them." Theoretically, then, the consumer was king. The housing industry, together with the appliance manufacturers and the house-design magazines, were now assuring the public that, for the first time in history, house designs reflected the desires of the people. Consumers would get exactly what they wanted. The perfect house was now within the reach of all middle-class Americans.[17]

In the decade of the fifties, the new construction techniques pioneered by William Levitt, the Long Island housing-tract developer, and others, together with the liberal loan policy which increased the Federal Housing

Administration's mortgage insurance commitments and lowered the down payments on FHA loans, resulted in an explosive surge in new construction. The volume of housing starts reached a record 1.65 million in 1955 and leveled off at over a million and a half for the rest of the decade. By the early 1960s, housing construction in the United States averaged $14 billion a year. Two-thirds of the construction consisted of private, one-family dwellings. The typical house had increased in size from nearly 800 to 1,240 square feet, sold for $14,585, and was a detached one-story home with three bedrooms, one-and-one-half baths, and a garage or carport. With the significantly increased availability of single-family housing, even working-class Americans were able to move to the suburbs in large numbers. Some families, like the Bernard Leveys on Long Island, changed homes the way they bought cars, purchasing a new model every year to take advantage of the latest changes in appliances and new features.[18]

To promote the thousands of new houses under construction, builders like William Levitt made lavish claims about the efficiency and convenience of the homes they built. The question was, Did the buyers like what they purchased? To what extent did the new suburban communities live up to the perfectionist assertions of their designers and builders?

Right from the start, some critics saw the new Levittown and Park Forest, Illinois, developments as potential disasters. A few planners argued that in the process of easing the housing shortage, the sheer volume of new homes put unacceptable pressures on schools, hospitals, and sewage facilities, creating a potential "slum of the future." "Nonsense," said Bill Levitt, and he blunted such criticisms in his subsequent housing development in New Jersey by providing schools, roads, water mains, and sewage plants so that the taxes of the home owners would be reduced and kept within manageable proportions. Since his firm used a comprehensive general plan, Levitt felt that his new communities were prototypes for the residential suburbs of the future.

But the critics remained skeptical. Sociologists, in particular, often saw the new housing developments as part of a creeping consumer conformity. Critical of the deluge of advertising which was appearing in the popular press, sociologist David Riesman published his best-selling book, *The Lonely Crowd,* which depicted the "other-directed" American as someone whose social radar was always focused on what others were doing. Although Riesman was careful to warn that no single person was completely "other-directed," many readers did not see the distinction. To them, most middle-class Americans seemed to be blindly following the herd instinct.

Vance Packard's *The Hidden Persuaders*, a biting critique of the advertising profession, and William H. Whyte's *The Organization Man*, an analysis of the conformist forces in the expanding corporate world of big business, also made Americans wary of excessive uniformity. Not surprisingly, then, other social critics were quick to add suburban housing developments to the long list of coercive and conformist institutions in modern society.[19]

The critique of suburbia pictured rows of identical houses, run by domineering wives, who were driven by spoiled children and absent husbands to the verge of mental breakdowns. In place of the house magazine's image of relaxed, informal, efficient home life, the social critics pictured loneliness, boredom, and despair. Commentators on contemporary architecture such as Lewis Mumford and Ada Louise Huxtable concurred. Mumford castigated the suburbs as "a multitude of uniform, unidentifiable houses, lined up inflexibly, at uniform distance, on uniform roads, in a treeless communal waste, inhabited by people of the same class, the same income, the same age group, witnessing the same television programs, eating the same tasteless pre-fabricated foods, from the same freezers, conforming in every outward and inward respect to a common mold." Huxtable agreed, adding that aesthetic disasters also produced social, cultural, and emotional problems for the people who lived there.[20]

So shrill and devastating were the attacks that even promoters like William Levitt were forced on the defensive. Writing in *Good Housekeeping*, Levitt admitted that mass-produced houses attracted younger families, exhibited some degree of uniformity, and encouraged a somewhat conformist behavior. His early developments had clear rules about when wash could be put out on the line (not on Sunday) and how often the grass should be cut. But he denied that there was any lack of privacy and asserted that the people who lived in housing developments were neither dull nor conformist. "Houses are for people, not critics," he asserted somewhat defensively. "We who produce lots of houses do what is possible—no more— and the people for whom we do it think that it's pretty good."[21]

A closer examination of the suburban housing developments by other sociologists, survey teams for house magazines, and the federal government showed that neither the defenders nor the critics were entirely accurate in their assertions about suburbia. The suburban ranch houses were neither the disasters the critics predicted nor the utopias that the promoters hoped for. In fact, careful surveys of new home buyers done by the federal government's Housing and Home Finance Agency in 1950 and by *Better*

Homes and Gardens in 1955 reveal that the reasons for the purchase of a single-family dwelling were more complex than either the promoters or the detractors had anticipated.

According to these surveys, two different kinds of families bought houses in the years 1949 and 1950. Nearly half of the home buyers were veterans of World War II. They were a younger group, whose median age was thirty-five, who had young children and had run out of space in their apartments. Dissatisfaction with the rental market, the desire for more independence and privacy, the ease of obtaining loans, and the belief that home ownership was a good investment prompted this younger group to buy its first houses. Buoyed by the expanding economy and confident that their future income prospects were good, these families decided to buy, usually in a new suburban development. When asked why they had moved, the "need for more space," "comfort and roominess for family members in a new house," and "privacy and freedom of action in owned home" were the reasons most often given. Contrary to the perfectionist visions put forth by architects and home magazines, the inadequacies of their previous housing were more important precipitants of the decision to buy than the emphasis on convenience or the lure of the new designs. As one interviewer confirmed, the increased space of the new home was the primary reason for its purchase.[22]

The other largest group of buyers in the 1950 housing market was made up of older families, whose median age was forty-five. Many of these families also moved from a previously owned house because the space was inadequate and their family needs had changed. Others preferred the quiet of being further from the central city or moved because of a change in job. This group had higher incomes, which allowed them to purchase more expensive homes on larger lots. Together with the younger families of the veterans, these home buyers helped fuel a massive exodus from the cities that was to increase suburban growth by more than fifty percent during the decade.[23]

When asked why they bought the particular house that they had, most buyers made a startling admission. They were forced to compromise their goals because of price and location. Most buyers wanted a larger lot, for more privacy, than the 11,000 square feet that was the median that year. Most also wanted a house with more than the 983 square feet that was the average of those being built and which represented a twelve percent *decrease* from the average size in 1940. Given this desire for more space, four buyers out of ten in 1950 were dissatisfied with the number of rooms in their new homes. Most wanted three bedrooms and were forced to compromise with two.

But not all deletions from the design of earlier homes were missed. For custom-built, two-story houses, the Federal Housing Administration recommended that the stairway be moved from the traditional central hall to a position between the kitchen and the living room. "Unnecessary traffic through the living room to reach the stairs thus is avoided," the federal housing authorities suggested. "Travel up and down stairs is given privacy from the living room, and vice versa." Certain areas of the ranch house—particularly the bedrooms—were to remain less accessible to outsiders.[24]

Despite the claims of the critics, therefore, that there was no consideration for privacy in the new rambler houses and that the big picture window served only to display the latest items for consumption, the 1950s ranch house retained the traditional nineteenth-century distinction between public and private spaces. The major difference was that kitchens, once considered private spaces, were redefined as public areas. As such, they now needed to be integrated into the decorative scheme of the house. For those who really desired privacy, the bedrooms and the bathroom, especially the separate bathroom attached to a master-bedroom suite, remained the most secluded areas.

From the federal government surveys done in the 1950s, therefore, it is evident that a major gap existed between the homebuyers' expectations and what they were able to afford. Larger rooms and more of them, larger lot sizes, porches, and more storage space were high on most buyers' lists. But builders were unable to supply these features at a cost that the average middle-class buyer could afford. Nevertheless, most home purchasers were more than satisfied with their new houses. And why should they not have been? Small though the houses were, they were still a good deal larger than the apartments in which most people had been living.

The satisfaction with the new suburban ranch houses came through most clearly when sociologists moved directly into the mass-produced middle-class suburbs and lived there, talking to the people and participating in community life. Although the development houses sometimes appeared to outsiders as monotonous, treeless wastes, those who lived there thought otherwise. "We're not peas in a pod," a mother with two children in a midwestern suburb told one interviewer. "I thought it would be like that, especially because incomes are nearly the same. But it's amazing how different and varied people are. . . . I never really knew what people were like until I came here." [25]

People in the new suburbs tried to retain their distinctive identities in several ways. They often customized the houses by adding a porch, garage, or new room. At other times, they sited the house on the lot differently. When the Delong family built a new house in Bennington, Vermont, in 1956, for example, they took the plans directly from *House and Garden* but reversed the house so that the main picture window looked out over the mountain valley in the distance instead of at the road. Other families individualized their houses through interior decoration.

Although the furniture that the family purchased was often modeled after what they had seen in the popular housing magazine, the large number of choices meant that the interior could be adapted to an enormous array of tastes. As one interviewer admitted, "In hundreds of houses I never saw two interiors that matched—and I saw my first tiger-striped wallpaper." In fact, most home owners believed that choosing the correct color and decorative scheme was one of the most important decisions that they would have to make. When the editors of *House and Garden* did a survey in 1955, entitled "The New House Next Door," they found that families ranked choosing the appropriate color scheme from a sparkling array of new, colored appliances, furnishings, and household accessories as the most frustrating problem in home decoration. Hours could be consumed in looking for wallpaper and trying to match colors. [26]

A second reason why people so easily accepted the mass-produced houses was that they considered their purchase as merely their "first" houses. Given the young age of many of the families in 1955—men averaged thirty-one years, women about twenty-six—most looked forward to increased buying power in later years. In the middle-class suburbs, where fifty percent of the men were college graduates, business transfers and increasing incomes made housing turnovers high. As one man told an interviewer, "After all, this is only the first wife, first car, first house, first kids— wait 'til we get going." [27]

A third reason for the widespread middle-class acceptance of mass-produced housing was that seventy percent of the new home buyers had held back enough money to make improvements as soon as they moved in. Some added a porch or an extra room. Others modified a bathroom or rearranged a kitchen. Still others added to the heating and cooling or the piping and wiring. Physically changing the house helped ease their discontent and preserved their hope that if the house was not all they wanted, they would be able to make further modifications in the future that would make it more acceptable.

Despite the obvious physical limitations of the houses, the optimism of 1950s home buyers was justified. By 1955, when *Better Homes and Gardens* did another national survey, the number of homes being built with six or more rooms had increased by six percent, and more than half of all new houses had three bedrooms. Substantial numbers of families were now willing to trade off a separate dining room for a combination living-dining room *and* kitchen eating area. The number of porches built had increased slightly, and, most significantly, the floor area for houses costing under $10,000 had increased from 983 square feet to 1,100.

How had the space in these houses been increased despite the inflation in building-material costs? The startling answer was that sixty-two percent of all home buyers now did some of the construction work themselves. A surprising twenty-three percent did all or most of the work themselves. The do-it-yourself movement had reached the stage where it had a substantial effect on middle-class housing.

The other feature of new suburban housing developments that made them attractive to the home buyers despite the limitations of the houses was their obvious separation from the congestion of the nearby city. Suburban home owners clearly wanted to leave the noise and insecurities of the urban metropolis. In this desire, they were substantially aided by the tremendous increase in highway development that was spurred by the $100 billion Interstate Highway Act of 1956. The rapid construction of new roads together with a massive increase in automobile ownership helped reinforce the suburbs' image as a haven of peace and safety. The middle-class image of the suburbs as a peaceful refuge was further reinforced by the use of restricted covenants to exclude blacks and other minorities, who were identified, through newspaper coverage, with urban crime and disorder. But perhaps the most important factor "pushing people to the suburbs," wrote the editors of *House and Garden*, "is the desire of families for elbowroom—the desire to get away from it all, where life is more informal, where there is plenty of yard room for the children, and where they can enjoy a maximum of outdoor living."[28]

The overwhelming evidence thus points to the fact that suburban home owners in the 1950s substantially accepted the perfectionist theories about family life and domestic architecture that were being promoted by the house magazines and family experts. To a greater extent than had been the case in 1880 or 1910, the new ideal of a relaxed, informal family life, with its emphasis on outdoor activities and its stress on enjoyment and personal satisfaction, was incorporated into the personal ideals of the suburbanites. To the older ideal of house as refuge they fused the new vision of the home as a center for recreation. Even when commuting to work for half an hour or more, which was the case in most of the larger suburban developments, meant that the husbands actually had *less* time to spend with their children than before, people in the suburbs argued that living in the new community had improved their family lives.[29]

Nevertheless, while the perfectionist ideal of the perfect home and family appealed to the middle-class suburbanites in the 1950s, home buyers, when they faced the reality of choosing among different housing alternatives, realized that their perfectionist dreams could never be completely fulfilled. Few families had the financial means to purchase the houses that they most wanted. Still, the tremendous surge of new building meant that middle-class Americans, if not attaining all that they wished, still substantially improved their family and home life. For a society that has never been completely content with what it had, this achievement was enough, at least until the end of the decade, to satisfy all but the most outspoken critics. No one in the 1950s clung more tightly to the American Dream than middle-class suburban Americans.

NOTES

1. For a more detailed account of the development of suburban-housing ideals, see Clifford E. Clark, Jr., *The American Family Home* (Chapel Hill: University of North Carolina Press, 1986), chaps. 7, 8; Benjamin DeMott, *Surviving the 70's* (New York: Dutton, 1971); Roland Stromberg, *After Everything: Western Intellectual History since 1945* (New York: St. Martin's, 1975); Paul A. Carter, *Another Part of the Fifties* (New York: Columbia University Press, 1983); William Leuchtenberg, *A Troubled Feast: American Society since 1945* (Boston: Little, Brown, 1973); Richard Polenberg, *One Nation Divisible: Class, Race, and Ethnicity in the United States since 1938* (New York: Penguin, 1980); Robert Wiebe, *The Segmented Society: An Historical Preface to the Meaning of America* (New York: Oxford University Press, 1975); Godfrey Hodgson, *America in Our Time: From World War II to Nixon* (New York: Doubleday, 1976); Robert Fowler, *Believing Skeptics* (Westport, Conn.: Greenwood, 1978), 4; Joseph B. Mason, *History of Housing in the U.S. 1930–1980* (Houston: Gulf, 1982), 46, 61.

2. Bruce W. Brown, *Images of Family Life in Magazine Advertising*, (Ph.D. diss., University of New Hampshire, 1979); Robert Coughlan, "How to Survive Parenthood: Theories on How to Raise Children Have Come Full-Circle as Parents Get Neurosis-Neurosis Wondering What to Do with and to the Kids," *Life* 28 (June 26, 1950): 113–26.

3. "Statistics of Average U.S. Marriage and Family," *Life* 29 (July 10, 1950): 43; Clifford Kirkpatrick, *The Family as Process and Institution* (New York: Ronald, 1955).

4. Billie Joyce Wahlstrom, "Images of the Family in the Mass Media," in *Changing Images of the Family*, ed. Virginia Tufte and Barbara Myerhoff (New Haven: Yale University Press, 1979), 193–227.

5. Brown, *Images of Family Life*, 69–77; Wahlstrom, "Images of the Family in the Mass Media," 26.

6. "The American Woman," *Life* 41 (December 24, 1956): 2; "Love and Marriage," *Life* 51 (September 8, 1961): 114.

7. "The Story of the Western Ranch House," *Sunset* 121 (September 1958): 74; "Eastward Ho: California Home Styles Invade the Rest of U.S.," *Life* 32 (March 17, 1952): 131–32.

8. "What's Happened to that Easy-going Western Favorite . . . The 'Ranch House'?" *Sunset* 112 (February, 1955): 54–59; "From the Rancho: A Contemporary Style," *Life* 40 (January 16, 1956): 58–59; "This Oregon Ranch House Lives as Well as it Looks: P. L. Menafe House near Yamhill," *House and Garden* 95 (March 1949): 104–11. "The Oregon Ranch House on the Cover . . ." *Sunset* 111 (September 1954): 56–57.

9. Will Melhorn, "Ranch Houses Suit Any Climate," *House Beautiful* 89 (January 1947): 66; "A Clean and Handsome Example of the West's 'Ranch House,'" *Sunset* 110 (April 1953): 74–75; George Nelson and Henry Wright, *Tomorrow's House* (New York: Simon and Schuster, 1956); "From the Rancho: A Contemporary Style," *Life* 40 (January 16, 1956): 58.

10. "It's Roomy, Ranchy and Buildable on a 54 Foot Lot: J. L. Rush House, Detroit," *American Home* 44 (November 1950): 147.

11. William H. Scheick, "What's Happened to Housing in the Last 30 Years," *Parents' Magazine* 31 (October 1956): 67.

12. "What's Been Happening to That Easy-Going Western Favorite . . . the 'Ranch House,'" *Sunset* 112 (February 1958): 56–58; Elizabeth Gordon, "Exploding the Box to Gain Spaciousness," *House Beautiful* 101 (October 1959): 256–58.

13. "How to Choose a Good One-level House," *Better Homes and Gardens* 41 (May 1963): 115–16; "Total Environment That Fosters a New Pattern of Living," *House and Garden* 119 (January 1961): 64–75; "Ranch House with One Open Wall . . ." *Sunset* 113 (September 1954): 83.

14. "House of Ideas," *House and Garden* 100 (July 1951): 51–52; J. Brenneman, "Modern Simplicity," *Ladies Home Journal* 76 (August 1959): 96.

15. Scheick, "What's Happening to Housing in the Last 30 Years," 93; "House of Ideas," 48–49.

16. J. D. Bloodgood, "Better Homes for All America—Plan No. 3309-A," *Better Homes and Gardens* 42 (March 1964): 40–43; "Total Environment That Fosters a New Pattern of Living," *House and Garden* 119 (January 1901); "House of Ideas," 45.

17. Scheick, "What's Happened to Housing in the Last 30 Years," 93.

18. Mason, *History of Housing*, 62; "Levitt Adds 1950 Model to His

Line," *Life* 28 (May 22, 1950): 141–47; "U.S. Building Boom Hits New Peak," *Life* 28 (March 20, 1950): 27–33; *Time* (July 3, 1950): 69.

19. *Time* (July 3, 1950): 69; Herbert Gans, *The Levittowners* (New York: Pantheon, 1967), 16–17; David Riesman, *The Lonely Crowd* (New Haven: Yale University Press, 1950), 19–23.

20. Lewis Mumford, *The City in History* (New York: Harcourt, Brace, 1961), 486; Ada Louise Huxtable, "'Clusters' Instead of "Slurbs,'" *New York Times Magazine* (February 9, 1964): 10, 37; Scott Donaldson, *The Suburban Myth* (New York: Columbia University Press, 1968), 60–77; Gans, *The Levittowners*, xvi.

21. William J. Levitt, "What! Live in a Levittown?" *Good Housekeeping* 147, no. 1 (July 1958): 47, 175–76.

22. Housing and Home Finance Agency, "What People Want When They Buy a House: A Guide for Architects and Builders" (Washington, D.C.: U.S. Department of Commerce, 1955), 5–7; Gans, *The Levittowners*, 31–41; Richard Polenberg, *One Nation Divisible* (Harmondsworth: Penguin, 1980), 128–29.

23. Polenberg, *One Nation Divisible*, 128.

24. Housing and Home Finance Agency, "What People Want," 23–25, 35–36, 46.

25. Ibid., 54.

26. Harry Henderson, "The Mass-Produced Suburbs. I. How People Live in America's Newest Towns," *Harper's* 30 (November 1953): 26.

27. Henderson, "The Mass-Produced Suburbs," 26; Better Homes and Gardens; *The New House Next Door 1955*, (Des Moines: Meredith, 1955), 10.

28. Henderson, "The Mass-Produced Suburbs," 27–29, 31.

29. Better Homes and Gardens, *The New House Next Door 1955*, 8, 12, 16, 23.

PART FOUR

The Search for Alternatives:
Art, Minorities,
and Popular Culture

10 *The Art of Cultural Politics: From Regionalism to Abstract Expressionism*

Erika Doss

During the 1940s, a remarkable shift occurred in American art from the anecdotal art of regionalism to the nonobjective art of abstract expressionism. Enormously popular throughout the Depression, the narrative pictures of such premier regionalist painters as Thomas Hart Benton were soundly denounced in the 1940s. Indeed, in 1946 art historian H. W. Janson equated regionalist art with Nazi art, claiming regionalism "has been nourished by some of the fundamental ills of our society—the same ills that in more virulent forms, produced National Socialism in Germany."[1] While regionalism was condemned as isolationist, parochial, and conservative, the nonobjective art of abstract expressionism was lauded as a sophisticated, innovative, and modern art. In 1945, critic Clement Greenberg praised Jackson Pollock as "the strongest painter of his generation and perhaps the greatest one to appear since Miro."[2] How did such a major shift, from narrative to nonobjective art, occur? Why did Jackson Pollock, who was Benton's foremost student in the early 1930s, reject the regionalist style of his mentor and move toward abstract expressionism?

Thomas Hart Benton is recognized as perhaps the foremost painter of his generation. Certainly, during the later 1920s and throughout the Depression, Benton was regarded as an important artist, a regionalist who painted dynamic murals seemingly representative of American life and legend. The members of the so-called regionalist triumvirate—Benton, John Steuart Curry, and Grant Wood—gave Depression-era audiences pictures of what seemed to be ordinary, everyday Americana: stoic farmers (Wood's 1930 *American Gothic*), a country christening (Curry's 1928 *Baptism in Kansas*), and men at work (Benton's 1930–31 mural panel *City Building*—fig. 10.1). Aimed at widespread public popularity, regionalism became a leading style of art during the Depression. Benton and other artists were adamant about creating a uniquely American art, an art intelligible and meaningful to all. Within this narrative and anecdotal framework, Benton especially promoted in his regionalist pictures an energetic America of

Fig. 10.1. Benton's vision of a reconstructed American scene celebrated the producer tradition. The artist himself is seen reading a blueprint in the lower right-hand corner. *City Building*, 1930 (from the America Today mural). Distemper, egg tempera, and oil glaze on linen, 92″ × 117″. (Courtesy of the Equitable Life Assurance Society, New York.)

workers, on the land and in the cities, driven to better themselves and their country.

In the 1940s, a very different kind of art emerged. In the previous decade, Jackson Pollock had worked in a regionalist manner while studying under Benton. By the end of the Depression, however, Pollock largely rejected Benton's style, in particular its subject matter and figure-ground relations, to concentrate on abstract expressionism. By the mid-1940s, Pollock, like Clyfford Still and Arshile Gorky, pioneered an improvisational painting style characterized by its thick, gestural application of paint, its ambivalent spacial relations, and its emphasis on aesthetic experimentation. Markedly dissimilar to his regionalist art, Pollock's abstract art was based on a personal and private aesthetic. In the nonobjective, poured paintings of the later 1940s and the 1950s, such as *Autumn Rhythm* (1950—fig. 10.2), Pollock revealed his primary concerns with the art-making process and with personal expression and made major contributions to the avant-garde style of abstract expressionism.

Much of the analysis of the shift to abstract art in postwar America has focused on the style's formal development. In 1944, Pollock made a since oft-quoted remark about his former teacher. When asked how his studies with Benton in New York in the early 1930s had affected him, Pollock replied, "My work with Benton was very important as something against which to react very strongly, later on; in this, it was better to have worked with him than with a less resistant personality."[3] Armed with this quote, art critics and historians after World War II suggested that the stylistic shift from Depression regionalism to postwar abstract expressionism was simply one of generational progress. Pollock "progressed" from the figurative and narrational art of his mentor to a gestural art of abstraction. He expanded on the rhythmic contours and vivid palette of his teacher's Americana anecdotes but rejected the content of regionalist art. His formal innovations, like those of other postwar abstract artists, were termed "breakthroughs," and their art was heralded as the "triumph of American painting."[4]

More recently, historians have turned away from this reading of abstract

Fig. 10.2. Pollock's abstract expressionist drip paintings expressed his alienation from postwar consensus culture. *Autumn Rhythm*, 1950. Oil on canvas, 105″ × 207″. (Courtesy of the Metropolitan Museum of Art, George A. Hearn Fund, 1957.)

art and have begun to examine the historical circumstances which led to its postwar triumph. Serge Guilbaut, for example, ties the postwar dominance of avant-garde abstract expressionism to its use as a "weapon against totalitarianism" by various cultural and political entities, remarking, "Avant-garde art succeeded because the work and the ideology that supported it, articulated in the painters' writings as well as conveyed in images, coincided fairly closely with the ideology that came to dominate American political life after the 1948 presidential election."[5] This ideology was inherent, Guilbaut explains, in the concept of "freedom," which became "the symbol most actively and vigorously promoted by the new liberalism in the Cold War period." For many, abstract expressionism became the perfect "expression of freedom: the freedom to create controversial works of art, the freedom symbolized by action painting, by the unbridled expressionism of artists completely without fetters."[6]

That the aesthetics of regionalism were formally expanded and revised within the abstract expressionist camp is an accurate analysis, as is Guilbaut's assessment of cold war ideology and its effect on postwar culture. What is of equal importance, however, and certainly merits further attention, is the simple fact that regionalism was a dominant style of American art throughout the Depression and yet failed to maintain its popularity after the Second World War. Neither interpretations which chart the internal, formal development of abstract expressionism nor those which focus on an external cause such as the cold war adequately explain this change from one leading style to the next. What is needed is an exploration of this radical shift in art in the context of a major cultural transition in the forties. To explore that generational shift, this study will examine the careers of Benton and Pollock. The choice of these two artists is not accidental: each was the major painter of the era, and Benton was, for a while, Pollock's mentor and close friend.

Perhaps the most important influence affecting the art of the 1930s and the 1940s was politics, not as party tactics or organization but as a set of cultural beliefs. Thomas Hart Benton, for instance, devoted his life to painting with the same kind of fervor his father, a U.S. attorney and congressman, and his great-uncle and namesake, the Missouri senator and statesman, had devoted to ninteenth-century politics. Born in Neosho, Missouri, in 1889, Benton was raised in an atmosphere of reformist political ideology. "Politics was the core of our family life," he noted in his 1937 autobiography, where he fondly recalled breakfasts with William Jennings Bryan and torchlight parades in support of free silver.[7] Exposure to his father's version of midwestern populism, that turn-of-the-century political movement which sought public control ("the hands of the 'plain people'") and government reform to regulate an increasingly corporate economy, certainly cultivated Benton's interest in creating art for the people.[8] Later, he would write, "I had been raised on the idea that the big capitalist monopolies, centered in New York, were against the 'people's' interests," and would even call himself a populist artist.[9]

During the mid-nineteenth century, the key figure in the burgeoning antislavery, free-labor organization of the Republican Party was the individualistic American entrepreneur, the small-scale farmer and businessman.[10] Benton's great-uncle and father (although elected to their political posts as Democrats) were committed to a "free-soil, free-labor" America, a nation where economic advancement occurred through labor mobility and equality, not corporate control. To the Benton clan of the nineteenth century, the potential for progressive reform in America was tied directly to an anti-aristocratic, anti-big-business society, where individual workers determined their own economic development and perpetuated a Jeffersonian sort of democracy.[11] Raised on this sociopolitical program, Benton, in his artwork, glorified a reformist producer tradition.

Benton's commitment to a public art of reform was further shaped by other ideas and other encounters. During the 1910s, he pondered Hippolyte Taine's *Philosophie de l'art* (1875) and was greatly impressed by the author's sociocultural and environmentalist theories: "Except for samplings of John Ruskin's works, this was the first philosophical treatise on the Arts I had ever read. . . . Revealing the close ties of the older arts to specific social backgrounds and cultures, it made me question many ideas about art."[12] And, in New York, immediately before World War I, Benton joined John Weischel's People's Art Guild, an organization "designed to bring art to the workers" through settlement-house art shows and classes. Through Weischel, Benton later recalled, he was introduced to Prudhon and Marx, and "ideas about the social meanings and values of art were germinated. . . . They were to bear fruit later."[13] Populism, Taine, Weischel, and Marx all conditioned Benton's aesthetic ambitions in the 1920s and 1930s: that art "regain a more purposeful place in society" and that it demonstrate either a need for or a confirmation of a certain "democratic idealism."[14]

If the overall impulse of Benton's regionalism was determined by his response to reformist politics and social concerns, the style of his art emerged from his assimilation of modern painting and contemporary popular culture. As an art student in Paris from 1908 to 1911, Benton dallied with the stylistic innovations of neo-impressionism, fauvism, and cubism, all of which became essential elements in the formal montage of his regionalist art.[15] Collage compositions, with awry perspectives and brilliant colors, characterize Benton's regionalist version of modern American art. But, uncomfortable with the abstraction of European modernism, Benton spent the years before World War I searching for subject matter to suit his emerging style. Later, he would write that following the much publicized Armory Show of 1913, he and other regionalists began to object to "the new Parisian aesthetics which was more and more turning away from the living world of active men and women into an academic world of empty patterns. We wanted an American art which was not empty, and we believed that only by turning the formative processes of art back again to meaningful subject matter, in our cases specifically American subject matter, could we expect to get one."[16]

The "meaningful subject matter" of Benton's regionalism was tied to political and social reform. He learned how such subject matter became "meaningful" during a five-year apprenticeship designing movie sets and painting backdrops for the Fox and Pathé movie studios in New York and New Jersey. From 1913 to 1918, Benton obtained such work through his roommate, Rex Ingram (destined for fame as the director of the 1921 film *The Four Horsemen of the Apocalypse*).[17] Movies, then and now, rely on a language of typology: the blonde, the cowboy, the Kansas farm, the Manhattan penthouse, are visual elements used to guide audience expectations. The movies Benton worked on, western shoot-'em-ups and two-reel melodramas, consisted of easily recognizable images in a narrational format. Further, the disjointed, fast-paced editing of these early movies aided in their appeal to their audiences.[18] As a participant in the creation of this new form of mass communication, Benton learned the parlance of popular culture. He relied on its methodology when he began creating art. The enormous size of the flats and movie backdrops he worked on from 1913 to 1918 led directly to his first Regionalist series, The American Historical Epic, which he worked on from 1920 to 1926. These mural-sized panels (the painterly equivalent of movie screens) were the beginnings of his regionalist style: dynamic "formal experiments" inlaid with a "social meaning, a cultural meaning, one attached to the United States."[19]

Benton called his epic a "people's history." A survey of American settlement and confrontation, the panels depict stereotypical pioneers and Indians, missionaries and soldiers. In painting generalized figures, not specific personalities, Benton emphasized the commonality of American history.

He tried to give a broadly democratic view of the making of a civilization: "I tried to show that the people's behaviors, their *action* on the opening land, was the primary reality of American life." [20] The series was Benton's ambitious interpretation of America's past. But, it was even more encompassing, for he aimed also to show how Americans had become "increasingly separated by advancing civilization and technology from the benefits of their settlements." [21]

During the 1930s, Benton's art continued to focus on the American people. More specifically, Benton promoted a revival of a worker-determined economy in the wake of what he perceived (and the Depression made clear) was the failure of corporate leadership. Much of Benton's Depression art was largely an attack against the consequences of a de-humanized organization of American life. He did not so much pine for a pre-industrialized America as he, like the Progressive politician of an earlier era, tried to "keep the benefits of the emerging organization of life and yet to retain the scheme of individualistic values that this organization was destroying." [22] Further, like nineteenth-century politicians who were as suspicious of aristocratic rule as they were of big business, Benton was opposed to elitism in American culture. A frequent critic of the "ivory tower boys and girls" of New York's art world, Benton blasted these "highbrowish disciples" and their reluctance to accommodate the "popularist leanings" of his art. [23] He was determined that his art be public art "which reflected the American people's life and history in a way which the people could comprehend." [24] Public accessibility was essential because Benton was determined that his regionalist art bear a liberal, progressive message to the American people.

Expected by his family to become a lawyer and eventually a reform politician, Benton chose art making. With regionalism, he continued the progressive political activism of his heritage and promoted the reform-oriented politics of the New Deal. Benton made the connection between his art and 1930s liberal politics in a 1951 essay: "Regionalism was . . . very largely affirmative of the social exploration of American society and resultant democratic impulses on which President Roosevelt's New Deal was based. The artistic projects of the New Deal were largely sparked by attitudes already affirmed by Wood, Curry, and myself. Roosevelt's early social moves were, as I have said, overwhelmingly Americanist and were concentrated on the solution of specifically American problems. This Americanism found its aesthetic expression in Regionalism." [25] An artist with a profound political and social conscience, Benton sincerely believed in the efficacy of both New Deal politics and regionalist art to facilitate sweeping social change in America. In his regionalist art of the 1930s, Benton transferred his personal politics into public art and thus, he hoped, into the realm of mass reform.

The progressive idealism of Benton's regionalism is confirmed in what and how he painted. Benton's preferred medium of aesthetic expression was the public mural. With their large scale and dynamic forms, Benton's murals demanded that their viewers pay attention to regionalism's optimistic message of social reform. From 1930 to 1931, Benton painted a large mural for the New School for Social Research in New York. To explicate the theme "America Today," Benton painted ten panels ranging in subject from urban recreation (*City Activities*) and urban labor (*City Building*—fig. 10.1) to the productive and playful atmosphere of the American countryside. With the skills he learned in the movie business, Benton painted scenes and figures a 1930s audience would find typical: *City Activities* reveals burlesque dancers and boxers, subway riders and movie watchers; *City Building* shows construction workers and ship builders. To make a cohesive visual statement about life in America around 1930, Benton arranged these vignettes into a single mural and united the sequences through decorative strips of wooden moldings. Such moldings were, Benton noted, common to the "illustrated pages of nineteenth century magazines and books" and could easily be seen in the rotogravure sections of popular twentieth-century tabloids.[26]

Benton expanded on the popular culture orientation of his murals by organizing particular scenes and shots in a cinematic manner. In *City Building*, for example, he edited certain motifs (skyscrapers, muscular workers) and sequences (men hoisting drills or hauling steel poles) and coordinated them in a seemingly haphazard way, with figures from one scene touching those in another. Benton's style is diametrically opposed to the long-standing pictorial conventions of scientific perspective, symmetrical order, realistic anatomy, modeling according to the incidence of light, and a fixed or static point of view. Instead, his regionalist murals are formally predicated on the modern spatial concepts of avant-garde art and popular movies. The action and energy of his New School mural is also a cinematic derivation. There is a fast-paced intensity to his spontaneous scenes of Americans at work and play, the same dynamic energy of early 1930s movies, with their "split screens, zip pans, moving cameras—all combine[d] to force the narrative pace relentlessly."[27]

Benton arranged his New School anecdotes about the American scene

in this cinematic, semitabloid, modern manner to attract the attention of a
1930s audience. He recognized their attentiveness to other media—movies,
magazine, modernist advertising—and relied on a similar look to lure
them. But, if Benton appropriated a popular culture style to attract his audience, he used it in quite a different way: to convey his regionalist message
of social reform. Although the "America Today" mural appears to be merely
painterly reportage, it is actually Benton's vision of the nineteenth-century
producer tradition carried into the twentieth century. In the panels *City
Building* and *Steel*, Benton emphasized the significance of the producer
in the development of modern industry. Heroic workers, their straining
muscles conveying their capable strengths, are seen purposefully building
America. Unlike other murals of similar subjects (such as Deigo Rivera's
1932 *Detroit Industry* frescoes), Benton's mural shows men towering over
their machines.[28] Clearly, in this visionary workplace, Benton's ideal of a
producer-controlled economy has been achieved.

Benton made only a few references in his New School mural to the
speculators and financiers of the twentieth century whose greed necessi-
tated the rebirth of the producer tradition. At the top of *City Activities with
Dance Hall*, Benton painted a sangfroid ticker-tape operator reading the
day's final tallies while a few brokers anxiously check the Stock Exchange
board. Nearby, middle-aged financiers are seen dancing the night away
with sexy sirens, celebrating their market manipulation with bottles of
speakeasy whiskey. Flanking this panel was *Outreaching Hands*, a small
frieze which clearly reveals his political message. The desperate hands
of black and white workers are seen reaching for breadline coffee, while
speculators, dressed in the requisite white shirt, dark suit, and top hat of
the successful businessman, stand in front of either a bank or a prison and
clutch wads of greenbacks. A purple dawn breaks in the distance. In this
final panel of his New School mural, Benton seems to project the end of
an unjust and inefficient capitalist system. In *City Building* and *Steel*, he
paints the new age: the restoration of a worker-based economy.[29]

Obviously, to make the assumption that Benton's regionalist art was a
species of social realism, or documentary illustration, is to ignore both what
the artist intended and the facts of the Depression. Benton's paintings were
largely mythical, his visions of an idealized America. To his Depression-
era audience, the simple fact that people were working in *City Building*
and *Steel* was optimistic since by the early 1930s the jobless rate in Depression America was high and rising. By 1932, steel plants were·operating at
only twelve percent of capacity, industrial construction had dropped from

$949 million to $74 million, and the unemployed numbered some thirteen million (out of a population of 120 million). And, it was only to get worse: "U.S. Steel's payroll of full-time workers fell from 225,000 in 1929 to zero on April 1, 1933."[30] Yet *Steel* shows men at work in the foundries, pouring molten metal and tending the furnaces of industry. For his intended 1930s viewers, Benton's "America Today" assumed mythical dimensions when measured against the realities of life.

Still, Benton's regionalist pictures were not escapist fare. Rather, realizing America was in a state of upheaval, Benton responded, and with a visionary art. The social function of his murals involved the potential for reform not the objective scrutiny of Depression conditions (or their complete avoidance). His regionalist art was meant to inspire its audience to change America by restoring its producer tradition. Benton hoped his art would encourage the making of a society where capitalist and speculative elements had been expunged, where corporate hegemony was halted, and where popular culture maintained a credibility previously reserved for only high-brow culture. Benton's illustrations of the vital strength and importance of the American worker, and his overwhelmingly positive visions of humanity, visually coincided with, as Benton noted, "the democratic impulses on which President Roosevelt's New Deal was based."[31] With a visually dynamic style derived from modern art and the movies, Benton ensured the public accessibility of his reform-oriented aesthetic. Benton's regionalism was meant as an inspiring, socially significant art which would help to persuade the American public of the possibilities of the New Deal.

Painted in an accessible, narrational style easily understood by the public, and with an optimism similar to that of New Deal politics, regionalism was broadly popular in the 1930s. Benton's art was described by critic Tom Craven in 1935 as "the collective American spirit":

> It is my guess that in . . . the future, this great drama of lawless change, which he has painted, will stand as one of the supreme arts. . . . The rushing energy of America, the strength and vulgarity, the collective psychology, are embodied in his art. The subordination of artistic tradition to actual experience with American life has enabled Benton to create the outstanding style in American painting, perhaps the only style.[32]

Craven's jubilant support of "American scene" painting (of which regionalism was a subdivision) snowballed: *Time*'s 1934 Christmas eve issue featured Benton on the cover, *Life* carried regionalist art from its first

(November 23, 1936) issue, the art was steadily acquired by major museums during the 1930s, and through well-publicized campaigns (verbal, literary, and aesthetic) many of the regionalists became household names.[33] Regionalism's popularity was certainly due to its liberal sentiments but also to its use by the commercial sector in advertising and in Hollywood. By the mid-1930s, middlemen began to see popular regionalism as an enormous aid in wooing public attention.

The regionalists were managed by the quintessential arts entrepreneur, Reeves Lewenthal, who later remarked, "I saw the potential of the arts, and I wanted to organize, publicize them."[34] Accordingly, in 1934 Lewenthal opened the first art agency, the Associated American Artists, which specifically promoted regionalism. To rouse public demand for the art, Lewenthal hired Benton and other regionalists and sold their commissioned lithographs and etchings for only five dollars apiece by direct mail order. Advertisements for these prints appeared in magazines like *Time* and *American Artist*, boasting: "This is the moment you have been waiting for! Through this vital new Art Project you can now get museum-perfect Originals, personally signed by the artists. . . ."[35]

While selling regionalist art to a middle-class audience of art patrons, Lewenthal also began promoting it to American business, convincing corporate America of the immediate cash rewards of using a popular American art in advertising. Throughout the 1930s and into the early 1940s, Lewenthal's New York gallery served as a regionalist clearing house for a large business clientele, among them Standard Oil and Twentieth Century-Fox.[36] Regionalism was one of the nation's most popular art styles during the Depression not just because of its idealized iconography of reform but also because it was regularly featured and often commissioned by popular magazines of the period, because the American Tobacco Company hired regionalist artists to paint for a cigarette promotion, because it was commissioned and seen by thousands in movie theaters across the country to promote movies.[37]

At first, the regionalists accepted these commissions willingly. For Benton, particularly, it was the opportunity to put further into practice his aesthetic aspirations, and he was optimistic about "the possibilities of a fruitful relation between big business and art."[38] Working in the advertising industry, creating art for mass media, enabled him to perform the role of a truly public artist and reach a far greater number of people with his regionalist message. Benton harbored no hostility toward American industry or commerce; rather, he wanted to reform it. He painted regionalist pictures for corporate America under two assumptions: first, that his art would aid in the reform of the corporate workplace, and second, that through this socially significant action, American art would be "returned to some functional place in the full stream of life." [39]

One of Benton's most important art-for-business commissions was the 1937 picture *Hollywood* (fig. 10.3). He had just finished a number of drawings for *Life* of a UAW picnic in Flint, Michigan, and was hired to paint a picture of the movie industry for a magazine cover. [40] Sent to the California studios of Twentieth Century-Fox, Benton likened his movie mural to "sex, melodrama and machinery." More specifically, he noted, "I wanted to give the idea that the machinery of the industry, cameras, carpenters, big generators, high voltage wires, etc., is directed mainly toward what young ladies have under their clothes." [41] Indeed, the "machinery of the industry" surrounds *Hollywood's* central blonde, the axis on which movieland revolves. Machines (spotlights, movie cameras, microphones, wind machines, electric generators, soundboards) and those who make them work (technicians, directors, actors, and actresses) fill *Hollywood*. Clearly, Benton saw it as a place of labor, and a place for labor reform.

In 1937, the movie industry, like the auto industry he had sketched just before his California visit, was embroiled in unionization struggles. The call to unionize was widespread, and everyone who worked in the industry was urged to join. Being in this hotbed of activism and committed to the reform of the American workplace, Benton filled *Hollywood* with the many movieland figures who were potential union members. This included everyone, as one author of the period noted:

> Hollywood is a union town. From the highest-paid directors to the lowly electrician, every group is organized. At labor rallies, its glamorous stars and suave writers hobnob with carpenters and painters. The popular conception of Hollywood as a land of make-believe is a figment of the imagination. The true Hollywood is just as firmly rooted in reality as Middletown. For every shining star there are thousands of little lights struggling to gain or keep a place. These men and women are interested in wages and hours, in working conditions, in union agreements, and in economic security. [42]

Although industry officials fought hard against any organized attack on their control of the studios, Hollywood was wracked by union battles, particularly in the 1930s. In 1933, an industry-wide strike by members of the

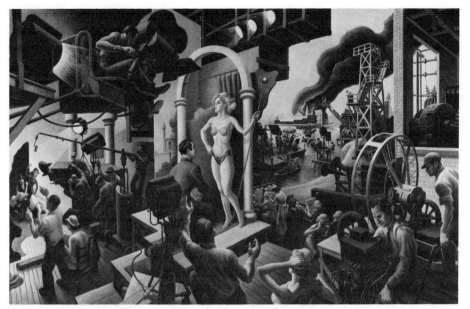

Fig. 10.3. Benton's view of workers in the movie industry, painted on commission for *Life*. *Hollywood*, 1937. Oil and tempera on canvas, mounted on panel, 53½″ × 81″. (Courtesy of the Nelson Atkins Museum of Art, Kansas City, Missouri.)

International Alliance of Theatrical Stage Employees and Motion Picture Machine Operators closed some studios and threatened to paralyze production.[43] The enactment of the National Labor Relations Act on April 12, 1937, revived union activity nationally, and during the spring and summer of 1937 various groups, including painters, plasterers, scenic artists, and utility employees, walked out on the movie studios.[44] During these same months, screenwriters, directors, and actors tangled in factional labor politics, and the trade papers bulged with anti-union commentary from studio chiefs.

Hollywood clearly shows that Benton sided with the workers and supported their struggle to control the movie industry. Like Leo Rosten, author of the 1941 *Hollywood: The Movie Colony, the Movie Workers*, Benton recognized the vital role movie producers played. In his book, Rosten noted: "The dazzling spotlight which Hollywood turns upon its Personalities throws into shadows the thousands who work in the movie studios—technicians and craftsmen, musicians and sound engineers, painters, carpenters, laboratory workers."[45] Correspondingly, in *Hollywood*

Fig. 10.4. Regionalist art was used in several 1940s advertising campaigns, including this one for the American Tobacco Company. *Outside the Curing Barn*, 1942. Advertisement in *Time* July 20, 1942. (Courtesy of the University of Colorado Libraries.)

Benton painted mostly the people working behind the scenes, the true producers of movieland's product. He painted Hollywood as a working place, a place like the steel foundries and coal mines he depicted in the "America Today" mural. In his paintings and in the many sketches he made of the movie industry, Benton focused on workers: common Americans collectively joined in the producer tradition. However, Benton's positivist vision of these workers controlling their workplace and thus participating in the reform of the American scene was not shared by the editors of *Life*. They preferred the mythical view of movieland as a place of stars and swimming pools. Not surprisingly, Benton's picture of Hollywood was rejected by *Life*, which depended on movie advertising revenue and openly promoted the glamour and glitter of the industry in regular features like "Movie of the Week." [46]

Although Benton's efforts to portray publicly the realities of work in Hollywood were unsuccessful, he persevered by accepting other business commissions. In 1941, he and seventeen other artists were hired to promote Lucky Strike cigarettes for the American Tobacco Company. The pictures Benton and others made were featured as full-page ads in popular magazines and seem to portray tobacco country as an agricultural paradise full of bountiful fields and enthusiastic farm laborers. Benton's picture, *Outside the Curing Barn* (fig. 10.4) appears to endorse the land of tobacco as a rural utopia. But this was not what he had actually seen in southern Georgia while on location for the assignment. His original work, which showed black sharecroppers, was rejected by the American Tobacco Company's advertising firm, which informed him:

> Don't you know you cannot show Negroes doing what looks like slave work. . . . The Negro reform institutions would boycott our products and cost us millions. . . . They want the Negro shown as a respectable well-dressed member of society. . . . If we did this the whole of the white South would boycott us. So the only thing to do is to avoid the presentation of Negroes in the tobacco business. [47]

In other words, Benton was advised to paint pictures which looked as if they were in the popular regionalist style but lacked any of its social and political import. *Outside the Curing Barn* has no offensive or provocative content and simply shows white field hands sorting huge golden tobacco leaves (a mandate for the entire advertising campaign). As this picture demonstrates, regionalism, which for Benton was an art of social responsibility and populist reform, was shaped into an art of business-product promotion. Instead of suggesting a better world with the possibilities of labor reform, it was used for immediate business profit in the status quo. Benton was noticeably vitriolic: "Every time a patron dictates to an artist what is to be done, he doesn't get any art—he just gets a poor commercial job. For that reason I thought the series of paintings the American Tobacco Company used in its advertising was a failure. Advertising is a lying art—it depends upon suggestions that are not wholly true. And you can't expect art to deal in half-truths." Business cannot expect art to tell its lies for it.[48]

Although he expected the merger of regionalist art and big business to lead to the reform of American society, Benton's experiences taught him otherwise. As he admitted, his regionalist work for mass media was a failure. It created neither social reform nor a "fruitful relation" between corporate America and regionalist art. Recognizing the manipulation of his regionalist art into something commercial, not reformist, Benton was understandably angered. Perhaps sympathizing with the Hollywood workers and the farm laborers he had painted on commission, he may have felt a keen loss of control and the inability to maintain his own artistic individuality. By the mid-1940s, Benton ended his efforts to change the corporate workplace through art and was seriously questioning the nature and efficacy of his regionalism.

Benton's sense of disillusion and his growing despair about the chances for social reform in America are reflected in his noncommercial art, which by the late 1930s had changed in style and subject matter. As international tensions mounted—the Spanish Civil War, the Sino-Japanese war, the Rome-Berlin Axis—national attention shifted from domestic to foreign policy. As American business, labor, and agriculture began to profit from supporting the Allies, New Deal programs were cut and neither the president nor the public did much to fight for them. Likewise, the coming of war made Benton's painted program of labor and social reform less and less viable, especially since the very nature of this war focused on maximizing corporate mobilization and control of the economy. Benton, like many American artists, reacted to this changed American scene with a very different style of art. As Benton biographer Matthew Baigell observes, "The general drift of realistic American paintings through the last years of the decade turned toward a greater reliance on imagination and fantasy and toward concern for the manipulation of color, as well as texture, and pattern."[49]

Benton began to break with his commitment to paint an America transformed through labor reform, and his work began to resemble the hallucinatory surrealist (or magic realist) pictures of American artists like Peter Blume or Walter Quirt. He turned from outdoor to in-studio painting, from generalized views of workers to scenes of pure fiction. *Persephone* (1938), for instance, depicts a pin-up girl plunked down nude in a Missouri hay field, and *Fantasy* (1945) is an utterly abstract play of textures and colors with no reference to subject matter. Benton had always painted small nonobjective works for aesthetic exercise, but his larger shift from reform to fantasy can only be explained by an increasing disillusion he felt about fulfilling his aesthetic ambitions with regionalism. Much later, he would write that "gnawing suspicions of failure" gripped him at this time:

> How difficult it was for me to paint significantly about the social situation that developed. . . . I began giving much of my attention to the details of the natural world, flowers, trees, and foliage. I had had a lifelong interest in such growing things, but my major painting themes, when I turned my attention to our native scene, were nearly always about the activities of people. . . . Now, however, people began to be accessory. . . . Although I did not realize it at the time, I was thus myself moving away from Regionalism, at least from Regionalism as I had heretofore conceived it. [50]

The "social situation" to which Benton referred was the Second World War, which destroyed, he noted, "that national concentration on our American meanings out of which the images of Regionalism grew and in which the movement found its justification and its successes." [51] Benton did try to reckon with isolationist America's involvement in an international war with the war pictures of his Year of Peril series. These gruesome paintings were his contribution to stirring war consciousness among the American public. After its purchase in 1942 by Abbott Industries (the major wartime pharmaceutical firm), more than 55 million reproductions of the eight paintings were distributed by the Office of War Information. [52] Largely derived from Benton's imagination, with help from war photographs and editorial cartoons, the Year of Peril series was not painted onsite, as was Benton's earlier regionalist art. Newspaper photos of the exploded USS *Shaw* and the sinking of the *West Virginia* furnished the artist with the imagery for *Starry Night*, which depicts a drowning midshipman, and for *Casualty* (fig. 10.5), a grotesque vision of bodies and barbed wire. On the whole, the series was not so much an inspirational call to arms as a horrific vision of apocalypse. Obviously, Benton's hideous Year of Peril pictures bear as little relation to his earlier reformist regionalist art as the film

Fig. 10.5. Benton's grotesque war pictures suggest disillusion with regionalist and New Deal efforts to transform American culture. *Casualty*, 1942 (from the Year of Peril series). Oil on canvas, 47″ × 56″. (Courtesy of the State Historical Society, Columbus, Missouri.)

noir movies of the 1940s, like *Spellbound* (1945), do to the essentially optimistic movies of the 1930s, like King Vidor's *Our Daily Bread* (1934).[53]

If the 1930s are characterized by an auspicious regionalist folk aesthetic which focused on the reform of American society, the 1940s were marked by the completely different style of abstract expressionism, which related to growing international and personal tensions. Regionalism dominated American culture during the Depression through its popular culture appeal and its promotion of liberal sentiments similar to those expressed by the New Deal. Yet, it failed to maintain its dominance after the Depression. While it is customary to see the change from regionalism to abstract expressionism as a tremendous alteration in art form, the art of both Benton and foremost abstract expressionist painter Jackson Pollock demonstrates a larger cultural transition at work. For Benton, regionalism was a vehicle which promoted the rebirth of the producer tradition in the twentieth century. But for the students trained in that tradition, for artists like Pollock, regionalism was seen as a failed style. Its subject matter and form lost popular and artistic credibility because its vision of social reform had not materialized. In the 1940s, the artists of Pollock's generation shifted to a largely apolitical art that was a personal response to both regionalism's and the New Deal's failure to transform American society. In the 1940s, Benton noted: "Regionalism was as much out of place as New Dealism itself. It declined in popular interest and lost its grip on the minds of young artists. Shortly after our entrance into the War, what was left of it turned to a swift and superficial representation of combat and production scenes, to a business of sensational reporting for the popular magazines. There it had its grass-roots substance knocked out." [54]

The major proponent of a passé art style in a changed American scene, Benton felt a sense of defeat. His "gnawing suspicions of failure" were shared by his partners in regionalism: Wood, on his deathbed in 1942, said he wanted to "start all over again with a new style of painting," and Curry, shortly before he died in 1946, said, "Maybe I'd have done better to stay on the farm." [55] The sense of failure that Benton, Wood, and Curry felt was reinforced by 1940s critics who attacked regionalism as commercialized "escapist material." [56] Such criticism helped regionalism lose support, especially among other artists. Later, Benton wrote that by the time of America's entrance into World War II, regionalism had begun to lose its influence "among the newly budding artists and the young students. The band wagon practitioners left our regionalist banner like rats from a sinking ship." [57]

Among those who turned away from regionalism was Benton's most promising student, Jackson Pollock. In the early 1930s, Pollock, a young man from the West (born in Cody, Wyoming, in 1912), enrolled in Benton's classes at the Art Students League in New York. This relationship was very close, as many have noted: "There was a rhythm, a flow between them from the beginning to the end of their lives. It was a physical, gestural rhythm; teacher and student were *bonded*, you might say." [58] Pollock's western roots and boot-tromping, hard-drinking "frontier behavior" led at least one critic of the period to comment that he carried "regionalism with him." [59] A classmate of Pollock's recalled, "There was that pride in being a Westerner. Like Benton, Pollock looked down then on the East and Europe." [60] Beyond Pollock's imitation of his teacher's personal mannerisms and attitudes, the small oils he painted in the early 1930s certainly reveal Benton's aesthetic guidance. *Going West* (1934–35, fig. 10.6) shows Pollock's assimilation of both regionalist subject matter (the American landscape, its workers, and history) and regionalist style (the dynamic composition and textural handling of paint). In Benton's mural painting classes, Pollock was introduced to grand-scale public art and the "problems inherent in keeping all of a large surface. . . . alive and interesting."[61] Later works, such as the monumental *Autumn Rhythm* (fig. 10.2) of 1950, indicate Pollock's mastery of energetic form and scale. Benton thought highly of his protégé's talents: "I have no doubt that his contributions to Regionalism, had he continued to make them, would have been quite as original as were the purely formalistic exercises to which he finally devoted himself."[62]

But the personal and aesthetic relationship between Pollock and Benton dissipated by the 1940s, when Pollock moved toward abstract expressionism. In a 1950 interview, Pollock commented, "Modern art to me is nothing more than the expression of contemporary aims of the age that we're living in."[63] It is the kind of statement Benton might have made twenty years earlier, but for Pollock these aims were expressed in quite a different way: "My opinion is that new needs need new techniques. And the modern artists have found new ways and new means of making their statements. It seems to me that the modern painter cannot express this age, the airplane, the atom bomb, the radio, in the old forms of the Renaissance or of any other past culture. Each age finds its own technique."[64] In his age, that of the 1940s and the postwar era, Pollock made no effort to project social progress onto his canvases, which Benton noted: "I don't think Jack ever adopted my ideas about the functions of art in society. I don't think they even interested him."[65] Pollock expressed the aims of his age through a spontaneous, personally expressive style.

Pollock's rejection of Benton's style could be read simply as a stereotypical example of youthful rebellion against parental authority. More astutely, Pollock recognized that his age, particularly that of the postwar era, was a changed culture. The hopeful, reformist society posited by Benton's regionalism and the New Deal had dissolved, replaced by a tense consensus culture and its cold war anxieties. And the abstract expressionist response to this dissolution, according to avant-garde painter and critic Robert Motherwell, was "rebellious, individualistic, unconventional, sensitive, irritable. . . . This attitude arose from a feeling of being ill at ease in the universe. . . . Nothing as drastic an innovation as [their] abstract art could have come into existence, save as the consequence of a most profound, relentless, unquenchable need. The need is for felt experience."[66]

Motherwell's comment, made in 1951, hints of the insecurities American artists felt in the 1940s, especially after World War II. In the 1940s, as it became obvious that Benton's (and Roosevelt's) worldview would not

Fig. 10.6. Pollock's 1930s pictures show his assimilation of regionalist style and subject matter. *Going West*, c. 1934–35. Oil on fiberboard, 15⅛″ × 20¾″. (Courtesy of the National Museum of American Art, Smithsonian Institution, Washington, D.C.)

come to pass, a sense of uneasiness spread, particularly as no new positivist worldview was perceived. Feeling themselves caught in a trap of reactionary hysterics, of international tensions and Cold War stress, Pollock and other artists responded with the art of abstract expressionism. With their tangled, tormented lines and lack of central focus, Pollock's all-over drip paintings, like *Autumn Rhythm*, were discerned by at least one postwar critic as the physical "disintegration of our culture."[67] Pollock's webbed-style and self-proclaimed effort to "literally be in the painting" can be seen as the artist's irretrievable entrapment in a painterly impasse.[68] Like Benton, Pollock aimed to express himself in his age. Unlike Benton, Pollock expressed personal and social alienation, not social reform.

Abstract expressionism was, like regionalism, an art of myth. But the mythical quest in this postwar art was mostly private. Pollock, for example, used myth and an automatic painting style to delve into the realm of his unconscious. Stimulated by Jung's *Psychology of the Unknown* and its emphasis on the role of myth and the importance of the collective unconscious in the creation of art, works like the 1943 *Pasiphae* have been described as Pollock's "means of scourging private demons."[69] He entered Jungian psychotherapy in 1939, his doctors using his drawings for "therapeutic purposes."[70] In the transformation from regionalism to abstraction, the expressionist contours and coarse textures of paint were maintained, and so was an interest in myth, but the myth itself was altered. Revelation of this personal mythology came through Pollock's innovative painting methods. Working in a frenetic but controlled way with poured and dripped oil and enamel paints on unprimed canvas, Pollock revealed his improvisational style in pictures like the huge *Autumn Rhythm* (8'10 1/2" × 17'8"). Pollock once said that "painting is self-discovery"; his style was his vehicle for personal exploration.[71]

Pollock's private revelations of social strain were lauded as the best art for a new generation by such critics as Clement Greenberg. In 1948, he noted, "The level of American art has risen in the last five years, with the emergence of new talents so full of energy and content as Arshile Gorky, Jackson Pollock, David Smith. . . . The main premises of Western art have at last migrated to the United States, along with the center of gravity of industrial production and political power."[72] But, America's stunning political and industrial postwar growth created an ironic situation for its avant-garde artists. Painted to express personal anxieties, Pollock's abstract pictures were celebrated by American critics and borrowed by postwar "new liberals" to express national freedoms. Through the auspices of the Museum of Modern Art and under the subsidy of the State Department, abstract expressionist art was exhibited throughout postwar Europe to promote America's creative freedom—in direct opposition to the Soviet Union's style of social realism. Abstract expressionism became, as several authors have noted, a weapon in the cold war, as its abstracted anxiety was translated, ironically, into a symbol of uniquely American freedom.[73]

The real irony is that Pollock was, as much as Benton, alienated from this emerging structure of American society. With abstract expressionism, Pollock, like Benton with regionalism, was trying to sustain the one powerful motif remaining of an earlier culture—that of the individual. Pollock's explorations were personal, and Benton's were social, but both were artistic efforts to envision the freedom of the individual—the individual worker, the individual artist—in America. Despite the aims of both men, their art was used for other purposes, to support commercial, political, and social ideologies that neither subscribed to. The continuity of their efforts lies in the cultural links between teacher and student, between regionalism and abstract expressionism, and between the Depression and postwar America.

NOTES

1. H. W. Janson, "Benton and Wood: Champions of Regionalism," *Magazine of Art* 39 (May 1946): 184.

2. Quoted in Irving Sandler, *The Triumph of American Painting: A History of Abstract Expressionism* (New York: Harper and Row, 1970), 103.

3. "Jackson Pollock," *Arts and Architecture* 61, no. 2 (February 1944): 14.

4. Sandler, 103. See Stephen Polcari, "Jackson Pollock and Thomas Hart Benton," *Arts Magazine* 53, no. 7 (March 1979): 120–24.

5. Serge Guilbaut, *How New York Stole the Idea of Modern Art: Abstract Expressionism, Freedom, and the Cold War* (Chicago: University of Chicago Press, 1983), 3.

6. Ibid., 201.

7. Thomas Hart Benton, *An Artist in America*, 4th rev. ed. (Columbia: University of Missouri Press, 1983), 5, 7, 10. Benton died in 1975.

8. Populism is discussed in Peter N. Carroll and David W. Noble, *The Free and the Unfree: A New History of the United States* (New York: Penguin, 1977), 290–91.

9. Benton, "American Regionalism, A Personal History of the Movement," in *An American in Art: A Professional and Technical Autobiography* (Lawrence: University Press of Kansas, 1969), 167.

10. Eric Foner, *Free Soil, Free Labor, Free Men: The Ideology of the Republican Party before the Civil War* (New York: Oxford University Press, 1970).

11. Benton discussed the political ideology of his great-uncle, Senator Thomas Hart Benton (1782–1858), and his father, Colonel M. E. Benton (1848–1924), in *An Artist in America*, 4–16, 23–30.

12. Benton, *An American in Art*, 25.

13. Benton, "A Chronology of My Life," in *Thomas Hart Benton* (Lawrence: University of Kansas Museum of Art, 1958), unpaginated entry for years 1913–16.

14. Benton, *An American in Art*, 36, and "After," a 1951 essay appended to *An Artist in America*, 315.

15. Benton, *An American in Art*, 13–27.

16. Benton, "After," 314.

17. Benton recalled his early studio work in *An Artist in America*, 37–38. See also Karal Ann Marling, "Thomas Hart Benton's *Boomtown*: Regionalism Redefined," *Prospects* 6 (1981): 106–13, and my "Regionalists in Hollywood: Painting, Film, and Patronage, 1925–1945" (Ph.D. diss. University of Minnesota, 1983), chaps. 2–6. For information on Ingram, see Liam O'Leary, *Rex Ingram: Master of the Silent Cinema* (New York: Harper and Row, 1980).

18. On the visual aesthetics of early movies, see Lary Mary, *Screening Out the Past: The Birth of Mass Culture and the Motion Picture Industry* (New York: Oxford University Press, 1980), 72, 123.

19. Benton, *An Artist in America*, 44, and *An American in Art*, 25.

Benton quoted from a July 1973 interview with Paul Cummings included in *Artists in Their Own Words: Interviews by Paul Cummings* (New York: St. Martin's, 1979), 39.

20. Benton, "American Regionalism," 149.

21. Matthew Baigell, *Thomas Hart Benton* (New York: Abrams, 1974), 70.

22. Richard Hofstadter, *The Age of Reform from Bryan to FDR* (New York: Vintage, 1955), 217.

23. Benton, "After," 316.

24. Benton, "American Regionalism," 189.

25. Ibid., 192.

26. Benton, *An American In Art*, 64.

27. John Baxter, *Hollywood in the Thirties* (New York: Paperback Library, 1970), 74.

28. Benton rejected preparatory sketches which showed machines more prominent than men. See Karal Ann Marling, *Tom Benton and His Drawings* (Columbia: University of Missouri Press, 1985), 105.

29. For a general account of Benton's images of workers, see Douglas Hyland, "Benton's Images of American Labor," in *Benton's Bentons* (Lawrence: Spencer Museum of Art, University of Kansas, 1980), 22–31.

30. William E. Leuchtenburg, *Franklin D. Roosevelt and the New Deal, 1932–1940* (New York: Harper and Row, 1963), 1, 19.

31. Benton, "American Regionalism," 192.

32. Tom Craven, *Modern Art: The Men, the Movements, the Meaning* (New York: Simon and Schuster, 1934), 335, 339. Craven was also a good friend of Benton's in the 1920s and 1930s.

33. "Art, U.S. Scene," *Time* 24, no. 26 (December 24, 1934): 24–27.

34. Interview with Lewenthal, New York, November 24, 1981.

35. *American Artist* 9 (November 1940): 29.

36. See my "Borrowing Regionalism: Advertising's Use of American Art in the 1930s and 1940s," *Journal of American Culture* 5, no. 4 (Winter 1982): 10–19.

37. Ibid., 13–16.

38. Benton, "After," 292.

39. Ibid.

40. On the UAW sketches, see "Artist Thomas Hart Benton Hunts Communists and Fascists in Michigan," *Life* 3, no. 4 (July 26, 1937): 22–25.

41. Benton, in a February 8, 1938, letter to Daniel Longwell, the *Life* editor who arranged the commission. See the Benton File, Longwell Papers, box 32, Rare Books and Manuscript Library, Columbia University, New York.

42. Murray Ross, *Stars and Strikes: Unionization of Hollywood* (New York: Columbia University Press, 1941), 3.

43. Robert Sklar, *Movie-Made America: A Cultural History of American Movies* (New York: Vintage, 1975), 172, and Ross, 144–48.

44. Ross, 193. Also see Lary May, chapter 7 of this volume.

45. Rosten, *Hollywood: The Movie Colony, the Movie Workers* (New York: Harcourt Brace, 1941), 32.

46. *Life* could not afford to offend an industry it depended on to generate advertising and subscriber dollars. It devoted over 250 of its 1,864 covers (from

1936 to 1972) to Hollywood personalities. See *Life Goes to the Movies* (New York: Time-Life, 1975), 4.

47. Benton, "After," 294–96.

48. "Business and Art as Tom Benton Sees It," PM (December 24, 1945), Benton Papers. See also Benton's essay "Business and Art," in *Work for Artists: What? Where? How?* ed. Elizabeth McCausland (New York: American Artists Group, 1947), 21–26.

49. Baigell, *Thomas Hart Benton*, 152.

50. Ibid., 151, for a discussion of Benton's change in style in *Persephone. Fantasy* is reproduced in *Benton's Bentons*, 68. Benton, quoted in "And Still After," a 1968 essay appended to *An Artist in America*, 368–69.

51. Benton, "And Still After," 326.

52. The paintings are in the vaults of the Missouri State Historical Society in Columbia. For illustrations, see *The Year of Peril: A Series of War Paintings by Thomas Benton* (North Chicago, Illinois: Abbott Laboratories, 1942).

53. For a discussion of this change in painting and movie aesthetics, see my "Regionalists in Hollywood," chap. 6.

54. Benton recognized that postwar America supported neither regionalism nor the New Deal, in his 1951 essay "American Regionalism," 192.

55. Benton, "After," 320–21.

56. Janson, "Benton and Wood," 184, 199.

57. Benton, "After," 319.

58. Painter George McNeil noted this in Jeffrey Potter's *To a Violent Grace: An Oral Biography of Jackson Pollock* (New York: Putnam, 1985), 36. For Pollock's chronology, see Francis V. O'Connor, *Jackson Pollock* (New York: Museum of Modern Art, 1967), and B. H. Friedman, *Jackson Pollock: Energy Made Visible* (New York: McGraw-Hill, 1972). Pollock died in 1956 in an automobile accident.

59. In his essay on Pollock in *American Masters: The Voice and the Myth* (New York: Dutton, 1974), 107, Brian O'Doherty notes Harold Rosenberg saying this.

60. Cartoonist Whitney Darrow, Jr., quoted in Friedman, *Jackson Pollock*, 25.

61. Friedman, 25.

62. Benton, "And Still After," 338.

63. From "An Interview with Jackson Pollock," taped by William Wright for the Sag Harbor radio station, although never used. See the transcript in O'Connor, 79.

64. Ibid.

65. Benton, in letter to Francis V. O'Connor, n.d., Benton Papers.

66. Motherwell, quoted in Sandler, 30.

67. John Berger, "The White Cell," *New Statesman* 56 (November 22, 1958): 722–23.

68. Pollock made this remark in *Possibilities* (Winter 1947–48): 78ff., a one-time New York publication edited by Motherwell and Rosenberg. See O'Connor, 40.

69. Sandler, 106.

70. Ibid.

71. Pollock, quoted from a 1956 interview with Selden Rodman, in *Conversations with Artists* (New York: Devin-Adair, 1957), 76–87.

72. Greenberg, quoted in Guilbaut, 172.

73. Ibid., 202, 207–9, 248–49.

11 *Things to Come: Swing Bands, Bebop, and the Rise of a Postwar Jazz Scene*

Lewis A. Erenberg

In 1946, a young veteran of many black swing bands recorded "Things to Come," a tune that presaged a new era in jazz. Like other bop melodies, it was filled with dissonance, a frenetic pace, and extended solo lines. The war, observed Dizzy Gillespie, had forced radical changes in his playing: "Fast and furious, with the chord changes going this way and that way, it might've looked like bedlam, but it wasn't."[1] Musicians and listeners nurtured on swing, the dominant big band style of the late 1930s and early 1940s, considered bebop an attack, a musical and social revolution. As Ralph Ellison, the most noted black novelist of the postwar era, declared, bop "was itself a texture of fragments, repetitive, nervous, not fully formed; its melodic lines underground, secret and taunting; its riffs jeering—Salt Peanuts! Salt Peanuts!"[2] Yet, even more important, Ellison and Gillespie both saw the music as more than a technical innovation. Rather, it expressed a desire to break from the minstrel stereotype required of black entertainers: "Musically we were changing the way that we spoke, to reflect the way that we felt."[3]

Given this new sensibility, the rise of bop music as the major jazz innovation of the era was as much a change in style as it represented a significant perceptual shift in the world. Initially, this new musical form found expression after the war as the entire band world plunged into musical and social turmoil. "The musicians were so good," observed trumpeter Red Rodney, "yet we were so screwed up. It was a period of being very bugged. Why, I'll never know, but we were."[4] As swing bands declined in the late 1940s, the music world fragmented into warring cults, each side protraying

Research for this article was completed with the aid of a Loyola University of Chicago leave of absence and a summer grant, and with the aid of an NEH summer grant. I wish to thank my research assistants, Lilia Kulak, Donna Neary, and Lori Witt, for their invaluable help and the many people who provided critical readings of the manuscript in its various stages: Anthony Cardoza, Susan E. Hirsch, J. Fred MacDonald, Donald B. Meyer, Russell B. Nye, and the late Warren Susman. Finally, I wish to thank Lary May for his superb organizational and editorial assistance, as well as for his faith in the efficacy of this project.

itself as the true heir of jazz. The war erupted among Dixieland revivalists who sought greater individualism and natural freedom in past music, white and black boppers who sought these values in a contemporary musical mode, and the remaining proponents of swing, the popular jazz sound of the 1930s and war years. Partisans hurled charges of "Nazism," "Fascism," and "commercialism" at each other. Modernist critic Leonard Feather, in referring to the revival of Dixieland music, for example, declared that "Moldy Figs are to music what Rankin and Bilbo are to politics and Pegler to the press. They are the extreme right-wingers of jazz, the voice of reaction in music." At the same time *Ebony* declared: "The long war between boppist and anti-boppist factions was almost political in its defenses. Boppists likened themselves to revolutionary leftists, their opponents as money-grabbing capitalists. Now, as the battle draws to a close, boppists find themselves in a musical equivalent of a political underground."[5]

Forty years after these battles, such vituperative political language seems bizarre when applied to popular music. Indeed, most jazz historians have ignored this battle between swing and bebop, preoccupied as they are with the musical evolution of jazz forms.[6] Yet what is most notable about the music of both the 1930s and 1940s, however, is how its creators saw it as a manifestation of not just a new art form, but a new way of life. Similar to the boppers, Benny Goodman, the most noted popularizer of swing, linked his music to a revival of American traditions. The innovations he helped to pioneer were a vital dance music and a contribution to jazz, according to the King of Swing, but they were also much more. Improvisation lay at its heart. It was "the expression of an individual kind of free speech in music," and he likened it to the freedom accorded a newspaper editor or an architect. "One music has grown out of our brand of government," he said, and, if swing dies, "it will die over the body of American freedom."[7] It is not that these musicians were politicians or that they had political platforms. Rather, as the language of Goodman, the boppers, and the traditionalists suggest, their music carried important hopes for personal freedom as well as larger civic concerns. To understand the bitter musical battles of the 1940s, and their relationship to the culture created after World War II, one must first grasp how swing music had become synonomous with personal freedom, important national values, new cultural hopes, and Depression-era dreams.

It is important, however, first to put swing in perspective. Modern popular culture emerged in the early years of the twentieth century. Until this time, several cultures dominated popular entertainments. The dominant value system was part of Anglo-Saxon middle-class life. On the basis of male individualism and female restraint, most middle-class Americans felt removed from the more vibrant life of the lower classes. But out of Victorian values, an organized, rationalized society and family emerged that produced a crisis for the middle classes. In the search for expressiveness, whites turned to modern popular entertainments. Movies, Tin Pan Alley popular music, cabarets, and personal life became the loci of individualism, but by the 1920s, those were removed from the larger world of organized society and the workplace. Prohibition played a large role in the separation of play from social values, for it rendered illegal the search for a moral revolution in cabarets and nightclubs. The result was that into the early 1930s urban popular culture was a vibrant part of American life, but it was not fully "American." The secretive style of speakeasy nightclubs, the exotic foreign movie-palace decor, the fact that this occurred in cities and not the heartland, all meant a fragmented relationship between modern popular culture and official values.[8]

In this context, jazz rose from the position of a music consumed overwhelmingly by Afro-Americans to one that was patronized by urban whites. As the middle class turned away from the more organized realms of work and civic life to new leisure realms, they became attracted to the formerly forbidden music of American blacks. Yet, when whites first encountered jazz in the 1920s, it had a dangerous as well as liberating aura, for the new music that first emerged in black urban areas in the early twentieth century had an enormous vitality and spontaneity. Segregated from white society, blacks had created their own expressiveness in the area that was least policed—their music and dance. Jazz bore the free, improvisatory energy of this one realm of freedom and expressed the body as a natural and divine feature of human existence. It also held out the hope for group and individual liberation from the oppressive existence of the present. In black jazz as in black churches, the individual soloist interacted with the community in an organic connection of call and response, improvisation and polyrhythm. These were carried over into jazz, and the music was thus based on group improvisation, where everyone played different lines at the same time. By the middle of the 1920s, however, the soloist, in the person of Louis Armstrong, emerged as the central personage in jazz as he or she played out deeply personal and emotionally authentic inner feelings.[9]

By the 1920s, moreover, jazz had attracted many white artists who saw it not just as a new music, but also as a means to reorient their own lives. Throughout the era, the music attracted numerous young, white Chicago musicians like Eddie Condon, Dave Tough, Bud Freeman, Jimmy McPartland, Jess Stacy, and Goodman, who sought alternatives to Victorian values of success and marriage. As a challenge to Victorian culture, jazz offered a personal and emotionally authentic expression, and these white artists often romanticized the black community as a spontaneous community of unrepressed individuals. Mezz Mezzrow eventually considered himself black because of the sense of natural freedom he witnessed in Harlem, while Artie Shaw considered Harlemites the only communal and human element in impersonal New York City. In contrast to the "straight" world, these musicians reveled in a hard-drinking, spontaneous style of life and music. As such, they preferred smaller combos where they could improvise uninhibitedly.[10]

Audiences, however, were ambivalent about the meaning of jazz. The new music was often considered a racial and ethnic attack on middle-class and Protestant values of self-discipline, sexual propriety, and self-advancement. Consequently, while audiences were drawn to "hot" music as an exciting, exotic expression, they preferred Paul Whiteman's refined, symphonic jazz. Indeed, Whiteman responded to external moral criticism as well as to his internal conflicts to bridge the gap between civilized public values and the new music by making "a lady of jazz." According to the New Yorker, the result was "a sweet jazz . . . with his violins, muted brasses, and soft symphonic effects." Polyrhythms and syncopation were adapted to the large society orchestra, "but improvisation was held in check and the hot stuff was dispensed only in teaspoonfuls." At the same time, the black originators were kept segregated in their own units. Whiteman hired hot jazz players in the late 1920s, but they felt dissatisfied, as their solos virtually disappeared in the refined arrangements and the section playing, and only Whiteman, the showman-conductor, stood out as the star. Further, as the music business centralized in the late 1920s, the marginal character of jazz increased. Radio, movies, and record companies attempted to reach a national audience and to do so squelched jazz playing and bawdy lyrics.[11]

At first, the crash and the Depression made things worse. During the early 1930s, jazzmen found it difficult to ply their trade, as nightclubs, ballrooms, hotels, and theaters closed, and the movie and record industries plummeted. Worried entertainment proprietors were reluctant to alienate remaining patrons with hot jazz. Audience mood proved a factor, as jazz became the symbol of a decadence which had contributed to the society's collapse. According to one music critic, "the public, suffering from . . .

retribution for material overindulgence and neglect of spiritual values, was in no mood for the reckless promptings of jazz."[12] Faced with declining opportunities, many white musicians sought refuge in radio orchestras or commercial bands, which became, according to Albert McCarthy, even sweeter and more rhythmically conservative as they sought to soothe older audiences with muted trumpets and "schmaltzy" saxes. Artie Shaw found the experience galling: "On most of the programs I did there was little or no room for any sort of individual musical expression." Benny Goodman also found it difficult to conform to authoritarian conductors who tried to tell him what to improvise.[13]

Goodman and Shaw's plight paralleled the larger mood of entrapment and insecurity during the worst years of the Depression. Unlike the "shouters" of the 1920s—Al Jolson, Sophie Tucker, and Bessie Smith—crooners and torch singers, the dominant vocalists of the early 1930s, sounded plaintive, guilty, and apologetic. "Dancing in the Dark," on a "Gloomy Sunday," under a sky of "Stormy Weather," listeners seemed afraid of what life might bring. Even the "happy" songs, such as "Life is Just a Bowl of Cherries," suggested that one's fate was subject to forces like the weather that were beyond control. Male crooners, such as Rudy Vallee, Russ Columbo, and Bing Crosby, and the female torch singers, such as Ruth Etting, Helen Morgan, and Libby Holman, took on a ruminative, introspective quality as they lowered their voices to sing into mega- or microphones. Of all the crooners, Crosby stood out. When he performed "I'm Sorry," "Just One More Chance," or "I Apologize," with a half sob in his voice, he seemed to be atoning for past sins. Raising interpretation of song lyrics to an art form, Crosby sang for a generation faced with adversity and uncertainty. In "Brother, Can You Spare a Dime?" he also gave vent to the masculine impotence that could no longer build skyscrapers up to the sky or make railroads run at high speed. The machine age had ground to a halt, and with it masculine power. During the same period, torch singers performed tortured love songs. They too sang of a world of blasted dreams, where male providers were emotionally and financially unreliable, and women remained helpless victims.[14]

By 1936, this downbeat mood gave way to a tremendous resurgence in jazz. Only now jazz was a different, more complex musical form called swing. Why this occurred has perplexed music historians. Looking back from the perspective of bebop and Dixieland, historians usually interpret the rise of swing as the gross commercialization of jazz, pushed by the established industries of the music world. Yet, while radio, records, and theaters did jump on the bandwagon once swing showed itself capable of garnering big audiences, the music business was initially hesitant. From the perspective of 1935–36, in fact, swing posed a cultural challenge to the control that "icky," "Mickey Mouse," and high-hat sweet bands held over the hotels, airwaves, and band agencies. Having experienced rejection by conservative audiences and his own band agency, Goodman viewed sweet music as "a weak sister incapable of holding its own in any artistic encounter with the real music of America." Swing devotees railed against "commercial corn." George Simon, an editor of *Metronome*, for example, called Shep Fields, a popular sweet band of the day, a "cute, Mickey-Mouse-like" band that makes "you feel like getting up and, hoping [*sic*] very daintily all around the room on tip-toe, squeaking in a very high falsetto, 'o-o-o-h, lookie, don't you think I'm a cutey iddy biddy thing too.'" Another reviewer added, "To the average person, reared within the refined cloisters of the Whiteman-Kemp-Duchin cult," Jimmy Lunceford's band "carries a tremendous 'sock,' . . . the music parallel of Joe Louis' gloved fists."[15]

Behind that "sock" lay a renewed sense of vital dance movement that enabled the new sound to challenge the remnants of sweet jazz for audience loyalty. This renewal also overlapped with the shift in public mood stimulated by the coming to power of Franklin Delano Roosevelt and his New Deal programs. On material grounds alone, there were reasons to stand up and cheer. Through its economic measures, the new administration stimulated the band business, for people now had money to spend on entertainment. But it was the repeal of Prohibition in December 1933 that had the most dramatic impact. Historians have often ignored this fact, but repeal played a major role in reviving entertainment, especially the band circuit. For one thing, in ending the reign of temperance that had divided the cities from the rural areas and Catholics and Jews from Protestants, the New Deal made it possible for bands to find larger audiences in the city and countryside. New revenues from the sale of alcohol, moreover, encouraged the operators of restaurants and ballrooms to reopen and present bands and entertainment. Soon swing's power attracted young high school and college dancers and listeners as radio, records, theaters, and even conservative hotels joined in. As a result, jazz, in the guise of swing, unexpectedly captured the institutions of mass communications and achieved for the first time an unprecedented popularity.[16]

It was no accident that a new group of bandleaders took advantage of these possibilities to end the dominance of the "society" bands and establish a more jazz-oriented and democratic ethos in American music. Most swing bandleaders had been part of the "hot clique" of the 1920s. Now, according to Goodman, the "players took over," bringing jazz, with all its irreverence and honesty, into the mainstream. The new bands avoided the hokum and gimmicky doubling on funny instruments (kazoos, for example) associated with bands like Whiteman's. According to Willard Alexander, an important band agent, Goodman "was even different physically, contrary to what everybody expected in a band leader. No glamour. No sex appeal. But a well-grounded musician. Once he hit, in came the others in the same pattern. Tommy Dorsey, Glenn Miller. Like Goodman, they were not the typical Hollywood glamour boys. They wore glasses. They had musical experience." Part of their appeal lay in their purging hot jazz of its decadent associations, and making the music seem more honest and accessible to a wider audience. What also set them off from previous bandleaders was that they were both excellent musicians and ordinary people. They were also older, seemingly less rebellious, and they enforced this professional image on their men. Musicians continued to drink, smoke marijuana, and engage in anarchic behavior, but leaders frowned on these excesses, and encouraged instead professionalism, teamwork, and discipline.[17]

At the same time, swing musicians made a virtue out of what formerly had been repressed. Unlike the homogenous, hierarchical groups of the sweet era, the swing bands celebrated the fact that the jazz world was one of the most egalitarian and pluralistic realms in American life. Whether one was immigrant, black, or old-stock American, who one was, was less important than how one played. As a result, swing was profoundly cosmopolitan, including blacks, Jews, Italians, Poles, Irish, and Protestants as leaders, players, and singers. It had wealthy Charlie Barnet, who rejected his background to lead the exciting jazz life, and Artie Shaw, the former Arthur Arshawsky, who sought in big-band success an American alternative to his parents' Jewish identity. The big swing bands fostered what Frank Sinatra called "collaboration, brotherhood and sharing rough times." In this context, swing offered a new model of social democracy and group life and in turn attracted players of mixed backgrounds and varied social groupings.[18]

Equally important, swing held out the hope of greater inclusion for blacks in American life. Nationally, despite the continued segregation of the music industry, black bands and musicians were increasingly defined as contributors, if not the originators of, a new national musical culture.

Many white bandleaders hired black arrangers, for example, and Goodman succeeded in breaking the color barrier by hiring black musicians. Although, initially, commercial pressures forced Goodman to present Teddy Wilson and Lionel Hampton in trio and quartet settings apart from the full band, by the end of the 1930s numerous black artists played in white bands. As Hampton observed, "A man can be pink, white, black or orange. But, as long as his stuff is what the doctor ordered, he's got something." Formerly excluded black bands also received greater attention from the music press. Repeatedly, public music polls usually had white bands and players on top, but *Metronome* often measured white players by how they compared with blacks. And in New York, black musicians moved from the separate world of Harlem to the more mainstream jazz clubs of midtown 52nd Street (fig. 11.1).[19]

With this shift in popular taste, many black musicians saw swing music as incarnating the possibility of their greater inclusion in American life, a life made richer by the fusion of black and white musical forms. Under the direction of bandleaders and arrangers like Fletcher Henderson, Don Redman, Duke Ellington, and Count Basie, the Afro-American improvisatory tradition fused with a white European arranging legacy. By the late 1920s and early 1930s, the black arrangers pioneered a jazz aesthetic that allowed for coordination and improvisatory soloists.[20] The results were often electrifying. At the heart of the new music was a natural rhythmic emphasis that created a dynamic sense of propulsion. In fact, it was this building momentum that made the music "swing" for its fans and musicians.

Numerous commentators observed in these early years that swing had liberated the power of the beat. Now, the drummer assumed a new importance, whereas previously he had been submerged in sweet music. In swing, however, he emerged at the front and center of the band. Gene Krupa, the most noted white drummer of the era, and a hero to millions of fans, reached stardom with his powerful steady 4/4 beat that electrified dancers and his bandmates. His longtime interest in African tom-toms also made him a star soloist, rare before the swing era. By the early 1930s, bands were emphasizing a steady 4/4 beat in the rhythm section rather than the 2/4 of the bands of the 1920s. Similarly, the string bass replaced the tuba, and the more fluid guitar took over from the up-down banjo. As a result, according to Andre Hodeir, the whole rhythm section took on a unity and suppleness that enabled them to speak with one voice. The hard-driving beat loped along in a steadier, flowing rhythm, making it superb for dancing. "To know what swing music," is, Goodman added, "you have to

Fig. 11.1. Benny Goodman band, Meadowbrook Lounge, Cedar Grove, N.J., September, 1941. In 1935–36, Goodman startled the music world by hiring black performers, but he was forced to showcase them as part of a featured trio or quartet to avoid hostility toward integrated bands and, hence, canceled bookings. By 1941, Goodman and other bandleaders integrated black musicians into the larger band. The black musicians are, from left, John Simmons, bass; "Big" Sid Catlett, drums; Cootie Williams, trumpet. Note the rapt listeners, standing transfixed around the bandstand. (Frank Driggs Collections, Brooklyn, N.Y.)

feel it inside." Once a unified rhythm section laid down the beat, the entire organization could "get in the groove" and move with the power and punch of a modern locomotive.[21]

A firm rhythmic foundation also enabled the other sections to interact in new ways. First, bandleaders dispensed with string sections and more than one tenor sax of the sweet style and replaced them with full-strength brass sections composed of trumpets and trombones. Swing-era brass sections opened up and blasted with confident power. Harry James, Ziggy Elman, and Roy Eldridge achieved stardom playing variants on "Bugle Call Rag."

In fact, the robust brass section distinguished swing and served as a call to a new musical era. As the brass played powerfully and in unison, it worked against a full-strength sax section. Using Henderson-style arrangements, Goodman and his followers treated sections as individual voices, playing them off against each other in an improvisational manner. Each would play particular figures, comment on the general melody, and help propel the music. Bands also added the Afro-American call and response pattern, which, together with the repetition of simple riffs, helped the bands achieve a free musical style and a sense of drive.

The merging of Afro-American traditions and European style also promised to accomplish what had seemed impossible in older musical forms: the creation of a highly organized group that provided the platform for both coordination and personal freedom. As Benny Goodman phrased it, "The most important element is still improvisation, the liberty a soloist has to stand up and play a chorus in the way he feels . . . as an expression of *himself*." As complex organizations, the big swing bands thus created specialized roles for soloists and singers: "The people who can play virtuoso jazz solos have the same sort of color that a good ballplayer or trapeze performer has. . . . This is something the mouse bands don't have." Soloists added the elements of surprise and adventure. Comparing swing to baseball, Goodman noted, "You may have a fair idea of what Joe DiMaggio is likely to do . . . but with a *swinging cat sending*, you can never tell where he's going—only that he is going 'out of the world.'" Also, swing bands pioneered the featuring of soloists as stars on theater marquees and on records. Solo instrumentalists received higher pay and had greater freedom of expression than ordinary section men. "Who knows the names of any of the men in Sammy Kaye's band," the top sweet outfit, asked one *Metronome* article sarcastically, "or even if they are men?" In Goodman's band, soloists were enhanced by the larger organization, and singers contributed to the group effort, doing one chorus of a song but fitting in with the group's overall interpretative effort.[22]

At the same time that individuals found greater freedom of expression, they also had to strike a proper balance with the overall group dynamic. Goodman disdained "just isolated exhibitions." According to one review, good swing men avoided "barrel house," where "it's every man for himself." The jamming style of the 1920s was associated with anarchic individualism and connoted excessive self-indulgence, which produced a breakdown in music. "Because it's likely to end up in a dog fight," the *New Yorker* noted, "it is frowned upon by good musicians." In contrast, Goodman emphasized coordination and symmetry, where "the solo was treated as a consistent element of the entire performance, as the development of an idea that had gone before, as a preparation for something that was to follow." As the King of Swing phrased it, he sought "consistency rather than genius," consummate professionals rather than touchy artists.[23]

Finally, to create a recognizable group sound, the wide array of musical voices had to work together smoothly. Swing arrangements added a logical and rational structure to this improvisatory mode to prevent individual overindulgence. Swing was thus "arranged improvisation," a term which combines freedom and order, liberty and security. Holding to the liberating qualities of jazz, swing arrangements also got rid of the high-hat, stuffy, tricky angular elements of twenties arrangements and instead emphasized rhythm, motion, and drive. These arrangements unified the direction of the solos and gave the bands a "tight small band quality. A driving beat, a rhythmic brass section and a sax section that would be smooth but with lots of punch."[24]

Yet, as arrangements produced freedom and movement, they could not be imposed entirely from above. In pursuit of a democratic ideal, arrangers and leaders built arrangements around their personnel and tested these arrangements against the advice of musicians and experience with dancers. "Most of the numbers," noted the New Yorker, "are really built up during working hours, on the bandstand, for creative swing depends a good deal on inspiration." Arrangements also helped create professionalism in swing and also merged the individual with the group effort. Otis Ferguson, music critic for the New Republic, noted the musicians' superb teamwork: "The feeling that the whole band is effortless and right will give individual power to each man as he stands out to play alone, and in turn each man who plays his few individual bars with inspiration will inspire all the rest as a unit, until they come as near to forgetting selfish pride and ego as any artist has come."[25]

At the same time, the modern band expressed intense audience dreams for personal fulfillment in an organized world. As Goodman noted, the power of swing offered dancers and listeners an "outlet for fear, inhibitions, dreams, hopes." " 'Out of the world' . . . they are free from . . . the pressures of depression and war clouds, from nagging friends and duty-calling love." Indeed, much of the appeal of swing among the young was its power to push them toward a new future where the self was forgotten and some semblance of spiritual freedom resulted. This was the underlying momentum or "drive" or push in swing toward ecstatic release. As the arrangements unified the solos, they also used the interaction of the sections to push the tunes bolero-like toward a climax. And as the bands revved up, the soloists, each contributing to one overall direction, began to "take off," until, like Benny Goodman's clarinet, they were flying. Listeners then enjoyed an immersion in the driving, coordinated sound that emulated the power of a streamlined locomotive.[26]

In this process, audiences were not passive. Goodman's signature tune called them to "Let's Dance," and he was not happy unless the floor was filled with activity. Dancers worked up to an ecstatic state in which, through a physical activity, they could leave this earth and fly through the air. Parallel to the music, the new dance steps spread out from black culture—especially New York's Harlem—as whites copied black dances such as the Lindy and the Big Apple. Both dances were extremely active and complex, perfect for the young. They were also open-hold styles, in which couples often held each other at a distance while they danced. This distance helped them improvise and strut in a fashion hitherto unknown in white dancing. The bodies shook, the shoulders moved, the legs strutted, all in natural, streamlined ways quite different from the choppy, vertical movements of the Charleston, the major dance innovation of the 1920s. Like the instrumental soloists, dancers ultimately built on the accelerating groove, jumped through the air, or lifted their partners. In the swing groove, dancers took off.[27]

At any dance hall where a swing band played in the thirties, the message was as clear as Harry James's trumpet: ecstasy and personal freedom still existed in the modern world. Nowhere was this more evident than in the intensification of personal dreams as a good swing band focused its "hot" sound on songs devoted to romantic love. Unlike the sweet style, swing fused love songs to a "hot" jazz style. The result was a heightened desire for more out of personal relations with the opposite sex. In "Rose Room," "Body and Soul," "It's All Yours," "I'll Never Smile Again," "Green Eyes," "Moonlight Serenade," and a host of other ballads, love became an all-consuming endeavor. The themes of personal transformation through love, the desire for absolute fulfillment, and the devastation of loneliness occurred again and again. In "It's All Yours," Helen Forrest offers "everything you see" to encourage her lover to come out of his "cloister" and stop moping, while Frank Sinatra mused that the dream of his girl made "a cloudy day sunny." The versatile instrumentation of the bands helped communicate the singers' messages. Band singers borrowed from Billie Holiday and Bing Crosby the style of singing directly to the listener in a natural speaking voice. As the singers spoke their one chorus of lyrics, the reeds and brass played out every element of the feeling, so that the entire arrangement heightened young people's intense involvement in songs of love and romance.[28]

Furthermore, the band's image radiated more than romantic love and hot sounds. In front of large audiences, a coordinated band—made up of shining trumpets, shimmering saxophones, and drums—took on the sleekness of streamlined trains speeding toward excitement and personal freedom. Indeed, as machines embodying adventure, power, and speed, trains were an important part of the swing lexicon. "Take the A Train," "Chattanooga Choo Choo," "Lunceford Special," "Big John Special," "Skyliner," and "Happy Go Lucky Local" combined with the airplane songs—"Flying Home," "Air Mail"—to offer images of speed, romance, mystery, and adventure. It is not too much to surmise that this brassiness, rhythmic urgency, and power might have restored phallic strength, while the sax's rounded musical figures united them to female fulfillment. Yet where was this hot vibrant life to be found? Nowhere but the big city. The bands and their glimmering sounds conjured up an inviting modern urban world of hotels, ballrooms, and supper clubs. As the big train rhythm took dancers outside their everyday existence, it also reestablished the city as the locus of natural freedom in the modern world.[29]

What is more, the utopian possibility of swing found its major audiences among young people aspiring to break from the past and affirm a more vigorous urban experience. Perhaps more than ever before, popular music came to mean a new life for a growing mass audience composed of young people—especially of high school and college age—of various class and ethnic backgrounds. There is a remarkable passage in John Okada's No-No Boy, a powerful novel of a college-educated Japanese-American war resister, that suggests the attraction of swing. Having served a jail sentence during World War II for remaining true to his mother's Japanese nationalism, Ichiro summarizes his conflicts by references to swing. "Quite frequently," he noted, his mother "would slip into his room where he was studying and listening to Glenn Miller or Tommy Dorsey and firmly switch off the set." Matters worsened when he learned to dance: "The phonograph was methodically smashed to bits. Nothing survived." Out of jail and embittered, Ichiro blamed his mother: "All she had wanted from America for her sons was an education, learning and knowledge which would make them better men in Japan. To believe that she expected that such a thing was possible for her sons without acquiring other American tastes and habits and feelings was hardly possible and, yet, that is how it was." Only when dancing to swing music at a roadhouse with his girl does Ichiro accept his new American identity: "This is the way it ought to be, he thought to himself, to be able to dance with a girl you like and really get a kick out of it because everything is on an even keel and one's worries are only the usual ones of unpaid bills and sickness in the family." And he concludes, "There's a place for me and Emi and Freddie here on the dance floor and out there in the hustle of things if we'll let it be that way." [30]

This child of immigrants was not alone. By the mid-1930s, swing defined a new, more inclusive vision of American culture that cut across ethnic and class lines. In ballrooms and open-air festivals, from radio and records, young people absorbed the new music. In "Bei Mir Bist Du Schein" and then Ziggy Elman's "And the Angels Sing," Jews of all ages found their traditional melodies and *frailiches* performed with great sophistication by swing bands. In "Cirribbin," Harry James performed the same function with an Italian folk melody. It was not just whites. Vernon Jarrett, now a major black columnist in Chicago, recalled that listening to swing music as a youth in the rural South conjured up a new world of possibility: "When I used to listen at night, it was not to only hear Duke Ellington from the Cotton Club. You also heard the man say 'Fatha Hines from the Grand Terrace in Chicago.' It seemed as though from the noise in there the people were just free. White people and black people in there together." And the train songs, so important in black culture, connoted a sense of mobility and promise, a world different from the South. [31]

Indeed, young people committed themselves to swing because it heralded a more optimistic future, capable of uniting the organic with modern individuality. When Goodman played New York's Paramount Theatre in 1937, for example, 4,400 young people awaited the opening of the box office. When the band hit the stage, a near riot ensued. *Variety* reported a "roar of handclapping, whistling, stamping, hallooing . . . tradition-shattering in its spontaneity, its unanimity, its sincerity, its volume, in the child-like violence of its manifestations." The optimism was contained in the "Killer Dillers" and "Flagwavers" (the loud, raucous, full-throated band anthems) that rocked the house, got the audience "off," and "sent them" "out of this world." The fact that swing had moved closer to traditional standards with its discipline and its Tin Pan Alley songs made this mass appreciation possible, but it was also true that swing took listeners and dancers away from the failed world of the present to a dream world of the future. [32]

In hindsight, it is not hard to see that swing was the music of the Great Depression because it offered this dream of a more abundant life, with its possibilities of freedom in the group, a more pluralistic society, and the ecstasy of romantic love. Yet it would be a mistake to see swing as just escapist music for hard times. In fact, most political and economic historians separate the periods of Depression and war, interpreting the coming of conflict as the beginning of affluence and the end to Depression-era concerns.[33] Yet, when one examines the swing phenomenon from the 1930s through the early 1940s, there exists a surprising continuity. In fact, as the country entered a war to rid the world of racism and tyranny, the optimism and élan of swing music was now transferred to the international arena. For one thing, the great wartime leader, FDR, was an icon in swing as he was in many elements of Depression culture. Swing bands and singers performed "The President's Birthday Ball," and "FDR Jones." And references to the president existed in Gershwin's "Can't Get Started" and "How about You?" As these tunes suggest, the New Deal tapped the interest of youth throughout the country with its vigorous leadership and its promise that modern life would work more securely and inclusively.[34]

Furthermore, swing bands and musicians enlisted in the armed forces, joined USO tours and bond rallies, and made V-discs. Artie Shaw led a swing unit in the Pacific, and Glenn Miller became a national hero when he died in the European Theater. According to Billy Rose, show business was to "make us love what is good in America and hate what Hitler and the minor thugs around him stand for." Swing musicians thus stood for "home" values and became symbols of a war to defend the American way.[35] The movie *Airforce* (1943) illustrates this point. On the eve of Pearl Harbor, an "All-American" crew, made up of a Pole, midwestern farmer, Jew, and southerner, flies toward Hawaii. Their group cohesion is troubled by the Pole, played by moody John Garfield, who thinks only about himself. As FDR announces the Japanese attack over the radio, midwesterner Harry Carey urges them to pull together like a football team; Duke Ellington's "It Don't Mean a Thing If It Ain't Got That Swing" wafts through the plane, and Garfield ultimately re-enlists. Swing had become a symbol of a re-vitalized, pluralistic national team under attack.

Yet the highly organized war effort also altered swing and its relation to American society. In a total war dominated by large-scale bureaucracy and rigid military hierarchy, air force Major Glenn Miller fused the spontaneity of popular culture and a new social purpose. No longer was swing an outsider to the establishment. Rather, Miller superbly wove together

swing and nationalism. Under Miller's lead, the music became more organized as well as more sentimental. Bands grew to twenty and even thirty
players and became more hierarchical in the process. Miller became an
officer, his band a military orchestra, and his style an "arranged" one,
where the coordination of the group meant players' roles were laid out
from on high and improvisation was severely diminished.[36]

The result was a subtle taming of the musical and utopian vision of
swing. For one thing, in Miller's hands, the regimentation of the armed
services began to curb the ecstatic rhythm of the music, and the lyrics became more expressive of personal security and happiness. Tex Beneke, the
singer-saxophonist in the band, observed that as early as 1939 Miller
"found that [the public] liked sweet ballads, reminiscent melodies, sentimental words. He found that it liked new pleasant sounds which did not
clash." Unlike earlier swing, his songs were of an America already per-
fected and not something to be made over anew in the future. True, his
bands played city songs, such as "Pennsylvania 6-5000," "String of Pearls,"
"In the Mood," "Tuxedo Junction," but they were also known for their
music about distinctively American regions and symbols: "Dreamsville,
Ohio," "The Little Brown Jug," "Kalamazoo." In 1941, "Chatanooga
Choo Choo," with dreams of "carry me home," became the first million-
record seller since 1927. Miller also consciously shaped his band in an all-
American image by demanding that his singers adopt the look of innocent
boys and girls from the heartland. Yet, while the band included musicians
of ethnic extraction, whom he stereotyped as proper for certain instruments, it excluded blacks.[37]

At the same time, the desire for personal ecstasy within the group meant
something entirely different when that larger group was the armed forces.
Miller himself resented the struggle he waged with the military "brass" to
get the type of band he wanted, while many of his bandsmen felt alienated
from him as a rigid military authority figure. A host of other musicians
found the military intolerable and became nostalgic for the spontaneous,
free life of the road or for the big cities of peacetime. They saw the watered-
down, sentimental character of swing as symptomatic of the lost energy. In
response, one group during the war revived old-style Dixieland as the only
truly authentic voice of freedom. One proponent observed that "the individuality of a hot musician became a liability when orchestrators, who are
the draftsmen of the music business, started to devise arrangements of
popular music for bands of twenty or thirty men."[38]

Disaffection from swing, however, reached its apogee in bebop, a musical style that matured among young black performers during the war years and then spread to younger white players and other black musicians after the war. In the hands of many younger white and black musicians, the new music—called bop for blacks, progressive for whites—represented a revolt against the dreams of their swing fathers. Significantly, many white "progressives" were ex-army men, restless under military authority, and uncomfortable in the postwar musical world. Bob Graetinger, one of the chief composers for Stan Kenton, a major progressive band leader, received a psychiatric discharge from the armed services and remained a nonconformist after 1945, living on the fringes of society. Woody Herman's "herds" were also composed of white boppers who were outsiders. These younger men saw a world that was highly regimented and threatening to one's individuality, and they confronted a moribund swing tradition. Accordingly, many boppers, white and black, felt alienated from organized society, which they viewed as "square," and some turned to heroin so they could "tune out the honking of the world." [39]

Yet alienation from the swing and the "square world" hit young black musicians the hardest. On all fronts, the war magnified awareness among young blacks of their secondary racial and economic status in the new national culture symbolized by Glenn Miller's band. To some, the war ended possibilities of social reform of American life. Fighting a racist foe in a segregated army pointed out the hypocrisy of national ideals of unity. To others, it might seem that the movie *Airforce* used black swing as a symbol of a united team effort, but black people were absent from the screen. To still others, the problems that black bands had with the shortages and rationing of wartime (they had more difficulty getting the buses, tires, and gasoline needed for touring) confirmed their belief that it was American society, and not they, that was lacking. One of the major contributors to the new bebop style, Dizzy Gillespie, for example, used his draft-board hearing to express hostility toward white society and was classified 4-F. As he exclaimed, he and others refused to accept "racism, poverty or economic exploitation, nor would we live out uncreative humdrum lives merely for the sake of survival." [40]

In this context, the new music created by these alienated musicians was more than a technical innovation in form. Rather, it was a protest against the failed expectations of the past, particularly those embodied in swing. Indeed, we miss the full meaning of bop if we do not see it as a profound criticism of the failure of swing's ecstatic hopes for a modern America rooted in pluralism and individualism. Along these lines, many boppers considered the music business inherently racist because whites had prospered with black music while most black bands had not. In his autobiography, Gillespie still resented the fact that Jimmy Dorsey would have hired him had he been lighter colored. Much of their bitterness was directed against the great "father" figures of jazz who had become popular with both whites and blacks. Gillespie rejected the "plantation" images enforced upon black musicians: "We didn't appreciate that about Louis Armstrong, and if anybody asked me about a certain public image of him, handkerchief over his head, grinning in the face of white racism, I never hesitated to say I didn't like it. I didn't want the white man to expect me to allow the same things Louis Armstrong did." At Harvard, Gillespie thanked an audience member for handing up a chair for the band, saying, "Mighty white of you, old man." They were not humorless, but their humor, like their music, was conscious of the racial nature of American life and entertainment (fig. 11.2).[41]

In bebop, thus, black performers were a new community of avant-garde outsiders in rebellion against racism and the failures of a rationalized, exclusive world. Yet boppers were not without hope. Instead, they reinvigorated the improvisatory power of the individual, who drew from his own emotional self a burst of creative power and meaning. The high value placed on the outsider searching for honest self-expression perhaps explains the importance of Charlie Parker. A child of the Kansas City ghetto, Parker was an outsider from an early age. Instead of sticking with big bands in the early 1940s, he took his rejection from the armed forces (for drug use) as his call to the underground. Hearing sounds that no one had played, he spent a lifetime pursuing them and in the process invented a new chordal improvisatory style. A formidable soloist, Parker was most comfortable in smaller bop combos, where he made his alto sax an extension of himself, playing, improvising, creating, as his mood changed. The supreme performer-creator, he spurned written lines to create anew each time he played. In fact, struggling to establish his identity through his playing, Parker, like other boppers, attracted a hip cult of young whites and blacks in the late 1940s who were drawn to the emotional wellsprings of jazz and the world of darkness. For hipsters, "Bird" became, in the words of Ralph Ellison, a "suffering, psychically wounded, law-breaking, life-affirming hero," fighting to affirm his individual identity in an oppressively rationalized society.[42]

Yet Parker was not alone. He was merely the most salient hero of the bop world where artists rebelled against swing in the name of individualism

Fig. 11.2. John Birks "Dizzy" Gillespie, the promoter and genius of bebop, San Antonio, Texas, c. 1952. Dizzy looks bebop hip: horn-rimmed shades, suitable for night vision; snappy beret; lip goatee; long-draped jacket. Numerous devotees copied Dizzy's attire. From left, L. D. Harris, trumpeter; Dizzy; unknown; Don Albert, ex-bandleader and owner of the Keyhold Club. (Frank Driggs Collection, Brooklyn, N.Y.)

and modernism. In the process, they also created a new and complex musical expression that revolutionized jazz. Swing players, for example, had improvised on popular *melodies* suitable for dancing. Boppers followed Charlie Parker in improvising on the *chord* patterns underlying popular songs, thus transforming elements of the older swing culture with new energy and spirit. "Cherokee," for example, a swing standard, became the startlingly different "Ko Ko." While swing moved steadily, bop was often frenetic, resembling a train about to go off the tracks. These unexpected qualities removed familiar signposts, making the sound unstable and the world of the listener anxious and restless. By changing chords, bop made the tunes more abstract and less representational and conventionally sooth- ing. As a result, it was up to the listener to supply, unconsciously but ac- tively, the missing threads in the music. As pianist and composer Mary Lou Williams noted, bop "was like riding around and taking in the scenery rather than having a steady beat going." Bop, thus, was more a "head," or listening, music.[43]

Changes in the entire rhythm section of the bop combo also under- scored the emphasis on the soloist. Under Kenny Clarke and Max Roach, drums moved away from the steady 4/4 timekeeping function of the bass drum to a polyrhythmic emphasis and a subtler beat. Time itself became more abstract and fractured, as drummers used cymbals for rhythm and placed accents on the drums between beats. Similar to their reaction to changes in pace and chordal improvisation, listeners had less assurance the beat was going anywhere, as emphasis shifted to the player's psychological interpretation of the meaning of time itself. In this fragmented, jagged world, the other rhythm instruments, guitar, bass, and piano, were solo ones too. Indeed, in bop combos, nearly everyone fed the soloist or soloed himself. This implied a rejection of the father-leader and new sense of equality: "We had to be as sensitive to each other as brothers in order to express ourselves, completely, maintain our own individuality, yet play as one."[44]

Finally, the music revolutionized the swing canon by looking to non- American sources for inspiration. Dizzy, for one, revitalized jazz by incor- porating Afro-Cuban elements and by exploring non-Western sounds, as in the motif that dominated "Night in Tunisia" and "Congo Blues." Others experimented with the Muslim religion and Arabic names, abandoning white Christianity long before others. Their musical stance mirrored their social and racial attitudes. Artists, according to Gillespie, were "in the van- guard of social change, but we didn't go out and make speeches or say, 'Let's play eight bars of protest.' We just played our music and let it go at that. The music proclaimed our identity. It made every statement we truly wanted to make." Dizzy, Charlie Parker, Kenny Clarke, Milt Hinton, Thelonious Monk, Max Roach, and others searched for a musical form that, unlike swing, could not be stolen by whites.[45]

The desire for a new identity, however, conflicted with the desire to spread the message to a wider audience. While most boppers followed Parker in disdaining the big band tradition, Gillespie tried repeatedly from 1945 on to build a big bop band. By 1947, he began to find an audience, but his experience only added to the boppers' sense of conflict with American society. Gillespie's attempt to integrate the new innovations with a big band format foundered because big bands were no longer economically feasible. It was difficult to get lucrative bookings, it was hard to discipline the free-spirited bebop musicians, and it was painful to work for audiences who expected them either to play for dancing or to attack middle-class life. Dizzy held on through the 1940s to spread the message of "our music," but his example only underscored what a difficult road inclusion in the mainstream would be. As one early fan noted, "Jazz had broken itself free of the middle-class world's *social* conception of what it should be. It gave no quarter and asked none. It was probably more than at any other time in its history, including the present, absolutely non-popular."[46]

Ironically, it was swing that had encouraged black musicians to want more from life, to dream of an egalitarian, ecstatic community. During the thirties, they had created a swing music which bound personal fulfillment with the promise of social regeneration. The organic freedom of the soloist would unite with the organized band to provide a utopian sense of progress within the modern organized world. Swing had also promised a pluralistic society, one that offered ecstasy and fulfillment to mass audiences. Paradoxically, this vision had been heightened by the war and exhausted by it. Now, the organic was replaced by the bureaucratic army, and the individual lost much of his sense of personal transformation. Many who had served in the army or on the home front sought personal dreams apart from regimented life. And there were doubts that these dreams could be achieved amid inflation and postwar reconversion. For swing players, the future was bleak. For revivalists, the only answer lay in the past. For boppers, the search lay in a conflict-ridden present. Similarly, faced with a bleak future and the necessity to struggle for identity, audiences made up of blacks and whites were drawn to bebop. "Everybody was trying to look like me," Gillespie mused. "Now, why in hell did they want to do that? They even pretended to laugh like me . . . and it was not a racial phenomenon. These were black and white people alike, by the tens of thousands, willing to stand up and testify for bebop."[47] For many in the postwar era, an age of anxiety, and a search for personal identity, had begun.

NOTES

1. Dizzy Gillespie, with Al Fraser, *To Be, or not . . . to Bop* (Garden City, N.J.: Doubleday, 1979), 201.

2. Ralph Ellison, "The Golden Age, Time Past," in *Shadow and Act* (New York: New American Library, 1966), 201.

3. Gillespie and Fraser, *To Be, or not. . . . to Bop*, 141.

4. Interview with Red Rodney, in Ira Gitler, *Swing to Bop: An Oral History of the Transition in Jazz in the 1940s* (New York: Oxford University Press, 1985), 236. For more on the decline, see George T. Simon, *The Big Bands* (New York: Schirmer, 1981), 32, and the files of *Billboard* and *Metronome.*

5. Leonard Feather, "On Musical Fascism," *Metronome* (September 1945): 16–31. Editorial, *Ebony Magazine* (n.d., c. 1949), Bebop file, Institute for Jazz Studies, Rutgers University, Newark, N.J. (hereafter known as IJS).

6. For work on swing, see LeRoi Jones (Amiri Baraka), *Blues People* (New York: Morrow, 1963); Neil Leonard, *Jazz and the White Americans* (Chicago: Univeristy of Chicago Press, 1962). J. Fred MacDonald, "'Hot Jazz,' the Jitterbug and Misunderstanding: The Generation Gap in Swing, 1935–1945," *Journal of Popular Music and Society* 2 (Fall 1972): 35–45 sees swing as a central element in the youth culture of the era. The best on music are Marshall Stearns, *The Story of Jazz* (New York: Mentor, 1964), and James Collier, *The Making of Jazz: A Comprehensive History* (New York: Dell, 1986). George T. Simon, *The Big Bands* (New York: Schirmer, 1981), is the best general account of its subject. Thomas Hennessey, "From Jazz to Swing: Black Jazz Musicians and Their Music, 1917–1935," (Ph.D. diss. Northwestern University, 1973), is a superb account of changes in black culture, music, and bands.

7. Benny Goodman, "Is Swing Dead? Was Swing Ever Alive?" unidentified periodical (in all likelihood *Downbeat*, c. 1940), Benny Goodman file, IJS.

8. For the development of popular culture in the twentieth century, see Lewis A. Erenberg, *Steppin' Out: New York Nightlife and the Transformation of American Culture* (Westport, Conn.: Greenwood, 1981; reprint, Chicago, University of Chicago Press, 1984); Lary May, *Screening Out the Past: The Birth of Mass Culture and the Motion Picture Industry* (Chicago: University of Chicago Press, 1983); Warren Susman, "'Personality' and the Making of Twentieth Century Culture," in *New Directions in American Intellectual History*, ed. John Higham and Paul Conkin (Baltimore: Johns Hopkins University Press, 1979), 212–26; John Kasson, *Amusing the Millions* (New York: Hill and Wang, 1980); Kathy Peiss, *Cheap Amusements* (Philadelphia: Temple University Press, 1986). Paula Fass, *The Damned and the Beautiful* (New York: Oxford University Press, 1978), analyzes the development of college youth culture in the 1920s.

9. For the general development of black culture and its applicability to jazz, see Jones, *Blues People,* and Lawrence Levine, *Black Culture, Black Consciousness* (New York: Oxford University Press, 1977).

10. Neil Leonard, *Jazz and the White Americans*, 55–68, is the best discussion of the Chicago group and their attraction to jazz.

11. On refined, symphonic or sweet jazz, see Leonard, *Jazz and the*

White Americans, 73–89; Albert McCarthy, *The Dance Band Era: The Dancing Era from Ragtime to Swing, 1910–1950* (Radnor, Penn.: Chilton, 1971), 19–72; Thomas A. DeLong, *Pops: Paul Whiteman, King of Jazz* (Piscataway, N.J.: New Century, 1983), 64–65. Henry Anton Steig, "Profiles (Benny Goodman)," *New Yorker* (April 17, 1937): 31, discusses Whiteman's holding hot stuff in check; Russel B. Nye, "A Word About Whiteman," *Popular Music and Society* 1 (Summer 1972): 231–41, has the best analysis of Whiteman's contributions to music.

12. For the general decline of show business, see *Variety* (December 29, 1931): 3. Barbara Zuck, *A History of Musical Americanism* (Ann Arbor: UMI, 1980), 94–95, discusses unemployment among musicians. Gama Gilbert, "Swing: Is It a Passing Fad?" *New York Times Magazine* (November 19, 1939): 15–19.

13. McCarthy, *The Dance Band Era*, 36–72, notes that by 1936 the band world was diverging, with sweeter bands eschewing experimentation to play in staid hotels, plusher nightclubs, and radio venues. Shaw, *The Trouble with Cinderella*, (New York: DaCapo, 1951), 256–60, and Goodman and Kolodin, *The Kingdom of Swing* (New York: Stackpole, 1939), 117–22, discuss their radio experiences.

14. H. F. Mooney, "Popular Music since the 1920s: The Significance of Shifting Taste," *American Quarterly* 20 (1968): 67–85, and "Songs, Singers and Society, 1890–1954," Ibid. 6 (Fall 1954): 221–32; Henry Pleasants, *The Great American Popular Singers* (New York: Simon and Schuster, 1974), analyze the new singing styles as a result of the Depression and the centrality of radio.

15. George Simon, "Review of Shep Fields," *Metronome* (June 1936): 16. Goodman and Kolodin, *The Kingdom of Swing*, 142–44, 197–98; McCarthy *The Dance Band Era*, 122; and Steig, "Profiles (Benny Goodman)," 33–34, note the failures, discouragement, and difficulties Goodman had and how his success at the Palomar Ballroom in August 1935 came as a complete surprise to him and to MCA, his own agency. For "weak sister," see Goodman, "Is Swing Dead?"

16. David Kyvig, *Repealing National Prohibition* (Chicago: University of Chicago Press, 1979), analyzes the lobbying groups behind repeal. Little has been done on the effects of repeal, however.

17. Goodman and Kolodin, *Kingdom of Swing*, 100, note that the hot men were originally a clique. "Players Take Over," in Irving Kolodin, "What About Swing," *Parents Magazine* (August 1939): 18. John S. Wilson, "Benny Goodman, King of Swing," *New York Times* (June 14, 1986): 30. Leonard, *Jazz and the White Americans*, 129–32, for the leaders' professional style.

18. Shaw, *The Trouble with Cinderella*, 33, 38, notes that after being labeled a Christ-killer in his youth, he wanted to "*belong*, to have some feeling of roots, to become part of a community, all out of a terrible sense of insecurity coupled with an inordinate desire to prove myself worthy." Sinatra, quoted in introduction to Simon, *The Big Bands*, xiii.

19. Lionel Hampton, "Tell Me What's on My Mind! Begs Hampton," *Metronome* (March, 1938): 16, for "pink, white. . . . " Arnold Shaw, *52nd St., Street of Jazz* (New York: DaCapo, 1977), covers the emergence of black jazz in midtown New York clubs. Jones, *Blues People*, 142–72, interprets swing as a desire for inclusion by black musicians of the middle classes. White bands hired numerous black arrangers.

20. Hsio Wen Shih, "The Spread of Jazz and the Big Bands," in Nat Hentoff and Albert McCarthy, *Jazz* (New York: DaCapo, 1978), 173–87. Goodman, *The Kingdom of Swing*, 156–70, explicitly credits his success to the Henderson style.

21. Andre Hodeir, *Jazz: Its Evolution and Essence* (New York: Grove, 1956), 195–217, analyzes the new style of black jazz that emerged in the late 1920s and early 1930s and the change in the rhythm section. On drums, see Gene Krupa, "Drummer's Dope," *Metronome* (May 1938): 36; and "Krupa's Band," ibid., 37, for tom-toms. Leonard Feather, "Helen Ward Comes Back," *Metronome* (March 1943): 12, noted the "kick" of the original Goodman band. Goodman, *The Kingdom of Swing*, 135, observes that no white band until then had gotten together such a rhythm section. Benny Goodman, "What Swing Really Does to People," *Liberty Magazine* (May 14, 1938); Benny Goodman file, IJS, 6, for "to know what swing. . . ."

22. Goodman and Kolodin, 237, on improvisation; Goodman, "What Swing Really Does," *Liberty Magazine*, 6, for baseball. Robert Deeley, "I Accuse," *Metronome* (November 1946): 57.

23. *The Otis Ferguson Reader*, ed. Dorothy Chamberlain and Robert Wilson (Highland Park, Ill.: December, 1982), 74–80. Steig, "Profiles (Benny Goodman)," 31, for disdain of barrel house; Goodman, *Kingdom of Swing*, 172–73, for solos as part of arrangement; 238, for consistency.

24. Goodman, *The Kingdom of Swing*, 173, for "arranged improvisation," and Leonard, *Jazz and the White Americans*, 123, for "small band."

25. Steig, "Profiles (Benny Goodman)," 32, for creating. Chamberlain and Wilson, *The Otis Ferguson Reader*, 79, for "band is effortless."

26. Goodman, "What Swing Really Does," *Liberty*, 6.

27. Marshall and Jean Stearns, *Jazz Dance* (New York: Macmillan, 1968), is a beginning effort to understand modern social dancing.

28. On the new style of singing, see Henry Pleasants, *The Great American Popular Singers* (New York: Simon and Schuster, 1974), 127–40, 159–64. See also, Helen Forrest, with Bill Libby, *I Had the Craziest Dream* (New York: Coward, McCann and Geoghegan, 1982), and Anita O'Day and George Eells, *High Times, Hard Times* (New York: Berkley, 1982).

29. In sound, swing is comparable to the streamlined modern architecture discussed in Jeffrey Meikle, *Twentieth Century Limited* (Philadelphia: Temple University Press, 1979).

30. John Okada, *No-No Boy* (Seattle: University of Washington Press, [1957] 1977), 204–5, 209.

31. Interview with Vernon Jarrett, in Studs Terkel, *American Dreams: Lost and Found* (New York: Pantheon, 1980), 87. Jarrett's remarks suggest that there were possibilities in American culture during the 1930s that challenge the current view of the era as conservative.

32. Steig, "Profiles (Benny Goodman)," 31, for *Variety*'s reaction and the swing lingo.

33. John Morton Blum, *V Was for Victory* (New York: Harcourt Brace Jovanovich, 1976), perceptively traces the important shifts of the World War II years. My point is that both changes and continuities were present.

34. See Kristi Andersen, "Generation, Partisan Shift, and Realignment: A Glance Back to the New Deal," in *The Changing American Voter*, ed. Norman H. Nie, Sidney Verba, and John Petrocik (Cambridge: Harvard University Press, 1979), 85–93.

35. Billy Rose, "'Escapology' Not the Answer, Showmen Must Sell Americanism to Everybody," *Variety* (November 7, 1942): 28. *Variety* and *Metronome* ran innumerable stories about show business's duty to the war effort, and the latter featured bands and musicians in the service.

36. George T. Simon, *Glenn Miller and His Orchestra* (New York: Crowell, 1974), 363.

37. Tex Beneke, "Swing was Never Really King," *Metronome* (February 1947): 20–21 for the new sound. Simon, *Glenn Miller*, 357, discusses the all-American image.

38. Simon, *Glenn Miller*, 365, on Miller as officer. Rogers E. M. Whitaker, "Profiles (Eddie Condon)," *New Yorker* (April 28, 1945): 30, for New Orleans revival.

39. Carol Easton, *Straight Ahead: The Story of Stan Kenton* (New York: DaCapo, 1973), 133–34, for Graetinger. Art and Laurie Pepper, *Straight Life: The Story of Art Pepper* (New York: Schirmer, 1979), 72, 186, for his reaction to army life. On drugs, see Ira Gitler, *Swing to Bop*, 186–218, 275–90.

40. Jones, *Blues People*, 175–207, for young boppers, and Gillespie, *To Be*, 119–20 on the draft; 287, for "humdrum."

41. Gillespie, *To Be*, 210, for Dorsey incident; 157, for reaction discrimination; 195, for battles with Armstrong. For Armstrong's position, "Armstrong Blast at Bebop Creates West Coast Furor," *The Capitol News*, (n.d.): 7, in Bebop file, IJS; and George Simon, "Bebop's the Easy Out, Claims Louis," *Metronome* (February 1948): 14–15. On the seriousness of boppers, see Barry Ulanov, "Miles and Leo," Ibid., (July 1947): 19.

42. Ross Russell, *Bird Lives!* (New York: McKay, 1980), for Parker's biography. Ralph Ellison, "On Bird-Watching, and Jazz," in *Shadow and Act*, 218–27, is most perceptive on Parker. Dennis McNally, *Desolate Angel: Jack Kerouac, the Beat Generation and American Culture* (New York: Random House, 1979), 82–83, 147–49, notes the similarity of Parker to writers like Kerouac and Ginsberg and artists like Jackson Pollock.

43. Stearns, *The Story of Jazz*, 155–67, for musical changes. Williams, quoted in Gillespie, *To Be*, 151.

44. Jones, *Blues People*, 193; Stearns, *The Story of Jazz*, 166–67; Gillespie, *To Be*, 98–100, discuss the changes in the rhythm section, especially the drummer. Gillespie, 134, for "sensitive."

45. Gillespie, *To Be*, 289–91.

46. Gilbert Sorrentino, "Remembrance of Bop in New York, 1945–1950," in *Things in the Driver's Seat: Readings in Popular Culture*, ed. Henry Russell Huebel (Chicago: Rand McNally, 1972), 127.

47. Gillespie, *To Be*, 342.

12 To the Battle Royal: Ralph Ellison and the Quest for Black Leadership in Postwar America

John S. Wright

In the fall of 1947, five years before the appearance of *Invisible Man*, Ralph Ellison published in *Horizon* magazine a fictional fragment that presaged the panoramic novel to come.[1] Nightmarishly surreal, grotesquely comic, hyperbolically absurd, the scenes of "Battle Royal," for all their Marx Brothers modernity, nevertheless had discernible roots in a hidden history of color-caste codes and "race ritual" traceable at least as far back as the fugitive slave narratives of the 1840s. The tale, however, directed no more attention to its place in a submerged vernacular history than it overtly promised the novel a 1965 *Book Week* critics' poll would ultimately acknowledge as the most distinguished single work of fiction published in post–World War II America.

"Battle Royal's" most immediate accomplishment was the rhetorical innovation of addressing its midcentury audience from the vantage point of a black memoirist whose intensely personal account of the preceding two decades of Depression and world war compressed its deepest meanings into this now famous anecdotal frame. A young black high school graduate, a would-be leader of his people, has been invited to repeat, before the leading white citizens of his segregated small southern town, his recent graduation speech urging blacks—à la Booker T. Washington—to "social responsibility" and cooperation with the ruling whites. Before being allowed to give his speech, however, he and nine other "little shines" are herded to the ballroom through a servants' elevator, outfitted with shorts and boxing gloves, titillated erotically by a nude blonde stripteaser, then blindfolded and led into a boxing ring where they battle to the last survivor and finally scramble for counterfeit coins on an electrified rug—all for the orgiastic entertainment of the onlooking whites. Delivering his speech at last as a finale to the evening's program, choking on his own blood and saliva, the self-described "invisible man" turns the sideshow atmosphere deadly serious for a moment by accidently uttering the forbidden phrase "social equality." He humbly retracts it, completes his speech, wins a brief-

case containing a scholarship to a black college, and goes home to a night
of haunting dreams that prophesy his fate as the butt of a white folk's joke
that is to "Keep This Nigger-Boy Running"—under the taunting tutelage
of his own outwardly meek but inwardly Machiavellian grandfather.

In contrast to the soberly strident protest fiction Richard Wright had created during the preceding decade, Ellison's experimental yarn revealed
much in common with the new metaphysically "black" humor and "tragic
farce" toward which postwar literary sensibilities were drawn.[2] Its dramatization of zealous public rituals and perverse ceremonial compulsions aligned
it with the developing body of mythopoetic motifs and New Critical concepts then rising to prominence among artists, academics, and reviewers.[3]
The tale deflected explicitly "racial" themes from the realm of moral melodrama to that of comic absurdity, and from the grotesqueries of the still-
prevailing American literary race ritual—lynching—to the slapstick antics
of the ballroom smoker. The deflection made it seem disarmingly distant
from the nonfictional specter of black-white confrontation signaled in the
forties' then expanding national pattern of organized black protests, boycotts, and "Freedom Rides," and from the urban race riots that had convulsed Mobile, Los Angeles, Detroit, and Harlem during the war years.[4]

"Battle Royal," however, would attract little critical attention until its
reappearance in 1952, opening the novel that, for all the reviewers' emphasis on generic identity crisis, existentialism, political disengagement,
and all-American questing for self, nonetheless pursued its larger meanings
through the medium of intensely "racial" experience and a corollary nexus
of political engagement, failure, and rededication. In the course of moving
its anonymous hero from childhood to manhood, from feudal southern
province to northern machine-age city, from the margins of power to the
center, *Invisible Man* traversed a disconcerting multiplicity of institutional, technological, and psychological environs while telescoping a hundred years of American history, official and unofficial.[5] Although, like
Wright's *Native Son*, Ellison's completed novel would find its explicit politics to be its greatest burden and its most often cited artistic failure, it was
precisely in *Invisible Man's* attempt to "politicize" the nonpolitical—to reveal the protopolitical jumble of human motive embedded in the ritual
and psychic substructure of American racial codes—that Ellison offered
the most startling new insights about American culture. Most crucially, in
creating a "conscious hero" able ultimately to comprehend this bewildering modern context and still to "believe in nothing if not action," *despite*
all his "sad, lost period" of naive political enthusiasms, Ellison's narra-

tive prophetically distilled the prototype Afro-American sensibility whose phoenix-like resurgence in the postwar Freedom Movement would ultimately transform American social and political life.

That such a sensibility would conceive its own circular life history as beginning and ending in riot was a matter of more than the rhetoric of fiction—a matter indeed of a newly consolidated radical black historicism. In recognition of it, the structure of Ellison's narrative was undergirded phenomenologically by a nonmechanistic, nonlinear concept of time that constituted no mere storytelling device but rather what Ellison knew to be an increasingly pervasive element of Afro-American consciousness. In a chiliastic mixture of fatalism and hope, Spenglerian visions of white Western nations spiralling downward in deference to a Rising Tide of Color had been in popular currency in black sermons and street-corner oratory since the Jazz Age.[6] In that tradition, for Ellison's "thinker-tinker" and chronicler of personal catastrophe, what he would call the "boomerang of history" represented this historically minded generation's awareness that, with the Second World War, what had happened to the Jazz Age "New Negroes" who had preceded them a generation and a world war earlier was repeating itself, only now on a broader scale. The great migration from South to North and country to city that had been spurred by World War I and that had been buoyed by hope and had buoyed in turn the Negro Renaissance and Garveyism, was now, with the stimulus of World War II, greater and nationwide. The military experience itself, which in World War I opened to black soldiers the internationalizing vistas of European battlefields and cosmopolitan cities, in World War II spread more than a million young black men across the globe and transformed their worldviews. World War I's covert colonialist underpinnings and accompanying "Scramble for Africa" had impressed on its black participants the international import of racial ideology and the rising anticolonialist fervor. Correlatively, World War II's undisguised fascist talk of master races, its genocidal Hitlerian assault on the Jews, and the heady symbolism of Mussolini's preparatory war on ancient, unbowed Ethiopia combined to help forge a new consensus among the black war generation. They henceforth would inseparably link foreign and domestic racisms and would be dedicated to breaking the cycle of institutionalized white supremacy in America as decisively as the cycle of colonial empire in Africa and Asia would be broken in the aftermath of the war for the Four Freedoms.[7]

Against this panoramic history, the most acclaimed novel of the postwar era took shape. Ellison's imaginary memoir would recapitulate the strivings and debates of a whole generation of black intellectuals who looked out on an expanded postwar world as pregnant with dangers as with new possibilities. For them, unlike for Anglo-American intellectuals, it was not a time when the old progressivist faith lost meaning or when consensus politics and an "end to ideology" dominated thought. Rather, it was a time when the twin specters of world war and race war drove them on a quest for a new kind of leadership that would draw on the rich resources of Afro-American life and liberate them from the myths and psychic shackles of the past. A "usable" past had to be won, the still magnetic career of W. E. B. DuBois taught them, from "the propaganda of the past"; and by fleshing out that proposition in the sweeping Depression-era prose poem of *Black Reconstruction* (1935), DuBois had, with partisan rigor, vivified an old millennial vision:

> The most magnificent drama in the last thousand years of human history is the transportation of ten million human beings out of the dark beauty of their mother continent into the new-found Eldorado of the West. They descended into Hell; and in the third century they arose from the dead, in the finest effort to achieve democracy for the working millions which this world had ever seen. It was a tragedy that beggared the Greek; it was an upheaval of humanity like the Reformation and the French Revolution. Yet we are blind and led by the blind. We discern in it no part of our labor movement; no part of our industrial triumph; no part of our religious experience. . . . And why? Because in a day when the human mind aspired to a science of human action, a history and psychology of the mighty effort of the mightiest century, we fell under the leadership of those who would compromise with truth in the past in order to make peace in the present and guide policy in the future.[8]

Having immersed himself in these issues during the early forties as researcher, as polemicist, and as apprentice novelist, Ralph Ellison enthusiastically witnessed the new black historical consciousness consolidate itself intellectually in the immediate postwar years through allied scholarly assaults on "The White Masters of the World" in the adamantine Pan-Africanist rhetoric of DuBois's *The World and Africa* in 1946 and in the quieter but no less revisionary cadences of John Hope Franklin's *From Slavery to Freedom* in 1947. The new historicism required a global context and a need to "re-tell the story of the evolution of the people of the United

States in order to place the Negro in his proper relationship and perspective."[9] The earlier publication of Gunnar Myrdal's *An American Dilemma*, in 1943 (the year of the cycle of urban race riots Ralph Ellison first helped report and then later re-created fictionally), had documented exhaustively both the ethical "schizophrenia" of the white American mind and the debilitating black adjustments to it that the dislocations of war now made unnecessary and untenable.[10] Acutely attuned to sociological as well as literary assessments of American race relations, Ellison had accepted Myrdal's anatomy of the white man's racial dilemma, but he took issue with Myrdal's account of a rigid psychology of victimization and a corresponding culture of deviant imitativeness ostensibly dominant in black communities.[11]

More in accord with Ellison's interpretation, *Black Metropolis*, St. Clair Drake and Horace Cayton's middecade sociological classic of participant observation, instead described the world of America's black "Bronzevilles" as a complexly differentiated amalgam of defensible norms, values, and prophylactic styles of living. Among them, the conscious, uncompromising struggle for "racial advancement"—through the labor-union movement, through left-wing politics, through the panoply of black nationalist enclaves, and more and more through a radicalized social gospel in the church—was increasingly ascendant, and the *new* New Negro "Race Men" and "Race Women" increasingly the leadership prototypes for the kind of disciplined public protests and politicoeconomic organization that ultimately would surface in the energetic civil rights movement of the early fifties.[12]

The postwar Freedom Movement's leadership would confront in turn a powerful deflation, however, in sociologist E. Franklin Frazier's *Black Bourgeoisie* (1957), which portrayed the new black white-collar novitiate as a pathetic subsociety of culturally deracinated, economically marginal, guilt ridden, and politically apathetic new dark-skinned entrants into the make-believe world of the American middle classes.[13] Amid the storm of controversy his study generated, however, Frazier later acknowledged one important aspect of the developing black bourgeoisie that he had omitted, an omission his *American* but not his foreign critics had strangely overlooked: those "recent accessions to the Negro middle classes who are prominent in the sit-ins and in the other protest movements against racial segregation" and who had evolved, Frazier believed, not so much from the old black bourgeoisie's fusion of mulatto aristocrat and southern peasant as from the migrating black folk and working classes, newly educated, newly urbanized, and conditioned by depression and war and the specter of race riots.[14]

It was the emotional history of precisely that pivotal segment of black America that Ralph Ellison's panoramic narrative, perhaps more than any other "document" of the early postwar era, finally made dramatically visible. And in the emotional distance between the fictional portrait of martyr-murderer Bigger Thomas with which Richard Wright had opened the decade of the forties, and the portrait of the anonymous would-be political leader with which Ralph Ellison synoptically recounted and closed it lay a whole generation's disillusioning experience of migration and work and war and education. But in the imaginative confrontation with this disillusionment lay also the psychological and social roots of an optimistic postwar rededication to political struggle and mass civil disobedience. For that, the long underground "hibernation" of Ellison's prototypical Invisible Man would be, by his own carefully prophetic definition, the "covert preparation for more overt action" that the decade ahead would disclose. As underground guerilla at odds with Monopolated Light and Power, as Brotherhood political operative turned saboteur and traitor like his grandfather, the Invisible Man would turn to military metaphors—retreat, reconnaissance, redeployment—to rationalize his hibernation, and to war and its symbolic equivalents for the emotional terms on which life perforce had to be lived and art's saving graces conceived.

As Ellison would remark many years laters in a prefatory essay on the "war-haunted" imagination of Stephen Crane—the one American writer between Twain and Faulkner whom Ellison could credit with having looked "steadily at the wholeness of American life"—war and its symbolic equivalents had perennially formed the background for the high periods of the novel.[15] Civil wars especially, Ellison thought—agreeing with Hemingway—because they are never really won, their most devastating engagements "fought within the individual human heart" and continuing long after military hostilities have ceased.[16] In accord with the World War II truism that every writer who had seen combat carried in his barracks bag a war novel or a plan for one, Ellison charted his own preliminary foray into the world of fiction with the military experience as his metaphor and microcosm of that inner civil war he early saw as a conscious obsession in Afro-American life and a suppressed but no less obsessive force in the literary and political imagination of the nation at large. As oblique preliminaries to "Battle Royal," his early short stories ("In a Strange Country" and "Flying Home," both published in 1944) and the framework of his un-

published first novel dramatized the dilemma of young black men, soldiers, who like Ellison himself had "wanted to contribute to the war, but
didn't want to be in a Jim Crow army." [17]

But in none of these was military combat or the atrocities and horrific
carnage of modern warfare the experiential or metaphorical focus. Nor
was war conceived as some inverted or alien world apart. Ellison's military
tales treated war most crucially as an intensification and continuation of
peacetime social existence: war was not a dislocation but a defense and
even an entrenchment of the social order's class and caste hierarchies and
racial mystique. Ernest Hemingway and André Malraux as war novelists,
for all the ways in which their importance as literary "ancestors" would
later be acknowledged by Ellison, did not provide that vantage point in
space, time, and circumstance from which the prospective black heroes of
Ellison's war fiction might come to see how "democratic ideals and military valor alike were rendered absurd by the prevailing mystique of race
and color." [18] Ellison had originally conceived *his* war novel's hero as a captured American pilot in a Nazi prisoner-of-war camp, where he, by virtue
of rank, is the spokesman for white fellow prisoners who despise him and
where, by virtue of a Machiavellian German camp commander's sadistic
sense of amusement, he is pitted against his erstwhile comrades:

> For him that war-born vision of virile fraternity of which
> Malraux wrote so eloquently is not forthcoming, and . . .
> while Hemingway's hero managed to put the war behind
> him and opt for love, for my pilot there was neither escape
> nor a loved one waiting. Therefore he had either to affirm
> the transcendent ideals of democracy and his own dignity
> by aiding those who despised him, or accept his situation as
> hopelessly devoid of meaning; a choice tantamount to re-
> jecting his own humanity. [19]

Sent home to recuperate during the winter of 1944 from the stress of his
service in the Merchant Marine, acutely aware that his original idea for a
novel would not work, Ellison floundered, he later acknowledged, "into a
state of hyperreceptivity" which yielded two creative seeds: first, an inner
voice that declared "I am an invisible man," in ironic rebuttal to the sociological truism that "most Afro-American troubles sprang from our 'high
visibility'"; and second, a realization that "war could, with art, be transformed into something deeper and more meaningful than its surface violence," an insight afforded by his conjunction of brooding recollections
about the experience of black soldiers first in the Civil War and then in the

war of his own time.[20] Out of a complex train of associations recorded only in fragments by Ellison over the years, two other oft-noted "explanations" stand out. He was absorbed with reading Lord Raglan's *The Hero: A Study in Tradition, Myth, and Drama* (1936). And he was, as an outgrowth of the current black struggle with the Roosevelt administration over discrimination against blacks in the war industry and among combat personnel, immensely "concerned with the nature of leadership, and thus with the nature of the hero . . . [and] with the question of just why our Negro leadership was never able to enforce its will. Just what was there about American society which kept Negroes from throwing up effective leaders?"[21]

Ellison's expressed concern with the problem of the hero and black leadership reflected political anxieties common to Americans and the modern world at large in the years between the Great Depression and the second Great War. The flood of studies of the hero-leader by political scientists, mythographers, philosophers, and historians and the rise of a formal sociology of leadership during the forties are not to be understood apart from the spectacular rise of Adolph Hitler and Benito Mussolini and fascist authoritarianism, of Roosevelt, Stalin, and Churchill, or from the interest rekindled thereby both in the perplexing role of great men in history and in the fatalistic popular attitudes and scientific determinism that denied such heroic interpretations of history.[22] Ellison's encounter with Lord Raglan's effort to separate the myth from the history of heroes took place against the intellectual gyrations of wartime 1943, during which philosopher Sidney Hook's *The Hero in History: A Study in Limitation and Possibility* and historian Gerald Johnson's *American Heroes and Hero Worship*, for example, affirmed the current claim that "never has the world been more in the grip of hero mythology than today, and never has the voice of sense and science been more needed to bring the beast to bay."[23]

Debated more abstractly as an expression of the ancient philosophical conflict between free will and determinism, framed most often as echoes of Carlyle's "Heroes and the Heroic in History" and of William James's "Great Men and Their Environment," the forties' discussions on whether the hero-leader (Hook termed him "the event-making man" as opposed to the merely "eventful" man) was the product of a particular age, or of his or her own prodigious will and creativity, became polarized between the touting of the leader's role by contemporary authoritarians and the correspondingly extravagant deification of impersonal "social forces" by Marxist thinkers.[24] Much of the debate on the hero in history, though, evaded or equivocated on the issues of particular interest to Ellison. The conventional emphases on military and political leadership largely ignored folk and popular culture heroes on the one hand and, on the other, the role of ideas and the heroes of the arts, sciences, and religion. A frequent failure to distinguish the hero from the leader led typically to a confusion of the former's honor or charisma with the latter's power and to the particularly American practice of associating honor with democratic heroes and power with authoritarian ones. Moreover, the overlooked relationships between the leader and the led, the shifting reasons for *their* obedience and the personal traits of *his* or *her* power, were, as C. Wright Mills shrewdly insisted, crucial to understanding the pivotal situations in which the hero acts, or can act, and the symbolic character of the process of "heroizing" by which the hero's power is socially bestowed. [25]

All these matters, of course, had also beleaguered the ongoing tactical disputes in Afro-American communities, where leadership and heroic action, as problem and possibility, had preoccupied black political strategies from the era of nineteenth-century abolitionist oratory and national conventions to the brief, betrayed experiment of Reconstruction to the turn-of-the-century Washington-DuBois controversy and the New Negro-Garveyite clashes of the twenties. Alongside the official heroes and leadership of the rising black middle-class's civil rights and racial uplift organizations, a popular tradition of millenarian cult heroes, religious revivalists, charismatic revolutionaries, and skilled confidence men had evolved. And parallel to and interpenetrating both of these from below, black folk traditions, shifting and diversifying with migration, urbanization, and industrialization, articulated the pantheon of alternative heroic images in tales, toasts, blues, and ballads, which Lawrence Levine's recent scholarship has helped illuminate. [26]

For Ellison's generation of literary radicals, the confluence of the tangled traditions of the hero and the perceived crisis in letters and public leadership galvanized both a rebellion against the intraracial old guard and a series of manifestos within their own radical ranks that realigned the black political and literary imagination. Two influential critiques of black leadership bracketed the decade of Ellison's literary apprenticeship: political scientist Ralph Bunche's anatomy of black organizational leadership and programmatic policies in 1939 and sociologist Oliver Cox's historical overview of black leadership styles and psychological types, which appeared at the end of the decade in 1950 as part of Alvin Gouldner's pathbreaking *Studies in Leadership*. [27] Bunche's bleak assessment described an unbroken chain of black leaders deluded, disorganized, and chauvinistic:

They flounder about, desperately and often blindly, in their
ghettoes of thought, seeking a break in the dams of oppression through which they may lead their flock to a more
dignified and secure existence. The tiniest crevice in the
barriers is magnified into a brilliant ray of hope. So great
is the desperation that daily disillusionments are angrily
shaken off; they pound away at impregnable walls, dash tri-
umphantly down blind alleys, yet dare not stop to calculate
lest it is learned that ultimate escape is generations, even
centuries removed. . . . Color is their phobia, race their
creed. . . . They, like Hitler, even though for different
reasons, think that "all that is not race in this world is
trash. . . ." Unless the Negro can develop, and quickly, organization and leadership endowed with broad social perspective and farsighted, analytical intelligence, the black
citizen of America may soon face the dismal prospect of
reflecting upon the tactical errors of the past from the gut-
ters of the black ghettoes and concentration camps of the
future.[28]

Cox's less lurid but no less urgent reading emphasized the forces in
America antagonistic to "genuine" black leadership, forces which mis-
directed would-be leaders into a variety of "spurious" attitudes. In Cox's
view, after the decay of the heroic abolitionist leadership in the crucial
post-Reconstruction years, collaboration, placation, compromise, and
opportunism had become the preeminent dynamics of self- and white-
appointed black leaders, while the disaffected black masses had been driven
increasingly toward the ambiguously emotional politics of revolutionary
nationalism and the dysphoric symbolism of martyrdom.[29]

The impact of the war experience and its internationalizing outlook in
part made these dilemmas of black leadership seem less a peculiar racial
inheritance and more a common condition of modern humanity. Richard
Wright's creation of Bigger Thomas in 1940 had embodied the point
metaphorically. And in his afterword to *Native Son*, "How Bigger Was
Born," Wright had made Bigger's *leaderlessness*, his hunger for a "highly
ritualized and symbolized life" and for the true leader who would organize
it, one measure of the global condition in which all Bigger Thomases,
black and white, American, Russian, German, were primed to follow the
"gaudy, hysterical" magnifico who would promise to fill the void left by
vanished moral and metaphysical meanings and by the cataclysms of material change, conflict, and dispossession.[30]

Wright proposed that writers themselves become the leaders of their generation and undertake "the task of creating with words a scheme of images and symbols whose direction could enlist the sympathies, loyalties, and yearnings of the millions of Bigger Thomases in every land and race."[31] Less imbued than Wright with the image of the artist-hero as the creator of values and a leader of people, Langston Hughes, emphatically reversing the emphasis on the common citizen and the independent artist that he had taken in his 1926 Jazz Age manifesto, "The Negro Artist and the Racial Mountain," in 1941 issued a new, more strident manifesto in tune with the temper of the times. He proclaimed "The Need for Heroes" and the social duty of black writers to turn away from the endless depictions of victimization and defeat and "caged animals who moan, who cry, who go mad, who are social problems, who have no guts"—and to document instead "the deep reservoirs of heroism within the race."[32] Citing himself along with his literary peers for insufficient attention to the pantheon of black heroes, historic and contemporary, ordinary and extraordinary, Hughes called for a cycle of literary odysseys about black men and women who, in contrast to Hollywood and popular culture stereotype, faced life unafraid and unhumbled: "For we are not endlessly funny, nor always lazy, nor forever quaint, nor eternally defeated. . . . For ourselves there is a need, more than anything else, of great patterns to guide us, great lives to inspire us, strong men and women to lift us up and give us confidence in the powers we, too, possess."[33]

The psychology of heroic inspiration both Wright and Hughes advocated, however differently, with its dark, Hitlerian tendencies at one pole and its liberating possibilities at the other, served as an implicit point of reference in the dialogue Ralph Ellison and Angelo Herndon fostered in 1942 and 1943—as editors of the short-lived journal the *Negro Quarterly*—among black and white radical writers concerned about the progress of the war and the developing forms and functions of black fiction.[34] Conceived by Ellison and Herndon as "a review of Negro thought and opinion" and as a medium for the "training and orientation" of young writers, *Negro Quarterly* recorded crucial aspects of the forties' attempt to divine the techniques for revitalizing black leadership in letters and life. And it charted, in the essays Ellison contributed, his own conscious progress toward a new war-born concept of heroic fiction.

The New Negro Renaissance, for all its pride in race, in the folk tradition, and in the African heritage, had cultivated no conscious *literary* historicism and, perhaps not surprisingly, given the underdeveloped state of black historical scholarship, had produced no genuine historical fiction. As suggested in Ellison's 1941 *New Masses* review, "Richard Wright and Recent Negro Fiction," Arna Bontemps's two historical novels, *Black Thunder* (1936) and *Drums at Dusk* (1936), and Edward Turpin's family chronicles, *These Low Grounds* (1937) and *O Canaan!* (1939), were the thirties' only significant black fictional vehicles of conscious history.[35] But Bontemps's tales of slave insurrection dramatized discrete periods long past rather than modern ongoing historical *processes*, and Turpin's attempts to trace the generations of a single black family through several periods of the country's development betrayed "the lack of a fully integrated world-view" and clung correspondingly to "obsolete technical devices."

The effect of all the recent black fiction, Ellison felt, was "one of incompleteness, something . . . not fully formed," a disjunction "between the themes of which Negro writers are becoming aware and the technique necessary for their expression."[36] Reviewing William Attaway's *Blood on the Forge* (1941) in *Negro Quarterly*'s first issue, Ellison made clear his own standards for integrating technique with conscious historicism. And in critiquing Attaway's work, he apparently moved close to having discovered his own potential subject matter and conceptual innovations. By choosing the World War I–spurred great migration as his subject, the review acknowledged, Attaway had appropriately made the processes of broad social transformation his historical theme. He showed himself naturalistically deft in depicting both rural and industrial milieus and psychologically scrupulous in identifying symbolically the principal attitudes with which his novel's three farm-family brothers—who flee a Kentucky lynch mob to become Allegheny Valley steel workers—face the changing social factors in their lives. Ellison charged, however, that Attaway's narrative nonetheless ultimately disintegrated "into a catalogue of meaningless casualties and despairs" and into a simple "lament for the dying away of the Negro's folk values."[37] The novel left one brother dead at the end, one blind, and the last a mere survivor, and left Ellison objecting not so much to the author's depicting them defeated by circumstance as to denying any of them a conscious understanding of their experience and, with it, genuine grounds for hope and endurance.

Counterposed here against the book's fatalism was Ellison's own belief in fiction's role as a means of "heightening" consciousness and of preserving pivotal historical traditions of black heroism. If not always expressed in the terms Hughes prescribed—of remaining undefeated, unhumbled, unafraid—those traditions always ought to achieve at least the victory of *con-*

scious perception, Ellison inferred, even under circumstances of defeat or
humiliation. "Attaway grasped the destruction of the folk," he noted, "but
missed its rebirth at a higher level." Consciousness was the narrative's potential, though unactualized, hero. But in *Blood on the Forge* "There was
no center of consciousness, lodged in a character or characters, capable of
comprehending the sequence of events." [38] Foreshadowing the conscious
hero he himself would create to traverse some of the same symbolic history, Ellison acknowledged that "this, possibly, would have called for *an
entirely new character*." Nor, he insisted, would such a character's higher
consciousness be "a mere artistic device; it would have been in keeping
with historical truth." [39] Neither wish fulfillment nor Jamesian artifice,
then, but historically evolved if not yet incarnated fictively, this consciousness Ellison hypothesized would be one capable, first, of understanding
the chaotic patterns of a complex mechanical world and, second, of distin-
guishing potential allies from natural enemies amid the two types of Western man then waging war—the democrat and the fascist—and between
whom the unending *social* warfare which had so powerfully conditioned
Afro-American life would persist. [40]

In a subsequent editorial in *Negro Quarterly*, Ellison probed in directly
political terms the meaning of such consciousness for black leadership.
Under the pressure of wartime experience, he noted, three principal political attitudes were being expressed by Afro-Americans toward the forms of
violent and discriminatory domestic fascism they faced. The first was a
self-abasing acceptance of racial subordination which revealed "almost
psychopathic" fear or uncertainty along with a "disintegration of the sense
of group personality" that produced, rather than leaders, "the spy, the stool
pigeon, and the agent provocateur." The second attitude, only seemingly
opposed to the first, was one of unqualified rejection of the entire war
against fascism as a "white man's war" because of its fascist racial practices.
This, he argued, was "a political form of self-pity," impotent and fatalistic
and inclined toward passivity, martyrdom, and "magical" solutions that
promised to make the problem—"Negroness"—simply disappear. The
third attitude, implied in group sentiment but barely articulated by figures
of official authority, was an unapologetic "manifestation of Negro nationalism" that proposed to transform both of the others into strategies of
struggle through its triple commitment to the life of the group's conscious
personality, to its nationally redemptive quest for freedom, and to that
sense of independent Afro-American interests in the war for the Four Freedoms which made rational give-and-take possible on the interracial home
front "in the interest of national unity." [41]

Such an attitude's leadership potential, Ellison contended, lay in carefully equilibrating modern social and technological innovations to reinforce Afro-American objectives, in consolidating the group's historical
consciousness as a guide to strategic possibilities and limitations, and in
deciphering psychologically just how those energies necessary for social
transformation might be repressed, channeled, and released through cultural symbols. The ability to centralize and direct group power, Ellison
surmised, would come only from those who realized that "much in Negro
life remains a mystery; perhaps the zoot suit conceals profound political
meaning; perhaps the symmetrical frenzy of the Lindy-hop conceals clues
to great potential power—if only Negro leaders would solve this riddle."[42]
The need to see leadership, democratic *and* fascist, as bound up in *symbolic transactions* with the led, and thereby linked like hero worship to
shifting social mythologies, dominated Ellison's probings. No mere plan-
ner, policymaker, ideologist, or exemplar, the leader he hypothesized here,
like the uncreated hero he had proposed for Attaway's unhopeful novel,
was first of all a center of consciousness and, by extension, perceptive, self-
critical, adaptive, technically skilled. Such a leader would be disciplined
but experimental, would be energized by personal will while directed by a
vision of freedom and fraternity, and would be necessarily unsentimental
about human virtues *and* vices.

Ellison's broodings over the idea of leadership, leadership as an explicitly
symbological problem rooted in the workings of a society in unprecedented
flux, ultimately exploded his unities-bound and more narrowly conceived
war narrative into a vision of politicized philosophical picaresque that developed as he pondered his prototypic leader and the corresponding need
to "work out some imaginative integration of the *total* American experience and discover through the work of the imagination some way of
moving a young black boy from a particular area and level of the society as
close as he could be 'realistically' moved to sources of political power."[43]
He needed a model, a "structure of symbolic actions," which could depict
how the mystique of race had been wedded to that of power and kept from
consciousness in the body politic through "the anesthesia of legend, myth,
hypnotic ritual and narcotic-modes of thinking."[44]

Aesthetic solutions emerged from Ellison's enthusiastic absorption of
critic Kenneth Burke's evolving philosophy of literary form.[45] Ellison had
gleaned how heroic myth might mask pathological leadership through
Burke's 1937 critique of Adolph Hitler's autobiography, *Mein Kampf*. In
the book that had become "the well of Nazi magic," the rhetoric of Hitler's
battle for Aryan ascendancy had modeled a masterful insinuation of heroic

biography's ritual logic into the quest for power by a man of self-described "domineering apostolic nature."[46] Richard Wright, analyzing the Nazi phenomenon in relation to Bigger Thomas's inner void, had admitted being fascinated by Hitlerian rhetoric and being "reminded of the Negro preacher in the South telling of a life beyond this world, a life in which the color of men's skins would not matter, a life in which each man would know what was deep down in the hearts of his fellow man."[47] The will to solidarity and certainty central to the oratorical traditions of black leadership were mirrored darkly in Hitler's autobiographical rhetoric, the sense of redemptive mission, and other psychic forces possibly delusive or dangerous: the evocation of a world to be fought for and won from an oppressor who appears in many guises and is an enemy to all; the total unspoken identification of the would-be leader with the people, of his suffering, his struggles, his rebirth with theirs—and at the same time a denial of his personal ambition; the assumption of specious group unity and the obsession with enemy spies and disunifiers; the sexualization of political conflict fostered in the verbal imagery of the hypermasculine leader-lover of the people who would keep his group "pure" and woo "her" from the seducer-rival; the advocacy of armed violence in the name of reason, humility, peace, and love; the enticing rhetoric of religious conversion and self-sacrifice grafted onto the processes of secular empowerment; the satisfactions of ritual itself, detached from moral ends; the studied presentation of the leader's political activities as the creative extension of his artistic ambitions.[48]

Because the ingredients of leadership might, through such word magic, concoct a "snake oil" as well as a curative for the body politic, Ellison conceived his novel as a Burkean "comic corrective" to the various pathologies of actual and idealized leadership impinging on the prototypic central character. Burke's comic frame, in its constant two-way measurement of human aspiration against human limitation, counteracted one-dimensional polemicism and made it possible for human beings to transcend being cheated or brutalized by turning such losses into the asset of "experience" and, by observing themselves *while* acting, able to convert passiveness into maximum consciousness.[49] It was just such an attitude, ritualized in the blues, that Ellison saw intimated in Wright's *Black Boy* (1945), the same year he began *Invisible Man*. And it was the attitude with which he would endow the disembodied narrative voice of the novel, whose ritual progress, like the blues, would become "an autobiographical chronicle of personal catastrophe expressed lyrically." That voice's comically corrective self-observations would give form in *Invisible Man* to what, in *Black Boy* again as in the blues, was an "impulse to keep the painful details and episodes of a brutal experience alive in one's aching consciousness, to finger its jagged grain, and to transcend it, not by the consolation of philosophy, but by squeezing from it a near-tragic, near-comic lyricism." [50]

His 1944 short story, "King of the Bingo Game," had left Ellison confident of having mastered technically the means for projecting, in his own distinctive voice, an arrestingly tragicomic and surreal rendering of modern life's absurdity. And Ellison was finally able to unveil, in 1947, the Burkean "representative anecdote" that compressed into a single dramatic scene the whole system of symbolic actions his meditations on war, leadership, heroic action, and the nation's hidden history had precipitated. [51] The idea of war as a grim microcosm of society and the soldier-hero as the prism through which to view it had given way finally to the image of a social battle royal, of human beings still warring but having disarmed themselves militarily and ideologically and facing each other instead in painfully comic confrontation. As the first clearly crystallized prototype of his newly conceived picaresque world, the battle royal was manufactured race riot and Dionysian orgy and coon show and circus entertainment and scapegoat sacrifice. It was an object lesson in humiliation, a sexual torture and castration rite, an acting out of crab barrel sociology, and, as Ellison would later name it in its structural context, a "ritual in preservation of caste lines, a keeping of taboo to appease the gods and ward off bad luck . . . and the initiation ritual to which all greenhorns are subjected." [52]

Perhaps most important, it dramatized a preliminary answer to Ellison's controlling query, "What was it about American life that kept Negroes from throwing up effective leaders?" The political lesson, inculcated earlier in Ellison's essays, that his fictive would-be Booker T. Washington fails to learn in the course of this grotesque graduation into adult life and leadership, the failed lesson that will dog him as cursedly as his grandfather's deathbed admonition, is that in a ruling Anglo-American culture dominated by ethical schizophrenics fearful of deep thought and feeling, political issues assume nonpolitical forms; ideologies are masked in sexual, cultural, and pseudoreligious guises. And in that white world of repression and among *its* leaders, it is practically impossible to think of entertainment, of sex, of economics, of women or children, of crime, or of social equality or social responsibility or sweeping sociopolitical changes "without summoning into consciousness fear-flecked images of black men." [53]

The battle royal Ellison's novel proceeded to chronicle—confined quite precisely by the narrator's chapter 1 exordium to the years between 1930 and 1950—pushed the events of the Second World War outside its conscious margins, but the book's denouement was no less a picture of apocalypse. Ellison's nameless narrator closed his metahistory of the Depression and World War II decades with not the slightest allusion to the cessation of international military hostilities or the onset of the atomic age and the cold war, or to the rise of suburbia, corporate culture, and an expanding consumer society. The closing scenes of the novel instead are of the introductory battle royal exploded finally into full-scale urban race war—the wartime race riots that actually convulsed Harlem in 1943 here transmuted into nightmarish scenes of black-white conflagration with all the military-minded incendiary strikes, deployments of racial combatants, guerilla maneuvers, and, perhaps most crucial, the loss of faith in potential alternatives that such warfare presumes.

That *Invisible Man*, however, does not rest in apocalyptic disillusion, that the historical consciousness framed in the book's circular prologue and epilogue finally posits the rebirth of the hero-leader and not his sickness unto death, discloses no unreasoning authorial leap of faith, no unearned catharsis, no indecipherable sociological mystery.[54] Rather, it simply but insistently inscribes a full historical sensitivity to the peregrinations of consciousness that so unexpectedly and "mysteriously" spawned the generation of hero-leaders Martin Luther King, Jr., would soon come to symbolize, those "accidents of history" who emerged from their invisibility in the official accounts of postwar consensus historians to "boomerang" the nation's psyche.[55] In the confidence games, shape-changing, and "spiritual technologies" of Ellison's urban trickster, B. Proteus Rinehart, *Invisible Man* intimated also the rise to power of King's leaderly alter ego, Malcolm X—alias Malcolm Little, alias Satan, alias Detroit Red, alias El Hajj Malik el Shabazz—though Ellison's fictional emphasis on the misleaderly dark side of Rinehart's multifarious omnicompetencies seemed thereafter to shade the novelist's recorded commentary on the Muslim minister's public odyssey from insurgent princeliness to martyrdom.[56] In Ellison's view, the belief that leadership, any more than progress, could ever again be stable, predictable, programmatic, defied the logic of modern change. The illusions on which such faith was based had been shattered by the Depression and the Second World War, and Ellison in the midfifties reiterated the sobering view he had consolidated more than a decade earlier during the war years:

> In fact there is no stability anywhere and there will not be
> for many years to come, and progress now insistently asserts

its tragic side; the evil now stares out of the bright sunlight. New groups will ceaselessly emerge, class lines will continue to waver and break and re-form. . . . The fundamental problems of the American situation will repeat themselves again and again and will be faced more or less by peoples throughout the world.[57]

It was out of this sense of an age of anxiety's crisis in letters and leadership that Ralph Ellison's career as a fiction writer had evolved in the late thirties and early forties. As the genesis of his literary experiment reveals, World War II brought to a focus tensions in Afro-American cultural thought that had developed over the course of three decades. And, if critical historians are correct in describing the forties as a productive period for black novelists, characterized by heightened technical merit and less chauvinistic perspectives, then in Ellison's maturation we see how much that achievement was forged out of black writers' sense of their collective engagement in a war-within-a-war. That war for leadership in letters and in life was fought with a double consciousness, both at the level of the international politico-military conflagration over fascism and at the level of black artist-activists grappling simultaneously with the obdurate rhetoric of fiction and with the unshouldered, reciprocal responsibility on both sides of the DuBoisian Veil of Color for leaders and the led to confront political realities that Americans, white and black, had conditioned themselves not to see. Making those realities visible is the creative animus of postwar America's most acclaimed novel.

NOTES

1. Ralph Ellison, "Invisible Man," *Horizon* 23 (October 1947): 104ff.

2. See David Grossvogel, *The Blasphemers: The Theatre of Brecht, Ionesco, Genet* (Ithaca, N.Y.: Cornell University Press, 1966); Arnold Hincliffe, *The Absurd* (New York: Barnes and Noble, 1969); Lionel Trilling's discussion of "anticulture" in *Beyond Culture* (1965); and Gerald Graff, *Literature against Itself* (Chicago: University of Chicago Press, 1979).

3. See René Wellek, "Philosophy and Post War American Criticism," in his *Concepts of Criticism* (New Haven: Yale University Press, 1963); and C. Hugh Holman, "The New Criticism," *A Handbook to Literature*, 4th ed. (Indianapolis: Bobbs-Merrill, 1980).

4. See Alfred McClung Lee and Norman D. Humphrey, *Race Riot* (New York: Dryden, 1943), and *Report of the National Advisory Commission on Civil Disorders* (New York: Dutton, 1968). On the history of lynching as a literary race ritual, see Trudier Harris, *Exorcising Blackness: Historical and Literary Lynching and Burning Rituals* (Bloomington: University of Indiana Press, 1984).

5. A variety of critics have discussed the historical dimensions of *Invisible*

Man. See, for example, Richard Kostelanetz, "The Politics of Ellison's Booker: Invisible Man as Symbolic History," in *The Black Novelist*, ed. Robert Hemenway (Columbus, Ohio: Merrill, 1970); Edward Margolies, "History as Blues: Ralph Ellison's *Invisible Man*," in his *Native Sons* (Philadelphia: Lippincott, 1968); and Russell Fischer, "Invisible Man as History, *CLA* 17 (March 1974): 338–67.

6. See Wilson Moses, "The Rising Tide of Color," in his *The Golden Age of Black Nationalism* (Hamden, Conn.: Archon, 1978), 251–71.

7. See Robert G. Weisbord, "Black America and the Italian-Ethiopian Crisis," in his *Ebony Kinship* (Westport, Conn.: Greenwood, 1973), 89–114.

8. W. E. B. DuBois, *Black Reconstruction in America: An Essay toward a History of the Part Which Black Folk Played in the Attempt to Reconstruct Democracy in America, 1860–1900* (Cleveland, Ohio: Meridian, [1935] 1964).

9. John Hope Franklin, preface to *From Slavery to Freedom* (New York: Knopf, 1947).

10. Gunnar Myrdal, *An American Dilemma* (New York: Harper and Row, 1944).

11. Ellison's review of Myrdal's study, written in 1944 for the *Antioch Review*, remained unpublished until the release of his *Shadow and Act* (New York: Random House, 1964), 290–302.

12. St. Clair Drake and Horace Cayton, *Black Metropolis: A Study of Negro Life in a Northern City* (New York: Harcourt, Brace, 1945; enlarged editions, 1962, 1970). In their appended notes and documentation, Drake and Cayton acknowledged using Myrdal's criteria for the "ideal study" of a black community to judge their own work—finding themselves ultimately disagreeing with Myrdal's structuralist disregard of distinctive black "class" formations and the *ethos* of various black subgroups (788–89, 1970 ed.).

13. E. Franklin Frazier, *Black Bourgeoisie: The Rise of a New Middle Class in the United States* (New York: Macmillan, 1957). *Black Bourgeoisie* created tremendous controversy in black communities because of its focus on the psychopathology of black marginalism and on the derelections of the black middle class— themes Drake and Cayton had largely suppressed.

14. E. Franklin Frazier, *Black Bourgeoisie*, 2d ed. (1962), 7–14. By the time of Frazier's 1962 reissue of his study, the emergence of the civil rights movement and its new leadership cadre made it clear that such a phenomenon was inexplicable in the terms *Black Bourgeoisie* had offered. Frazier admitted as much, but offered no full reassessment. Drake and Cayton, in fact, had provided the more clearsighted and prophetic reading back in 1945.

15. Ralph Ellison, "Stephen Crane and the Mainstream of American Fiction," in *Shadow and Act*, 74–88.

16. Ellison, "Stephen Crane," 79.

17. Ralph Ellison, quoted in Richard Kostelanetz, "Ralph Ellison: Novelist as Brown-skinned Aristocrat," in Kostelanetz, *Master Minds: Portraits of Contemporary American Artists and Intellectuals* (New York: Macmillan, 1967), 42.

18. Ralph Ellison, introduction to the thirtieth anniversary edition of *Invisible Man* (New York: Vintage, 1982), x.

19. Ibid., ix.

20. Ibid., xiii–xiv.

21. Ellison, "On Initiation Rites and Power: Ralph Ellison Speaks at West Point," ed. Robert H. Moore, *Contemporary Literature* 15 (1974): 185.

22. The consolidation of the new "science" appeared at the end of the decade in *Studies in Leadership: Leadership and Democratic Action*, ed. Alvin Gouldner (New York: Russell and Russell, [1950] 1965).

23. Adrienne Koch, review of the *The Hero in History: A Study in Limitation and Possibility*, by Sidney Hook, in *Weekly Book Review* (June 6, 1943): 16.

24. See C. Wright Mills, "Prometheus as Democrat," review of *The Hero in History*, by Sidney Hook, in the *New Republic* (June 21, 1943): 834.

25. Ibid., 834.

26. Lawrence Levine, *Black Culture and Black Consciousness: Afro-American Folk Thought from Slavery to Freedom* (New York: Oxford University Press, 1975).

27. Ralph Bunche, "The Programs of Organizations Devoted to the Improvement of the Status of the American Negro," *Journal of Negro Education* 8 (July 1939): 539–50; and Oliver Cox, "Leadership among Negroes in the United States," in *Studies in Leadership*, 228–71.

28. Ralph Bunche, "The Programs of Organizations Devoted to the Improvement of the Status of the American Negro," 550.

29. Oliver Cox, "Leadership among Negroes in the United States," 228–71.

30. Richard Wright, "How Bigger Was Born," introduction to *Native Son* (New York: Harper and Row, 1966), xx.

31. Ibid., xix.

32. Langston Hughes, "The Need for Heroes," *Crisis* 48 (June 1941): 194.

33. Hughes, "The Need for Heroes," 185.

34. See Abby Johnson and Ronald Johnson, *Propaganda and Aesthetics: The Literary Politics of Afro-American Magazines in the Twentieth Century* (Amherst: University of Massachusetts Press, 1979), 125–60.

35. Ralph Ellison, "Richard Wright and Recent Negro Fiction," *Direction* 4 (Summer 1941): 12.

36. Ibid.

37. Ralph Ellison, "Transition," review of *Blood on the Forge*, by William Attaway, *Negro Quarterly* 1 (Spring 1942): 90.

38. Ibid.

39. Ibid.

40. Ibid., 91–92.

41. Ralph Ellison, "Editorial Comment," *Negro Quarterly* 1 (Winter–Spring 1943): 296–99.

42. Ibid., 301.

43. Ellison, "On Initiation Rites and Power," 171.

44. Ibid.

45. Ellison, in "The Essential Ellison," 148.

46. Kenneth Burke, "The Rhetoric of Hitler's Battle," in his *The Philosophy of Literary Form*, 3d ed. (Berkeley: University of California Press, 1973), 192.

47. Richard Wright, "How Bigger Was Born," xviii.

48. Burke, "The Rhetoric of Hitler's Battle," 191–220.

49. Kenneth Burke, "Comic Correctives," in his *Attitudes toward History*, 2d ed. (Los Altos, Calif.: Hermes, 1959), 170–71.

50. Ellison, "Richard Wright's Blues," in *Shadow and Act*, 90.

51. Ellison's introduction to the thirtieth anniversary edition of *Invisible Man* demystifies the genesis of the novel, if not its "representative anecdote," by consolidating various facets of the novel's creative origins—the military associations in particular—that had been recounted only in scattered pieces over the years.

52. Ellison, "The Art of Fiction," in *Shadow and Act*, 175.

53. Ellison, "Beating That Boy," in *Shadow and Act*, 109.

54. The continuing critical debates over *Invisible Man's* problematic resolutions and denouement have had nothing in common so much as a fulsome detachment from the concrete intellectual and cultural history of black literary radicals during the 1940s. Carl Milton Hughes's pioneering study, *The Negro Novelist, 1940–1950* (New York: Citadel, 1953), remains the only broad survey. No satisfactory study has yet appeared.

55. The inability of Anglo-American postwar "consensus" historians to account for the emergence of the civil rights movement and its successor, Black Power, though partly anatomized in recent years, has yet to be contrasted explicitly with the comparative prescience of postwar Afro-American historians, who indeed shared many progressivist assumptions about the nature of the postwar world, but who could consent not at all to Daniel Bell's presumptively representative dictum that "for the radical intellectual who had articulated the revolutionary impulses of the past century and a half, there was now an end to chiliastic hopes, to millenarianism, to apocalyptic thinking—and to ideology"—Daniel Bell, *The End of Ideology: On the Exhaustion of Political Ideas in the Fifties* (Glencoe, Ill.: Free Press, 1960). For representative views about black historical contexts during the postwar years, see Samuel DuBois Cook, "A Tragic Conception of Negro History," and William B. Hixson, Jr., "The Negro Revolution and the Intellectuals," both in *Understanding Negro History*, ed. Dwight Hoover (Chicago: Quadrangle, 1968).

56. See, for example, Ellison's oblique but readily deciphered allusions to Malcolm X in his interview with Ishmael Reed and others, "The Essential Ellison," 149–50.

57. Ralph Ellison, "Society, Morality, and the Novel," in *The Living Novel: A Symposium*, ed. Granville Hicks (New York: Macmillan, [1957] 1962), 66.

13 Land of a Thousand Dances: Youth, Minorities, and the Rise of Rock and Roll

George Lipsitz

> . . . perhaps the zoot suit conceals profound political meaning;
> perhaps the symmetrical frenzy of the Lindy-hop conceals clues
> to great political power.[1]
>
> *Ralph Ellison*

One of the most persistent preoccupations in popular culture in the 1970s and 1980s has been nostalgia for the 1950s and 1960s. Amid recurring economic and political crises, restrospective portrayals of beach parties, drag races, and sock hops in television programs and feature films like "Happy Days," *American Graffiti,* and *Grease* display a pursuit of innocent pleasures and suggest an era when the nation had the luxury of savoring the calculated foolishness of postwar youth culture. Much of this memory revolves around rock and roll music as the core icon linking the present with the past. From the enduring public fascination with Elvis Presley to the sudden popularity of the film *Back to the Future,* the early years of rock and roll constitute an important period marker in collective popular memory. A promotional video for televised wrestling in 1986 used the mid-1960s song "Land of a Thousand Dances," and in the summer of 1987, Columbia Pictures released *La Bamba,* the story of the 1950s Chicano rock and roll star Ritchie Valens.

Although severe inaccuracies and oversimplifications pervade these images, their focus on the birth of rock and roll as an important shared memory reveals a sensitive appreciation of the recent past. The true story of the "Happy Days" of the 1950s and 1960s is every bit as significant as current nostalgic imagery suggests. In that era, young people identified themselves as a self-conscious and rebellious social group, they made music that reflected an unprecedented crossing of racial and class lines, and their actions posed serious challenges to traditional American cultural attitudes and values. The calculated foolishness of the 1950s and 1960s was quite serious; its imagination and sense of play went a long way toward transforming American culture from the domain of a privileged elite into a "land of a thousand dances."

The retrospective approval of rock and roll music pervading so much of popular culture in the 1970s and 1980s stands in sharp contrast to rock and roll's reputation in its early years. The music industry resisted rock and roll, despite its demonstrated popularity with a mass audience, and civic and church leaders condemned it as immoral and debilitating. Intellectuals and moralists during those years tended to see rock and roll music as just another facet of an alienating and potentially anarchic society, one suffering from too many unsocialized youths and too much populist energy. Subsequent social critics, themselves raised amid the mass popularity of rock and roll, have shown more appreciation for the important racial and social implications of the music's mass appeal, yet these critics have rarely connected rock and roll music to the social history that gave it determinate shape. They have underestimated the significance of a mass popular music capable of speaking the language of everyday life and articulating the experiences and activities of the streets. Awed by the formal properties or commercial successes of rock and roll, these critics have overlooked the reasons for the music's successful challenge to elite culture as well as its mobilization of youth across racial, class, and ethnic lines.[2]

The acceptance of rock and roll music as a core icon in popular memory stems from its historical significance as a conduit for cultural change in postwar America. Rock and roll's popularity reflected changes in race relations as white teenagers accepted as their own a music that originated among racial minorities. It reflected changes within minority communities as black and brown musicians staked unprecedented claims for themselves as participants in shaping American popular culture. Finally, rock and roll music reflected the rich cultural interactions in American cities in the wake of social changes emanating from war mobilization and mass migrations during World War II. This inquiry revolves around the relationship between rock and roll music and those social changes. But, instead of exploring art disengaged from social context, this study will examine its subject historically—in one specific community over a period of time. My point of entry will be "Land of a Thousand Dances," the mid-1960s song revived by the recent wrestling promotional video. A hit song for black singers Chris Kenner, Round Robin, and Wilson Pickett, "Land of a Thousand Dances" established itself as a conduit for the many cultural streams flowing through rock and roll music in 1965, when it was recorded by Cannibal and the Headhunters, a Chicano group from East Los Angeles.[3] Recent writing about popular music has acknowledged the significance of rock and roll as a shared creation by young whites and young blacks in postwar America, but little has been written about the contribution of Chicano artists and audiences to that fused culture. To understand the era in which rock and roll emerged, we must also understand the complex cultural mediations taking place in communities like the East Los Angeles barrio where Cannibal and the Headhunters developed their musical aspirations and ambitions. The rock and roll music made by Mexican-American musicians like Cannibal and the Headhunters reveals important connections among music, memory, class, ethnicity, and race, and it illumines the enduring usefulness of rock and roll as a vehicle for collective popular memory.

Frankie "Cannibal" Garcia and the other members of his group grew up in a public housing project in East Los Angeles. [4] They originally learned to play music as folk artists in Mexican *mariachi* and *jarocho* bands, but like other brown, black, white, red, and yellow youths all across America, they blended the traditional music of their community with the sounds they heard on records and radio, drawing inspiration from the diversity of urban life and the excitement of the city streets. The Los Angeles environment that nurtured and shaped their music reflected the oppressive and exploitative hierarchies that had done so much to distort American culture in the past, but the postwar years brought radically new social formations that encouraged the development of alternative forms of cultural expression.

During the 1940s, defense spending and war mobilization changed the face of Los Angeles, stimulating a massive in-migration of whites, blacks, and Chicanos. Traditional residential segregation confined Afro-Americans to the south-central area while limiting Chicanos largely to housing near downtown and in east-side neighborhoods. [5] Private bankers and government planners encouraged housing segregation by class and race, viewing ethnic heterogeneity in Los Angeles (as in other cities) as a defect of urban life rather than as one of its advantages. In this way, vicious prejudice became written into federal loan policies and private commercial practices. For example, the Home Owners Loan Corporation City Survey File on Los Angeles for 1939 contained a confidential memorandum that argued against the feasibility of loans to Mexican-Americans because, "While many of the Mexican race are of high caliber and descended from the Spanish grandees who formerly owned all of the territory in Southern California, the large majority of Mexican peoples are a definite problem locally and their importation in the years gone by to work the agricultural crops has now been recognized as a mistake." [6]

Translated into public policy, that perception of Mexican-Americans meant that Chicano neighborhoods would not be eligible for housing loans, thereby ensuring residential segregation in the region. Federal appraisers rated the eligibility of each Los Angeles neighborhood for home loans, giving the highest rating to areas reserved for the exclusive use of white Christians while assigning the lowest rating to black, Chicano, and mixed neighborhoods. The Federal Housing Authority gave its lowest possible rating to Boyle Heights in East Los Angeles because its mixture of Chicano, Jewish, and Eastern European residents convinced the appraisers that "This is a 'melting pot' area and is literally honeycombed with diverse and subversive racial elements. It is seriously doubted whether there is a single block in the area which does not contain detrimental racial elements and there are very few districts which are not hopelessly heterogeneous. . . ."[7]

Yet the opening of new shipyards and aircraft-assembly plants combined with Los Angeles's severe housing shortage to produce unprecedented interethnic mixing in Los Angeles. Official segregation gave way bit by bit as Chicanos and European ethnics lived and worked together in Boyle Heights and Lincoln Park and blacks and Chicanos lived in close proximity in Watts and in the San Fernando Valley suburb of Pacoima.[8] On the factory floor, on public transportation, and on the streets of thriving commercial districts, diverse groups mixed with each other as never before. Wherever one traveled in the city's barrios, ghettos, and mixed neighborhoods, one could easily find the potential for intergroup conflicts and rivalries; sometimes they took the form of actual racial and ethnic violence. But there also existed a vibrant street life built upon communication and cooperation in community organizations and in neighborhood life.

In this milieu, small entrepreneurs catering to the local market sensed a demand for cultural commodities that reflected the social life of the new urban environment. Before RCA's purchase of Elvis Presley's contract from Sun Records in 1955, the major studios ignored the music emanating from working-class neighborhoods, leaving the field to the more than four hundred independent labels that came into existence after the war. Existing outside corporate channels, the smaller firms in working-class areas produced records geared to local audiences, especially in minority communities. The invention of magnetic recording tape made it possible to enter the record business with relatively little capital, and concentrations of transplanted war workers provided a ready market for music based on country music and blues.[9]

Recruiting performers from the communities they knew best, small-scale local record producers responded to trends in the streets. In addition, the proliferation of local radio stations in the postwar years offered exposure to new audiences. Juke-box operators, furniture-store owners, and musicians responded to the consumer demand for a popular music that reflected the folk roots and multiracial ethos of the new urban streets. For example, a 1948 hit record by Los Angeles's Don Tosti Band titled "Pachuco Boogie" sold more than two million copies, an extrordinary total for any Spanish-language record in the United States, but especially for one that glorified one of the barrio's more reviled subcultures—the pachucos.[10]

In many ways, pachucos embodied the defiance of conventional authority that came to symbolize the appeal of rock and roll. Pachucos were teenage gang members sporting zoot suits, ducktail haircuts, and distinctive tattoos; they had attracted public attention during the war years when newspaper stories blamed them for much of the youth crime in Los Angeles. Tensions peaked in June 1943, when hundreds of sailors invaded the East Los Angeles community to beat up Mexican-American youths who wore zoot suits. The police, prosecutors, and city council joined forces to praise this criminal attack, lauding the sailors for their efforts to "clean up" the city. But the racism manifest in the attacks caused many Mexican-Americans to start looking at the pachucos as defenders of the community against outside encroachment and as symbols of Chicano victimization and marginality.[11]

The Don Tosti Band's "Pachuco Boogie" captured the spirit of that new-found admiration for street rebels. The song's lyrics employed *calo*, the street slang associated with pachucos but considered vulgar by "respectable" Mexican-Americans. "Pachuco Boogie" blended Mexican speech and rhythms with Afro-American scat singing and blues harmonies to form a provocative musical synthesis. Some Spanish-language radio stations refused to play the song, but Anglo disc jockeys programming black rhythm-and-blues shows aimed at white teenagers put it on their playlists, to the delight of their listeners. Itself a blend of Chicano, Anglo, and Afro-American musical forms, "Pachuco Boogie" garnered commercial success by uniting a diverse audience into a new synthesis—a "unity of disunity."[12]

"Pachuco Boogie" signaled the start of creative new links among previously divided groups. Anglo youth, especially, imitated the distinctive dress of Mexican-American "cholos" with their khaki pants and long-sleeved Pendleton shirts over sleeveless white undershirts, and "cholo" became a hip slang word with larger meanings. The word "cholo" probably derives from an Aztec word meaning servant, and it connotes someone with low status, usually a recent immigrant from a rural area. Cholos spoke a bilingual slang, displayed elaborate tattoos, and staked their claims to urban neighborhoods by covering walls with stylized graffiti. The studied disinterest and cultivated detachment affected by cholos echoed the oppositional postures of other postwar subcultures, including bop musicians and Beat poets. But in Los Angeles, the cholo relationship to rock and roll made that subculture the most accessible model of "otherness" for middle-class white youths. When Anglo, black, or even Chicano youths embraced the cholo image, they flaunted their alienation by openly identifying with one of society's most despised groups. [13]

Behind that flaunting lay a source of fresh inspiration for musicians and song writers. White popular songwriters in the United States had long envied and copied the idioms and styles of black and Hispanic musicians. But their tendency had been to absorb these "primitive" forms into the musical vocabulary of respectable or refined culture. During the rock era, white artists acknowledged their debts to Third World musics more honestly than ever before, and audiences accepted the idea of black artists in positions of privilege and honor to a greater degree than they had previously. The ability of musicians to learn from other cultures played a key role in their success as rock and roll artists. For example, in 1952, black saxophonist Chuck Higgins had a hit recording with "Pachuko Hop"—a song he wrote as a tribute to the dancing, style, and slang of the Mexican-American youths he encountered while playing dances at East Los Angeles union halls. [14] Mike Stoller, an Anglo piano player and songwriter, became fascinated by the street culture of Chicanos when he moved to Los Angeles in 1949 at the age of sixteen, and that fascination led him to a career in music. "I learned the pachuco dances and joined a pachuco social club," Stoller later explained when asked how he got his start as a musician. [15] He played piano with the Blas Vasquez band, which exposed him to Chicano appropriations of Afro-American and Euro-American forms and styles as well as to indigenous Mexican music. Within a year after joining the Vasquez band, Stoller began writing rhythm and blues songs for black vocal groups with his writing partner, Jerry Leiber, another white teenager. "We found ourselves writing for black artists," recalls Leiber, "because those were the voices and rhythms that we loved. By the Fall of 1950, when both Mike and I were in City College, we had black girlfriends and were into a black lifestyle." [16] Leiber and Stoller went on to write the original "Hound Dog" for Big Mama Thornton, and they fashioned dozens of best-selling songs for black artists and celebrated the speech, folklore, and subcultures of Afro-American city life.

Perhaps the artist who best exemplifies the new cultural fusions engendered by rock and roll music is Johnny Otis. The son of a Greek immigrant
grocer and shipyard worker from northern California, Otis first came to
Los Angeles in 1943 as the white drummer in a black band playing at the
Club Alabam on Central Avenue in Watts. Otis had developed his interest
in black music while growing up in a mixed but mostly black neighborhood
in Berkeley, where he accompanied his friends to "sanctified" churches
to listen to the gospel preachers, singers, and choirs. "This society says
no white kid can stay in black culture," Otis observes, "but see, that culture had captured me. I loved it and it was richer and more fulfilling and
more natural. I thought it was mine." [17] When a high school teacher suggested that he spend less time with blacks and associate more with whites,
Otis capped a long battle with his teachers and principals by dropping out
of school in disgust. He became a drummer with Count Otis Matthews's
West Oakland House Rockers and then went on the road to tour with
a variety of Afro-American bands, including Lloyd Hunter's Territory
Jazz Band.

In Los Angeles, Otis worked with black musicians, married a black
woman, and thought of himself as "black by persuasion." But part of the
consciousness of the black community he joined there involved staking a
claim for full participation in American life and culture, and that claim
led to interactions with other groups and other cultures. "I got here in '43
and at that time the Avenue [Central] was just swinging. It was like a transplanted Harlem Renaissance," Otis remembers. [18] One night at the Lincoln
Theater, he saw the blues singer and piano player Charles Brown win a
talent contest by playing "Clair de Lune." Otis recalls,

> He kind of apologized for what he played, but they loved
> him, they made him do an encore—"Rhapsody in Blue"—
> he just broke it up. And it was a good lesson for me, because
> in later years people would tell me that "You can't take Big
> Mama Thornton to New York because she's too rough and
> bluesy, and you can't take Sally Blair to the Apollo because
> she's not bluesy enough." Well, bullshit on both counts.
> The people just liked it. If it's really strong and it has artistry,
> they like it. [19]

Otis began promoting rhythm and blues shows for mixed audiences,
offering Chicano and white youths a chance to hear the music of the black
community. He promoted and starred in weekly rhythm and blues shows
at Angeles Hall on the east side that demonstrated the powerful appeal of
black music for Mexican-American audiences and that helped stimulate

the growth of rock and roll music within the barrio.[20] Otis had rock and roll television programs on three Los Angeles television stations in the early 1950s and promoted dances all over the city, despite harassment from local authorities upset about a music that crossed racial and class lines. "The cops would come and hassle the kids standing in line to get into the television show," Otis recalls. "They see black kids and Hispanic kids and Asian kids and they don't like it. They just didn't want to see that. If it were all Asian and Hispanic and black they wouldn't care, but there were whites there, and they're mixing with the blacks and what not."[21] But despite the official harassment, the teenagers kept coming out to Otis's shows, and, despite rumors of gang violence and racial incidents about to happen, Otis remembers that "We never had any trouble, the people got along great."[22]

Exemplifying the fusion of small entrepreneur and musician that often brought rock and roll to the public, Otis started a small record label and recording studio in the mid-fifties featuring many of Los Angeles's leading rhythm and blues singers, including L'il Julian Herrera, the city's first commercially successful Chicano rock and roller. Otis produced Herrera's 1956 local hit "Lonely, Lonely Nights," a classic do-wop ballad, and featured him in his stage shows as part of a special effort to attract Chicano audiences. As Otis tells it, "L'il Julian came to me as a kid, a young Mexican-American guy and sang. He wasn't great, but he could sing and he was charming and it was nice and real. I put him on stage, and the little Mexican girls loved him, and our Chicano audience was a big part of our audience in those days. I put him in the band, and then he lived in my house."[23]

Herrera's relationship with Johnny Otis illustrates the ways in which rock and roll music became a common ground for people from diverse backgrounds in Los Angeles in the early 1950s. After all, "Lonely, Lonely Nights" presented a Chicano's rendition of a black vocal style on a record produced by a white man who thought of himself as black. But Otis found out that the story of L'il Julian Herrera was even more complicated than he knew. One day, a juvenile officer walked into Otis's record company in search of Ron Gregory, a runaway youth from the East. When the officer showed Otis a picture, he realized that Ron Gregory was L'il Julian Herrera. "He ran away from home, hitchhiked out here, and this Mexican lady in Boyle Heights takes him in and raises him as her son," Otis relates.[24] It turned out that Los Angeles's first Chicano rock and roll star was born a Hungarian Jew and became "a Chicano by persuasion," just as Johnny Otis had become "black by persuasion."[25]

The pinnacle of this brown-white-black mixing in rock and roll music in Los Angeles came with the enormous popularity of Ritchie Valens, East Los Angeles's best-selling and most significant rock and roll artist. Independent record producer Bob Keane discovered Valens when he noticed that the car-club cholos of East Los Angeles responded to a band called the Silhouettes and their lead singer, Richard Valenzuela. Shortening (and Anglicizing) the youth's last name to Valens, Keane signed him to a contract and recorded the singer with the same back-up musicians that Keane used on sessions by the black gospel and rock singer Sam Cooke. These session musicians brought a wealth of musical experience to Valens's recordings—bass player Red Callendar had played with jazz great Art Tatum, and drummer Earl Palmer had recorded with rhythm and blues artists in New Orleans, including Roy Brown, Fats Domino, and Little Richard.[26] But Ritchie Valens did not have to learn his cultural pluralism in a studio; life in postwar Los Angeles had already prepared him well for the mixing of forms and styles that would come to characterize his recorded music.

More than any other artist, Valens brought the folk traditions of Mexican music to a mass audience through rock and roll, but his music also reflected an extraordinary blending of traditions and styles from other cultures. Born in 1941 in the San Fernando Valley suburb of Pacoima, Valens learned music listening to his relatives sing Mexican songs as they gathered at each other's homes in the evenings. At the age of five, Valens made a toy guitar out of a cigar box and learned to fret it with the help of an uncle who taught him how to play his first song—the traditional Mexican *huapango*, "La Bamba." In Pacoima, Valens met William Jones, a black musician who lived across the street from the youth's Aunt Ernestine. Jones taught Valens how to tune a guitar and play chords. After building a green and white electric guitar for himself in his junior high school wood-shop class, Valens began to experiment with the Afro-American rhythm and blues songs that he heard on the radio. In 1957, he joined the Silhouettes, a band put together by Chicano vibraphonist Gil Rocha that featured Valens on guitar, William Jones's sons Conrad and Bill on drums and clarinet, and Japanese-American Walter Takaki on tenor saxophone. Valens became the featured vocalist with the band, and his tributes to the black rhythm and blues singer Little Richard moved his admirers to start calling him "Little Ritchie."[27]

In the brief period between Valens's emergence on the best-selling record charts and his death in a plane crash early in 1959, he brought an extraordinary range of musics before pop audiences. He borrowed from white rockabilly, black blues, and Mexican folk musicians because they all made up parts of his cultural environment in postwar Los Angeles. "La Bamba" and "Come On, Let's Go" featured variations on melodies and harmonies common to Mexican fiesta music, while "Ooh My Head" employed the boogie-woogie form and vocal mannerisms common to Afro-American music. One of Valens's unfinished records included an attempt to lay the rhythm popularized by blues guitarist Bo Diddley underneath the Latin guitar standard "Malaguena." Radio programs and phonograph records made Eddie Cochran's rockabilly and Bo Diddley's rhythm and blues songs an organic part of barrio life, and the limited but nonetheless real cultural mixing in working-class neighborhoods enabled young people to explore the culture of their neighbors. Valens wrote his big hit song "Donna" about a failed romance with an Anglo classmate whose father ordered her to stop going out with "that Mexican," and he recorded a version of his favorite rhythm and blues song "Framed," which had originally been recorded by a Los Angeles rhythm and blues group, the Robins, but which had been written by Mike Stoller and Jerry Leiber.[28]

Valens's tragic death at age seventeen deprived the Los Angeles Chicano community of its biggest star, and it cut short the career of one of rock and roll's most eclectic synthesizers. But other artists carried on his propensity for blending the folk musics of the barrio with the styles and forms circulating within popular music. In the late 1950s and early 1960s, groups such as the Salas Brothers, Carlos Brothers, Rene and Ray, and the Romancers had regional and national hit songs that reflected the barrio's dialogue with mainstream rock and roll music. Just as Ritchie Valens established himself as a commercial performer by playing rhythm and blues–styled versions of Anglo and Mexican songs for a mixed audience, later Chicano musicians played a combination of different musics for a combination of audiences. In concerts at East Los Angeles College and at El Monte Legion Stadium, at dances held in youth centers and union halls, and at popular nightclubs like the Rhythm Room and Rainbow Gardens, Chicano rock and rollers learned to blend Mexican and rock musics into a synthesis that won them admirers both inside and outside the barrio.[29]

Nothing illustrates this synthesis more completely than the song and group with which we began—"Land of a Thousand Dances" by Cannibal and the Headhunters. Garcia got his start as a rock singer when the lead vocalist for the Royal Jesters (another East Los Angeles rock group) became sick, and the band recruited Garcia to take his place "because I sang in school with a mariachi band, doing traditional Mexican music."[30] Garcia later joined with some friends from the Ramona Gardens Housing Project to form Cannibal and the Headhunters, taking their name from Garcia's "street" (gang) name of "Cannibal," gained when he bit an opponent in a fight. One of their most effective songs in live performances had been Chris Kenner's "Land of a Thousand Dances," but at one show Garcia forgot the words at the beginning of the song and ad-libbed "na-na-na-na-na," to the delight of the crowd. In the studio, they retained Cannibal's accidental improvisation to give the record a captivating introduction that helped it become one of the best-selling records of 1965. They also borrowed the double-drum sound prominent in Stevie Wonder records to forge a synthesis that attracted the attention of audiences all over the country.

Other Chicano musicians in the 1960s combined a fusion of popular and Mexican musics with lyrics that addressed one facet of their lives that distinguished them from previous generations—a fascination with the automobile. They celebrated cars as a means to pleasure, joy, and excitement, not as transportation to work or as a means of accomplishing mundane tasks. In 1965, Thee Midnighters scored a national hit with "Whittier Boulevard," a song honoring the main traffic artery of the East Los Angeles barrio. Drawing inspiration from the energy and imagination of the car customizers and cruisers who claimed the boulevard as their own territory on weekend nights, Thee Midnighters presented the activities of the car-club cholos to the outside world while elevating the self-image of the cruisers by inserting their subculture into the discourse of mainstream popular culture. As Thee Midnighters' lead singer Little Willie G (for Garcia) once explained, "A lot of people say you guys made Whittier Boulevard famous, but we just took the action off the boulevard and made it into a song."[31]

The car culture's quest for fun and good times expressed a desire for the good life of material success, but it also provided a means for satirizing and subverting ruling icons of consumer society. Just as Chicano car customizers "improved" upon the mass-produced vehicles from Detroit, Chicano rock songs like "Whittier Boulevard" celebrated Mexican-American appropriations of automobiles as part of a community ritual. By the late 1960s, that dialogue between the images of mass culture and the realities of barrio life increasingly took on an expressly political cast. At that time, changes in urban economics and politics threatened to destroy the social basis for the cultural pluralism of Los Angeles rock and roll by undermining the social and economic infrastructure of the central city. The cumulative effects of postwar highway and housing policies had subsidized suburban growth at the expense of the inner city, had exacerbated racial and class polarizations, and had encouraged residential segregation. For Chicanos, increased migration from Mexico, inadequate access to decent housing, and discrimination in a segmented labor market all combined to help create a new consciousness.[32]

The failures of 1960s social programs including the War on Poverty, the effects of the Vietnam War on poor and working-class youths, and the repressive policies of the Los Angeles Police Department all contributed to a growing political activism and cultural nationalism. On August 29, 1970, the Chicano community mobilized for a massive antiwar demonstration that expressed anger over many pent-up grievances and complaints. Taking their opposition to the war and their growing nationalism to the streets, demonstrators relied on their cultural traditions to give form to their protest activity. As one participant chronicled the start of that day's events, "The boulevard was filled with *gente*, doing Latino chants and playing musica right in the streets. It started taking on the atmosphere of a carnival. Some even danced."[33] This demonstration involved an attempt to reclaim city streets as a terrain for culture, politics, and celebration. But its aggressive festivity provoked a violent reaction from the authorities. Los Angeles police officers used force against the demonstrators; one officer shot and killed *Los Angeles Times* columnist Ruben Salazar. The Salazar killing outraged many people in the Mexican-American community and helped mobilize subsequent activism and demonstrations.[34]

The political ferment surrounding the 1970 demonstration found its way into Mexican-American rock and roll music in significant ways. Thee Midnighters recorded a song titled "Chicano Power" in 1970, and the group the V.I.P.'s changed their name that same year to El Chicano. In the early 1970s, East Los Angeles musicians began to feature Latin musical forms and Spanish-language lyrics more prominently in their songs, and they attached themselves to a variety of community icons and subcultures. A series of outdoor music festivals, known popularly as "Chicano Woodstocks," showcased the community's musicians and provided a forum for displaying and celebrating diverse images of Chicano identity. The band Tierra emerged as a favorite of the "low-rider" car customizers in the early 1970s, while Los Lobos got its start with an album recorded under the aegis of Cesar Chavez's United Farm Workers union. Mixing images from the past of pachucos and cholos with contemporary ones like low riders, these bands and their audiences placed current struggles in historical perspective, preserving a measure of continuity in a period of extraordinary change.[35]

Yet the music of East Los Angeles still had significant influence on artists and audiences outside the barrio. In 1975, for example, a mostly Afro-American jazz/funk ensemble from Long Beach calling themselves War recorded "Low Rider," a tribute to Chicano car customizers, cruisers, and musicians.[36] One of the year's best-selling records, "Low Rider" expressed War's own experiences playing dances and concerts for Mexican-American audiences throughout southern California, but the song also reflected demographic trends in Los Angeles that encouraged black-Chicano cultural interaction. In 1970, more than 50,000 Hispanics lived in the traditionally black south-central area of Los Angeles; by 1980 that figure had doubled, with Chicanos making up 21 percent of the total population of the south-central area.[37] The clear Latin influence on the subject and style of "Low Rider" testifies to the importance of Chicano music to American popular music, even when Chicano artists themselves might not enjoy access to a mass audience.

In striking contrast to previous eras when the music and experiences of racial minorities remained largely inaccessible to youths from comfortable economic backgrounds, Chicano and black music in the postwar years played a major role in defining the worldview of Anglo artists and audiences. Mass popular culture and especially radio offered young people an opportunity to expand their cultural tastes in private, away from the surveillance of adult authority. Indeed, young people in Los Angeles who had grown up listening to local disc jockeys Hunter Hancock, Dick Hugg, and Art Laboe (whose broadcasts from El Monte Legion Stadium focused particular attention on Chicano music) had gained their earliest knowledge of rock and roll from songs like "Pachuco Boogie" and "Pachuko Hop" along with scores of records voicing Afro-American music and lyrics. In the mid-1970s, rock musician Frank Zappa paid tribute to his memories of the early years of rock and roll in his album "Zoot Allures," and Captain Beefheart (Don Van Vliet) offered a song titled "Pachuco Cadaver" at the same time. Zappa designed a performance piece built around an imaginary Chicano rock band named Ruben and the Jets, whom he envisioned as the pure spirit of Los Angeles rock and roll. Zappa persuaded Ruben Guevara, a veteran of east-side rock bands, to form an actual group named Ruben and the Jets, who recorded several albums under that name in the early 1970s.[38]

Even outside Los Angeles, white rock and roll musicians playing to

largely middle-class audiences recognized and acknowledged their debt to
Chicano rock and roll. The popular British band Led Zeppelin remade
Ritchie Valens's "Ooh My Head" in 1976, and the New York "punk"
group, the Ramones, recorded his "Come On, Let's Go." Rock critic
Lester Bangs saluted Valens's "La Bamba" as the original punk-rock song,
and he identified it as the forerunner of the Ramones' "Blitzkrieg Bop." [39]
The national and international respect for Chicano music among rock and
punk musicians made itself felt in Los Angeles in the late 1970s when Chicano groups emerged as an important part of the local punk-rock scene.
Ruben Guevara told a reporter in 1980 that the Chicano punk groups attained popularity because of their ability to involve audiences in basic feelings and emotions that rarely surfaced in mainstream popular music.
"This music has a particular quality that's missing in most of the stuff that's
playing around town," Guevara noted. "For lack of a better word, it's raw,
primitive. Which reminds me of something Stravinsky said which I think
is relevant. When a culture loses its primitive music it dies." [40]

Chicano rock and roll music extended the perceptions of the Mexican-
American community to a mass audience that included young people
raised in affluent circumstances, cushioned by the privileges of white skin.
The tendency for the culture of aggrieved communities to form the core of
significant strains in popular culture characterized the vital center of an
unprecedented youth culture in postwar America, one that made a defini-
tive break with the historically sanctioned hierarchies of American life.
The increased purchasing power of the middle class and the likelihood of
postponed entry into the work force gave middle-class youths the resources
to begin experimenting with cultural forms that challenged sexual repression, racial oppression, and class suppression. At the same time, the
cultures and subcultures of seemingly marginalized outsiders held a fascinating attraction for privileged youths looking for alternatives to the secure but stifling and limited sexual roles and identities of middle-class life.

The kinds of ethnic and class interactions common to industrial cities
like Los Angeles in the 1940s and 1950s provided the subtext for the emergence of rock and roll as the central force in American popular music.
Even though a combination of public and private policies worked to destroy the very kinds of cities that made that music possible, a nostalgia for
the heterogeneity of the postwar industrial city has provided the impetus
for all the "great leaps" that have marked the history of rock and roll from
the 1950s to the present. Elvis Presley and Chuck Berry rose to popularity
in the 1950s by immortalizing in song the racial interactions they had ex-

perienced as young workers in Memphis and St. Louis (respectively) during the late 1940s and early 1950s. The "British Invasion" spearheaded by the Beatles and Rolling Stones in 1964 resonated with the echoes of the lost cultural fusions of the 1950s forged by Presley, Berry, and Bill Haley. The late 1960s Aquarian ideal, with its celebrations of unity across racial, cultural, and gender lines, drew its inspiration and focus from the real crossing of those lines that took place in the early years of rock and roll. Janis Joplin drew upon her memories of Afro-American blues and white country music in her childhood home in industrial Port Arthur, Texas, as she shaped her singing style and stage persona, and Jimi Hendrix created his fusion of psychedelic and soul sounds on the basis of his experiences with white rock and roll bands like Bobby Taylor and the Vancouvers, as well as with the Texas country blues that he heard in his home in the postwar production center of Seattle. Whether raised in industrial cities or the newly created residential suburbs of the 1950s, young rock and roll artists and audiences of the 1960s and 1970s savored the textures of cultural diversity present in popular music but increasingly absent from everyday cultural life in America. In the 1980s, Bruce Springsteen, Bob Seger, and John Cougar Mellencamp continue to infuse rock and roll music with the lost hopes and dreams of the postwar era and the interactions among diverse populations.[41]

Above all, the experience of rock and roll music in East Los Angeles over the past forty years illumines the social and cultural basis for a major shift in American life. By the mid-fifties, rock and roll music became a conduit for racial and class grievances as well as a determinate force in middle-class youth culture. As such, it was more than play. Real historical experiences and aspirations lay within rock and roll music, inside the life histories of individual musicians, and inside the collective memory of the audience. Often unacknowledged, these sedimented layers did much to undermine an older cultural hierarchy, and they shed light on where America has been, as well as where it may yet go. As demonstrated by the rock and roll music created in East Los Angeles over the years, seemingly neutral and frivolous forms of popular culture can contain the history of concrete communities of creation and reception. So, when popular films, television programs, and phonograph records hark back to the early days of rock and roll, they engage in something more than nostalgia for the carefree days of youth. They touch a resonant chord in collective popular memory because they recall the exhilaration of years when popular culture began to cross previously insurmountable barriers of race, class, and eth-

nicity—a time when young artists and audiences transformed the dissonance and noise of urban life into a chorus of many voices. In the face of
an increasingly standardized manipulation of urban spatial and cultural relations, they carved out a place in popular culture for a vision of America
as a land of a thousand dances.

NOTES

1. Ralph Ellison, "Editorial Comment," *Negro Quarterly* 1 (Winter–
Spring 1943): 301.

2. Dwight Macdonald set the tone for critical dismissals of rock and roll
music by liberal intellectuals with a series of articles in the 1950s, including
"A Theory of Mass Culture," *Diogenes* 3 (1953), and "Masscult and Midcult,"
Partisan Review, 27, no. 2 (Spring 1960) and 27, no. 4 (Fall 1960). Norman
Podhoretz's "The Know-Nothing Bohemians" struck a similar note on related
issues in *Partisan Review* 25, no. 2 (Spring 1958). In the 1960s, Jeremy Larner
offered a liberal critique of rock and roll in "What Do They Get from Rock'n'Roll?"
Atlantic Monthly 214, no. 2 (1964). A conservative (and essentially racist) critique
came from Richard Corliss in "Pop Music: What's Been Happening," *National Re-
view* 19 (April 4, 1967). Some of the more recent and more sensitive writing on the
topic includes Steve Chapple and Reebee Garofalo, *Rock'n'Roll Is Here to Pay*
(Chicago: Hall, 1977), Greil Marcus, *Mystery Train* (New York: Dutton, 1976),
Gerri Hirshey, *Nowhere to Run* (New York: Penguin, 1984), and Peter Guralnick,
Sweet Soul Music (New York: Harper and Row, 1986).

3. Bob Shannon and John Javna, *Behind the Hits* (New York: Warner,
1986), 94–95.

4. Steven Loza, "The Musical Life of the Mexican-Chicano People in
Los Angeles, 1945–1985" (Ph.D. diss., University of California, Los Angeles,
1985), 147. Ethlie Ann Vare, "Cannibal and the Headhunters," *Goldmine* (November 1983): 26. Don Snowden, "The Sound of East L.A., 1964," *Los Angeles
Times* October 28, 1984.

5. Eshrev Shevky and Marilyn Williams, *The Social Areas of Los Angeles*
(Berkeley: University of California Press, 1949); Ricardo Romo, *East Los Angeles*
(Austin: University of Texas Press, 1983). Romo also reveals some long-standing
ethnic interactions between blacks and Chicanos in Los Angeles neighborhoods.

6. City Survey Files, Los Angeles, 1939, 7, Home Owners Loan Corporation Papers, National Archives, Washington, D.C.

7. Ibid., D-53.

8. Gilbert G. Gonzales, "Factors Relating to Property Ownership of Chicanos in Lincoln Heights, Los Angeles," *Aztlan* 2 (Fall 1971): 111–14.

9. George Lipsitz, "'Against the Wind': The Class Composition of Rock
and Roll Music," *Knowledge and Society* 5 (1984).

10. Lindsey Haley, "Pachuco Boogie," *Low Rider* (June 1985): 34. *Los
Angeles Times* Calendar Section, October 12, 1980. Roberto Caballero-Robledo,
"The Return of Pachuco Boogie," *Nuestro* (November 1979): 4–17.

11. Mauricio Mazon, *Zoot Suit Riots* (Austin: University of Texas Press, 1984); George Lipsitz, *Class and Culture in Cold War America: A Rainbow at Midnight* (South Hadley, Mass.: Bergin and Garvey, 1982), 26–28.

12. Marshall Berman, *All That Is Solid Melts into Air* (New York: Simon and Schuster, 1982), 15.

13. Ruben Guevara, "The View from the Sixth Street Bridge: The History of Chicano Rock," in *Rock'n'Roll Confidential Report*, ed. Dave Marsh (New York: Pantheon, 1985), 118. Marjorie Miller, "Cholos Return to Their Roots and Find They Bloom," *Los Angeles Times* September 9, 1984): pt. 1, 3.

14. Ray Topping, "Chuck Higgins Pachuko Hop," liner notes, Ace Records Ch 81, 1983.

15. Robert Palmer, *Baby That Was Rock and Roll* (New York: Harvest, 1978), 19.

16. Ibid., 16.

17. Johnny Otis, interview with author, Altadena, California, December 14, 1986.

18. Ibid.

19. Ibid.

20. Ibid. Steven Loza, "The Musical Life of the Mexican-Chicano People," 124.

21. Johnny Otis, interview with author.

22. Ibid.

23. Ibid. Guevara, "The View From the Sixth Street Bridge," 118.

24. Johnny Otis, interview with author.

25. Johnny Otis, *Listen to the Lambs* (New York: Norton, 1968). *Los Angeles Times* Calendar Section, April 3, 1985. Joe Sasfy, "Johnny Otis' Fifth Decade," *Washington Post* (June 24, 1985): sect. B, 7.

26. Jim Dawson and Bob Keane, "Ritchie Valens—His life story," Rhino Records insert, 1981.

27. Jim Dawson, "Valens, The Forgotten Story," *Los Angeles Times* (February 3, 1980): 100. Dawson and Keane, "Ritchie Valens."

28. Dawson and Keane, "Ritchie Valens." Jim Dawson, "Valens, The Forgotten Story."

29. Don Snowden, "The Sound of East L.A., 1964," 6.

30. Ethlie Ann Vare, "Cannibal and the Headhunters," 26, 53. Don Snowden, "The Sounds of East L.A., 1964," 7.

31. Ibid., 6–7.

32. For a detailed explanation of the urban crisis of the 1960s and 1970s, see John Mollenkopf, *The Contested City* (Princeton: Princeton University Press, 1983).

33. Luis Rodriguez, "La Veintineuve," in *Latino Experience in Literature and Art* (Los Angeles: Los Angeles Latino Writers Association, 1982), 9.

34. Guevara, "The View From the Sixth Street Bridge," 120.

35. Ibid. *Los Angeles Times* Calendar Section (November 9, 1980): 69. El Larry, "Los Lobos," *Low Rider* (March–April 1984): 34.

36. Joel Whitburn, *The Billboard Book of Top 40 Hits* (New York: Billboard, 1984).

37. Melvin Oliver and James Johnson, Jr., "Inter-Ethnic Conflict in an Urban Ghetto," *Research in Social Movements: Conflict and Change* 6: 57–94.

38. *Los Angeles Times* Calendar Section (October, 12, 1980): 7.

39. Dawson and Keane, "Ritchie Valens—His life story."

40. *Los Angeles Times* Calendar Section (October, 12, 1980): 7.

41. George Lipsitz, "'Against the Wind.'"

14 *The Irony of American Culture Abroad: Austria and the Cold War*

Reinhold Wagnleitner

> They're killing me with inquiries about Walt Disney films.
> *Fantasia* is awaited with particular eagerness in a country where
> *Toscanini* can run as a feature. . . . *Snow White* was announced
> but, so they say, never released here. And they further say, the
> American occupation cannot be complete without Mickey
> Mouse and Donald Duck. . . . What about it?[1]
> Eugen Sharin, films officer, U.S. Forces in Austria, 1945

The preceding contributions to this volume analyze various developments of a unique postwar culture in the United States. Yet the study of that process must not remain confined to the geographical borders of the United States because what also makes American culture unique and interesting is the fascination and attraction it has had *outside* its continental borders.

American cultural products, of course, already had a strong effect on Europe before World War II, but these products had been (mostly) disseminated through commercial channels. Yet since 1945 foreigners have been confronted with a new situation: massive U.S. government support for the distribution of American images and values abroad. Although these new policies were felt most directly in the occupied territories (Austria, Germany, Japan, Korea), where all institutions—from governments to youth clubs, from political parties to the mass media—could be influenced, their effects can be found everywhere in Europe. Indeed, cultural products, broadcast through the channels of the mass media, know no political borders, as the frequent protest against jazz and rock 'n' roll by communist governments have proved. Yet most previous studies have concentrated on the political, diplomatic, military, and economic effects of the United States in cold war Europe. Less attention has been paid to the wider cultural implications of U.S. influence.[2]

This case study aims to overcome these limitations by concentrating on occupied Austria and the attempt to export the unprecedented political and cultural consensus forming in the United States after World War II; it may thereby add a new cultural dimension to our understanding of the cold war era. For the new Pax Americana did more than enlarge the geographic space to which the Monroe Doctrine could be applied. Reflecting upon the immense attraction of U.S. popular culture in this process, we can also detect a shift in form and content: from the Monroe Doctrine to the Marilyn Monroe Doctrine.

I

In postwar Austria, efforts to establish domination over cultural production and distribution were not limited to U.S. policymakers. All four occupation powers tried everything possible to impress the population with their respective achievements. In the first months after the war, the French, the British, and the Russians formed agencies for democratic reorientation and control. But while the French and, to a certain extent, British and traditional Russian cultures remained highly regarded by the Austrian elites, most Austrians, like many Europeans, scoffed at what they presumed to be the cultural wasteland of the United States.[3]

But the Americans in postwar Europe had several unprecedented advantages over their rivals. Indeed, the struggle for cultural supremacy had to be founded on a material basis. And while the Soviet Union could reach only a tiny minority in a strongly anticommunist Austria, the French and British efforts were handicapped by a lack of funds. The United States, however, was the only country whose industrial and economic system profited from the war and thus had large amounts of money and resources to focus on cultural diplomacy. The central agency in charge of that process in Austria was the Information Services Branch (ISB), which had been established by the Allied Forces Headquarters in Italy and began full-scale operations on May 15, 1945.[4]

As the ISB set up operations in Austria, its aim, in the words of one administrator, was to "utilize every possible material and psychological means to create a respect, if not admiration, for the American attitudes and purposes, and thereby vitiate the propaganda of competing political philosophies."[5] In that wide-ranging goal, the U.S. occupation authorities initially had absolute control over operas, concerts, movies, theaters, news agencies, the radio, newspapers, books, advertisements, circus performances, balls, processions, puppet shows, and street markets—a power that involved the paradox of enforcing democracy with possibly undemocratic methods that went far beyond the fairly liberal cultural policies of the Soviet Union in Austria. Reflecting that power and influence, the ISB grew from about 140 workers in 1945 to more than 730 in 1947.

That concentration of resources guaranteed influence and impact. Newspapers were either founded or licensed by the occupation powers. And those in the western zones became dependent, first on the American News Service and then on privately owned U.S. news agencies, which finally broke the near monopoly which the French and German news services had possessed before World War II. The U.S. services supplied more than 200 papers and journals, and their photographs and articles were readily accepted, even by the communist papers. In addition, the installing of conservative Austrian journalists as licencees for newspapers fostered United States interests, particularly since the journalists were fervently anticommunist. The most important paper, the *Wiener Kurier,* also remained under direct American control until the last phase of the occupation. The ISB produced and distributed a number of journals directed at opinion makers and special interest groups, one example being the *Gewerkschaftliche Nachrichten aus den USA,* which contested the image of the United States as the center of capitalist exploitation, bolstered the compromise policies of the Austrian trade unions, and emphasized stories about the high living standards and general happiness of the American workers.[6]

In addition to the print media, the Americans also had partial control of Austrian radio broadcasting. Until its dissolution in 1955, the U.S. radio station *Rot-Weiss-Rot* was the most popular in Austria. The news and political programmers of "Red-White-Red" saw their goal in Austria very clearly. As one memorandum noted, "One of the more delicate functions of American personnel in Austria is not to encourage people to say what they feel . . . but rather, as well as we can, to suggest to them the right thing to think." In general, the underlying assumptions of that policy were summarized by Leo Bogart as "Five minutes of propaganda with two hours of sugar coating. Music is the vehicle rather than the end in itself. We wouldn't have more than five minutes of propaganda in one hour. It's like a commercially sponsored radio program here. Our commercial is our political commentary."[7]

An even more direct way of implementing the cultural side of that political commentary flowed from the establishment of the "Amerika Häuser." These centers of American cultural distribution were not only established in various small Austrian towns and cities, but, by 1949, they were operating in 300 places all over the world, frequented by over 23 million visitors

Fig. 14.1. Exterior of Amerika Haus, Vienna, after World War II. Notice that in the entabulature frieze above the street there is a star and name for each state of the union. (Courtesy of the Washington National Record Center, Suitland, Maryland, reference no. 260/105/44.)

annually. The Amerika Häuser in Austria serviced about 200,000 people a month and functioned as libraries, reading rooms, galleries, concert halls, and centers of information (figs. 14.1, 14.2). Scientific lectures, classical concerts, and gospel performances were mixed with picture displays of "American Super Highways," "Baseball," "Mickey Mouse," and popular films like *Gone With the Wind*. Likewise, the agency distributed ISB posters and placed short propaganda films into most Austrian cinemas to be shown with the main features. Between January and March 1950 alone, more than 4,200 of these films were shown. Among the three ISB movies produced about Austria itself, one of the most stunning was *Project for Tomorrow*, which showed that a 4-H Club could be organized in Austria along the same lines as in the farming areas of the American heartland.[8]

In addition to shorts and propaganda films, the Amerika Haus in Vienna offered about 400 journals to its readers. The most popular were *Life*, *Esquire*, *Time*, *Reader's Digest*, and *Good Housekeeping*. The agencies in Graz, Linz, and Salzburg also used bookmobiles, each carrying some 4,000 volumes, record players, and film equipment on weekly trips into the remotest areas of the countryside. Each offering was widely advertised and promoted with such auspicious titles as "Uncle Sam's Bookstack," "Our Fighting Books," and "Campaign for Truth."[9]

By no means did the selection process reflect that truth campaign. As early as 1947, the Amerika Häuser served as a primary weapon in the struggle against the residues of fascism and, even more important, against the current "danger" of communism. Accordingly, more than 6.5 million anticommunist publications sat on the most accessible shelves, and anything that smelled of "left wing" and "liberal" ideas was anathema. Dedi-

Fig. 14.2. The reading room of Amerika Haus, Vienna, after World War II. The caption on the back wall says, America Helps Austria. (Courtesy of the Washington National Record Center, Suitland, Maryland, reference no. 260/105/44.)

cated to encouraging a political consensus similar to that unfolding at home, the selection guide of the State Department insisted in July 1953 that "no materials shall be selected which, as judged by their content, advocate the destruction of free institutions, promote or reinforce communist propaganda, or are of inferior literary quality, as evidenced by malicious, pornographic, sensational or cheap or shoddy treatment, or matter inherently offensive." Speaking to that purpose, the assistant secretary of state, William Benton, told Congress in 1947 that the Amerika Häuser in Austria "cannot be regarded as libraries in the same sense that we think of a library in this country. They are really information centers about the United States, to which we give the name of libraries as a more convenient and exploratory name." [10]

Between 1949 and 1953, the anticommunist outlook of the Amerika Häuser was particularly strong. But it was not strong enough for the McCarthyites at home. In February 1953, a new directive came to remove more books, some of them were even burned, and in April Roy Cohn and G. David Schine embarked on their much publicized (and ridiculed) tour through American libraries in Europe, screening the holdings of the information centers and finding eighteen titles by eight communist writers and seventy-eight works by twenty-one authors who had refused to testify before the House Committee on Un-American Activities. A rather meager result considering the fact that these libraries held more than six million volumes.

A list, which is anything but complete, of the authors deemed un-American includes Charles Beard, Pearl S. Buck, Erskine Caldwell, Aaron Copland, Joseph Davies, John Dewey, Theodore Dreiser, John Dos Passos, Philip Foner, Albert Einstein, George Gershwin, Dashiell Hammett, Ernest Hemingway, Norman Mailer, Arthur Miller, Lewis Mumford, Henry Thoreau, Henry Wallace, and Frank Lloyd Wright. Similarly, there is no record that the libraries carried the work of black authors, such as Richard Wright or Ralph Ellison, which was critical of race and class relations in the United States. In addition, the destruction of the 1946 edition of the *Annals of the American Academy of Political and Social Science* was ordered because it dealt with problems of world government. When a Fulbright scholar was trying to prepare a lecture at the Amerika Haus in Vienna, he found that though the collection was "safe and unobjectionable, it could hardly be called a monument to the freedom which is our boast and the basis to our claim to leadership." [11]

Yet, in spite of the political and cultural limits of that policy, it did not thwart efforts to spread the appeal of American books and journals. The

ISB publishing company, Neue Welt, understood the translation and pub-
lication of American fiction and nonfiction and subsidized Austrian com-
panies which published American books at cost. By December 1948, the
U.S. Publication Section had concluded more than 120 contracts with
Austrian publishers, and Austria provided a large market for the distri-
bution of American publications. Austrians also copied many practices of
American publishers, such as best-seller lists. By 1952, Walt Disney's
Bambi already had half as many fans as the long-time cartoon favorite
"Max and Moritz" in the age group of six to ten years. Austrian children
between ten and fourteen favored either Karl May's imagined stories of the
Wild West, James Fenimore Cooper's novels, Mark Twain's *Tom Sawyer*,
or Jack London's adventure stories.[12]

At the same time, Austrian authors were attracted to American literature
and the new world myth of "America." The end of Austria's intellectual
isolation, coupled with the rapid distribution of U.S. literature, created an
unusual responsiveness to American literary trends. The style of American
prose directly affected many German-language authors. But the United
States in these years seemed to be a myth completely separated from the
realities of U.S. politics and society. With the exception of the views of
some critical authors of the 1960s and of those publishing in East Germany, "America" in German-language literature since 1945 has been a
metaphor for a territory outside history.[13]

Without a doubt, one of the key policies affecting the reception of
American ideas and literature was ISB efforts to reform and modernize the
educational system. At first, the occupation authorities tried to alter the
Austrian *Hauptschule* and *Mittelschule* according to the integrated American pattern that offered more opportunity for children from the lower
classes. Yet American and Austrian socialist school reformers confronted
the opposition not only of most Austrian teachers but also of the Catholic
church and the Austrian People's Party, whose policy, an American memorandum insisted, was "on the whole . . . committed to the preservation of
existing practices and to the restriction of education opportunities to the
masses." And by 1948 any plans for a real democratization of the Austrian
school system had been abandoned by the U.S. authorities.

Nonetheless, there were dramatic changes in other areas. To promote
reform, the Educational Division distributed American textbooks as models
for Austrian authors, tried to update Austrian high school classes and attempted the training of Austrian *Gymnasium* teachers, whose competence
was thought to be "elementary, platitudinous and perfunctory." The Ameri-

cans also published the journal *Erziehung*, which promoted education reform through student parliaments and newspapers, group discussions, and the abolishment of the classroom teachers' platform, which had reinforced the authority of the teacher. The occupiers also used their financial resources to modernize some school buildings, and Austrian school architects soon copied stateside models.[14]

A similar process permeated university life. Before the occupation, the universities of Vienna and Graz had had a minor tradition of American Studies since the second half of the nineteenth century. But they had hardly been, as in most other European universities, a focus of study. Yet, after the war, the "Englisch Institut" of the University of Vienna was rechristened the "Englisch-amerikanisches Institut." But even then resistence occurred. When academic teachers were inclined to pay only lip service to "Americanizing" the curriculum, an official U.S. report on the situation of the Austrian humanities in 1949 proclaimed that the universities "threaten to be the victim of a policy based upon thinking of the years prior to the airplane, the rocket, and the atomic bomb," clinging to an "antiquated curriculum and methods of scholarship which in the present day amount to escapism."[15]

Yet change did slowly occur. Between 1946 and 1953, about one hundred courses were taught on American subjects in Vienna alone. Over the same period, about sixty Ph.D. students finished their dissertations on American subjects, and the Salzburg Seminar flourished as a center where visiting scholars from America exchanged ideas with European professors and students. In the secondary schools, English replaced French as the dominant foreign language. Twelve American authors were included in the curriculum of the last years of the Austrian *Mittelschulen*, and Austrian textbooks began to include material on the history and literature of the United States.[16]

The foundation of the Salzburg Seminar in Schloss Leopoldskron in 1947, moreover, probably amounted to the finest achievement for the advancement of American Studies in Europe. Although initially, U.S. army intelligence suspected the Salzburg Seminar of being a hotbed of subversive fellow travelers, the Seminar soon became the "most efficient center for the dissemination of American ideas in Europe." Yet, in spite of the success of that institution, visiting American intellectuals confronted a phenomenon which perhaps explains why so many German-language writers and their readers saw America as mythic place, divorced from social and political reality. As Henry Nash Smith noticed, "No one could stay at

Leopoldskron without realizing that the conception of the American character held even by cultivated Europeans was vastly oversimplified if not downright misleading." [17]

Furthermore, cultural diplomacy had been designed to overcome European prejudices and clichés about the United States, to oppose the Soviet Union and communist ideas, and to foster the integration of Europeans into one "Western World." Yet the continental elites were less than impressed with American "High Culture," and the European "masses" were rarely if ever reached by these attempts. Consider the U.S. Theatre and Music Section, which placed American drama and serious music in Austrian theaters and concert halls. Unfortunately, it hardly ever achieved any real success. And did not the American invaders prove their barbarism when they converted the sacred halls of the Salzburg Festival Building into a variety stage for the entertainment of their troops, with the name "Roxy" blazing over the top. Indeed, long-standing cultural prejudices were too strong to overcome, and they withstood the considerable efforts of U.S. cultural officers in most cases. [18]

The only exception to that rule was avant-garde art, especially abstract expressionism, and, later, pop art. Initially, these new styles were admired in Europe by a small elite of art enthusiasts who would not hesitate to agree with Jackson Pollock, who already in 1944 mocked all trends of cultural nationalism: "The idea of an isolated American painting, so popular in this country during the thirties, seems absurd to me just as the idea of creating a purely American mathematics or physics would seem absurd." An even stronger irony was involved because the new style was condemned by the American press and McCarthyites as subversive. Yet, as it achieved popularity, it was promoted by the Central Intelligence Agency and private groups as a model of American freedom—an irony unsuspected by the admirers of the new art in Europe. [19]

Far more effective in capturing the masses attention, however, were American films and other products of popular culture. Indeed, the lure of Hollywood and the Austrians' fascination with it were used as a powerful weapon by the ISB Film Section. The U.S. government during the war years had mobilized the stars and Hollywood to sell the new American Way at home and abroad. The aftermath saw the State Department's giving full support to exporting Hollywood films and cooperating with the new head of the producers' association, Eric Johnston, so that "the rifle that the film industry shouldered in World War II could not be put down: it had to keep marching to the drums of another martial conflict—the Cold War with international and domestic communism." In practice, the effort to "reflect credit on the good name of this country and its institutions" meant discouraging the distribution in the occupied territories of critical movies, like *The Grapes of Wrath*, or gangster films, such as *Key Largo*. As one American general phrased it, "*Key Largo* is not a film to export to any country where we may be interested in either re-education, reorientation or giving a positive picture of American life." The result was that the film "is not policy cleared and therefore not acceptable for release in Austria." [20]

Within Austria, the strategy to show only acceptable films appeared to be remarkably successful, for the Americans had a number of advantages. For one thing, the war had destroyed the German and Austrian film and record companies, leaving the way open for the American companies to nearly monopolize distribution and production. Furthermore, the ISB controlled not only the distribution of all American films but also large parts of the Austrian industry. Already by 1948, Austrians preferred U.S. movies to any other foreign films, and the market for American motion pictures, especially for Walt Disney products (as my opening quotation suggests), was to experience a tremendous expansion in the late forties. By 1948, officials at the Amerika Häuser recognized that

> Films are especially suitable for unsophisticated audi-
> ences. . . . It makes no difference what we have to show
> them. They will come to see anything you have to show
> them. You will find this true almost anywhere except per-
> haps among intellectual groups where they are blasé about
> it. There is a fascination that films have for people. Even
> among the intellectuals there, they come to be critical. . . .
> You can do anything you want with them as long as you
> don't drive them away. [21]

American popular music and jazz also had similar advantages. Before the war, the jazz of Benny Goodman and Louis Armstrong became a code for "unpolitical protest" of German and Austrian middle-class youth in underground "swing clubs," and the National Socialist regime had constantly denounced the *Niggermusik* as decadent, racially inferior, and subversive. Yet after the war those who owned radios could easily tune in to the American Armed Forces Network radio stations, and many of the young did. At first, the broadcasters and critics were wary of the new jazz sounds like bebop. As Senator Ellender of Louisiana proclaimed, "I never heard so much pure noise in my life. . . . To send such jazz as Mr. Gillespie, I can assure you that instead of doing good it will do harm and people will really believe we are barbarians. . . . " But when the critics saw that an anti-American crowd that had demonstrated against U.S. policies in Athens gathered to cheer Dizzy Gillespie the next day, the propaganda value of jazz became clear. An Athens newspaper pointedly commented, "Greek Students Lay Down Rocks and Roll with Diz," and the American jazz critic Leonard Feather even proclaimed a new kind of cold war: "Let Hot Jazz melt Joe's Iron Curtain. . . . How about parachuting some real cool tenor sax men and a couple of crazy trumpets into strategical Eastern European points, to start their own Iron Curtain concert tour. Heck, we could turn the cold war into a Cool War overnight." [22]

With the "Cool War" gaining many converts, the Voice of America program "Music USA" also became in many European countries the all-time favorite show, and the twanging voice of its disk jockey, Willis Conover, was widely emulated. The flood of fan letters from all over the world forced reporters in the homeside press to remark that the "Disc Jockey of 'Voice' Is Winning Goodwill for U.S. the World Over," and *Time* wrote that "in most parts of the world jazz is a kind of Esperanto to the young generation from 15 to 25, and even countries with boiling anti-American prejudices enjoy and respond to it." By the late forties, Austrians had formed their own jazz bands and played before American soldiers, and in the fifties, with the rise of rock 'n' roll music, German records sounded like a crash course in Pidgin English: "I love you, Baby" (Conny, 1957), "Sugar Baby" (Peter Kraus, 1959), or "Crazy Boy" (Ted Herold, 1959) (fig. 14.3). And when Elvis Presley arrived in Germany for his army service in the late fifties, the crowds of fans stalking him showed that he was as popular in Europe as in the United States. [23]

Consequently, it was not American high culture that won the European "masses," as idealistic, liberal universalists had hoped, but the new-world promise of abundance spread by advertising, movie stars, and popular music which accompanied the greatest propaganda victory of the United States in Europe—the Marshall Plan. It was the European Recovery Program that created a "pool of political capital" and dwarfed all efforts to promote American high culture. Indeed, by the fifties, Austrian newspapers and journals of all political persuasions expressed a profound admiration for the American kitchen and cars, nylons and cigarettes, automatic washing machines and supermarkets. And the teenage world, especially, became America. Already in the early 1950s, its international language was popular music, its symbols of rebellion and identification blue jeans and T-shirts, Coca-Cola and chewing gum, U.S. comics and movie stars. [24]

Fig. 14.3. Austrian tenor-saxophone player Josef (Jo) Wagner at a jam session with American GIs at the "Negro club" Royal Roost, in Salzburg in 1952. (Courtesy Josef Wagner.)

To be sure, the efforts of the U.S. occupation authorities to use American high culture for the reorientation of the Austrians were not completely unsuccessful—that would be a gross exaggeration. Yet the fascination with the material and popular culture of the United States predominated for two outstanding reasons. While American sociologists studied the phenomena of the lonely crowd and the generational division between parents and adolescents, many European countries had really lost a generation. After the war, the grandfathers still made the political, economic, and cultural decisions (within the limits allowed by the great powers), and the grandchildren tuned in to the new material and popular culture offered by the conquering Americans. If ever there has been a generation gap, it could be discovered in Europe after World War II.

Yet there was more to it than just the vast gulf between the young and old. In fact, Europeans who criticize the subsequent economic and cultural "Americanization" of the continent are inclined to ignore the second factor encouraging that process: the development of an American-European consumption-oriented society since World War II. What has—in many respects, correctly—been termed "CocaColonization" does at least show strong traces of self-colonization. For the fact that Europe and other parts of the world now appear to many as a homogeneous supermarket has less to do with "Americanization" than with the further development of an economic system on a worldwide scale: corporate capitalism.

Indeed, as the policy of the political and economic conversion unfolded, the essence of America's cultural diplomacy was to encourage the values appropriate to that new order. And it seemed to work, as the American Fulbright scholar Stanley T. Williams found when he tried to teach the heritage of American high culture in Scandinavia in 1952—Europeans were attracted to another facet of the modern United States. "I lectured," he recalled, "in Uppsala on Emerson: in an adjacent hall my wife spoke on the American kitchen. My audience numbered thirty; hers was three hundred. Some wished to know about the Sage of Concord; but more about the deep freeze." [25]

Little wonder, then, that the American authorities found that it was not the forms and values of the American educated classes that came to influence many Austrians, but popular culture and the American Dream as a dream of consumption. Yet, along with the obvious political and economic benefits of that new culture, there was also the mixed message that lay at the heart of the consensus emerging in the United States. True, the mass media and the advent of an affluent society could encourage, as Jackson Lears and Terence Ball have shown, the hegemony of postwar corporate capitalism and a new class of image makers and social scientists. Yet, as Lewis Erenberg, George Lipsitz, and Erika Doss have pointed out, the same culture produced jazz, rock 'n' roll and avant-garde art which emanated from those alienated from dominant institutions, serving as a means of inspiring criticism and youthful alternatives to the consensus at home and abroad. Indeed, twenty years after the end of World War II, many on both sides of the Atlantic would launch a criticism of the cold war. Europeans who had studied English were now able to tune in to the American pop singer Bob Dylan, who drew on that paradox when he sang,

> Well, the last I heard of Ahab
> he was stuck on a whale
> that was married to the deputy
> sheriff of the jail
> but the funniest thing was
> when I was leaving the bay,

I saw three ships a-sailin'
they were all heading my way
I asked the captain what his name was
and how come he didn't drive a truck
he said his name was Columbus
I just said, "good luck." [26]

What that counterculture sensibility meant for the legacy of postwar American culture in Europe is another story.

NOTES

1. Eugen Sharin (films officer, United States Forces in Austria) to the Office of War Information in New York, August 14, 1945, Washington National Records Center, Record Group 260/64/66, National Record Center, Suitland, Maryland (hereafter known as WNRC).

2. Among the several new studies looking at the culture of postwar diplomacy, see Emily S. Rosenberg, *Spreading the American Dream: American Economic and Cultural Expansion, 1890–1945* (New York: Hill and Wang, 1982), and Frank Ninkovich, *The Diplomacy of Ideas: U.S. Foreign Policy and Cultural Relations, 1938–1950* (New York: Cambridge University Press, 1981). Neither however examines the effect of cultural diplomacy on the receiving country or assesses which products succeeded, which failed, with their intended audience. For a general discussion, see *Superculture: American Popular Culture and Europe*, ed. C. W. E. Bigsby (Bowling Green, Ky.: Bowling Green University Press, 1975).

3. The cultural policies of the Soviet Union, Great Britain, and France in Austria still need close examination. The western zones in Germany have been studied more closely; see, for example, John Gimbel, *The American Occupation of Germany: Politics and the Military, 1945–1949* (Stanford: Stanford University Press, 1968); Henry Kellermann, *Cultural Relations as an Instrument of United States Foreign Policy* (Washington: Bureau of Educational and Cultural Affairs, U.S. State Department, Government Printing Office, 1978); *La dénazification par les Vainqueurs. La politique culturelle des occupants en Allemagne 1945–1949*, ed. Jerome Vaillant (Lille: Presses universitaires de Lille, 1981); Kurt Jürgensen, "Elemente britischer Deutschlandpolitik: Political Re-education, Responsible Government, Federation of Germany," in *Die Deutschlandpolitik Grossbritanniens und die Britische Zone 1945–1949*, ed. Claus Scharf and Hans-Jürgen Schroeder (Wiesbaden: Steiner, 1979), 103–27.

4. The best treatment of American cultural policies in postwar Austria is Oliver Rathkolb, "Politische Propaganda der amerikanischen Besatzungsmacht in Oesterreich in der Presse-, Kultur- und Rundfunkpolitik" (Ph.D. diss., University of Vienna, 1981). See also Alfred Hiller, "Amerikanische Medien-und Schulpolitik in Oesterreich 1945–1950," (Ph.D. diss., University of Vienna, 1974); Michael Schoenberg, "Amerikanische Informations-und Medienpolitik in Oesterreich 1945–1950" (Ph.D. diss., University of Vienna, 1975).

5. "ISB Policy," WNRC, Record Group 260, box 59372-1.

6. See Jeremy Tunstall, *The Media Are American: Anglo-American Media in the World* (New York: Columbia University Press, 1977); Herbert Schiller, *Communications and Cultural Domination* (White Plains, N.Y.: International Arts and Sciences, 1976).

7. Rathkolb, "Politische Propaganda," 452; Leo Bogart, *Promises for Propaganda: The United States Information Agency's Operating Assumptions in the Cold War* (New York: Free Press, 1976), 152.

8. See *Study of Amerika Haus Vienna* (Washington, D.C.: Government Printing Office, 1955), in United States Information Agency Library, Historical Collection, Washington, D.C. (hereafter known as USIAL/HC). Hiller, "Amerikanische Medien," 93, 145.

9. P. S. J., "Books Perform Vital Service in 'Campaign of Truth,'" *Publisher's Weekly* (November 18, 1950).

10. P. S. J., "Books"; *Pentagraph* (Bloomington, Ill.) December 27, 1955; *Watertown Times* (N.Y.) December 30, 1953; Circular Airgram, no. 1692, *Instructions for Selection and Retention of Materials in Book and Library Programs*, International Information Administration, Department of State, July 15, 1953, USIAL/HC. Testimony of William Benton, Special House Committee on Foreign Affairs, *U.S. Information and Educational and Exchange Act of 1947*, 80th Cong., 1st sess., May 13–20, 1947, 164.

11. See *Report on the Operations of the Overseas Book and Library Program*, International Information Administration, Department of State, July 15, 1953, USIAL/HC; John J. Criscitiello, "The Role of American Books," in *Propaganda and the Cold War: Princeton Symposium*, ed. John B. Whitton (Washington: Public Affairs, 1963), 106–12; Helmut Bonheim, "American Books in Vienna," *Nation* (January 14, 1961): 37–38.

12. *Verleger Informationen* 1 (December 1948): 1; Criscitiello, "The Role of American Books," 106–12.

13. Richard Ruland, *America in Modern European Literature: From Image to Metaphor* (New York: New York University Press, 1976); Hans K. Galinsky, "America's Image in German Literature," *Comparative Literature Studies* 13 (1976): 165–92.

14. Tyrus Hillway, "American Studies in Austria," in *American Studies Abroad: Contributions in American Studies*, ed. Robert H. Walker (Westport, Conn.: Greenwood, 1975), 89–94. Henry Brechbill, "Recommendations for Teacher Education in Austria, 1947," cited in Hiller, "Amerikanische Medien," 227, 270, 286.

15. *Report on the Humanities in Germany and Austria* (Washington, D.C.: Government Printing Office, 1949), 86, 95.

16. Sigmund Skard, *The American Myth and the European Mind: American Studies in Europe, 1776–1960* (Philadelphia: University of Pennsylvania Press, 1976). O. Tacke, "Die Bedeutung der westlichen Fremdsprachen für den demokratischen Schulunterricht," *Zeitschrift für Anglistik und Amerikanistik* 1 (1953): 66–72.

17. H. F. Peters, "American Culture and the State Department," *American Scholar* 21, no. 3 (Summer 1952): 265–74; Henry Nash Smith, "The Salzburg Seminar," *American Quarterly* (1949): 35.

18. "Contributions of U.S. Music to the Democratization of Austria," undated memorandum (November–December 1946), WNRC RG 260/35/12.

19. Jane De Hart Matthews, "Art and Politics in Cold War America," *American Historical Review* 81 (October 1976): 762–87. The Pollock quote is from Charles Alexander, *Here the Country Lies: Nationalism and the Arts in Twentieth-Century America* (Bloomington: Indiana University Press, 1980), 268. See also Erika Doss, "The Art of Cultural Politics," chap. 10 in this volume.

20. Rosenberg, *Spreading the American Dream*, 100–102. Department of State Inquiry, "American Motion Pictures in the Post-War World," cited in Larry Ceplair and Steven Englund, *The Inquisition in Hollywood: Politics in the Film Community, 1930–1960* (Garden City, N.Y.: Anchor, 1980), 248–49. The remark on *Key Largo* is from Robert A. McClure (brigadier general, chief, Department of the Army, Civil Affairs Division, New York Field Office) to Colonel S. S. Eberle (director, Information Services Branch, Headquarters, U.S. Forces Austria), August 13, 1948, WNRC, RG 260/42/45. For *Grapes of Wrath*, see WNRC, RG 260/35/2.

21. See Hiller, "Amerikanische Medien," 93, 145; Institute of Communications Research, International Motion Picture Service USIAL/HC. For the increasing number of American films shown in Austria and the influence of Eric Johnston, see Thomas H. Guback, *The International Film Industry: Western Europe and America since 1945* (Bloomington: Indiana University Press, 1969), esp. 48.

22. Detlev Peukert, "Edelweisspiraten, Meuten, Swing: Jugendsubkulteren im Dritten Reich," in *Sozialgeschichte der Freizeit: Untersuchungen zum Wandel der Alltagskultur in Deutschland*, ed. Gerhard Huck (Wuppertal: Hammer, 1980); Earl R. Beck, "The Anti-Nazi 'Swing Youth,' 1942–1945," *Journal of Popular Culture* 19 (Winter 1985): 45–53. Ellender is quoted in Joseph N. Acinapura, "The Cultural Presentations Program of the United States," (M.A. thesis, University of Colorado, 1970), 73, 71–80; Marshall W. Stearns, "Is Jazz Good Propaganda? Dizzy Gillespie Tour," *Saturday Review* 39 (July 14, 1956): 28–31; Leonard Feather, "Let Hot Jazz Melt Joe's Iron Curtain," *New York Journal American* October 4, 1952.

23. *New York Herald Tribune* (October 27, 1949): 1; *Wichita Eagle* December 2, 1955; "Jazz Around the World," *Time* (June, 25, 1956): 47; Elmar Kraushaar, *Rote Lippen: Die ganze Welt des deutschen Schlagers* (Reinbek bei Hamburg: Rowohlt, 1983), 78–80.

24. For the Marshall Plan and the rise of a new capitalism rooted in the politics and ideology of abundance, see Charles S. Maier, "The Politics of Productivity," *International Organization* 31, no. 4 (1977): 607–32. John Blum, *V Was for Victory: Politics and American Culture during World War II* (New York: Harcourt Brace Jovanovich, 1976), 107–8.

25. On the politics of the new economy, see Maier, "Politics of Productivity"; on the desire to export an appropriate culture, see Rosenberg, *Spreading*

the American Dream, and Ninkovich, *The Diplomacy of Ideas;* Stanley T. Williams, "Who Reads an American Book?" *Virginia Quarterly Review* 28 (Autumn 1952): 529.

26. "Bob Dylan's 115th Dream" (1965), from the album "Bringing It All Back Home." See also Bob Dylan, *Lyrics, 1962–1985* (New York: Knopf, 1985).

Contributors

TERENCE BALL is professor of political science at the University of Minnesota. A specialist in political theory and the history and philosophy of social science, he is the author of *Civil Disobedience and Civil Deviance* and the forthcoming work *Transforming Political Discourse*.

CLIFFORD E. CLARK, JR., is M. A. and A. D. Hulings Professor of American Studies and chair of the History Department at Carleton College. Interested in social and intellectual history, he is the author of *Henry Ward Beecher: Spokesman for a Middle Class America* and *The American Family Home, 1800–1960*.

ERIKA DOSS is assistant professor of art history at the University of Colorado, Boulder. She has written on Depression-era and contemporary public art for *Women's Art Journal* and *Arts Magazine* and is currently completing a study of regionalism and abstract expressionism.

LEWIS A. ERENBERG is associate professor of history at Loyola University of Chicago. He is the author of *Steppin' Out: New York Nightlife and the Transformation of American Culture, 1890–1930* and is presently working on a history of the big bands and national musical culture from the 1920s through the 1940s.

EDWARD GRIFFIN is professor of English and the chairman of the Program in American Studies at the University of Minnesota. He is the author of several articles on American literature and culture as well as *Old Brick: Charles Chauncy of Boston, 1705–1787*.

JACKSON LEARS is professor of history at Rutgers University. Best known for his *No Place of Grace: Anti-Modernism and the Transformation of American Culture, 1880–1920* and his articles on intellectual history and theory, he is working on a study of advertising and American culture.

GEORGE LIPSITZ is associate professor of American Studies at the University of Minnesota. He is the author of *Class and Culture in Cold War America: A Rainbow at Midnight*, and *A Life in the Struggle: Ivory Perry and the Culture of Opposition*, as well as several articles on television and rock and roll.

ELAINE TYLER MAY is associate professor of American Studies at the University of Minnesota. She is the author of *Great Expectations: Marriage and Divorce in Post-Victorian America* and *Homeward Bound: American Families in the Cold War Era*.

LARY MAY is associate professor of American Studies at the University of Minnesota. He has written *Screening Out the Past: The Birth of Mass Culture and the Motion Picture Industry* and is working on a study of the American motion picture industry, culture, and politics between 1930 and 1960.

DAVID W. NOBLE is professor of American Studies and history at the University of Minnesota. Among his numerous articles and books are *The Progressive Mind* and *The End of American History: Democracy, Capitalism and the Metaphor of Two Worlds in Anglo-American Historical Writing, 1880–1980.*

NORMAN L. ROSENBERG is professor of history at Macalester College. He has written several articles on the relation of the law and American society and is the author of *Protecting the Best Men: An Interpretive History of the Law of Libel.*

CARL E. SCHORSKE is professor emeritus at Princeton University, where he served as Dayton-Stockton Professor of History and director of European Cultural Studies. During his distinguished career, he has produced several noted articles and books on intellectual history and politics, among them the prize-winning *Fin-de-Siècle Vienna: Politics and Culture.*

WARREN SUSMAN was professor of history and director of the Institute for the Study of Contemporary American Culture at Rutgers University before his death in 1985. He was the author of numerous influential essays, many of which were published in *Culture as History: The Transformation of American Society in the Twentieth Century.*

REINHOLD WAGNLEITNER is assistant professor of history at the University of Salzburg, Austria, and has served as a Fulbright scholar at the University of Minnesota, where he taught American Foreign Relations. He has edited *Understanding Austria: The Political Reports and Analysis of Martin F. Herz, Political Officer of the U.S. Legation in Vienna, 1945–1948* and has published several articles on the influence of American culture in Europe. He is completing a book about the effect of U.S. culture in Austria, 1945–55.

JOHN S. WRIGHT is associate professor of English and chairman of the Department of Afro-American and African Studies at the University of Minnesota. He has written numerous articles on American literature and minorities. He is completing a study of Afro-American and African literary and intellectual history between the eighteenth and twentieth centuries.

Index